COST & EFFECT

Using Integrated
Cost Systems to
Drive Profitability
and
Performance

ROBERT S. KAPLAN
ROBIN COOPER

HARVARD BUSINESS SCHOOL PRESS
Boston, Massachusetts

Library of Congress Cataloging-in-Publication Data

Kaplan, Robert S.
    Cost and effect : using integrated cost systems to drive
profitability and performance / Robert S. Kaplan and Robin
Cooper.
        p.   cm.
    Includes bibliographical references and index.
    ISBN 0-87584-788-9 (alk. paper)
    1. Activity-based costing.   I. Cooper, Robin,
1951–
II. Title.
HF5686.C8K266   1997
658.15′52—dc21   97-26561
                                              CIP

The paper used in this publication meets the requirements of
the American National Standard for Permanence of Paper for
Printed Library Materials Z39.49-1984.

Contents

Preface

This book is a practical guide for managers on how cost and performance management systems can increase the profitability and performance of their organizations. It brings together, in an integrated, comprehensive way, the modern cost management methods we have helped develop during the past 15 years. Managers have likely heard about such innovations as activity-based costing (ABC), activity-based management (ABM), kaizen costing, target costing, and nonfinancial performance measures. But how do these innovative approaches fit together? Are they substitutes or complements? And are they compatible with existing financial systems, or do organizations have to replace their existing systems with a new, integrated one? The book provides definitive answers to these questions.

We use two powerful concepts—first, the accurate measurement of activity costs, and, second, the reduction of costs by continuous and discontinuous improvements—that enable the finance function to shift from being the passive reporter of the past to a proactive influencer of the future. The book illustrates the conceptual leap from feedback to feedforward cost management. Used in this way, cost and performance measurement systems become integrated with the formulation and implementation of strategies and operational improvements.

Today many organizations are installing, at considerable expense, new enterprise-wide systems (EWS) (also called enterprise resource planning systems). The availability of such systems raises two critical questions for modern cost management:

1. Will an EWS easily provide the accurate information about the cost of activities, processes, products, and customers that is currently available only through stand-alone PC-based ABC systems?

2. Will an EWS automatically supply the relevant, timely information needed by managers and employees to improve current and future operations?

The answer to both questions is no! Only if managers understand the fundamental concepts of activity-based costing and performance improvement will they be able to take full advantage of the cost management potential of their new systems.

We wrote this book to help managers capture the benefits both from recent advances in the theory of cost management and from the installation of new enterprise-wide systems. Many of these benefits can be achieved without EWS technology. Thus, companies not undertaking the journey to integrated financial systems on an enterprise-wide platform can still realize major benefits from the new approaches documented here. But to realize the full potential of modern cost management, companies may need the integration of information from many disparate sources. Such integration can be provided only by an EWS.

The book is organized around a four-stage model of cost system evolution. We describe how many companies have likely avoided Stage I, where cost systems are not even adequate for routine, periodic financial reporting. These companies, however, may still be in Stage II, where cost and performance information are available only from the system used to prepare periodic financial reports. We advocate that companies start their journey by migrating to Stage III, where they develop customized, stand-alone approaches, separate from their official financial system, for measuring organizational costs (the ABC approach) and providing relevant, timely performance measurement feedback to their employees.

Our first writings on activity-based costing and performance measurement appeared in the mid-1980s. Since then, we have developed several important insights to enhance the capabilities of cost management systems. But even today, many new ABC implementations fail to incorporate these newer ideas and concepts, particularly the critical role of organizational capacity. Consequently, most users are taking advantage of only a fraction of the potential benefits of modern cost management. In addition, even fewer firms are developing integrated cost management systems that incorporate both feedforward and feedback techniques.

This book articulates the full power and capabilities of advanced ABC systems. It clearly demonstrates that ABC is not limited to the four walls of the factory. ABC is not just for measuring and managing production costs for manufacturing organizations. The book provides ample illustrations of how companies are using ABC information for a wide variety of activity-based management applications: driving process improvement efforts; managing product variety; enhancing customer relationships in ordering, pricing, and distribution; managing supplier relationships to achieve low cost, not just low price; and influencing the design of future products, services, and customer relationships. We show how modern cost management can and should be applied to both manufacturing and service organizations, and across the entire value chain of a firm's activities. In addition, the book contains many examples of how activity-based management complements other organizational improvement initiatives such as reengineering, the theory of constraints, target costing, and economic value-added.

In addition to explaining how to gain greater value from activity-based cost systems, we also illustrate how Stage III companies are using financial information for direct feedback to front-line employees to support their continuous improvement activities.

We do not take the cookbook approach—describing 10 easy steps on how to implement an organization's first integrated cost management system. Instead we provide the conceptual foundations for activity-based costing and performance measurement, as well as the necessary understanding for managers to act upon and benefit from the information produced from their new cost systems.

The gains in Stage III, from both ABM and the financial feedback to employees, are now available to all companies. Both approaches can be implemented with modest expenditures on computer hardware and software. We hope the book will stimulate companies to begin the migration to modern cost management by elevating their existing cost and performance measurement systems to the much higher level of capabilities provided by these customized, stand-alone systems.

But we go beyond these Stage III extensions to existing systems; our second main objective is to demonstrate how companies can move to Stage IV, where cost and performance measurement information become integrated into the mainstream fabric of organizational reporting and managerial processes. This integration enables cost management and performance measurement to function in feedforward mode. Now the primary aim is to motivate improvements in future performance, not provide feedback on past performance. Target costing and kaizen costing play a role in this shift to a feedforward orientation.

Advances in information technology give companies the opportunity to create an integrated set of cost and performance measurement systems, designed explicitly to meet managerial needs. But the benefits from integrated systems will not be fully realized unless managers truly understand the capabilities as well as the limitations from the new cost and performance measurement systems. Without such understanding, managers may believe they have acquired a modern, integrated cost management system, but will only have re-installed the obsolete thinking from their old Stage II cost system onto a new (and much more expensive) information technology platform.

The book documents how to embed ABC concepts into the firm's organizational reporting and managerial processes such as budgeting, transfer pricing, and what-if simulations of the financial consequences from decisions made today about future products, services, processes, and customers. Most financial systems, even advanced ABC systems, still report on the past. They may report more accurately, and in a more timely way, than previous financial systems, but they still only provide a brilliant picture of the organization's past trajectory rather than helping the senior management team steer a new and more profitable path to the future. For example, many managers still view most organizational expenses as fixed. We show how the process to transform apparently fixed costs into variable costs occurs during the organization's activity-based budgeting process. So if managers want to influence their so-called fixed costs, they must have predictive information about the cost consequences of their decisions during the budgeting process. They must be able to simulate the cost consequences from alternative decisions before such decisions are made and new resources supplied to implement those decisions. Therefore, companies can only realize the full benefits from more accurate cost information if this information becomes embedded in their budgeting and resource allocation processes. Enterprise-wide systems make such activity-based budgeting a realistic possibility.

We start with the basics. The ideas evolve in an integrated, cumulative approach with each chapter building upon concepts previously established. Readers already familiar with the critique of existing cost systems may wish to skim Chapter 3, and those knowledgeable about ABC fundamentals can skim the introduction to this topic in Chapter 6.

The ideas in all chapters are illustrated with examples drawn from actual practice. Many of these examples are documented in considerable detail in our Harvard Business School case studies, which are referenced throughout the book. Interested readers can obtain more information about these studies by ordering the cases directly from Harvard Business School Publishing.

In developing the ideas in this book, we are obviously indebted to the many individuals and organizations in North America, Europe, and Japan with whom we have worked over the past 15 years. The several dozen case studies, drawn from innovative companies willing to share their experiences in implementing new cost management systems, required the cooperation of hundreds of people. We have learned from each of them. Rather than list them individually, we wish to thank them collectively for allowing us to enhance our research by studying their experiences.

We also have benefited from the support of the Harvard Business School and the Claremont Graduate School. A combination of collaborative teaching assignments and support for the extensive field work and case studies enabled us to learn from and influence practice.

We profited from the reviews of experienced practitioners: Ralph Canter of KPMG Peat Marwick, with whom we continue to share an ongoing learning relationship; Dr. Erwin Schneider, senior financial manager of Hoffmann-La Roche; and Aimeé Hampson of Gemini Consulting's London office. We are also grateful to our academic colleagues, Professor Srikant Datar of the Harvard Business School and Professor Jim Reeve of the University of Tennessee, who read an early draft and were particularly helpful in pointing out significant opportunities for improvement.

Carol Franco, director of the Harvard Business School Press, provided enthusiastic support and insight throughout the project. Barbara Roth, managing editor, kept the project on schedule, even as exhibits and text were altered. Kent Lineback and our development editor, Alice Fugate, gave us fresh perspectives on how to clarify and highlight key points throughout the book. Copyeditor Natalie Greenberg did her usual professional job. To all of these individuals and to their colleagues behind the scenes, we express our appreciation.

Robert S. Kaplan
Boston, Massachusetts

Robin Cooper
Atlanta, Georgia

August 1997

COST & EFFECT

1

Introduction: Cost and Performance Management Systems

Changes in business since the mid-1970s, triggered by global competition and technological innovations, have led to striking innovations in the use of financial and nonfinancial information in organizations. The new environment demands more relevant cost and performance information on the organization's activities, processes, products, services, and customers. Leading companies are using their enhanced cost systems to:

- Design products and services that both meet customers' expectations and can be produced and delivered at a profit;
- Signal where either continuous or discontinuous (reengineering) improvements in quality, efficiency, and speed are needed;
- Assist front-line employees in their learning and continuous improvement activities;
- Guide product mix and investment decisions;
- Choose among alternative suppliers;
- Negotiate about price, product features, quality, delivery, and service with customers; and
- Structure efficient and effective distribution and service processes to targeted market and customer segments.

Many companies, however, are not gaining these competitive advantages from enhanced cost systems. Their managers rely on information from a cost system designed for a simpler technological age, when competition was local not global, that featured standard not customized products and services, and when speed, quality, and performance were less critical for success. These managers do not have timely and relevant information to guide their operational improvement activities. Nor are they receiving accurate, valid information to shape their strategic decisions about processes, products, services, and customers.

One Cost System Isn't Enough

Companies need cost systems to perform three primary functions:

- Valuation of inventory and measurement of the cost of goods sold for financial reporting;
- Estimation of the costs of activities, products, services, and customers; and
- Providing economic feedback to managers and operators about process efficiency.

The first need is driven by the needs of constituencies *external* to the organization: investors, creditors, regulators, and tax authorities. The procedures for the external, financial reporting function are governed by a myriad of rules and regulations established by tax authorities, governmental agencies, private standard-setting bodies, and public accounting societies. The second and third functions arise from the needs of *internal* managers to understand and improve the economics of their operations. Managers need accurate and timely cost information to make both strategic decisions and operational improvements.

In the past, many companies attempted to meet these three different functions with a single costing system.[1] In an environment of limited product and process variety—where excellence in manufacturing processes was not critical for success—a single costing system might have sufficed. This is no longer possible. Traditional standard cost systems are still fine for financial reporting. Some companies, even today, have systems that use simplistic direct labor overhead costing systems, perhaps with only a single rate, despite operating plants with diverse processes, which might include both manual assembly and highly automated machining. Overhead rates can reach 500–1,000% of direct labor cost. Yet auditors, regulators, and tax authorities are perfectly content with these simple, aggregate cost systems for allocating manufacturing overhead to products. Companies receive clean audit opinions since auditors are more concerned with year-to-year consistency in method than with accuracy of costs at the individual cost center or product level. External users are not concerned that a company's simple standard cost system reports distorted costs on virtually every individual product as long as the reported inventory numbers are roughly correct in the aggregate.

But such aggregate methods for allocating factory overhead costs to products provide managers with poor information.[2] And the costs of many organizational resources, especially those for marketing, sales, and distribution, are not assigned to cost objects at all since such costs are not "inventoriable" in financial statements. Although these resources clearly help an organization meet the demands of individual customers, channels, and markets, the financial system does not assign their costs to users. Such a calculation is neither necessary nor, worse, allowable for financial reporting purposes.

Many companies, recognizing the arbitrary nature of factory overhead allocations in their inventory valuation system, have shifted to direct costing systems for facilitating managerial decisions. Direct costing systems ignore overhead costs entirely in calculating the costs of products, services, and customers. They assign only the materials and direct labor costs to individual products. Direct costing methods are fine if the ignored indirect and support costs are a small fraction of total costs, or if, as direct costing advocates claim, they are "fixed" costs. Yet organizations learned that not only were the indirect and support costs not fixed, they were not even variable. For many organizations, these costs are "supervariable"; they are increasing at a faster rate than production or sales volume. And direct costing methods can certainly not relate the growing chunk of below-the-line (gross margin) expenses for marketing, selling, distribution, product development, and general administrative support to customers, channels, and divisions.

Activity-Based Cost Systems

As competition increased, and as the basis of competition shifted away from the efficient use of direct labor and machines, managers needed more accurate information about the costs of processes, products, and customers than they could obtain from the system used for external financial reporting. Activity-based cost (ABC) systems emerged in the mid-1980s to meet the need for accurate information about the cost of resource demands by individual products, services, customers, and channels.[3] ABC systems enabled indirect and support expenses to be driven, first to activities and processes, and then to products, services, and customers. The systems gave managers a clearer picture of the economics of their operations.

The clearer picture from ABC systems led naturally to *activity-based management* (ABM): the entire set of actions that can be taken, on a better informed basis, with activity-based cost information. ABM enables the organization to accomplish its outcomes with fewer demands on organizational resources; that is, the organization achieves the same outcomes at a lower total cost. ABM accomplishes its objective through two complementary applications: *operational* and *strategic* ABM (see *Exhibit 1-1*).[4]

Operational ABM—doing things right—works to enhance efficiency, lower costs, and enhance asset utilization. Operational ABM can increase the capacity of resources (equipment and people) by reducing machine downtime, improving, or even eliminating entirely, faulty activities and

Exhibit 1-1   Using ABM for Operational Improvements and Strategic Decisions

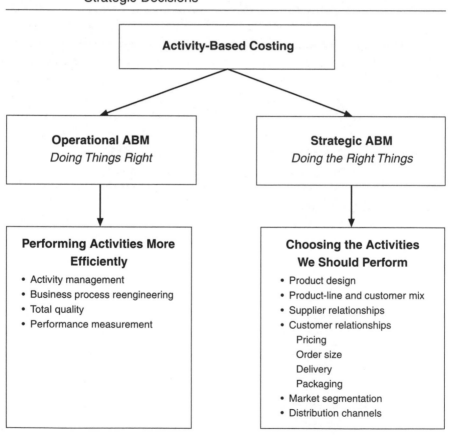

processes, and increasing the efficiency of the organization's resources. Operational ABM takes the demand for resources as given and attempts to either increase capacity or lower spending (i.e., reduce the cost driver rates of activities), so that fewer physical, human, and working capital resources are required to generate revenues. The benefits from operational ABM can be measured by reduced costs, higher revenues (through better resource utilization), and cost avoidance (the expanded capacity of existing resources obviates the need for additional investments in capital and people).

Strategic ABM—doing the right things—attempts to alter the demand for activities to increase profitability while assuming, as a first approximation, that activity efficiency remains constant. For example, the organization may be operating at a point where the revenues earned from a particular product, service, or customer are less than the cost of generating those revenues. Strategic ABM encompasses shifting the mix of demand for activities away from such unprofitable applications by reducing the cost driver quantities demanded by unprofitable activities. The ABC model signals when individual products, services, and customers appear to be highly profitable. This information can be used by marketing and sales experts to explore whether demand for those highly profitable products, services, and customers can be expanded to generate incremental revenues that exceed their incremental costs. Managers can then shift the activity mix toward more profitable uses. They can also use ABC information to choose suppliers that are low-cost, not just low-price.

Strategic ABM also encompasses decisions about product design and development where perhaps the biggest opportunity for cost reduction exists. Many observers now believe that 80% or more of manufacturing costs are determined during the product design and development stages.[5] With inadequate and distorted cost systems, product designers and engineers receive faulty signals about the economics of the products they are developing. They make decisions that ignore the costs of using unique versus common parts, new versus existing vendors, and simple versus complex production processes. Distorted cost systems also overestimate the cost of direct labor, thereby encouraging overinvestment in reducing new products' consumption of that labor. Many companies now use their ABC systems to provide product engineers and designers with better information at the best time to affect future costs.

Obviously, operational and strategic decisions are not mutually exclusive. Organizations will get the greatest impact when they reduce both the resources required to perform a given quantity of activities and, simultaneously, shift the activity mix to more profitable processes, products, services, and customers.

But ABC systems, by themselves, do not solve all the limitations of traditional costing systems.

Systems for Operational Control and Learning

Even with the more accurate cost information provided by innovative ABC systems, many companies continued to use their standard costing systems as the primary feedback mechanism to responsibility center supervisors and employees. Management accountants acted as scorekeepers. They preferred to be neutral observers, sitting on the sidelines, and often not even observing the processes that produced and delivered products and services. Instead, the management accountants issued periodic reports, derived from their financial accounting system, that reconciled actual with budgeted (or standard) expenses. The accounting and finance staff issued these periodic performance reports according to the monthly financial reporting cycle, so they appeared days or weeks later than the actual events they reported on. And the reports were filled with cost accounting jargon—allocations and variances calculated many different ways—that were incomprehensible to the people performing the actual work.

Apart from the delays and difficulty in interpreting these reports, their philosophic underpinnings were inconsistent with the demands of the new manufacturing environment. The traditional cost controlling systems emphasized stability, control, and efficiency of isolated machines, workers, and departments. Such an emphasis is not responsive to today's competitive world, which stresses continuous and discontinuous (i.e., reengineering) improvement and the cross-functional integration required to provide quick response and high-quality processes geared to customer demands.

Thus, both newly designed activity-based costing systems as well as new systems for operational control and learning are needed for the critical management challenges. These new systems supplement the traditional standard costing systems that are still used to prepare periodic financial reports.

Roles for Multiple Cost Systems

Some financial managers are concerned about having multiple cost systems. After all, one cost system is expensive to install and maintain; how can they justify three cost systems? Also, people with a high tolerance for ambiguity typically do not become financial managers. The financial accounting model provides a rigorous, logical framework for viewing the world and seems to attract people who value the objectivity and clarity (if not the relevance) of that framework. The idea of having three different costing systems can be highly upsetting for managers who have been educated and trained in the highly orderly and structured world of double-entry accounting.

Companies do not have to operate with three different and inconsistent cost reporting systems. In fact, companies should continue to operate with the existing financial system that captures and aggregates financial transactions into their general ledger or chart of accounts. But rather than use these financial reports directly for managerial purposes, managers can access the data from this financial transaction system as well as data from many other organizational information systems, such as the systems for production planning and control, inventory management, sales order entry, engineering, and customer management. They can process the data from these diverse systems to produce accurate and managerially relevant reports about the cost and efficiency of their processes, products, and customers.

Ideally, companies could have developed one integrated system that serves all these functions—financial reporting, strategic costing, operational improvement and performance measurement, plus inventory and production planning, engineering, sales order fulfillment and customer administration. Realistically, however, a leap to a completely integrated and managerially relevant set of costing, performance measurement, and operating systems was not possible, either technologically or, more important, conceptually. Neither the systems capabilities nor the theory for such integration was available (until very recently). Rather than wait, however, for the advanced hardware and software technology and a unified management theory to emerge, many companies retained their existing financial system and installed stand-alone or networked activity-based cost systems for specific managerial uses. Others, heavily committed to TQM, employee empowerment, and continuous improvement, installed innovative, new systems that provided front-line employees with timely and accurate information for operational learning and improvement.

These companies took an evolutionary approach to introduce 1) the innovations of activity-based costing and 2) specialized, local measurements to provide feedback for operational learning and improvement. These stand-alone systems leveraged new hardware and software technology that was inexpensive and already widely available in 1990 to supply valuable information for managers and employees. Thus, companies benefited, in the near term, from more accurate and more responsive cost and performance measurement information. This book will provide a comprehensive description of the innovations and the benefits that leading companies have received from their new operational learning and improvement systems and their activity-based cost systems.

Integration: Vision for the Future

In the mid-1990s, new hardware and software technology emerged that enabled companies to contemplate having an enterprise-wide system (EWS). An EWS can provide a company with an integrated set of operating, financial, and management systems. The EWS has a common data structure and a centralized, accessible data warehouse that permits data to be entered and accessed from anywhere in the world. With the new EWS technology, managers can bring together all their stand-alone ABC and operational improvement and learning systems into a single integrated system. And the integration offers new capabilities not realizable when financial reporting, product, customer, and process costing, and operational feedback and learning systems were separate.

Perhaps the most important benefit of integration occurs when managers use their cost systems on a prospective basis—as part of an organization's financial budgeting process. Existing cost systems, and even recently implemented activity-based cost systems, treat budgeted expenses as given, independent of the ABM actions taken. The real payoffs from ABC and ABM, however, cannot occur unless ABC information is an integral part of an organization's budgeting process. Activity-based costing gives organizations the opportunity to move from static to dynamic budgeting. Instead of authorizing the supply of resources in forthcoming periods based on historical spending patterns, managers can supply resources based on the anticipated demands for the activities that they expect will actually be performed.

When activity-based costing is used proactively in the budgeting process, it blows away conventional thinking about fixed and variable costs. The time when the spending on most resources is variable occurs during the budgeting process. Once, during the budgeting process, the spending is authorized, then indeed most organizational expenses seem to be fixed. But activity-based costing gives managers the information they need to make almost all organizational expenses variable; they can acquire, supply, and maintain only those resources needed to fulfill specific demands in upcoming years.

The explicit vision for an integration of cost and performance measurement systems, and the expansion of capabilities that can be accomplished with integrated systems, is the primary objective of this book. We proceed incrementally. Chapter 2 describes a four-stage model of cost system migration: from broken systems, to systems that are adequate for external reporting, but inadequate for managerial purposes, to systems that have been customized for managerial purposes, and, finally, to an integrated set of cost and performance measurement systems that serve both external and internal constituencies. In Chapter 3, we explain in more detail and specificity the precise limitations of traditional costing systems for serving managerial purposes. We can then see how innovative systems can provide adopting companies with more responsive, more accurate, and more relevant information for making operational improvements and strategic decisions. Chapter 4 describes how standard costing systems can be made more timely and responsive in providing feedback on financial expenses, and the role for supplementing financial systems with nonfinancial measures, especially on process quality and cycle times. Chapter 5 illustrates how Japanese and U.S. companies use new financial measurement systems, such as kaizen costing and pseudo-profit centers, as part of their continuous improvement efforts. We use these observations to develop the general design principles for operational control systems that promote improvement and learning.

Chapters 6–13 provide a comprehensive treatment of activity-based costing. Chapter 6 describes the foundations of ABC. Chapter 7 treats the measurement of capacity costs, and illustrates how ABC can switch from being an historic to a prospective costing system. Chapters 8–11 show how managers are using activity-based management to make better decisions about improving activity and process efficiency (Chapter 8), product pricing and mix (Chapter 9), customer relationships (Chapter 10), and managing supplier relationships and influencing product design and development (Chapter 11). Chapter 12 discusses the application of ABC and ABM to service companies like banks, telecommunications companies, and retailers. Chapter 13 identifies the technical advances that companies can make to their existing ABC systems.

By the end of Chapter 13, we have documented the current state of the art in operational control and activity-based cost systems. Chapter 14 describes our vision for the future: cost and performance measurement systems, tightly integrated to provide managers with valid, timely information for managerial purposes as well as for external reporting. Chapter 15 builds upon this vision to describe how the ABC system can be used as the foundation for budgeting, on a rational, analytic basis, the organization's future expenses and resource supply.

In summary, the book provides a guided tour for how companies can migrate from inadequate, traditional cost systems to a destination where cost and performance measurement systems are explicitly designed to produce the right information at the right time for essential managerial learning, decisions, and control.

2

Four-Stage Model for Designing Cost and Performance Measurement Systems

Managers can view the development of their integrated cost and performance measurement systems as a journey through four sequential stages[1] (see *Exhibit 2-1*).

Although today some companies have characteristics of the broken systems in Stage I, most are operating with Stage II systems, our baseline. Companies must then migrate to Stage III, developing customized, stand-alone systems for cost, profitability, and performance measurement before daring to venture to the somewhat uncharted shoals of Stage IV. Thus we concentrate on describing the excellent Stage III systems before moving on to Stage IV, where cost, performance, and financial reporting systems are integrated and provide timely, relevant, and accurate information for managers and for external constituencies.

Stage I Systems: Inadequate for Financial Reporting

Some companies have cost systems that are inadequate even for financial reporting purposes. Inadequacies arise from poor internal controls for recording transactions so that transactions are either not recorded or are recorded incorrectly. In addition, some Stage I systems have incorrect algorithms for allocating overhead costs to products as they pass through different processing stages and for updating old standard costs to current price levels. These incorrect algorithms introduce errors into the accounts so that book values of inventory are virtually guaranteed not to be reconcilable to physical inventory. Stage I systems often exist in newly emerging companies that have not yet had the time or resources to install an excellent financial system. But they can also exist in mature companies that continue to use what are now called legacy systems. These systems, installed decades

Exhibit 2-1   Four-Stage Model of Cost System Design

Systems Aspects	Stage I Systems *Broken*	Stage II Systems *Financial Reporting–Driven*	Stage III Systems *Specialized*	Stage IV Systems *Integrated*
Data Quality	• Many errors • Large variances	• No surprises • Meets audit standards	• Shared data-bases • Stand-alone systems • Informal linkages	• Fully linked databases and systems
External Financial Reporting	• Inadequate	• Tailored to financial reporting needs	• Stage II system maintained	• Financial reporting systems
Product/ Customer Costs	• Inadequate	• Inaccurate • Hidden costs and profits	• Several stand-alone ABC systems	• Integrated ABM systems
Operational and Strategic Control	• Inadequate	• Limited feedback • Delayed feedback	• Several stand-alone performance measurement systems	• Operational and strategic performance measurement systems

earlier, are technologically obsolete and almost impossible to maintain since their designers have left the company and there have been so many undocumented changes and updates that no one fully understands the mechanics or the logic of the existing system. But the system cannot be scrapped since it is the only mechanism for recording and maintaining financial transactions.

Even companies that once had systems adequate for financial reporting may now have inadequate systems because of acquisitions of new divisions or companies. Usually, the financial systems in the different operating companies will be independent of and inconsistent with each other. They likely make different assumptions about the way factory and indirect costs are assigned to products for inventory valuation.

The characteristics of Stage I cost systems are:

- Extensive amounts of time and resources required to consolidate different reporting entities within the company and to close the books each accounting period,
- Unexpected variances occurring at the end of each accounting period when physical inventories are reconciled against book values,
- Large writedowns of inventory after internal and external audits,
- Many postclosing adjusting entries to the financial accounts, and
- A general lack of integrity and auditability of the system.

Fortunately, most companies do not have Stage I cost systems, and those that do can acquire and install modern general ledger systems that avoid all the problems identified above. For example, many companies are now installing new and expensive enterprise-wide systems. These are valuable systems for providing a common, integrated view of data and information across the organization. But managers in these companies may believe that an EWS can meet all their cost and performance measurement requirements, that in effect they have a Stage IV cost system. In reality, they are most likely migrating from their obsolete (Stage I) financial system to a modern integrated financial system; they will have moved only to Stage II. A Stage IV system must be based on concepts and theory, not just the ready availability of data and information.

Stage II Systems: Financial Reporting–Driven

Most companies have financial systems best described as Stage II systems, which

- Meet financial reporting requirements,
- Collect costs by responsibility centers but not by activities and business processes,
- Report highly distorted product costs,
- Have nonexistent or highly distorted customer costs, and
- Provide feedback to managers and employees that is too late, too aggregate, and too financial.

Stage II financial systems are fine for valuing inventory for financial reporting purposes and for preparing periodic financial reports. They have common data and account definitions across different business units so that financial managers can readily compare and consolidate financial results across multiple units, divisions, and operating companies. The systems can prepare complete financial statements shortly after the close of an accounting period that require few, if any, postclosing adjustments. They prepare statements consistent with standards established by financial reporting, government, regulatory, and tax authorities; the systems of data recording and processing have excellent integrity so that they satisfy stringent auditability and internal control standards.

Stage II financial systems (see *Exhibit 2-2*), however, also report individual product costs, employing the same simple and aggregate methods used for external financial reporting, to value inventory and measure cost-of-goods sold. And Stage II systems provide financial feedback to managers and employees on the same reporting cycle used to prepare the aggregate organizational financial statements. Such Stage II cost systems are completely inadequate for the two key managerial purposes identified in Chapter 1:

1. Estimating the cost of activities and business processes, and the cost and profitability of products, services, and customers; and
2. Providing useful feedback to improve business processes.

Exhibit 2-2   Stage II: Cost Systems Driven from Financial Reporting Requirements

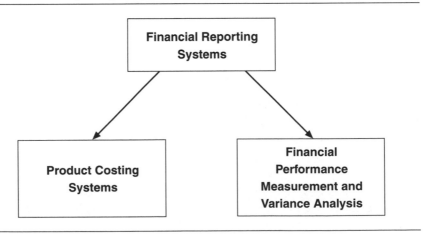

In fact, it is these Stage II systems that we and others have criticized for the past 15 years as inadequate for managerial reporting and control.[2]

Poor Costing of Activities, Products, Services, and Customers

The first defect in Stage II systems arises from the assignment of costs to products. The methods used to allocate factory overhead and other indirect costs to products for inventory valuation may be adequate for the aggregate inventory accounts on the balance sheet and the cost-of-goods-sold account on the income statement. Errors in product costing at the individual product-unit level cancel each other out as products are agglomerated together at the balance sheet and income statement levels. Also, whatever their defects in the method of cost assignment, the systems at least use the same method every year. As we have noted, auditors and financial accountants often prefer consistency to accuracy.

Many Stage II product costing systems continue to allocate indirect and support costs using direct labor measures (hours or dollars). These systems are easy to operate since information on direct labor has to be collected anyway to pay and monitor the direct labor workforce. Direct labor–based overhead allocation systems made sense 50–80 years earlier (when they were designed) because direct labor was then a high fraction of the company's total manufacturing conversion cost. As many companies automated their production processes, they introduced machine-hour allocation bases into their costing system. And some companies have shifted some of the costs of materials acquisition activities (such as purchasing, receiving, inspection, handling, and storage) to a materials overhead pool that can be allocated to purchased items based on a percentage markup over purchase cost. Some companies also attempted to improve their Stage II cost system by defining more cost centers, to match the increased diversity of different production processes and machines in their plants.[3]

But all these improvements—using additional allocation bases like material cost and machine hours, and increasing the number of cost centers—still do not reflect the underlying economics of companies with complex processes, multiple products and services, and diverse customers. These systems all assume that factory indirect and support costs vary with the physical volume or number of the units produced. They fail to recognize that many expensive factory resources are supplied to handle the production of batches of items (activities required for setup, ordering, receiving, moving, and inspecting products) and to design and sustain the myriad products the plant is capable of producing (activities required to design, improve, and maintain individual products). Stage II cost systems fail to capture the economics of production batches and product variety.

One particularly devastating loss from inaccurate Stage II cost systems is that product designers and developers receive either no information or highly distorted information about the production costs of products they are designing. Companies with Stage II cost systems force their product designers and developers to use obsolete and distorted information when making design choices and trade-offs. The erroneous choices and trade-offs made during this phase become locked in; they are costly and difficult to change when the actual cost behavior is revealed during the subsequent manufacturing phase.

Stage II cost systems also rely on responsibility cost centers for accumulating costs, both primary centers where actual fabrication or assembly production work is performed, and secondary cost centers, such as indirect labor, maintenance, and tooling preparation, that provide services and support to the primary cost centers. But assigning costs to responsibility centers gives little visibility to the costs of performing activities and business processes. Most activities and business processes use resources from many different cost centers. For example, one company discovered that an activity, like *respond to customer requests,* actually involved people from seven different departments. The customer service department, where the company thought this activity was focused, incurred only about 30% of the total cost of performing the activity.[4] The lack of information about the cost of activities and business processes has impeded many companies in setting priorities for eliminating inefficiencies, and make it essentially impossible to benchmark activity and business process costs across other units, either internal or external to the organization. Consequently, companies with Stage II systems often do not know where to focus their total quality and reengineering initiatives.

In addition, Stage II financial systems only allocate factory and other manufacturing costs to products. Large quantities of cash expended are reported in financial statements below the line under expense categories such as marketing and selling, administrative, distribution, research and development, and general (corporate). These cash expenditures are not assigned at all to cost objects (e.g., products, services, and customers) since periodic financial reporting does not require, in fact does not allow, these expenses to be assigned to cost objects. For financial reporting purposes, these cash expenditures are treated as period expenses. No attempt is made to causally link them to the activities and processes actually being performed or to the cost objects—services and customers, for example—that create the demand for or benefit from these expenditures. Again, treating such spending as a single line item in the income statement is fine for financial reporting. It is, however, totally inadequate for managerial decision making about the level of services to provide and the degree of support to supply individual customers, as well as about the control of expenditures on these resource categories.

Further, service companies, lacking tangible products, have no financial reporting requirements at all for allocating indirect and support expenses to the services they produce or the customers they serve. Consequently, most service companies do not suffer from distorted cost numbers; they have no cost numbers at all since they do not measure the costs of producing their individual products, delivering their individual services, and serving their individual customers. Service companies do have financial systems, which measure and control costs at responsibility centers. But they do not know the costs of individual products, services, and customers; nor do they know anything about the costs of the activities and processes they perform. Their Stage II systems provide no guidance to their TQM and reengineering initiatives.

In short, Stage II systems, which allocate costs adequately for financial reporting and for assigning costs to responsibility centers, provide either no information or distorted information about the cost of activities, processes, products, services, and customers.

Poor Feedback for Learning and Improvement

Stage II systems also provide inadequate information to support organizational continuous learning and improvement. The new competitive environment requires that managers and operators have timely and accurate information to help them make processes more efficient and more customer-focused. As noted, Stage II financial systems prepare and issue summary financial feedback according to a financial reporting cycle (typically monthly or every four weeks). Because of the complexities associated with closing the books, the reports are delayed for several days or weeks after the close of the accounting period, certainly too late for organizations to take corrective actions. So the feedback to responsibility center managers and supervisors is not only delayed but encompasses an extensive period of operations. One financial officer remarked:

To understand the problem of delayed and aggregate financial information, you could think of the department manager as a bowler, throwing a ball at pins every minute. But we don't let the bowler see how many pins he has knocked down with each throw. At the end of the month we close the books, calculate the total number of pins knocked down during the month, compare this total with a standard, and report the total and the variance back to the bowler. If the total number is below standard, we ask the bowler for an explanation and encourage him to do better next period. We're beginning to understand that we won't turn out many world-class bowlers with this type of reporting system.[5]

In addition, the monthly performance reports for many operating departments contain extensive cost allocations, so that managers are held accountable for performance that is neither under their control nor traceable to them. The costs of corporate- or factory-level resources, such as the heat and lighting in the building or the landscaping outside, are allocated arbitrarily to individual departments even though the departments are not responsible for these costs. For example, referring back to the bowling alley metaphor, think about having the accountants, after a ball is thrown down each of an establishment's 35 lanes, count every pin knocked down, divide by 35, and report back the average, say 8.25714,[6] to every bowler. The number may be quite accurate (it does represent the mean number of pins knocked down per alley), but it is completely useless to an individual bowler. Each bowler wants to know the number of pins she has knocked down so that she can improve on the next toss. She does not want the number contaminated or influenced by the actions of others over whom she has no control.

In summary, Stage II systems also fail to provide information to employees for their problem-solving and continuous improvement activities. Stage II systems reinforce a command-and-control philosophy. Companies now need a new philosophy—to inform and improve the work done by their employees.

Stage III Systems: Customized, Managerially Relevant, Stand-alone

The new costing philosophy is embedded when a company develops Stage III systems for financial reporting, cost measurement, and performance management. Stage III systems contain:

- A traditional, but well-functioning financial system that performs basic accounting and transactions-capturing functions, and prepares monthly or quarterly financial statements for external users, using conventional methods for allocating periodic production costs to cost-of-goods sold and inventory accounts.

- One or more activity-based cost systems that take data from the "official" financial system, as well as from other information and operating systems, to measure accurately the costs of activities, processes, products, services, customers, and organizational units.
- Operational feedback systems that provide operators and all front-line employees with timely, accurate information, both financial and nonfinancial, on the efficiency, quality, and cycle times of business processes.

In Stage III, companies retain their existing (Stage II) financial system to prepare financial reports for external constituencies such as shareholders, regulators, and tax authorities. Companies need a basic financial system to capture the transactions occurring continually throughout their operations, to assign these transactions to accounts in a general ledger system, and to aggregate and process them to prepare the statutory periodic financial statements. Given that many companies already have financial systems that are adequate for this purpose, it seems foolish to scrap these systems even though they are inadequate for managerial decision making and for employees' learning and improvement activities. Given the availability, in the mid-1980s, of powerful microcomputers and, subsequently in the 1990s, of networked client-server systems, the processing of available information into specialized managerial accounting systems is not a difficult or expensive task. Development times are measured in months not years, and total resource costs are in the tens to hundreds of thousands of dollars, not the millions required for entirely new financial systems. The powerful capabilities of new information technology—hardware, software, and networks—enable companies to introduce two customized cost and performance measurement systems for managerial purposes (see *Exhibit 2-3*), especially:

- Activity-based cost systems to provide accurate information about the costs of activities and business processes, and the costs of individual products, services, and customers.
- Operational control and learning systems to provide new and more timely feedback to employees, including nonfinancial and perhaps financial information, for their problem-solving and improvement activities.

Activity-based cost systems establish priorities for process improvement activities and help managers make strategic decisions. But ABC systems

Exhibit 2-3 Stage III: Specialized, Customized Managerial Systems

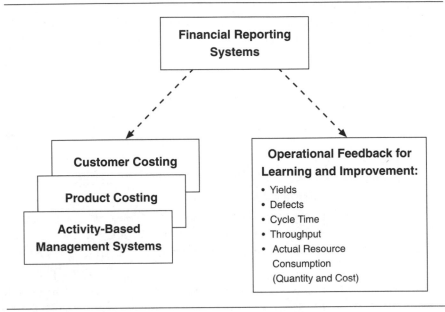

are not useful for short-term operational decisions and control. A second type of managerial financial system is needed to provide day-to-day feedback on the performance of business processes. Advances in cost assignment and timeliness of reporting can enhance traditional standard costing systems to provide more relevant information to responsibility center managers. But even with these enhancements, there are still limitations to even superbly designed and implemented standard costing systems. Companies can overcome these limitations in Stage III by deploying innovative cost systems for learning and improvement.

Activity-Based Costing and Operational Feedback: A Role for Multiple Systems?

In Stage III, therefore, managers may have three separate types of financial systems: 1) a traditional system for financial reporting; 2) ABC systems for information about the cost of processes, products, and customers; and 3) operational feedback systems to promote local efficiency and process improvements. Fortunately, activity-based cost systems and operational feedback systems can be developed without major investments in new computing hardware or software. The data and information for both systems typically already exist in the Stage II financial system, as well as in a variety of other information systems in the organization: production planning and control, inventory management, sales order entry, customer administration, and engineering, among other systems. Therefore, as new Stage III ABC and operational feedback and learning systems are developed, analysts develop protocols for accessing the appropriate data from multiple organizational systems and download the data into the local network, workstations, and microcomputers where the customized processing for ABC and operational feedback occurs.

Under this incremental approach, the ABC and operational feedback systems should be viewed as supplementary to the existing organizational systems, not as competitive or redundant with them. Also, although we use the word "system" to describe these two new sources of managerially relevant information, their systems aspects are minimal. The investment to perform the data access, processing, and reporting is far lower than what organizations normally expect when they hear the word "systems." That is why the Stage III approach is so powerful. With relatively modest expenditures, organizations can draw upon data already being collected to supply information that supports two vital managerial functions, which are inadequately addressed with existing systems. Improvements in decision making and process improvement with ABC information and with timely, relevant operational feedback can be achieved quickly and inexpensively.

Dangers of a Single System for Cost Measurement and Performance Improvement

Rather than develop two customized approaches to resource costing and for operational feedback, some organizations have attempted to perform both functions with a single additional system. Typically, they develop an activity-based cost system and then try to use it, as well, for feedback and control. Managers in such organizations fail to realize that the fundamental requirements of these two systems are so different that no single approach can possibly meet both purposes; more likely than not they end up with a system doing neither function well. ABC and operational feedback systems differ greatly in the assumptions they make about expense variability; frequency of reporting and updating; requirements for accuracy and precision; and the role for objective, historical data versus subjective estimates of future costs for measuring resource consumption. We discuss these differences in more detail in Chapter 14. For now, we assert—without documentation—that the two systems should be developed separately.

Many financial and operating managers, fully up to speed in Stage III with the three well-designed and well-functioning systems described above, will think they are in a state of heavenly bliss. They have an official system that their accountants and external constituencies are happy with, plus two additional systems that provide highly relevant sources of information that they can continually and inexpensively customize and update. For these managers, Stage III is *the* desirable goal, certainly a vast improvement over attempting to manage and improve a complex organization in a virulently competitive and technologically challenging environment with only a Stage II system.

Many other managers, however, are uncomfortable with multiple financial systems operating simultaneously but unlinked, especially when the information reported in two of the systems may conflict. For example, the standard product costs reported for cost-of-goods sold and inventory valuation may differ sharply from ABC-computed product costs. And the variance analysis performed by the official financial system to reconcile budgeted and actual data may turn up a very different view of efficiency than that reported by the operational feedback system, which works directly with data on actual throughput, quality, and response times. These managers may be willing to live with Stage III systems as an interim solution, but want to know how all the cost and performance measurement systems can be integrated with each other and with the official financial reporting system. This is Stage IV, to which we turn next.

Stage IV Systems: Integrated Cost Management and Financial Reporting

In Stage IV, the ABC and operational feedback systems are integrated and together provide the basis for preparing external financial statements (see *Exhibit 2-4*). No fundamental conflict exists between the product costs calculated by an ABC system and the external requirements for objective, consistent valuations of inventory and cost-of-goods sold. The cost drivers in an ABC system can be used to assign indirect and support costs to products for financial reporting. Expenses that have been assigned down to individual product units, but which cannot (according to generally accepted accounting principles, regulatory requirements, or tax rules) be allocated to inventory are automatically stripped away in the preparation of financial reports. For example, the cost of carrying inventory and of

Exhibit 2-4   Stage IV: Tomorrow

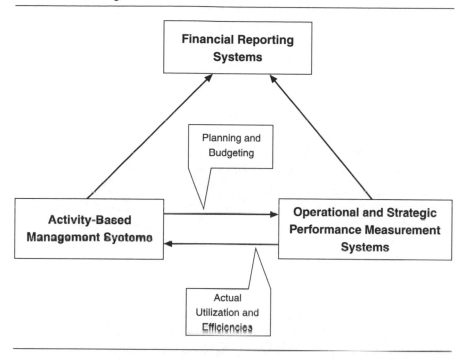

making product improvements may have been assigned to products in the ABC model, but these expenses are not inventoriable. A simple attribute field for each assigned activity can flag these noninventoriable expenses so that the system eliminates them from product costs in inventory accounts. Conversely, the ABC system may not have assigned some facility-sustaining expenses, such as the cost of the senior plant management staff down to product units. For financial, regulatory, or tax reporting, these expenses must be allocated (arbitrarily) to the product units. The Stage IV system performs the necessary and arbitrary allocation easily each time financial reports are prepared.

Similarly, the actual expenses required to prepare periodic financial statements can be found in the feedback systems that have been capturing data continually from actual operations. The financial elements in operational feedback systems can be aggregated together periodically and given to the financial accountants when they are needed to prepare external financial reports. In this way, the operational feedback system for managerial purposes becomes integrated with the system preparing periodic financial reports for external constituencies. What is remarkable is the shift in emphasis from the Stage II world to the Stage IV world. In Stage II, financial accounting and external reporting are king. Managerially relevant information—for costing of activities, products, and customers, for example—must be derived and extracted from financial accounting reports. As accountants in more than one company have been known to say when operating managers complained about how difficult it was to find managerially relevant information in the accounting reports they received: "All the information you need to know about your operations is there. You just have to learn where and how to look for it."

In Stage IV, the systems have been designed to maximize the benefits to decision-making managers and the front-line employees who work continually to improve the processes under their control. The information from Stage IV managerial systems is periodically distributed to the financial accountants who then reconcile the information with statutory needs. If the accountants complain about the information they receive, or the difficulty of meeting external reporting requirements, managers and operators will have to exercise great restraint to not point out: "This is the information we use to run the business. Try to learn how to use it to prepare your financial statements."

In addition to preparing periodic statements from the managerial systems, Stage IV systems will also integrate the information from the activity-based cost systems and the operational feedback systems. The ABC system becomes the basis for the organizational budget, authorizing the supply and expenditure of resources in all organizational units. These activity-based budgets are then used by the operational feedback system to compare and analyze the actual expenses incurred by each organizational unit throughout the year. In return, the operational feedback system provides the ABC system with information about the most recent efficiencies and capacity utilization of operations, which updates ABC cost driver rates when the organization has made demonstrable, sustained changes in operating efficiencies and practical capacity. This feedback enables activity cost-driver rates to track operating improvements quickly and reliably.

Stage II to Stage IV in One Step

Some companies, however, are impatient. Typically, their Stage II financial systems are so out of date that they wish to move directly to Stage IV, without passing through the recommended period of experimentation with ABC and operational feedback systems in Stage III. Often a company because of a major shift in its operating technology (e.g., it has eliminated direct labor reporting in its almost completely automated production environment) has an obsolete Stage II system. Since the company needs to replace its Stage II financial system, it reasons, "Why not go directly to Stage IV and use our new activity-based cost system for inventory valuation and periodic reporting as well?"

As we see in subsequent chapters, such attempts to migrate directly to an entirely new, integrated Stage IV system will almost surely fail. First, the requirements for simplicity, objectivity, and auditability for the financial reporting statements inevitably compromise the fundamental design principles of the ABC system so that it does not provide valid estimates of the costs of activities and business processes and of the cost of resources used for products, services, and customers. For example, in two cases of developing integrated ABC systems for electronics assembly divisions,[7] the system designers relied exclusively on unit-level drivers (such as number of insertions in a printed circuit board) and did not use batch and product-sustaining cost drivers (such as setups and engineering change notices) that would more accurately identify the cost of excessive variety and short production runs. Thus, the premature installation of a pseudo-Stage IV system risks compromising the main task for which ABC systems have been proposed.

Second, calculating actual cost driver rates for the most recent (monthly) period as the basis of feedback to front-line operators and employees about the efficiency of their operations uses the ABC information in an inappropriate and incorrect manner. Operators would, as in Stage II systems, get distorted and delayed information about the efficiency of their operations, rather than the more accurate, timely information from a Stage III operational feedback system. Both divisions in the company cases mentioned above provided employees with monthly reports on actual cost driver rates during the most recent period, which the system calculated by dividing the actual monthly expenses by the actual quantity of the cost driver (e.g., number of PC board insertions) during the month. Presumably, the actual monthly cost driver rate was a signal of how efficiently the process was performed during the month. But this calculation is not a valid signal of operating efficiency. First, the ex post cost driver rate reflects unexpected fluctuations in the quantity of activity performed which, although of managerial interest, does not indicate the efficiency with which the activity was performed during the preceding month. Second, the actual monthly expenses loaded on the ex post cost driver rate may reflect spending fluctuations or financial accounting accruals that bear little or no relationship to the cost of resources used during the month to perform the activity.

Another seductive migration path from Stage II to Stage IV arises as companies install sophisticated, extensive, and expensive enterprise-wide systems. Companies around the world are busy installing EWSs acquired from software companies like SAP, Oracle, PeopleSoft, and Baan. These systems can capture information from anywhere in the world, and make aggregated versions of the data available, on-line and in real time, to all authorized managers and employees. Having on-line, accessible, real-time, and consistent data available in an integrated fashion throughout the organization should be a major benefit. Such a technology platform would seem to offer companies an easy road to Stage IV cost-system capabilities. After all, it can track daily expenses by account code, activity, and business process, and measure physical quantities of activities performed so that managers have real-time, actual daily ABC driver rates and product costs.

But again, data and information are not the same as knowledge. Once an organization understands the conceptual theory underlying activity-based costing and activity-based management, it becomes clear that daily, actual cost driver rates are far from the desired information one wants from an ABC system. Rather than getting distorted information (as now provided by Stage II cost systems) once a quarter or once a year, managers would get distorted information every single day. Nor would data about such rates be of much use for operational improvement and learning. It's not that enterprise-wide systems are irrelevant in building better activity-based cost and operational feedback and learning systems. Undoubtedly, they will make such systems more accurate, responsive, and easy to install and operate. But the data and information from enterprise-wide systems are only an input to activity-based and operational feedback systems; they are not a substitute. Companies that think their ABC and operational feedback systems' needs will automatically be fulfilled once they have installed their brand new enterprise-wide system are likely to be severely disappointed.

Thus, rushing prematurely into a Stage IV system may compromise the managerial relevance and usefulness of that system. In effect, a company may boldly try to leap directly to a Stage IV system, but like a golfer buried in a sand trap near the green who attempts to sink the ball in the hole with a single shot, may find itself reburied in Stage II.

Companies need the experimentation and learning that occur with Stage III financial systems. They need to understand how to structure their activity-based systems for their particular managerial purposes, they need to solve some technical measurement issues, and they need to explore the structure of the financial and nonfinancial feedback they provide to employees for their learning and improvement activities.

Mike Roberts, former executive director of the CAM-I Cost Management Project, has a vivid metaphor that illustrates the benefits of Stage III experimentation. He recalls the example of wingwalkers, daredevils who entertained people at county and state fairs by walking back and forth along the wings of WWI-vintage biplanes flying thousands of feet in the air. A researcher studied their techniques by interviewing all the wingwalkers he could find. Naturally, he only interviewed successful wingwalkers since the unsuccessful ones were in no position to describe their experiences. Each wingwalker had his or her own style of presentation, but they all shared one technique in common. As they moved from one strut on the wing to the next strut several feet away, they kept one hand firmly on the strut already achieved, and reached out with the other hand to the next strut—making sure that the new strut offered the stability and security of the strut about to be left. In effect, wingwalkers did not abandon the security of the Stage II financial system, but they groped forward and reached out to Stage III financial systems farther down the wing. After they had operated with both systems, they felt confident abandoning their previous system as they prepared for the next one. The researcher learned that any wingwalker who attempted to get from one strut to the next by abandoning the previous hold before getting a firm grip on the next strut, with its perhaps new and unique characteristics, was blown away and could not be interviewed. Financial systems can be as fragile as handholds on planes flying thousands of feet in the air. Companies should be cautious in moving from Stage II to Stage IV. They should explore the new opportunities but without giving up the security of their tried and tested financial system that still must prepare statements for many important constituencies.

In the next chapter, we start the journey to Stage IV. We begin by defining the baseline of what the very best standard cost systems look like. These systems can provide a foundation for Stage III feedback and learning systems. We also identify, however, some specific limitations of even the best standard cost systems for managerial purposes.

3

Stage II: Standard Cost and Flexible Budgeting Systems

In this chapter we describe Stage II standard cost systems. Even with excellent designs, Stage II systems have serious limitations for the managerial purposes of costing processes, products, customers, and for providing timely, relevant feedback to front-line employees. This chapter provides the baseline for the improvements documented in the remainder of the book for making cost and performance measurement systems far more relevant and useful for managerial purposes.

History

We start by tracing a brief history of cost systems during the past two centuries that have led to the excellent standard cost/flexible budgeting systems used in many U.S. and European companies. The Stage II cost systems used by many manufacturing and service companies today are not new. They have been used for hundreds of years to control the performance of employees. This task can be traced back to the early stages of the industrial revolution—in textile mills, in armories that built weapons, and in ceramics and porcelain manufacturing operations. Managers of early nineteenth century textile mills received information about the hourly cost of converting raw material (cotton) into intermediate products (thread and yarn) and finished products (fabric), and the cost per pound of output by departments and for each worker.[1] The owners used such managerial accounting information to measure the efficiency of the process that converted raw cotton into finished yarn and fabric. Managers compared productivity among workers, and tracked the productivity of individual workers over several periods of time. They used this information to provide additional compensation for the most productive workers, and as production targets for less efficient workers. This data helped maintain and improve the efficiency of critical internal processes.

The railroad organizations that developed in the mid-nineteenth century were enormous and complex enterprises that could not have functioned effectively without extensive financial control information. Their financial managers developed summary measures of performance for decentralized and dispersed managers, such as cost per ton-mile for individual commodity types and for each geographic segment of operations. They developed a new performance measure—the operating ratio, which equaled the ratio of operating expenses to revenues. Managers used this measure to evaluate the efficiency of operations of local managers, and to measure the profitability of various types of business: passenger versus freight, region A versus region B. These measures enabled local managers to take actions, based on the unique information they had about local conditions, that were consistent with maximizing the economic performance (that is, profits) of the entire railroad.

Steel mills, such as those owned and operated by Andrew Carnegie, measured daily the cost of materials, labor, and energy inputs used to produce steel and rails. Carnegie used the cost information for operational control—to evaluate the performance of department managers, foremen, and workers and to check the quality and mix of raw materials. He also used the cost information to evaluate investments that offered improvements for processes and products.

Companies that manufactured discrete, customized products, such as machine tools, had to understand the costs of resources used to produce each item. This information was needed to determine the profitability of different product lines and to help determine the prices that would be offered, particularly for customized products, to prospective customers. Engineers in the scientific management movement, like Frederick Taylor, developed procedures to measure in considerable detail the quantity of materials and the labor and machine time required to manufacture individual products. This information was collected primarily to improve and control the efficiency of production operations. The costing techniques developed at that time provided the basis for the Stage II standard cost systems still used today by many organizations.

Flexible Budgeting and Standard Cost Systems

The innovations during the scientific management movement led to standard cost systems that have been the foundation for companies' cost control systems for most of the twentieth century. This approach has been taught for decades to business and accounting students around the world.[2] German academics and practitioners developed a highly structured and detailed approach to cost control through standard costs and flexible budgets.[3] *Grenzplankostenrechnung,* or GPK, as we will refer to it here (for obvious reasons), was developed by Kilger and Plaut in the early 1970s. It represents a widely used German approach for flexible, standard costing.[4]

The Kilger-Plaut GPK system incorporates two basic principles. First, responsibility (cost) centers are the focal point for cost planning, cost control, and product costing. This focus enables managers to monitor and control the efficiency of responsibility centers. In order to give the highest visibility to cost productivity and cost control, German companies define many distinct cost centers to avoid the averaging of heterogeneous cost behavior (e.g., similar machines, but with different productivities or operating characteristics) within a cost center. Consequently, German companies typically have far more cost centers than do companies in other countries. For instance, one medium-sized ($150 million annual sales) manufacturing company, producing electric and electronic switches with only three different manufacturing processes, has about 100 cost centers—15 direct production cost centers, and 85 indirect responsibility centers. Big plants of other companies, such as Siemens, can have upward of 1,000 to 2,000 cost centers.[5]

GPK's second fundamental principle is to make clear distinctions between fixed and variable costs at every individual cost center. The distinction between fixed and variable costs is made even when the percentage of variable costs in indirect cost centers is small and declining. These two principles are incorporated in companies' cost planning and control system. Annually, financial managers plan each cost center's expenses (e.g., labor wages and salary, consumable supplies, equipment depreciation). They then establish monthly budgets for each cost component at each cost center. The budgeted costs are set at standard levels, based on estimates of efficient resource consumption, as determined by industrial engineers.

During the year, the GPK financial reporting system prepares monthly statements of each cost center's actual and planned demand for resources, actual costs per expense item, standard costs, and different types of variances. Standard costs are allowable costs to meet actual demand for resources. Hence, standard costs are different from planned costs if actual demand for resources differs from planned demand for resources. We provide a sample illustration of a GPK cost system in the chapter appendix.

U.S. Standard Cost Systems

Some of the best U.S. cost systems are similar to the GPK cost systems used by companies in German-speaking countries. For example, Caterpillar's costing system[6] establishes responsibility centers for:

- Logistics cost pools that collect costs associated with purchasing, receiving, handling, and transporting materials;
- Machining cost centers that include automated machines, manufacturing cells, and work stations; and
- Assembly cost centers where products are assembled, tested, painted, and shipped.

For each cost center or cost pool, expenses are split between variable and fixed. The variable costs assigned to the logistics cost pools include freight of incoming materials; cleaning materials; receiving, inspection, and materials handling labor; and fuel and electricity for operating materials handling equipment. Period expenses (as Caterpillar refers to its short-term fixed costs) include purchasing personnel, depreciation and maintenance on materials handling equipment, utilities, insurance, property taxes, maintenance, and clerical support.

For machining cost centers, the variable expenses include wages and fringes of the direct labor assigned to the cost center, perishable tooling (e.g., drills, taps, and cutting tools), variable costs of operating the tool crib and grinding reusable tools, machine power, consumable supplies, spoilage and rework, quality auditing, first-line supervision salaries, and other variable support. Period expenses include machine-specific depreciation; building occupancy costs; depreciation and storage and maintenance of dies, jigs, and fixtures; repairs; and planning. Building occupancy costs include depreciation, utilities (heat and light), maintenance and repair, and plant security. These occupancy costs are assigned based on floor space occupied by the cost center.

For assembly cost centers, variable expenses include cost of assemblers, test people, painters, and shipping personnel, plus related costs for clerical support, quality assurance, housekeeping, factory accounting, product handling, tooling, indirect materials and expenses, power, gas, and supervision. Period assembly expenses include depreciation on assets used, occupancy costs, training, tool and equipment repair, and fixed supervisory and management costs.

Appropriate cost drivers are associated with each type of cost center. Logistics cost pools use materials weight, machining cost centers use labor hours (for direct labor expenses) and machine hours (for all other expenses), and assembly cost centers use labor assembly hours.

The Caterpillar system is somewhat less elaborate than the German GPK system since, instead of having an extensive array of indirect cost centers, it relies on analytic techniques for allocating indirect and support expenses to logistics, machining, and assembly production cost centers. The Caterpillar system also differs by allowing for multiple cost pools (labor-hour and machine-hour related) within the same cost center, a feature now adopted by more recent GPK systems (formerly, GPK systems required that each cost center be classified as either a labor-hour or a machine-hour cost center).

Both the U.S. and German (GPK) approaches represent excellent cost systems for monitoring and controlling costs via responsibility centers. They utilize many different cost centers so that the work done in each cost center is homogeneous with respect to an appropriately selected cost driver. The homogeneous cost centers with appropriate cost drivers provide highly transparent cost and performance information that facilitates effective discussions about cost control and productivity improvement among cost center managers, management accountants, and plant managers. The systems clearly separate fixed and variable costs to facilitate short-term cost control. And, by separating fixed (or period) expenses from variable, they permit flexible budgets to be prepared each period so that actual expenses for the period can be compared to a budgeted level that reflects the volume and mix of activity in the plant each period. In this way, supervisors and cost center managers are motivated to adjust the supply of variable resources to the short-term demand for these resources.

The systems record inefficiency variances (unfavorable spending and usage in a cost center) at the cost center where they arise, rather than allocating the variances either from indirect centers to direct (production) centers, or from direct production centers to products. Thus, costs are transferred between departments at budgeted levels, representing standard levels of efficiency. With this procedure, managers are held accountable for costs they can control—spending and usage variances within their cost center, quantities of services they use from other cost centers, valued at standard prices. They are not assigned costs they cannot control. And the use of flexible budgets allows the fixed costs to be assigned at a predetermined budgeted rate, calculated annually, with variable costs assigned based on actual usage (but at standard prices).

Consider an alternative (Stage I) cost system process in which no distinction is made between fixed and variable costs, nor between actual and standard costs. In any period, the total (actual) cost of a cost center is divided by the output produced by that cost center, and that actual cost driver rate is used to transfer costs to the direct cost centers or products that used the resources of the cost center during the period. This process introduces several severe distortions in the fully loaded cost center rate. First, any inefficiencies within the cost center are reflected in the actual costs incurred and passed on to products processed (in the case of a direct cost center) or to direct cost centers (in the case of an indirect cost center). Also, if demand for the output from the cost center is lower than expected in a period, the cost center burden rate will be inflated, since its full costs are spread over a smaller output.[7] By

1. Separating fixed from variable costs in all indirect and direct cost centers,
2. Applying fixed costs at a predetermined lump sum transfer, and
3. Applying variable costs based on actual quantities consumed multiplied by a standard rate per unit,

the cost shifting and distortion that arise in Stage I cost systems from arbitrary full cost allocations are avoided.

The standard cost, flexible budgeting system also calculates product and part costs at standard levels of efficiencies. Inefficiencies, as reflected in unfavorable spending and usage variances, are calculated each period and can be highlighted for management attention. They need not be rolled forward for sales and marketing to recover by attempting to realize higher prices from customers.

Limitations of Standard Cost/Flexible Budgeting Systems for Product Costing

Many companies today, much less 10–15 years ago, would dearly love to have costing systems that have the transparency and functionality of the German and U.S. systems described above. But these systems still have two limitations that severely impair their value for modern companies. First, they do not report accurately on the cost of processes, products, and customers. For product costing, the systems may identify the short-term variable costs associated with producing one more or one less unit of a product. But they fail to capture and trace accurately many other costs triggered by designing, producing, delivering, marketing, selling, and servicing individual products. Large categories of costs—in design and development, in logistics and distribution, in marketing and selling, and in postsales service—are not traced to individual products and customers with these Stage II cost systems. Largely because these other categories of costs are not considered inventoriable or part of the cost-of-goods-sold calculation in the periodic income statement, little attention has been given to tracing these categories of costs to individual products and customers. They are expensed each period on the income statement, appearing below the line as elements within large agglomerations of period expenses.

But even beyond the failure to trace nonfactory costs to individual products, the Stage II cost systems treat many factory expenses as fixed or period expenses. These period expenses are either ignored entirely, as in direct costing systems, or allocated using the same cost drivers (materials weight, labor hours, machining hours) used to assign variable expenses to individual products. Unfortunately, these expenses are not fixed with respect to the volume and mix of individual products manufactured within a plant. Plants producing a wide range of products—high-volume and low-volume, new and mature, standard and customized—have much higher levels of period costs than plants producing only one or two products in high volumes.[8]

The inability of flexible budgeting systems to relate the expenses of almost all factory resources to the demands made by individual products for these resources led to the development of activity-based cost systems, an innovation that will be discussed in subsequent chapters of this book. To foreshadow that discussion, initial Stage III ABC systems use historical actual, not standard, costs. Our vision for Stage IV ABC systems, however, advocates a return to using standard, not actual, activity cost-driver rates. Therefore, future ABC systems will retain some important benefits from the standard costing approach. But, as we explain, the ABC approach makes three important extensions to traditional standard costing for measuring the costs of products, services, and customers. ABC systems

1. Use activities and processes, rather than responsibility centers, as the focus of the costing system;
2. Trace the costs of using resources, not the cost of supplying resources, to cost objects; and

3. Use a richer set of cost drivers, to reflect the effects of variety and complexity, for assigning costs from activities to cost objects.

Thus, adopting the ABC approach does not sound the death knell for standard costing.

Limitations of Standard Cost/Flexible Budgeting Systems for Feedback and Learning

The second limitation of standard costing/flexible budgeting systems arises when companies use these systems for cost control and to monitor efficiency. This usage, providing feedback via monthly variances, is based on a system of engineered work standards and standard costs that was developed a century ago by engineers in the scientific management movement. This system of work and cost standards reflects a philosophy in which engineers and managers determine operators' tasks. Operators are told what to do, and the measurement system—including cost variances that compare actual results to the predetermined standards—checks whether the workers are following the prescribed procedures.

How are standards set for workers? Typically the standard and budget-setting processes are performed by and under the control of engineers and managers. The engineers are the descendants of the mechanical engineers in the scientific management movement. These scientific management engineers operated in an environment where relatively unskilled and uneducated workers produced quite complex products, whether discrete products like machine tools, automobiles, and household appliances, or continuously processed industrial products, like aluminum, steel, chemicals, and paper. The engineers broke the complex processes required to make these items down into much simpler tasks, that, collectively, enabled the production of the final product. The engineers established detailed procedures for unskilled workers to perform in a reliable fashion ("simple jobs for simple people"). The procedures also enabled the engineers to measure in considerable detail the quantity and cost of materials, labor time, and machine time required to perform each individual task. As noted by Frederick Taylor, the pioneer of the scientific management approach:

> In our scheme, we do not ask the initiative of our men. We do not want any initiative. All we want of them is to obey the orders we give them, do what we say, and do it quick. . . . [We hire workers] for strength and mechanical ability, and we have other men paid for thinking.[9]

The standard cost systems, still in use today, retain the top-down, elitist philosophy of Fred Taylor and the scientific management movement.

Today, however, performance that just meets historical standards is no longer adequate. Many managers have learned that often their best source of new ideas for continually improving performance is the people who are closest to the work being performed. These operators see firsthand the types and the principal causes of defects. Front-line employees, not engineers or managers, are expected to devise new approaches for how to perform work and satisfy customers. Employees must make the continuous improvements to ongoing processes to reduce and eliminate waste, improve quality, and reduce defects. As one plant manager stated:

> *The machines build the parts. They have been designed to run automatically. An employee's job is to think, to problem solve, to ensure quality, not to watch the parts go by. . . .*
>
> *In traditional factories, the financial system viewed people as variable costs. If you had a production problem, you sent people home to reduce your variable costs. Here, we do not send people home. Our production people are viewed as problem solvers, not as variable costs.*[10]

As problem solvers, employees cannot be held strictly accountable to predetermined standards. They need freedom to experiment with solutions designed to fix the root causes of defects. They also need information—first, to identify the source of defects and, second, to see immediately the consequences from attempts to fix the causes of the defects. With this total quality management philosophy,[11] operators find solutions for eliminating defective output, waste, and activities that do not add value for customers. They no longer just follow standard operating procedures and monitor the machines producing output. They now must quickly identify problems as they arise, devise countermeasures, implement those countermeasures, and test and validate that the problems have been solved. The new environment stresses cross-functional linkages to promote effective and efficient performance of business processes, not the individual tasks within a process.[12]

For these new responsibilities, the front-line employees need new and more timely forms of feedback information for their problem-solving activities, not to control them against preset and soon-to-become-obsolete standards. For operational control, companies need to shift away from their Stage II standard cost/flexible budgeting systems since these systems emphasize performance against historical standards.

Several advocates of the TQM approach claim that financial control systems should be discarded entirely—that financial information is at best irrelevant and at worst dysfunctional in the continuous improvement espoused by TQM. Such a claim presented a stark challenge to the financial community. Has the new basis of competition in the information era outpaced the financial measurement and control systems that have proven so vital to success in industrial-age competition?[13] Initially, the answer to this question was not clear. What was clear was that any financial information system that could meet the information needs of employees attempting to improve customer-focused, quick response, high-quality processes would be very different from traditional costing systems. Stage III financial systems should enable organizations to experiment and implement new systems for providing feedback to employees about the actual cost, efficiency, quality, and timeliness of their business processes.

Specific Limitations of Standard Cost Systems for Operational Control

Let us examine the problems of Stage II systems, and, by inference, the opportunities for Stage III systems for providing feedback for employees' learning and improvement activities. We can analyze the problems along several critical dimensions:

1. Delayed reports
2. Exclusive reliance on financial measures
3. Top-down direction
4. Focus on local task improvement
5. Individual control
6. Adherence to historical standards

1. DELAYED REPORTS

In Chapter 2, the metaphor of the bowler not being allowed to see how many pins he knocked down until the end of the month was introduced to highlight the foolish expectations of using a monthly cycle—perhaps appropriate for financial reporting—to provide feedback for monitoring and improving an ongoing, real-time process. Certainly, in the mid-1980s, most organizations did provide only monthly (or quad-weekly) financial feedback to cost center managers.

2. EXCLUSIVE RELIANCE ON FINANCIAL MEASURES

Competition, since the mid-1970s, has focused on a much broader set of parameters than just low cost. The TQM approach advocates zero-defect production. Standard cost financial systems may report on the cost of resources spent to produce products, but provide no information on the quality and defects associated with the production. Most standard cost systems even include an allowance for scrap and waste ("budgeted scrap"). But companies should not budget for scrap; they should eliminate it entirely. As companies implement continuous improvement programs, such as TQM and cycle-time reduction, they must supplement the exclusive financial information from their Stage II systems with direct measures of defects, scrap, yields, cycle times, and throughput.

3. TOP-DOWN DIRECTION

The scientific management standard-setting system works fine when knowledge about processes and how to improve them resides with highly trained engineers and at middle to upper levels of management. This system was appropriate for decades, but began to erode in the 1970s as new forms of competition arose. Particularly as engineers and managers learned the enabling conditions behind the new competition, based on total quality and highly responsive operating processes used by leading Japanese companies, they realized that front-line employees had to be empowered. For this radically new assignment, the front-line employees could not continue to follow standard procedures established by organizational elites—the engineers and managers.

Stage II cost systems, however, hold workers and local supervisors accountable to meeting standards established high up in the organization. Stage III systems must enlist the minds, motivation, and talent of front-line employees for them to make continual improvements in the processes they can control and influence. The design of a Stage III system for performance improvement must reflect the informational needs of individuals and teams who now are responsible for improving the quality, responsiveness, and cost of their local processes.

4. FOCUS ON LOCAL TASK IMPROVEMENT

Another legacy of the scientific management movement is the decomposition of work into individual microtasks. Workers achieved efficiency through specialization of knowledge. They were assigned microtasks, and they performed them over and over again until they achieved high levels of proficiency (as well as boredom). The theory was that if every individual microtask was performed efficiently, the overall production process would be highly efficient. Wrong! The emergence of the lean enterprise destroyed much of the intellectual underpinnings for the task-specialized organization.[14] Innovative Japanese manufacturers demonstrated the breakthrough improvements in cost, quality, and cycle time from switching from a batch-and-queue production system to a single-piece continuous flow production. The gains from lean-enterprise continuous flow work processes was subsequently adapted to white-collar work by the reengineering movement.[15] Michael Hammer, a pioneer of reengineering, illustrates his approach with a line from a movie in which a lawyer is investigating the death of a friend. The lawyer found no sign of overt incompetence or negligence: "Every person in the system did his or her job well, and yet my friend died." This syndrome occurs in highly fragmented organizations or systems, where each local piece is optimized, but not the entire organization or process. Consequently, gross inefficiencies build up between individual tasks. Hand-offs from one task to another are poorly managed, if managed at all, inventories and delays build up between stages, and vital information gets lost as work is passed from one stage to the next.

The system of local responsibility and controllability, embodied in factories with thousands of microcost centers, each controlled monthly or daily with its own standard cost and flexible budget report, illustrates exactly the failures from optimizing isolated, individual tasks. Each cost center, arguably, does its job superbly well, controlling actual costs to budgeted and authorized amounts, yet the entire factory could have low first-pass yields, many defects not detected until the product or service is received by customers, and incredibly long delays in converting raw materials (or even earlier, from receipt of a customer order) to a finished product arriving at the customer's location. Defects created at one stage, such as by high impurities in a chemical mixture or a poorly placed component, will likely not get detected until the product is several stages farther down the production process. At that point, the detecting cost center bears the cost of repair or scrap, and usually at a much higher cost than if the defect had been detected initially. Also, small delays in transferring goods from one department to another, early in the process chain, eventually lead to overtime, expediting, and rushed production at a much later stage in order to meet stringent delivery dates.

Hammer argues that reengineering is not about process improvement; it's about process abandonment, especially if you are looking for a ten-fold improvement, not a 10% improvement. Reengineering—defined as "the fundamental rethinking and radical redesign of business processes to achieve dramatic improvements in critical measures of performance (cost, quality, capital, service, speed)"—requires starting with a clean sheet of paper, a green field design, for designing a process to accomplish work. The financial system to provide feedback to employees working with a reengineered process will clearly be very different from the standard cost/flexible budgeting system used to provide feedback to supervisors about short-term cost performance in their isolated, local cost centers.

5. INDIVIDUAL CONTROL

When the world of work resembled Fred Taylor's neatly hierarchical and compartmentalized system of decomposed microtasks, the focus of measurement could clearly be on individual worker efficiency and productivity. As business processes become more complex, more integrated, and more reengineered, measurable work gets done by teams, not individuals.[16] Performance measures must track people's contributions to their team, and the team's contribution to the performance of the reengineered processes. This implies that generic costing systems, especially those focused on individual labor and machine efficiencies and local cost centers, are not likely to be the primary means for evaluating team performance. The performance measures must be derived by the nature of the process being controlled and the critical factors at which that process must excel. Standard cost/flexible budgeting systems, despite their sophisticated real-time capability to capture actual costs, daily, at thousands of individual cost centers, are not likely to promote team-based process improvement activities.

6. ADHERENCE TO HISTORICAL STANDARDS

Standard cost systems measure success when employees in local cost centers meet the cost standards established by industrial engineers. At best, these standards reflect best current practice; often, however, detailed studies have not been done for many years so the standards are historical, occasionally updated by engineers when local improvements have or should have been made. Alternatively, some organizations choose a period, such as the last three months of the year, measure the actual performance during that period, and use the actuals during that period as the standards for the upcoming year. The opportunity for gaming and sandbagging with this procedure are so obvious that no further comment seems necessary.

Again, the industrial engineering approach is internally focused. It examines existing ways of performing tasks and attempts to devise incrementally better ways for performing the work. The global competition that most companies now confront requires more than incremental improvements to local processes. Critical internal processes should be comparable—in cost, quality, and cycle time—to the best in the world. Otherwise, the company's competitiveness could be seriously eroded.

Summary

Traditional standard cost and flexible budgeting systems worked well for many decades for decentralized cost monitoring and cost control. But they are inadequate for managers and employees in today's competitive environment.

First, Stage II standard cost systems trace costs to cost centers and not to activities or processes. And when calculating product costs for inventory valuation or for measuring short-term incremental costs, these Stage II systems use traditional volume-based cost drivers such as labor and machine hours. Therefore, these systems cannot report accurately on the costs of resources used by activities, business processes, products, and customers. To overcome the limitations of inaccurate costing, companies need Stage III activity-based cost systems.

Second, Stage II systems focus on responsibility accounting and accurate tracing of costs to cost centers. In today's environment, however, such reporting fails to provide the accurate, timely, operational, process-focused, team-based measurements needed to drive continuous improvement and learning. These Stage II systems rely much too heavily on financial measures of performance, assume that efficient operating procedures can be determined by managers and engineers, focus on the performance of isolated and unlinked tasks, machines, and individuals, and concentrate on controlling costs to preset standards, not making continuous improvements in quality, cycle times, and actual costs. Stage III operational feedback systems must be specifically designed to promote employee learning and improvement that will enhance the efficiency, quality, and responsiveness of operating processes.

Appendix: GPK Cost System

We can illustrate the GPK approach with a simplified example of budgeting and charging for a secondary (indirect) cost center, #55, Inspection of Production Batches. This center inspects the output from injection molding machines in three different primary (operating or direct) cost centers.

Step 1: Develop the Annual Budgeted Expenses for Cost Center #55

COST ELEMENT	FIXED	VARIABLE	TOTAL
Personnel	$50,000	$250,000	$300,000
Supplies	300	1,200	1,500
Tools		4,000	4,000
Maintenance	1,000	3,500	4,500
Capitalized services	20,000		20,000
Occupancy	24,000		24,000
Energy		3,500	3,500
Total Expenses	**$95,300**	**$262,200**	**$357,500**

In general, the budgeted expenses for an indirect cost center, like #55, would include both expenses directly incurred within that cost center (like personnel salaries and supplies and energy consumed) as well as expenses arising in other indirect cost centers (like plant maintenance, finance, and information systems) that can be directly attributed to cost center #55. Thus, an initial stage using either a step-down or reciprocal method assigns indirect support expenses among all indirect cost centers.[17] For example, in the above calculation, the occupancy cost could include assignment of expenses from plant maintenance and plant utility indirect cost centers.

Step 2: Distribute Planned Costs from Indirect Cost Center #55 to the Primary Cost Centers Serviced by the Indirect Cost Center

Indirect cost center #55 services three molding production cost centers: #22, #25, and #27. Its costs are distributed to the three molding cost centers based on expected annual operating levels of the three centers.

OPERATING COST CENTER	ANNUAL OPERATING HOURS	PERCENTAGE OF OPERATING HOURS
22	4,350	38.3%
25	1,870	16.5
27	5,130	45.2
Totals	11,350	100.0%

Determine the budgeted variable cost rate for assigning cost center #55's variable expenses to the three production cost centers:

$$\text{Variable Cost Rate} = \frac{\text{Budgeted Variable Costs (Center \#55)}}{\substack{\text{Planned Operating Hours} \\ \text{(Production Centers \#22, \#25, \#27)}}}$$

$$= \frac{262,200}{11,350} = 23.10 \text{ per Hour Worked}$$

Develop the monthly budget for the three production cost centers.

COST CENTER	PLANNED EXPENSES		
	FIXED	VARIABLE	TOTAL
22	$36,500	$100,500	$137,000
25	15,700	43,200	58,900
27	43,100	118,500	161,600
Total Planned Expenses	$95,300	$262,200	$357,500

Step 3: Determine Monthly Actual Costs in Indirect Cost Center #55, and the Activity Levels in the Three Production Cost Centers It Services

COST ELEMENT	ACTUAL COSTS
Personnel	$27,000
Supplies	200
Tools	300
Maintenance	400
Capitalized Services	1,667
Occupancy	2,000
Energy	297
Total Actual Expenses	**$31,864**

OPERATING COST CENTER	ACTUAL HOURS WORKED
22	415
25	90
27	460
Total Hours Worked	**965**

Step 4: Analyze Actual Expenses Incurred in Indirect Cost Center #55

Budgeted monthly fixed expenses equal annual budgeted expenses divided by 12. Authorized variable expenses equal budgeted variable cost per unit multiplied by the actual hours worked in the three production cost centers during the month.

COST ELEMENT	AUTHORIZED EXPENSES FIXED	AUTHORIZED EXPENSES VARIABLE	ACTUAL EXPENSES	VARIANCE
Personnel	$4,167	$21,258	$27,000	$1,575
Supplies	25	102	200	73
Tools		340	300	(40)
Maintenance	83	298	400	19
Capitalized Services	1,667		1,667	—

COST ELEMENT	AUTHORIZED EXPENSES		ACTUAL EXPENSES	VARIANCE
	FIXED	VARIABLE		
Occupancy	2,000		2,000	—
Energy		297	297	—
Total Authorized Expenses	**$7,942**	**$22,295**	**$31,864**	**$1,627**

Alternatively, the total authorized variable expenses for cost center #55 can be computed as:

Allowed monthly variable expenses $-$ Actual monthly hours worked $\times$ 23.10

$$= 965 \times 23.10 = 22,295.$$

Step 5: Distribute Monthly Inspection Department (#55) Expenses to the Three Molding Production Cost Centers

Fixed expenses are distributed to the three cost centers based on the planned actual usage (see calculations in Step 2). Monthly variable expenses are distributed based on the annual planned variable rate (23.10 per hour) multiplied by the actual hours worked in each cost center.

COST CENTER	ASSIGNED EXPENSES		
	FIXED	VARIABLE	TOTAL
22	$3,042	$9,589	$12,631
25	1,308	2,081	3,389
27	3,592	10,625	14,217
Total Assigned Expenses	**$7,942**	**$22,295**	**$30,237**

Under the GPK system, all spending (or usage) variances that arise in the indirect cost center (#55) remain in that center as the responsibility of the manager of that cost center. Only budgeted fixed and authorized variable costs for the actual hours worked would be charged to the three production cost centers (#22, #25, #27).

In a subsequent step (not illustrated here), the expenses assigned to each production cost center are allocated to the products processed through that cost center each month. A measure of activity volume is selected for each cost center. The activity volume measure could be machine hours, as in the injection-molding production cost centers discussed in this example, or labor hours in a labor-paced cost center, such as assembly, or materials dollars in a materials handling or acquisition cost center. These expenses assigned to the production cost center are divided by the selected activity volume measure to obtain the production cost center burden rate. This rate is then used to assign the center's expenses to products processed through the cost center. Separate rates are calculated for assigning the production cost center's variable costs (which include the variable costs assigned by indirect cost centers, such as #55, as well as the variable costs incurred within the production cost center) and fixed costs. Some systems may not assign any fixed costs to products, except for a separate calculation used to value inventory for financial reporting purposes. These companies are using what they interpret as a marginal costing approach in which only short-term variable costs are assigned as product costs.

4

Stage III Systems for Learning and Improvement: Upgrading and Supplementing Standard Cost Systems

In this chapter we explore how Stage II systems can be modified and supplemented to provide more timely and relevant information to front-line employee teams. The teams use this information for their problem-solving activities to reduce cost, increase productivity, and improve the quality of processes under their authority. We start by describing the modifications to Stage II standard cost systems so that they can be more responsive to the needs of front-line employees. We also discuss how the financial feedback from even enhanced standard cost systems needs to be supplemented with extensive nonfinancial measurements.

Enhancing Standard Cost Systems for Operational Control

The standard cost/flexible budgeting systems described in Chapter 3 were generic systems that provided information according to the cycle of the organization's financial reporting process, typically monthly. Managers used the financial summaries from these Stage II systems to monitor and control front-line employees, to ensure that they followed the prescribed operating procedures designed by engineers and managers.

Stage III systems must provide timely information about the actions employees have recently taken to improve processes under their control. The feedback must incorporate both nonfinancial and financial information so that front-line employees, working in teams, can simultaneously take informed actions, based on their task-specific knowledge, to improve the quality, cycle time, and cost of processes. And the information should be directed to achieving outstanding, even breakthrough performance improvements in critical internal processes.

Some newer versions of standard costing systems, such as those developed by SAP/Plaut (incorporating GPK principles) and installed on modern mainframe or client-server computer systems, can overcome the timeliness problem of Stage II systems. The new systems can now prepare weekly or even daily reports on cost center expenses and variances. Many U.S.-based cost systems also have exploited powerful information technology to provide cost center managers with more frequent reports. For example, an automobile engine plant prepared a weekly report on scrap and total expenses for each cost center, plus a daily report, for each cost center, that displayed:

- Direct labor usage, including variances between actual hours worked and the budgeted work standard (BWS). The BWS equals the direct labor hours authorized for the actual parts produced that day; and
- Actual indirect labor (maintenance, cleaning, materials handling, and inspection) hours compared to daily authorized indirect labor hours, calculated as a budgeted percentage of the department's BWS that day.[1]

Thus, one of the previous limitation of Stage II standard cost systems for operational control—delayed information—can now be overcome. Supervisors and front-line employees can receive daily variance reports. The question is, are daily financial reports sufficient? Are daily variance reports meaningful?

Recall that another limitation of Stage II cost systems for performance improvement is their dependence on work standards established by engineers and managers remote from actual day-to-day operations. Stage III systems should not impose standards from above. The new systems must support local employees' experiments and innovations for continuously improving process performance. One approach is to use standards based on most recent efficient actual performance. And this updated standard should not just be met in the current period; it should be a standard that has to be *improved upon* by actual results in the current period.

Alternatively, many organizations now use benchmarking to identify best practices for critical internal processes. Benchmarking involves studying comparable internal processes of the best companies not only in your own industry, but also in any industry using the same process. For example, Xerox learned a great deal from L.L. Bean about the order fulfillment process. When feasible, benchmarking sets stretch targets for cost performance based on external, not internal, considerations.

Setting stretch targets for internal operating processes represents a distinct departure from the Stage II system philosophy of being content when actual costs do not exceed historically determined standard costs. Stage III systems evaluate the cost performance of teams and processes against standards established by the most efficient internal or competitive processes. And the standards should continually be reset to reflect organizational continuous improvement activities.

With timeliness and standard-setting practices upgraded from Stage II to Stage III systems, we must still examine whether financial information alone is sufficient for cost reduction and performance improvement.

Role for Nonfinancial Measures

Cost reduction is an important managerial objective. But cost improvement alone may not be sufficient. Customers want not only lower prices and costs; they also greatly value quality, responsiveness, and timeliness. Consequently, employees must have information about both the cost consequences of their activities and the quality and cycle time of processes under their control. Stage III systems for learning and improvement must supplement financial feedback with information on critical nonfinancial measures, especially measures of process quality and time.[2]

One can think of a process as converting a set of inputs to a set of outputs:

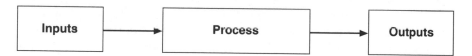

Assuming that the output of the process meets the functionality requirements of customers, we can describe such a process with three parameters:

1. Quality: Defect rates—for every 1,000,000 inputs, how many defective items are produced?
   Yields—what is the percentage of zero-defect finished items to total items started into production?
2. Timeliness: Cycle time—from the time an item starts into production, how long until it is completed?
   Lead time—from the time an item has been ordered, how

long until it starts production?

On-time delivery—is the finished item delivered at the time promised?

3. Cost: For each item produced, what are the costs of resources used (materials, labor, energy, machine time, indirect support) for its production?

Stage III cost systems can provide timely and accurate answers to the third question, measuring the cost of resources used in operating processes. But they can certainly not provide information about the first two parameters, quality and timeliness. For this, Stage III systems must also include an appropriate set of nonfinancial indicators.

Process Quality Measurement

As organizations adopted the TQM philosophy, they introduced a broad array of nonfinancial measures to monitor and improve the quality of their products and processes. These included:

- Process part-per-million (PPM) defect rates
- Yields[3] (ratio of good items produced to good items entering the process)
- Waste
- Scrap
- Rework
- Returns
- Percentage of processes under statistical process control

Motorola, a leading company in applying the TQM philosophy, adopted an aggressive approach to quality, setting a quality target of 6 sigma for its manufactured products, a level representing fewer than 12 defects per one million parts.

Service organizations also needed to identify the defects in their internal processes that could adversely affect costs, responsiveness, or customer satisfaction. Some developed customized measures of quality shortfalls, for example:

- Long waiting times
- Inaccurate information
- Access denied or delayed
- Request or transaction not fulfilled

- Financial loss for customer
- Customer not treated as valued
- Ineffective communication

Thus, front-line employees in any manufacturing or service organization must receive signals on process quality, not only on the cost of performing their task or process.

Western managers were slow to recognize the benefits from higher quality processes. Their financial model did not incorporate how improved quality could lead to higher profits. Many companies felt that defect rates in the parts per hundred were optimal. For example, Texas Instruments, before it bought into the TQM philosophy, emphasized financial control measures and expected a certain amount of defective product to be returned by the customer.[4] Financial measures are lagging indicators. Employees, if they are to lower the cost of their processes, need leading indicators that they can control, such as defect rates and yields, not reports about the cost performance of last period's production.

Process Time Measurement

Managers, in the 1980s, learned that competition was taking place along a time dimension as well as a quality dimension. New time-based competition strategies were being deployed by superb Japanese manufacturers to compete both on rapid time-to-market for new products as well as short lead times and highly reliable delivery times for existing products.[5] For example, Olympus Optical reduced its product development cycle from 10 years (1970) to 18 months (1990), a reduction that enabled it to compete more aggressively on product functionality. Nissan Motor Company adopted a policy of delivering its cars "while the paint was still wet," a euphemism for extremely rapid order-manufacture-delivery response times. A customer could order a car, have it manufactured, and delivered to his or her residence in about the same time that it took to get a parking permit from the Tokyo city government.

Many customers strongly value short lead times—the time between when they place an order and the time when they receive the desired product or service. They also value reliable lead times, as measured by on-time delivery. Reducing cycle or throughput times of internal processes becomes a critical internal process objective.

Choosing starting and ending points for measuring cycle or throughput time is determined by the scope of the operating process for which cycle time reductions are being sought. The broadest definition, corresponding to an order fulfillment cycle, could start the cycle with receipt of a customer order and would stop when the customer has received the order. A much narrower definition, aimed at improving the flow of physical material within a factory, could correspond to the time between when a batch is started into production and when it has been fully processed. Whatever definition is used, the organization continually measures cycle times and sets targets for employees to reduce total cycle times.

More advanced organizations combined quality and time-based measures when they focused on on-time delivery—the percentage of orders that arrived within the promised delivery window which could be ± 2 days for nondemanding customers or ± 1 hour for excellent just-in-time (JIT) manufacturers like Toyota and Honda. Another quality/time-based measure is the percentage of promised delivery dates that met customers' requests, a useful measure to avoid quoting long lead times in order to be sure to hit demanding targets for on-time delivery.

An especially powerful metric used by many organizations that are attempting to move to JIT production flow processes is manufacturing cycle effectiveness (MCE), defined as:

$$\text{MCE} = \frac{\text{Processing Time}}{\text{Throughput Time}}$$

This ratio is less than one because:

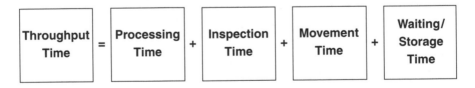

$$\text{Throughput Time} = \text{Processing Time} + \text{Inspection Time} + \text{Movement Time} + \text{Waiting/Storage Time}$$

For many operations, processing time, the time when the product is actually being worked on (machined or assembled), is less than 5% of throughput time. In an ideal JIT production-flow process, the throughput time for a part equals its processing time. In this ideal situation, the MCE ratio equals one, a goal that, like zero defects, may never be attainable but is worth striving for.

The theory behind the MCE ratio is that all time, other than processing time—that is, time used for inspection, reworking defective items, moving items from one process to the next, and having items wait until processed at the next stage—is waste or non-value-added time. This time is wasted because the physical form of the product is not being enhanced to meet a customer need. And the product is being delayed for delivery to the customer, with no value added during the delay. As the MCE ratio approaches one, the organization knows that the amount of time wasted moving, inspecting, repairing, and storing products is decreasing, and its ability to respond rapidly to customer orders is improving.

While just-in-time production processes and the manufacturing cycle effectiveness ratio were developed for manufacturing operations, they are applicable to service companies as well. If anything, eliminating waste time in a service delivery process is even more important than in a manufacturing process, since consumers are increasingly intolerant of being forced to wait in line for service delivery. As in manufacturing, most service delivery processes revealed the existence of long cycle times for customer service, during which actual processing time was remarkably low. A few companies have reengineered their service delivery processes. Automobile rental companies and a few hotel chains have automated, for targeted customer segments, all aspects of check-in and check-out, enabling valued customers to bypass all wait lines. Thus, companies attempting to deliver products and services on demand to targeted customers can set objectives that have MCE ratios approach one, thereby producing dramatically shortened lead times.

Clearly, in the new competitive world where customers demand high quality and rapid response times, cost summaries of manufacturing performance and, in fact, of all organizational processes, must be accompanied with measures of quality, timeliness, and responsiveness.

Quality and Timeliness Measures: Are They Sufficient?

Some people believe that in a world of TQM and customer satisfaction, financial and cost measurement may be unimportant. For example, a group of professors, enamored of the continuous improvement philosophy in operations management, argues against tinkering with the costing system:

> . . . *when cost accounting data of any kind does not help, "better" cost accounting data will not help either. . . .*
>
> *Several companies had even gone beyond tinkering with their cost accounting systems. These companies cut the Gordian knot by finding simple, innovative, yet bold solutions to the performance measurement problem.*[6]

The companies praised above just used direct costing, no analysis or reporting of spending on indirect and support resources, and relied extensively on quality and timeliness measures such as cycle time, defect rates, and yields, for their front-line employees. The theory that advocates the elimination of financial measures for front-line employees and replaces financial measures with measures of quality and timeliness, apparently assumes: ". . . if the operational measures are good, the result is on-time delivery and product-line budget cost. If operational measures are bad, these results should not occur."[7] In other words, the authors argue that good operational measures are both necessary and sufficient for achieving good financial performance, so employees do not need to see cost-based measures. The authors conclude:

> *Accounting-based performance measures become less useful as the following situations occur:*
>
> 1. *The market environment in which the firm competes becomes more dynamic; and*
> 2. *The level of management at which performance is being measured becomes closer to physical activities.*[8]

The authors clearly believe that cost signals are, at best, irrelevant and, at worst, distracting and dysfunctional to front-line employees in innovative, quick-response, high-quality environments.

H. Thomas Johnson, another academic advocating total quality, continuous improvement, and the Japanese approach to manufacturing excellence, claims:

> *Managing with information from financial accounting systems impedes business performance today because traditional cost accounting data do not track sources of competitiveness and profitability in the global economy. Cost information, per se, does not track sources of competitive advantage such as quality, flexibility and dependability. . . . Business needs information about activities, not accounting costs, to manage competitive operations and to identify profitable products.*[9]
>
> *What information should a company have to evaluate its power to compete and profit in the long run? We have already concluded that it is not accounting information about financial results, such as revenue or cost information. Revenues and costs . . . provide no insight about customer needs or about the causes of profit. . . . Cost information . . . tells how much was spent, on what, and where, but it never indicates what caused the cost. . . . [O]ld cost-oriented mindsets still impede competitiveness even where companies compile reliable activity-based product costs for strategic decisions.*[10]

Johnson concludes by advocating that companies focus on the most important information—what it takes to create and keep satisfied customers—and argues that cost and financial information are not relevant for this purpose: "Always keep information that is used to control operating activities separate from the financial information that is used for planning and budgeting."[11] Johnson argues forcefully against sharing financial and cost information with employees to promote their continuous improvement and customer satisfaction activities: "Whatever form management accounting takes . . . never again should it be seen as a tool to drive people with measures."[12]

These academic critics claim that financial measures should *not* coexist with nonfinancial measures to promote employee learning and improvement activities. Their quite explicit recommendation is that in a world where quality, responsiveness, and customer satisfaction are primary, organizations should direct their front-line people to achieving excellence along these dimensions. They assume that companies that improve quality, reduce cycle and lead times, and keep customers satisfied will be rewarded with both low costs and high profits. If this view is correct, indeed there would be little apparent need for financial measurements for front-line employees. They should just focus on quality and time. Low cost and expense control will inexorably follow. And there should be no provision in Stage III systems for cost measurements to enhance employee learning and improvement activities.

Facts, unfortunately, occasionally intrude on academic theories. Many companies made enormous commitments to improving quality and satisfying customers, yet still had disappointing, if not disastrous, financial performance. This is not surprising. It would be curious if among these three core process measures, two—quality and timeliness—were vitally important for continuous improvement activities, but one—cost—was irrelevant or even counterproductive for process improvement. It would be even more curious since clearly there are trade-offs in performance along the three measures. For example, to improve timeliness, managers could add redundant machines, labor, and other resources so that there was always capacity to process a new order, whenever it arrived. Also, to improve quality, employees and machines could work at a much slower pace, to avoid any chance of an error. But a slow pace clearly adds to the labor and machine resources required to produce a single finished item, and may also conflict with the timeliness criterion.

In addition, decisions to add functionality to the product will typically require additional resources, thereby adding to the cost of the process.

Without a cost measure of the process, managers and engineers have little guidance about whether any anticipated increased revenue from the added functionality will exceed the additional process costs.

Finally, and more important to our argument here, we have seen many outstanding organizations, deeply committed to improving quality, reducing cycle times, and satisfying customers, provide their front-line employees with innovative measurements of cost and financial performance. These innovations in cost and financial measurement, however, were not, necessarily, the daily variances from standard costing/flexible budgeting systems described earlier in this chapter.

Thus, at one level the skeptics of financial measurement are correct in their criticism that traditional costing systems are inadequate for performance improvement. The critics overreach, though, by making blanket statements about all cost and financial systems, not recognizing the opportunity for innovation in financial information provided to front-line employees.

Managers in Japanese companies, where the lean enterprise evolved, have developed sophisticated cost management systems to enhance their employees' ability to develop very fast cycle times and high quality levels. If the critics of the use of financial measures were correct, Japanese cost systems should be nonexistent. They would not have predicted the sophisticated cost systems—*kaizen costing* and *pseudo-profit centers*—actually found in leading Japanese and U.S. companies.[13] We turn to these in Chapter 5.

Summary

Companies wanting to foster a spirit of continuous improvement in their employees often espouse a rhetoric of employee empowerment. Senior managers urge employees to take actions every day to improve quality, reduce cycle times, increase yields and output, and lower costs. But unless the employees are provided with timely and accurate feedback about the results of their continuous improvement experiments, employee empowerment cannot occur. Employees need an appropriate mixture of financial and nonfinancial measurements, especially cost, quality, yields, and cycle time, of processes under their control.

5

Stage III Systems for Learning and Improvement: Kaizen Costing and Pseudo-Profit Centers

Chapter 4 described the upgrading of traditional standard costing systems into systems that provide more frequent feedback on cost performance to cost center managers. We also explicated the need to supplement financial information with nonfinancial measures on process quality and cycle times. But the financial information, even if provided more frequently, still has some serious limitations. The information is related to a cost or responsibility center view of the organization. The information on variances against standards promotes a controlling, not a learning, view. The variances are not easily understandable by front-line employees, do not promote an integrated process view of the organization, and do not directly encourage continuous improvement activities.

The kaizen costing and pseudo-profit center systems described in this chapter are meant to provide direct financial feedback to employees. These systems may replace standard cost systems in Stage III since their designs are based on the actual production processes in the organization and they have been explicitly customized to promote specific learning and improvement opportunities by front-line employee teams. They, like many contemporary feedback systems, use extensive nonfinancial information so that employees can improve process quality and cycle time. But their distinguishing characteristic is that financial information is also provided to empowered employees so that they can develop more efficient processes. And underlying all these systems is a common philosophy that the systems have been designed to provide *information* for local team improvement activities, not to *control* the employees and teams and monitor their adherence to preset standard operating practices.

Kaizen Costing

Kaizen is the Japanese term for continuous improvement: "gradual, unending improvement, doing 'little things' better; setting—and achieving—ever-higher standards."[1]

Most Western observers first became familiar with kaizen by studying the Japanese approach to improving quality and cycle time performance. The observers are somewhat less acquainted with how Japanese companies apply kaizen to reducing cost. Cooper, in his extensive study of Japanese cost management practices, has documented kaizen costing systems used by several important companies.[2] Kaizen costing is the "continuous improvement applied to cost reduction in the manufacturing stage of a product's life."[3]

Kaizen costing reduces the cost of producing existing products by finding ways to increase the efficiency of the production process used in their manufacture.[4] In many firms with very short-lived products, the life of production processes is longer than the life of products. Therefore, greater savings can be achieved by focusing on the production processes in the manufacturing phase of a product's life than on the product itself.

Kaizen costing focuses on where managers perceive the greatest opportunity for cost reduction. Citizen Watch, with a labor- and machine-intensive production process, concentrated its kaizen costing program on increasing the running speed of machines and on increasing the number of machines that could be operated or supervised by a single employee.[5] Sumitomo Electric, a mass producer of copper wire, mainly used its kaizen costing program to reduce materials cost.[6]

For kaizen costing to be effective, work teams are provided with detailed cost information on a continual basis. Most of the companies had traditional (Stage II) standard cost systems that they used for inventory valuation and financial reporting. But the standard cost systems did not provide the primary information to the work teams. At Citizen, workers focused on improvements in labor hours per watch produced. The entire workforce engaged in efforts to reduce direct labor cost. Even minor efficiency improvements were valued, and pictures and stories circulated continually about how small changes led to reductions in labor-time requirements. Production engineers focused on how to get more output per machine and how to have more machines operated by a single employee. Separately, engineers and technical staff worked to reduce the cost of parts purchased from suppliers.

At Sumitomo, the emphasis was on reducing materials cost. Its employees focused on a standard loss ratio of materials. This ratio had three components:

- *Loss Ratio of Surplus:* the extra length of product that was unavoidably produced in the production process (by running a little extra for each run so that the customer would be guaranteed getting at least the length of usable wire it ordered) plus that consumed by inspection;
- *Loss Ratio of Giveaway:* the extra materials consumed by running a slightly larger diameter of wire, again to ensure that customers got at least the diameter they ordered; and
- *Loss Ratio of Scrap:* the extra materials wasted at the beginning of a run, while the process was stabilizing, and at the end of the run when the process was terminating.

The work teams also monitored the operating expenses of the process by calculating an actual cost per hour, obtained by summing the salary and fringe benefits of the work team, plus the energy, maintenance, and lubricants cost of the machines, and dividing the whole by the group's hours of useful production.

Continual information on actual costs was used by the work teams to direct their attention to areas (labor time at Citizen, materials loss at Sumitomo) where improvements would have the largest impact on product and organizational profitability. The cost information also helped the teams assess the impact of their implemented improvements. The implemented reductions in labor time, material loss, lubricants, and energy use, even in indirect personnel supporting the local work team, could all be denominated in a common unit (¥1,000 saved). And knowing the cost of processes under their control, the work teams generated investment proposals where they balanced front-end costs of new equipment against the ongoing cost savings from the new equipment.

The relationship between standard costing in Stage II systems and those required to support kaizen costing is highlighted by the approach taken by Shionogi Pharmaceuticals. Shionogi's cost system uses two sets of standards, budgetary and updated. The budgetary standards are set once a year based upon the actual performance achieved in the last month of the prior year. These standards are modified to reflect any anticipated improvements in production equipment and process planned for the upcoming year. For example, if a new piece of equipment is expected during the year or there will be a major change to the production process, the standards reflect the expected actual operating efficiencies.

The updated standards are revised throughout the year based on the progress of the kaizen program. They are used to evaluate the workforce's current performance. For example, usage variances, calculated from these standards, provide up-to-date feedback on progress. Production supervisors have on-line access to the updated standards and the actual production results for each lot and, hence, the kaizen variances. Their access, however, is limited to variances specified in terms of units produced. They do not see the variances measured in monetary terms; managers feel that on-line availability of quantity variances is sufficient to motivate the workforce to be highly cost conscious. Workers are neither rewarded nor punished for creating variances, but overall performance, including variances, is taken into account in reviews that lead to both promotion and pay raises.

The workforce reports to the technical development department after every lot is completed to discuss the effectiveness of their kaizen activities. They are expected to identify the portion of the variance that is due to kaizen. Once the standard setter and the workers responsible for that chemical process have agreed on the level of kaizen improvement, the updated standards are adjusted accordingly, but the budgetary standards remain the same.

Updating standards is done in three steps. First, the technical development department tests any new process in a laboratory or pilot plant to see if it can replicate the anticipated improvement. Second, once the improvement is confirmed, the technical development staff asks the production staff to run the new process on the production line, and check the result. Finally, when the anticipated result is attained, the production staff repeats the same process alone so it can independently confirm the improvements. When all three steps have been successfully completed, management officially endorses the new standards and the firm's databases are updated.

If negative variances occur after updating the standards, because they were too difficult to achieve consistently, the updated standards are reduced to reflect reality. Thus, the variances determined from the updated standards are expected to be either zero or slightly positive because of kaizen activities that have yet to be reflected. Natural variations in the yield of the chemical processes, however, can occasionally cause the usage variances to be negative.

Thus, the updated standard costs in kaizen costing are used to create pressure on the workforce to reduce costs. Unlike the static standards described in Chapter 3 (which are equivalent to the budgetary standards at Shionogi), the updated standards for kaizen costing are revised continually. In kaizen costing, the objective is not to achieve the standard but to outperform it. For this objective, the workforce is empowered to find ways to reduce costs.

In summary, kaizen costing systems have several important characteristics in common:

- The focus is to inform and motivate process cost reduction, not to obtain more accurate product costs.
- Cost reduction is a team, not an individual, responsibility.
- Frequent, even batch by batch, actual costs of production are calculated, shared, and analyzed by the front-line employees. In many instances, the team itself, not the accounting staff, collects and prepares the cost information.
- The cost information used by the teams is customized to their production environment so that learning and improvement efforts are focused on the areas for highest cost-reduction opportunities.
- "Standard costs" are continually adjusted to reflect both past reductions in actual costs and targeted improvements in future costs. This ensures that proven innovations in process improvement will be sustained, and will set a new level for further improvements.
- Work teams are responsible for generating ideas to achieve cost reduction targets; they have authority to make small-scale investments if these can be demonstrated to have cost reduction paybacks.

Most important (and perhaps obvious by now), the goal under kaizen costing is not stability of a production process to predetermined work standards. The goal is to constantly improve critical processes so that costs can be continually reduced in product lines that are mature, highly price-sensitive, and not amenable to product innovation.

U.S. Systems for Continuous Improvement

Systems that supply continual process information to empowered work teams are no longer confined to Japanese companies. Romeo Engine Plant, a refurbished Ford tractor plant, reopened in the late 1980s with a new mission and a new philosophy.

The Purpose of the Romeo Engine Plant is to produce the highest quality production engines in the world that meet all of our customers' requirements at a cost lower than the competition, and to develop teams of employees who are the best engine builders in the world.[7]

Unlike a similar engine plant, Peoria (with the daily variance report on labor and overhead described in Chapter 4), Romeo's plant manager encouraged initiative, creativity, and prudent risk taking in the work teams that would support growth in capabilities and continuous improvement of processes.

His plant was organized by independent work teams. Every employee in the Romeo plant was assigned to a single work team, which operated as an independent business unit, with its own team manager and support staff, including engineering, maintenance, and administration. The teams had complete responsibility and autonomy over their assigned production process, including safety, quality, engineering, productivity improvement, housekeeping, and equipment maintenance. Work teams received extensive education and training, especially in quality, team problem solving, safety, information systems, process technology, and productivity.

For operational improvement, Romeo's work teams received information about machine downtime and scrap. The plant manager wanted Romeo to bid for new engines to be built on site, so expanding plant capacity without adding new machines was a high priority. Work teams focused on improving operations at bottleneck machines and processes. The teams received daily reports on machines and a summary of the principal causes of shutdowns on each machine. Workers were expected to use these reports to identify the machines and processes that were the current bottlenecks. The work teams had frequent discussions with higher management about progress in reducing and eliminating recurring faults with bottleneck machines. The teams also received a detailed daily report on scrap—plus weekly and monthly scrap reports that traced defects to components, fault code, and part. Each team had weekly meetings to discuss actions taken to eliminate the principal causes of scrap, meetings that might include direct discussions between the team and suppliers.

In addition to the daily information on machine downtime, throughput, and scrap (all nonfinancial measures), the teams received a daily report on their spending on indirect materials such as supplies, tools, scrap, and maintenance goods. The teams had an authorization for spending based on production quantities, and had a goal, similar to that of a Japanese kaizen costing team, to reduce the actual spending per engine produced. The teams implemented internal process improvements and had direct negotiations with suppliers to reduce spending on indirect materials.

The teams also received a weekly report on total overhead expenses charged to their departments, including telephone, utilities, indirect labor, and salaries of engineering and technical assistants. Although these expenses are often considered fixed by many companies and cost systems (such as the Stage II flexible budgeting systems used in its sister Peoria plant), Romeo's finance staff believed: "The teams are responsible for their own expenses. They are billed for everything that relates to their department. If they leave the lights on, their costs go up."[8]

Romeo management wanted the teams to influence their use of the salaried people. They could ask them for advice on how to increase productivity, and they had the option of not replacing salaried people who left because of retirement or attrition. Obviously, this is a complete reversal of power. The expense of managers and engineers was now visible to the front-line employees who were authorized to decide whether the costs of additional engineers or salaried people were too high relative to the benefits they could provide for enhancing productivity and quality.

Monthly, managers at the Romeo plant looked at the unit cost of the engines they produced. Historically, engine plants relied on a system that reported labor and overhead expenses, by account, compared to budgeted amounts (as did the Peoria Engine Plant with its daily variance reporting). Romeo managers and supervisors preferred their system of reports of actual, daily machine downtime, scrap, and spending to the company's official variance reporting system. They felt that watching trends in critical operating parameters, including cost, was more consistent with their continuous improvement philosophy. Also, the budgeting system at Peoria encouraged game playing, manipulation, and sand-bagging to build more slack into budgeted quantities and to avoid short-term unfavorable variances. As the controller noted:

> *People soon learn that there are two ways to avoid unfavorable variances. Reduce actual costs or increase your budget. Initially people work hard to reduce costs, but at some point a manager finds it easier to develop a case and argue for an increased budget allowance because of product design, mix changes, external economic factors, and machine deterioration. The manager might get a higher allowance but how does this help to reduce spending in the plant?[9]*

An area manager agreed: "At Romeo, I spend my time *improving* actions, not *tracking* actions. Instead of focusing on how much my area spent yesterday on tooling and overhead, I am coaching and problem-solving with teams on how to enhance line productivity."[10] Even the company's divisional finance staff endorsed the new performance reporting system at Romeo:

> We believe the emphasis on actual costs in a team environment was the right thing to do. . . . By having employees concentrate on actual costs rather than the traditional budget variance approach, the Romeo systems provided employees with the opportunity to learn how their actions drive costs and formed the basis for continuous improvement.[11]

The contrast between the traditional (Peoria) plant, treating its workers as variable costs and meeting top-down targets for cost, and the plant (Romeo) committed to continuous improvement in quality, yields, throughput, and cost reduction was remarkable. Note that the traditional plant used a (Stage II) controlling system with standard cost targets, and a flexible budgeting and variance analysis system operated by middle-level supervisors and managers. The continuous improvement plant, in contrast, used a (Stage III) informing system of daily reporting of actual outcomes on nonfinancial and financial measures—quality (scrap), throughput, machine downtime, and spending—to empower its front-line work teams.

As another example, an automobile supply plant had adopted a TQM program.[12] It organized the factory into work teams dedicated to producing a particular product for a designated customer. As at Romeo, the employee work teams were almost completely self-contained. Each team performed its own customer scheduling, inspection, job assignment and rotation, training, recruiting, and supplier scheduling. As with the Japanese kaizen costing systems, each team had a goal for annual reductions in labor and materials cost; 10% for labor costs and 5% for materials costs. To measure performance improvements, the employee work teams received a weekly "profit index" report on the costs of key resources under their control.[13] For example, the profit index of one team included the measured cost of:

- Inventory
- Equipment (weekly cost of each piece of equipment in the work cell)
- Floor space (calculated at $55 per square foot)
- Efficiency (machine time per piece produced)

- Materials savings (through substitution of less expensive materials)
- Scrap

The plant held weekly meetings of the profit index managers from each team to compare improvements and share ideas that had improved the profitability (by reducing costs and enhancing productivity) of their teams.

These examples show how plants, looking to employee work teams for suggestions and actions for continuous improvement (kaizen) in process quality, cycle time, and cost, need frequent, accurate information on both physical parameters and actual costs incurred for producing output. Employee work teams constructively use their daily actual cost and financial information for continuous improvement activities.

Pseudo-Profit Centers

We have seen some companies go beyond providing financial feedback on traceable and controllable costs to their front-line employees. Some companies are motivating their employees by providing them with *profit* information about their operations. Profit is a more comprehensive financial signal than cost, and profit enhancement is proving to be a more powerful motivator for improvement than cost reduction. These systems provide real psychological benefits by focusing the teams on the positive action of increasing profits as opposed to the negative action of decreasing or avoiding costs. In addition, having a measure of team profitability helps the team see the alignment of their actions with overall firm performance.

What is quite remarkable about the use of profit as a signal for continuous improvement is that the companies have not organized the employee work teams into true profit centers. Employees do not have authority for pricing, product mix, or output; these decisions remain with higher management. Given that employees cannot make the decisions normally associated with being a profit center, what advantage does feedback on profits offer beyond feedback on costs? Let's answer this question with some specific examples.

One dramatic experience with use of profit information for continuous improvement occurred in Department 3B, a hydrocarbon-cracking unit of a large chemical company.[14] The company had made a deep commitment to a total quality approach, built on a three-pronged approach of teamwork, performance management, and statistical quality control. The performance management component had identified key result areas for driving improvement and for developing measures for each area to determine how well the employee work team was performing its mission. The intense focus on measurement and statistical quality control had led to a major investment in information technology so that department managers received thousands, often tens of thousands of observations about physical operating parameters, throughput, and quality every two to four hours.

In this environment, a chemical-engineer department manager had developed, on his own, a daily income statement for the operators in his department, 3B. One's first reaction to such an innovation is a virulent skepticism. After all, U.S. managers have been roundly criticized for their short-term orientation when using a quarterly income statement. Could a daily income statement motivate employees to engage in long-term process improvement? A second reaction, similar to that of the academic skeptics quoted in Chapter 4, concerns the enormous quantity of computer-accessible information that operators were already receiving. What incremental benefit could an aggregate financial measure, like daily profit, add to their extensive information set?

The construction of the daily income statement was elegantly simple. The existing system already measured, on a continual basis, quantities of inputs used—hydrocarbon feedstock, energy, cooling water, and machinery—and the quantities of outputs produced—ethylene, propylene, and several by-products. It also measured the quality of the outputs produced, defined by the incidence of impurities in the intermediate products produced by the cracking unit. The department manager created the daily income statement by estimating the cost of each input and an approximate price for the value of each output. The primary output products could be purchased or sold in external markets so estimates of output prices could be easily made. The manager even included the cost of capital by estimating the daily mortgage payment (calculated using an estimate of the replacement value of the assets employed, the division's cost of capital, and the expected useful life of the assets) required to pay back the company for use of the assets. The operators may have found depreciation an obscure concept, but all were familiar with repaying loans for cars, trucks, homes, and family farms.

The really clever innovation was a penalty for poor-quality production. The employees would only earn the full revenue from production of output products if the output was within statistical control limits ($\pm 3\sigma$). Output outside the control limits, but still within rated specifications (it was still usable), was priced at only 50% of the standard price (a 50% penalty), and output that was unusable received a 100% penalty; no revenue credit was given for output produced that had critical parameters outside rated specifications.

As a final motivator, the manager issued stock certificates to all operators, showing that they were the owners of the 3B company. As owners, they were entitled to an income statement describing how well their company did each day. The manager launched the program by promising the employees a new kitchen in their control unit if they could hit a stretch profit target for a 90-day period.

The daily income statement proved a big hit. The team soon set new records for throughput and quality. In fact, quality got so high that a subsequent process, three stages later, malfunctioned. It seemed that trace elements were required for the subsequent chemical reaction, and these trace elements were carried by impurities. As employees in 3B succeeded in purging all impurities from their output, the trace elements disappeared as well. The 3B manager received an urgent request to allow some impurities to remain in the intermediate products. Prior to the daily income statement, and despite a highly successful quality program, the 3B plant had never before achieved such extraordinary levels of quality.

The daily income statement functioned effectively in several ways, some of which could have been accomplished with accurate cost information alone, without pricing the output produced. But several critical benefits were realized by having a simulated revenue figure that enabled daily profits for 3B to be calculated. The statement

1. Provides rapid, easily understood feedback,
2. Internalizes cost of nonconformance,
3. Informs trade-offs,
4. Sets priorities and justifies spending for improvements and investment, and
5. Empowers employees for local decision making.

We discuss each benefit, in turn.

Provides Rapid, Easily Understood Feedback

The daily income statement provided operators with a quick summary of the operations just completed, including the efficiency of the conversion process and the quality produced. Despite, or because of, receiving thousands of observations, operators appreciated seeing a single financial figure that summarized yesterday's performance. The summary income number was simple to understand and communicate, and it provided a rapid guide to short-term actions that would increase quality and throughput.

For example, after a major cleaning of a heat exchanging unit, the daily income statement showed a decline in profit. This anomaly led to a problem-solving exercise where the operators concluded that the temperature differential across the heat exchanger was now much too high and should be reduced significantly. Perhaps they could have detected this problem without the decline in daily income. But amidst the myriad of operating statistics they were receiving, the fall in income provided a powerful signal that an unexpected and major problem had occurred.

The 50% penalty for off-spec production also provided a highly visible signal of the importance of maintaining high quality levels. Workers soon learned which operating parameters were associated with quality fluctuations, and focused their efforts on ensuring those parameters stayed within very carefully controlled limits.

Internalizes Cost of Nonconformance

Previously, if output was of poor quality, the consequences would show up in a subsequent department, not in the performance report of 3B. Equipment in downstream processes would have to be taken off-line while impurities were purged from the system. So the operating performance of downstream processes would be adversely affected while 3B showed good throughput and yield ratios. Assigning a cost to off-spec output enabled the 3B plant to internalize the cost of poor quality output. Rather than treating quality as something different from output, the financial penalty integrated quality considerations into the aggregate performance of the 3B plant. The success of this signal was manifested in the record quality levels achieved in the 3B plant (even to the unexpected detriment of a downstream process, as related above, and which could be easily remedied, once known about).

The more general lesson from this calculation is how seemingly intangible (to financial accountants) parameters, like quality and timeliness, can be incorporated into a profit figure. For example, if on-time delivery of intermediate product from a pseudo-profit center is important, the "revenue" figure from the center can be penalized by a cost of late delivery. This would internalize, to the pseudo-profit center, the future revenue losses incurred by a downstream department because of late deliveries of finished products to customers.

These two benefits, of rapid feedback with a simple financial summary, and incorporating the cost of nonconformance (or more generally, the cost of not achieving specified quality or delivery targets) could also be achieved by an aggregate cost figure. Such a treatment would be consistent with the kaizen costing approaches described above. What is the benefit of calculating a profit figure obtained by estimating the value of the intermediate outputs produced each day? To answer this question, we have to look at the three additional benefits.

Informs Trade-offs

Employees, especially those empowered for continuous improvement, are urged to reduce defects, increase yields, and lower operating costs, as if these functions could all be done simultaneously. Perhaps in the highly inefficient, low-quality production environments of the 1970s, quality was indeed "free." Production processes were so far from optimal levels that investments (in employees, training, problem solving, or equipment) to improve quality would be quickly repaid in higher output and lower operating costs. At some point, however, the low-hanging fruit had been picked and the slack in operations eliminated. Additional improvements in quality can only come at a cost that is not immediately repaid. At this point, financial information becomes vital to inform employee quality-enhancing activities.

For example, at the 3B plant, yield could be increased by operating the cracking unit at higher temperatures. But this required more energy consumption and also made the introduction of impurities more likely. How should this trade-off between higher output requiring higher operating costs, and lower quality be made? Or consider the trade-off between maintenance and output. When preventive maintenance is required to sustain high-quality, high-yield operations, should it be performed on regular shifts using regular work crews, or should it be done continually, requiring overtime and midnight shift premiums for the work crews? Again this is a trade-off among quality (the need to perform preventive maintenance), output, and operating expense.

At a motivational level, one of the products, propylene, was more expensive to produce. So when the production plan calls for shifting a higher percentage of the output mix from ethylene to propylene, the measured productivity declines and the cost per unit of the 3B plant increases. Employees told to increase productivity and lower actual costs would find that the mix shift has thwarted their best efforts for improvement. But when productivity is measured by pricing out each output, not just by measuring the quantity of output produced, employees can see that the net *value* of what they produce has increased, even when the quantity has declined. The approach of measuring throughput by the value of production not by physical units is also similar to that advocated by Goldratt in his Theory of Constraints (TOC).[15]

In effect, having pseudo-prices for the departmental output provides an alternative way to control for variations in the mix of outputs produced during a period. Historically and traditionally, variations in mix are handled through a standard cost system where input allowances are determined for every product. Each period, an overall flexible budget is calculated based on the expected consumption of inputs for the product mix actually experienced. With pseudo-profit centers, as a more complex product mix is produced, actual expenses may rise but so would the revenue credit for the product mix produced. Thus, by pricing intermediate outputs, managers can encourage continuous reduction in the actual consumption of input resources to produce a given quantity and mix of output, without using a standard costing system.

Sets Priorities and Justifies Spending for Improvements and Investment

The operators of the 3B plant use the daily income statement to set priorities for their improvement efforts. They could assess where improvements in operating performance had the highest impact on improving the daily profit of the plant. Without a financial signal, employees in a continuous improvement mode could make huge improvements to local subprocesses that had negligible impact on total operating performance. A 100% improvement in a subprocess that costs $100 per day to operate is much less significant than a 10% improvement in a $10,000 per day subprocess. The financial figure also provides the appropriate benchmark for justifying investments in new equipment and technology. The payback from such investments can be quantified in operating savings, higher quality, or higher output. Employees quickly learn the ground rules for suggesting where money should be spent to save even more money. Again, the advantage of internalizing the value of outputs produced is that improvement projects and new investments can now be justified either by operating cost savings (the usual criterion) or by quality improvements and yield increases (the new criteria enabled by the daily profit calculation).

Empowers Employees for Local Decision Making

The final payoff from the daily income calculation is undoubtedly the most important. The operators at 3B felt they truly owned the process. They took far more interest in process improvements when their results were measured by a daily profit figure than by cost reduction and defect avoidance. The profit figure was a positive target rather than a negative outcome (extra cost, a defect) to be avoided. This motivational aspect proved highly important as a tangible illustration demonstrates.

One night, during the midnight shift, a hydrogen compressor in the 3B plant failed. Since hydrogen venting to the atmosphere is not a toxic or lethal condition, the standard operating procedure would have the shift supervisor log the failure in the shift report. When the department manager showed up for his normal shift the next morning, he would learn of the outage, request a repair crew to fix the problem, and later that afternoon the hydrogen compressor would come back on stream.

Instead of following the SOP, however, the shift supervisor ordered up an emergency work crew to make immediate repairs. When the department manager arrived in the morning, he read about the incident and asked the supervisor why he did the emergency repair, at an incremental expense that would surely show up in the manager's monthly report. The supervisor responded simply and elegantly:

> *This was a no-brainer. I knew from the daily income statement that following the standard procedure would lead to a loss of hydrogen gas measured in thousands of dollars by the time the compressor would be repaired 12 hours later. I wasn't sure exactly how much the emergency work crew would cost, but I figured it was measured in hundreds of dollars. I didn't go to engineering school, but my sense is that when the benefits are measured in thousands and the costs in hundreds, I don't need to know the first digit in either answer to figure out the right decision.*

How can we empower employees to make prompt, correct decisions, unless we provide them with information about the economics of processes under their control? Empowerment without information about the economics of operations is rhetoric. If managers are truly committed to employee teams using specific knowledge to continually improve the quality and productivity of processes under their control, economic information, not just operating parameters, seems essential.

By sharing with work teams the approximate prices of the output they continually produce, employees understand the value of lost output. Cost reduction or cost minimization treats the output as predetermined and asks employees to reduce resources required to produce that output. The profit figure, while retaining the benefits from cost reduction, also encourages employees to increase yields and throughput, avoid situations when output cannot be produced, and provides a better benchmark when output shifts to products that may be more difficult (and costly) to produce, but that provide more benefits to customers, as signaled by higher prices.

Japanese Pseudo-Profit Centers

Cooper, in his exploration of innovative Japanese cost management practices, came across several companies that also used pseudo-profit centers.[16] The motivation was identical to that in the 3B plant. By having the work teams take responsibility for revenues, as well as costs, the companies motivated the groups to improve the yields and quality of the outputs they managed. The impact of any improvements—in cost reduction, yield improvement, and quality enhancement—would show up immediately in their bottom-line performance measure. As did the 3B workers, the Japanese employees could appreciate the benefits from operating as a pseudo-profit center: "The [pseudo-profit] system is important because it allows us to identify our own plans and run our own group. The amount of profits we generate each month allows us to see the results of our efforts. Seeing these results gives us an incentive to work even harder."[17]

The Kyoto brewery of Kirin Beer adopted the pseudo-profit center approach because it felt that years of cost reduction programs (i.e., kaizen costing) had fostered a negative attitude among the workers toward continuous improvement.[18] Kyoto management identified four specific benefits from its pseudo-profit center approach:

1. Employees would have a stronger sense of belonging to the company because they could see their own contribution to company performance.
2. Public display of profit center results would motivate the work teams to achieve high targets, and provide reinforcement and recognition of the work teams that achieved superior performance.
3. Work teams could compare their performance against targets with that of other teams, thereby motivating an internal rivalry for improvement.
4. The new system would revitalize interest in cost reduction activities.

As did the 3B plant, the Kyoto brewery soon enjoyed improvements in water and energy consumption, indirect materials usage, and yield.

Olympus Optical Company, one of the major Japanese manufacturers of 35mm cameras, turned to pseudo-profit centers to motivate employees to generate increases in outputs while continuing to focus on cost reduction.[19] There are two interesting aspects to the Olympus Optical approach. First, it illustrates the application of pseudo-profit centers in a discrete parts manufacturing setting and second, the application of the technique to the purchasing function. At Olympus's Tatsuno plant, each production line is treated as a separate profit center. The revenue of each line is calculated by multiplying the quantity of output by the estimated external acquisition cost. This external cost is estimated by the Technical Department, which is responsible for negotiating with suppliers. The costs of each team include their direct costs and allocations for the space and other factory resources it consumes. Each production line is expected to be profitable. If a line were to become consistently unprofitable, the parts it manufactured would be outsourced. By using the data and evidence from the pseudo-profit centers, Olympus managers shift the outsourcing decision from a traumatic, and often unexpected, event to a natural fact-based decision. To date, all production lines at Tatsuno have not only remained profitable, but have increased their overall level of profitability.

Olympus also extended the pseudo-profit center concept to the purchasing process. The revenue for purchasing is the expected purchase price of each component times the quantity purchased in the period. The cost is the actual purchase price. With this approach, purchasing attempts to find ways to reduce the costs of the items it purchased. The intense dedication to quality throughout the company, plus the long-term nature of supplier relations, makes it impossible for purchasing to take dysfunctional actions normally associated with purchasing departments' attempts to avoid unfavorable purchase price variances (to be discussed in Chapter 11). At Olympus, purchasing works with the technical department to visit suppliers to find ways to reduce costs. As supplier costs are reduced, the savings are shared between the two firms, enabling purchasing to earn profits.

In all the pseudo-profit centers examined, the shift in focus from cost reduction to profit enhancement generated much new energy and interest among the work teams to find innovative ways to lower costs, increase yields, and enhance productivity. At the heart of this energy was the positive overtones of increasing profit compared to the negative ones associated with decreasing costs. In the Japanese companies, this shift reenergized cost reduction activities. Kaizen costing and other systems had been used for more than 15 years and had begun to lose their effectiveness.

Kaizen Costing and Pseudo-Profit Centers as Stage III Systems for Learning and Improvement

Pseudo-profit centers are a relatively new innovation (based on our limited set of observations) so we can offer only some tentative ideas about where their benefits will have the greatest impact. All the company examples were striving for improvements in cost, quality, and productivity of *repetitive* operations. Three of the four examples were in process industries (chemicals, soy production, and beer) where yields and quality are critical success factors. The discrete-part camera manufacturer (Olympus) had a similar continuous process because of its high-volume production and assembly of standard components. Thus, kaizen costing and pseudo-profit centers seem most applicable in mature industries or products where there are limited opportunities for achieving cost reduction through product redesign or changes in product functionality.

The techniques would seem less applicable in facilities handling products with short life cycles or products that are highly customized. Job shops that produce thousands of unique products each year would not be good candidates as pseudo-profit centers nor would a shipyard producing one product every 24 months. Service organizations with repetitive operations, such as many banking and insurance processes, health care facilities performing standardized tests and procedures, or government processing offices (think of an Internal Revenue Service processing center) would be good candidates. But at the other extreme, one would not expect to use kaizen and pseudo-profit centers to create motivation and incentives to improve the performance of software program designers, cardiac surgeons, investment bankers, and venture capitalists.

Accurate measurement of quantities of input resources consumed (such as energy, water, labor, machine time, and materials), quantities of outputs produced (cubic feet of propylene, liters of soy sauce, gallons of beer, units of camera subassemblies), and quality of all outputs produced is essential for both kaizen costing and pseudo-profit centers. The organizations are striving for continual small improvements in yields and quality that would be impossible to detect unless the systems can accurately measure the actual quantities used and quantities produced as well as quality. The prices (or costs) of the resources do not have to be accurate. All the organizations used estimates of prices. They made no effort to continually track actual input costs or output prices. The unit cost or prices serve as relative weights among input and output resources. Employee motivation and decisions were not greatly affected by small shifts in these weights. Of course, the expenses of support resources—such as maintenance, repair, energy, and information systems—have to be accurately assigned, not allocated, to the cost centers. Otherwise, the cost centers would not have a clear picture of the indirect resources they can control and influence, nor would they gain the full benefits of potential cost reductions when they learn to reduce their demands for support services.

The use of actual quantities and standard costs (and prices) still enables these systems to be described as *actual cost systems*. Standard costs and prices are used, not short-term actual prices, because, in addition to these standards being easier to measure, managers want employee work teams to achieve their kaizen cost reduction or profit targets by concentrating on improving the efficiency, productivity, and quality of production processes, not by shifting the mix of products to respond to short-term changes in input or output prices. That is why these responsibility units are still basically cost centers, not profit centers. They do not have the authority to change output mix or suppliers as input or output prices fluctuate.[20] Managers who deploy pseudo-profit centers want employees to increase output through higher yields and quality, an incentive that is difficult to achieve when organizational units are treated as mere cost centers.

Pseudo-profit centers offer improvements over cost-based (kaizen) systems, in motivation, employee empowerment, and information for improvement initiatives and investment proposals. But pseudo-profit centers require additional information—estimates of prices for the intermediate output. At 3B this was simple because the intermediate outputs were commodity chemicals that could be purchased or sold in quite competitive markets. At Olympus, the knowledge of manufacturing engineers, and an adequate supply of alternative contractors for each stage of the production process, enabled reasonable prices to be estimated for the intermediate outputs. At Kirin's Kyoto brewery, managers used arbitrary markups over standard cost to simulate market prices. These arbitrary markups did motivate and empower the work teams, but they may be less reliable for decisions to increase output that require incremental spending or new investments.

Timeliness of the data relates to the time cycle of the process that converts inputs into outputs. At the 3B plant, where inputs were being continually converted to outputs, a short-term (daily) income report on yields, quality, and resource consumption was appropriate. At the Japanese plants, or for the total payroll expenses in the cost centers at Romeo Engine Plant, where some emphasis was placed on reducing use of support resources, monthly reports could track the gradual decreases in expenses on these resources. In general, one might have short-term (daily, batch-by-batch) reports on yields, quality, materials, labor, machine, and energy consumption, and longer-term (monthly) reports on actual expenses incurred for support resources. This explains why traditional (Stage II) reporting of actual expenses versus budgeted amounts may still be part of Stage III systems; this reporting would track spending on support and discretionary resources, whose consumption would not be expected to vary in the short run, based on employee continuous improvement activities. Their spending would be expected to decrease over longer periods of time, say monthly or quarterly, so that daily reporting would not be that informative.

A final consideration is whether kaizen costing and pseudo-profit centers could be extended to production facilities, like the German plants described in Chapter 3 that produced a wide variety of products. The standard cost and flexible budgeting systems used by the German companies and U.S. companies like Caterpillar allow for spending authorizations (the flexible budget) to vary based on the volume and mix of products produced. The actual unit-cost systems, such as those used at Romeo Engine Plant and at the process companies described in this chapter, work well for narrow, homogeneous product lines. This allows a summary financial statistic like cost per engine, cost per cubic foot, or cost per liter to be a valid summary of operating performance. But managers at Romeo discovered that when a second and more complex engine was introduced, the plant's actual unit cost rose; not a surprising outcome since a more complex engine requires more resources for its production. Therefore, shifts in product mix confound efficiency and productivity improvements in an actual unit-cost system.

There would seem to be two approaches for dealing with the problem of measuring and motivating continuous improvement in production settings with products of varying complexity and where the product mix can shift each period. One is to develop a flexible budget for total expected costs based on the standard costs for each product produced during the period, and hold employee work teams accountable for consistently beating the flexible budget. In effect, the target for improvement becomes the percentage or actual dollar improvement between actual expenses and the flexible budget.

For example, consider a department with budgeted fixed expenses of $120,000 and standard costs of variable expenses—materials, labor, and support—as shown below for the three products produced in the department:

	PRODUCT			VARIABLE EXPENSE BUDGET
	1	2	3	
Quantity per Product	3,200	4,800	2,100	
Materials Cost	$4.60	$8.30	$6.80	
Subtotal: Variable Expense Budget for Materials Cost	$14,720	$39,840	$14,280	$68,840
Labor Cost	$2.80	$3.20	$1.00	$26,420
Variable Support Costs	$1.20	$1.80	$1.50	$15,630
Total				$110,890

In a period where the production quantities were as shown, a kaizen target to reduce costs by 6% would establish a target of .94 × [120,000 + 110,890] = $217,037 for actual expenses incurred. The employees would be free to seek reductions in whatever categories seemed the most promising. The budget for variable expenses, at historical standards, controls for the changing mix in the plant so that if the mix shifts to the more complex product (Product 2 above), a bigger budget is created for the expenses incurred.

This system would certainly work for a while. The challenge would be to maintain the accuracy of the individual product variable expense standards, in light of all the process improvements being implemented and sustained. Without periodic recalibration, the flexible budget would soon become obsolete and would no longer be able to control the budgeted cost target effectively for changes in product mix.

The second approach would adapt the pseudo-profit center approach of controlling for the varying mix of output through the pseudo-prices of the intermediate outputs. That is, treat the organizational unit as a pseudo-profit center, not a cost center. As a more complex product mix is produced, costs would rise but so would the revenue credit for the product mix produced. Thus, one can use either standard costs for inputs or standard prices of intermediate outputs to control for fluctuations in product mix, even in an environment of high product variety.

These examples indicate that some aspects of reporting against standards and budgets may remain in Stage III systems. But such information will be provided, as today, less frequently—say monthly—than measures specifically designed to provide feedback and learning to employee daily improvement activities. The periodic reporting of incurred expenses provides a summary, and a validation, of employee improvement activities, but is not a substitute for information that will directly support and promote the activities themselves.

Summary

In this chapter, we have illustrated several innovative approaches—organized around kaizen costing and pseudo-profit centers—in which employee work teams receive financial feedback on their performance. This feedback enables employees to see the cost and revenue impact of their actions, enabling them to set priorities for their continuous improvement efforts, evaluate trade-offs that may have to be made, and understand the opportunities for investments that can reduce future operating expenses, or improve quality and cycle time performance. Most important, the financial signals empower the employees to take local actions that maximize overall company performance. Companies, in Stage II, use standard costing systems to control employees to meet standards set high up in the organizational hierarchy. In Stage III, managers provide relevant and customized financial and nonfinancial information that empowers employees to continually improve their operating performance.

We now turn to the other major component of Stage III cost systems: activity-based costing for measuring the costs of organizational activities, business processes, products, services, and customers.

6

Activity-Based Costing: Introduction

We discussed, in Chapter 3, the failures of Stage II standard cost and flexible budgeting systems to provide relevant information about operational improvements and about the costs of organizational processes, products, and customers. Chapters 4 and 5 dealt with the first major component of Stage III cost systems, the systems to provide financial and nonfinancial measurements that will promote employee continuous improvement activities. In this chapter we introduce the innovation of activity-based costing (ABC) as the second major component of Stage III cost systems.

ABC systems require a new kind of thinking. Traditional (Stage II) cost systems are the answer to the question, "How can the organization allocate costs for financial reporting and for departmental cost control?" ABC systems address an entirely different set of questions:

1. What activities are being performed by the organizational resources?
2. How much does it cost to perform organizational activities and business processes?
3. Why does the organization need to perform activities and business processes?
4. How much of each activity is required for the organization's products, services, and customers?

A properly constructed ABC model provides the answers to these questions. An ABC model is an economic map of the organization's expenses and profitability based on organizational activities. Perhaps referring to it as an activity-based economic map rather than as a cost system clarifies its purpose. Can one drive from one location to another without a map? Can one build a house without a set of architectural drawings? Absolutely. If a manager is working in familiar territory (either a drive we've taken or a house we have built hundreds of times before), the manager can rely on experience and good judgment for a successful outcome. But when the territory is new, and conditions have changed in important ways from prior experience, that's when an information system like a good map or a good set of drawings becomes invaluable.

For companies operating in stable environments, with mature products that the company has extensive experience producing and with stable customer relationships, the company's traditional Stage II cost system, or perhaps no cost system at all, can guide operations. But if the company is producing many new products, introducing new processes, reaching new customers, and satisfying many more customer demands, it is easy for the company to get lost, economically, as it operates in a new environment. An activity-based cost system provides companies with an economic map of their operations by revealing the existing and (as we will see in subsequent chapters) forecasted cost of activities and business processes, which, in turn, leads to knowledge of the cost and profitability of individual products, services, customers, and operating units.

The economic map produced by Stage II cost systems averages resource costs between high- and low-volume products, and between simple and complex products (see *Exhibit 6-1*). Stage II systems flatten the quite different resource consumption pattern between these different types of products. The map produced by Stage II cost systems looks like the Great

Exhibit 6-1 Traditional Systems Distort Product, Customer, and Segment Costs

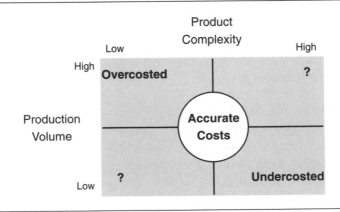

Plains in the U.S. midwest—the terrain looks the same wherever you look. Managers don't know where to devote their energy and attention. The map produced by a Stage III ABC system, as we will see in the next several chapters, looks like the southeastern part of California, and makes visible the Sierra Madre peaks of profitable products and the Death Valley craters of losses. Managers now have directions about where and how their scarcest resources—energy, time, and attention—should be committed to bring the losses to at least sea level (breakeven), and eventually to modest hills of profitability.

Why ABC Systems? The Pen Factories

The motivation for ABC systems is easy to articulate. We have often introduced the subject by asking people to think about two hypothetical and almost identical factories.[1] Simple Factory makes one million pens, all the same color: blue. Complex Factory also makes one million pens, but of many different colors, sizes, and varieties. This factory, in a typical year, produces about 2,000 different types (SKUs) of pens, ranging from specialty pens, with annual production volume as low as 50–100 per year, to higher volume standard pens (blue and black), whose annual production volumes are each about 100,000 per year.

Although both factories make the same basic product, Complex Factory requires many more resources. Relative to the blue pen factory, Complex Factory would have a much larger production support staff to schedule machines and production runs; perform setups; inspect items after setup; move materials; ship orders, expedite orders; rework defective items, design new products; improve existing ones; negotiate with vendors; schedule materials receipts; order, receive, and inspect incoming materials and parts; and update and maintain the much larger computer-based information system. Complex would also operate with considerably higher levels of idle time, setup time, overtime, inventory, rework, and scrap. Since both factories have the same physical output, they would both have roughly the same cost of materials (ignoring the slightly higher acquisition costs in Complex Factory for smaller orders of specialty colors and other materials). For actual production, if you assume that all pens are of about the same complexity, both Simple and Complex factories would require the same number of direct labor hours and machine hours for actual production (not counting the higher idle time and setup times in Complex Factory). Complex would likely have about the same property taxes, security costs, and heating bills as Simple. But Complex Factory would have much higher indirect and support costs (i.e., overhead) because of its more varied product mix and complex production task.

Consider now the operation of a Stage II standard cost system in these two plants. Simple Factory has little need for a cost system to calculate the cost of a blue pen. The financial manager, in any single period, can simply divide total expenses by total production volume to get the cost per blue pen produced. For Complex Factory, the costs of the indirect and support expenses would be traced to its various production cost centers, as described in Chapter 3. Once expenses were accumulated in each production center, they would be applied to products based on the cost driver for that cost center: direct labor, machine hours, units produced, or materials quantity processed. On a per-unit basis, high-volume standard blue and black pens require about the same quantity of each of these cost drivers as the very low-volume, specialty products. Therefore, Complex Factory's overhead costs would be applied to products proportional to their production volumes. Blue and black pens, each representing about 10% of the plant's output would have about 10% of the plant's overhead applied to them. A low-volume product, representing only .01 of 1% of the plant's output (100 pens per year) would have about .01 of 1% of the plant's overhead allocated to it. Therefore, the Stage II standard costing system would report essentially identical product costs for all products, standard and specialty, irrespective of their relative production volumes.

Clearly, however, considerably more of Complex Factory's indirect and support resources are required (on a per-unit basis) for the low-volume, specialty, newly designed products than for the mature, high-volume, standard blue and black pens. Stage II cost systems, even those with hundreds or thousands of production cost centers, will systematically and grossly underestimate the cost of resources required for specialty, low-volume products and will overestimate the resource cost of high-volume, standard products. The distortion in reported costs between standard and specialty products can only be avoided if the standard and specialty pens are manufactured on separate machines in different cost centers.

Abandoning the assignment of support resource costs entirely and moving to direct costing systems does not solve this problem. Under direct or marginal costing, blue and black pens, which have about the same materials and direct labor cost as the low-volume, specialty pens, will have the same variable costs. Also, direct costing systems fail to explain why the two factories with the exact same physical units of production (e.g., one million pens) have dramatically different levels of so-called fixed costs.

Fundamentals of ABC Systems

Activity-based cost systems extend traditional Stage II cost systems by linking resource expenses to the variety and complexity of products produced, not just the physical volumes produced. To see the contrast, let's start by examining the structure of a traditional cost system (see *Exhibit 6-2*). Here, factory overhead costs are allocated to production cost centers. Many traditional cost systems fail in the allocation of overhead expenses to cost centers by using arbitrary bases, such as direct labor hours or headcount, to assign overhead costs to production cost centers. As described in Chapter 3, the best Stage II cost systems, such as the GPK and Caterpillar systems, can be quite thoughtful and accurate as they directly

Exhibit 6-2 Traditional Cost Systems Allocate Overhead Costs to Production Cost Centers and Then to Products

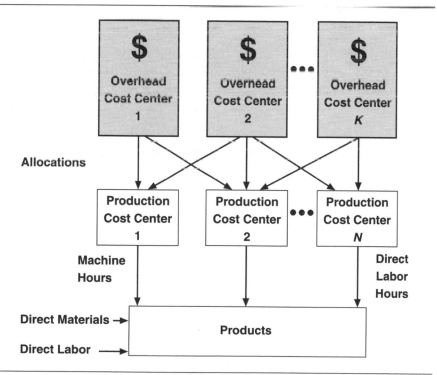

Exhibit 6-3 Activity-Based Cost Systems Trace Resource Expenses to Activities and Use Activity Cost Drivers for Tracing Activity Costs to Objects

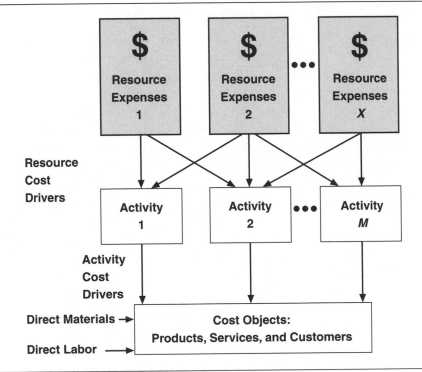

attribute, based on actual usage, overhead expenses to production cost centers. Even these excellent systems fail, however, in the next stage, when the costs accumulated in production cost centers are assigned to the products processed through each center. As in the pen factory, Stage II cost systems use drivers, like direct labor dollars, direct labor hours, machine hours, units produced, or materials processed, to allocate production cost center costs to products.

Such Stage II systems provide a simple, inexpensive way to meet the financial reporting requirement to allocate factory overhead costs to production. In fact, were it not for the desire to use the same system to monitor and control costs at the individual cost center level, Stage II cost systems could be even simpler for financial reporting, using only a single cost center for the entire plant, and a single allocation base, such as direct labor. *Exhibit 6-3* shows the structure of an activity-based cost (ABC) system for factory operations. At first glance the ABC system appears similar. But the underlying structure and concept are quite different. ABC systems are developed through a series of four sequential steps.

Step 1. Develop the Activity Dictionary

Organizations spend money on indirect and support resources so that important activities get performed (for example, scheduling, purchasing, customer administration, and improving products) or to obtain the capabilities being supplied by these resources (such as information technology and suitable production and customer support space). The focus of ABC has already shifted, from how to allocate costs to why the organization is spending money in the first place. In developing an ABC system, the organization first identifies the activities being performed by its indirect and support resources. Activities are described by verbs and associated objects: schedule production, move materials, purchase materials, inspect items, respond to customers, improve products, introduce new products, etc. The identification of activities culminates with construction of an activity dictionary that lists and defines every major activity performed in the production facility.[2]

Initially, when ABC systems were first introduced in the mid- to late 1980s, ABC project teams had to invent activity dictionaries virtually from scratch. Now, with nearly a decade of implementation experience, companies and consulting organizations have developed standard activity dictionaries that provide a template for selecting the appropriate activities to be used in any particular application. The chapter appendix shows a high-level structure for organizing activities within business processes developed by the International Benchmarking Clearing House. Some organizations, however, like to use their front-line employees, in a bottom-up process, to define the activity dictionary. Doing so engages the entire organization in the ABC-modeling exercise and helps build confidence that the model reflects the reality of the organizational setting. This is a longer, more expensive process that may yield compensating benefits in terms of commitment and ownership of the final model.

In some initial applications, engineers and accountants defined activities at a very microlevel, perhaps at an individual task level, leading to several hundred or more activities. This was both expensive and confusing. Now, ABC project teams use rules of thumb, such as ignoring activities that use less than 5% of an individual's time or a resource's capacity. Activity dictionaries can be relatively brief, say 10–30 activities, especially where the prime focus of the ABC system is to estimate product and customer costs. In other applications, ABC systems continue to be built with hundreds of activities. Typically, such highly detailed systems have been constructed to serve as the foundation for process improvement and process redesign efforts, as we will discuss in Chapter 8. The number of activities, therefore, is a function of the purpose of the model, and the size and complexity of the organizational unit being studied.

With organizational activities identified, we can now move to step two.

Step 2. Determine How Much the Organization Is Spending on Each of Its Activities

The ABC system now maps from resource expenses to activities, using resource cost drivers (see Exhibit 6-3). The resource cost drivers link spending and expenses, as captured in the organization's financial or general ledger system, to the activities performed.[3] As the internal training manual of an organization states:

> *The resources represent the cost base for the model. A resource comprises a distinct and homogeneous grouping of existing costs fulfilling a similar function or, in the case of people, having a similar work profile. The sum of all resources for a model equals the total cost for an organization, with a set time frame.*[4]

Classifying resource expenses by activities performed accomplishes a 90 degree shift in thinking about expenses (see *Exhibit 6-4*). Data from the organization's financial system categorizes expenses by spending code; for example, salaries, fringe benefits, overtime, utilities, indirect materials, travel, telecommunications, computing, maintenance, and depreciation. The resource cost drivers collect expenses from this system and drive them to the activities being performed by the organizational resources. Thus, after going through this step, organizations learn, usually for the first time, how much they are spending on activities like purchasing materials and introducing new products.

The actual mechanics of selecting resource cost drivers and estimating the quantity of each resource cost driver are reasonably well documented.[5] For our purposes, you can think about employee surveys in which individuals, other than the front-line employees who are doing the production work, are asked to fill in a form on which the activity dictionary appears and estimate the percentage of time they spend on any activity (in excess,

Exhibit 6-4 Activity-Based Costing Shifts Analysis from Expense Categories to Activities Performed

Salaries and Fringes $313,000

Occupancy $111,000

Equipment and Technology $146,000

Materials and Supplies $30,000

Total $600,000

Activity-Based Costing

Activity	Salaries and Fringes	Occupancy	Equipment and Technology	Materials and Supplies	Total
Process Customer Orders	$ 31,000	$ 5,300	$ 12,600	$ 800	$ 49,700
Purchase Materials	34,000	6,900	8,800	1,500	51,200
Schedule Production Orders	22,000	1,200	18,400	300	41,900
Move Materials	13,000	2,100	22,300	3,600	41,000
Set Up Machines	42,000	700	4,800	200	47,700
Inspect Items	19,000	13,000	19,700	800	52,500
Maintain Product Information	36,000	2,800	14,500	400	53,700
Perform Engineering Changes	49,000	32,000	26,900	2,400	110,300
Expedite Orders	14,000	900	700	500	16,100
Introduce New Products	35,000	44,000	16,100	18,700	113,800
Resolve Quality Problems	18,000	2,100	1,200	800	22,100
Total	**$313,000**	**$111,000**	**$146,000**	**$30,000**	**$600,000**

say, of 5% of their time) on the list (see *Exhibit 6-5* for a sample screen of an interactive computer program to elicit activity information from employees).

For nonpersonnel resources, the ABC project team either relies on direct measurement (how much power, computer, or telecommunications time) or estimates the percentage of the resource used by each activity in the dictionary. In fact, this procedure does not really differ substantively from that done by the excellent standard cost/flexible budgeting systems described in Chapter 3. The main difference is that Stage II standard cost/ flexible budgeting systems drive indirect expenses only to other responsibility centers, typically production cost centers. ABC systems, like Stage II systems, can drive expenses to production cost centers—where the activity is part of the actual product conversion process like *fabricate parts, mix chemicals,* or *assemble products.* But, in addition, the ABC system drives operating expenses to activities that are not directly involved in converting materials into intermediate and finished products like *set*

Exhibit 6-5 Activity Surveys Estimate the Quantity of
Resource Cost Drivers

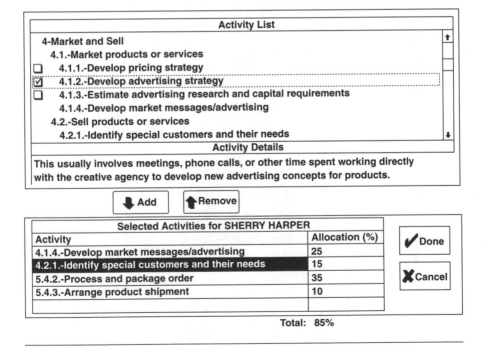

Source: KPMG Peat Marwick LLP. Reprinted by permission.

up machines, schedule production runs, and *perform engineering change notices.* Stage II systems, in contrast, drive the expenses of such activities to production cost centers where they are arbitrarily allocated to products proportional to production volumes.

One does not need extensive time-and-motion studies to link resource spending to activities performed. The goal is to be approximately right rather than precisely wrong, as are virtually all traditional product-costing systems. Many traditional standard cost systems calculate product costs out to six significant digits ($5.71462 per unit) but, because of arbitrary allocation procedures, the first digit is wrong.

HIERARCHY OF ACTIVITIES

Once resource costs have been traced to activities, managers obtain powerful insights from identifying critical attributes of the activities. One of the most important attributes classifies manufacturing activities along a cost-hierarchy dimension: unit, batch, and product, customer, and facility-sustaining (see *Exhibit 6-6*).[6]

Exhibit 6-6 ABC Hierarchy of Activities

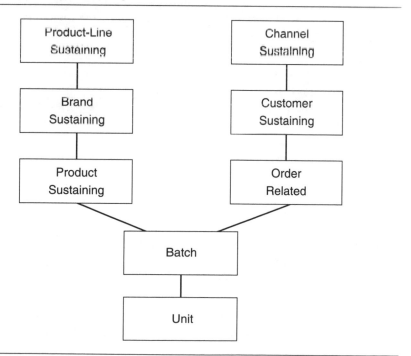

Unit-level activities *are the activities that have to be performed for every unit of product or service produced. The quantity of unit-level activities performed is proportional to production and sales volumes. Examples include drilling holes in metal parts, grinding metal, and performing 100% inspection.*

Traditional cost systems, which use allocation bases such as labor hours, machine hours, units produced, or sales dollars to assign indirect costs to cost objects, rely exclusively on unit-level cost drivers. One of the principal differences between activity-based and traditional cost systems is the use of nonunit cost drivers (e.g., batch, product-sustaining) for assigning resource costs to products and customers.

Batch-level activities *are the activities that have to be performed for each batch or setup of work performed. Batch activities include setting up a machine for a new production run, purchasing materials, and processing a customer order.*

The resources required for a batch-level activity are independent of the number of units in the batch. Activity-based cost systems measure and assign the cost of handling production orders, material movements, setups, customer orders, and purchasing to the products, customers, and services that triggered the activity.

Product-sustaining activities *are performed to enable the production of individual products (or services) to occur. Extending this notion outside the factory leads to* customer-sustaining activities *that enable the company to sell to an individual customer but that are independent of the volume and mix of the products (and services) sold and delivered to the customer. These product- and customer-sustaining activities include maintaining and updating product specifications, special testing and tooling for individual products and services, and technical support provided for individual products and to service individual customers.*

Product- and customer-sustaining activities are easily traced to the individual products, services, and customers for whom the activities are performed. But the *quantity* of resources used in product- and customer-sustaining activities are, by definition, independent of the production and sales volumes, and quantity of production batches and customer orders. Traditional cost systems, relying only on unit-level drivers, cannot trace product- and customer-sustaining resources accurately to individual products and customers.

Beyond unit, batch, product, and customer-sustaining activities, other resources supply capabilities that cannot be traced to individual products and customers. Some activities, such as product development and advertising, can be classified as *brand* or *product-line sustaining* since they support an entire *brand* or product line. Some activities, such as pricing and invoicing, may be *order-related,* specific to a particular order, but independent of the volume or content of the order. Others provide general production or sales capabilities (*facility-sustaining* expenses—a plant manager and administrative staff) and *channel-sustaining* expenses—trade shows and advertising, catalogs—that cannot be traced to individual products, services, or customers. The expenses of product line, facility, and channel resources can be assigned directly to the individual product lines, facilities, and channels but should not be allocated down to individual products, services, or customers within these categories.

The ABC cost hierarchy, applicable to manufacturing, marketing, and research and development expenses, enables all organizational expenses to be mapped to a particular hierarchical or organizational level where cause and effect can be established. That is, a customer-sustaining expense is not allocated to the products or services purchased by the customer since this expense is incurred independent of the volume and mix of products or services acquired by the customer. The customer-sustaining expense can be avoided or controlled only by operating at the customer level (dropping the customer, changing the level of support provided to the customer), not by changing the volume or mix of the individual products and services the customer acquires.

Returning to our pen factory example, the batch, product-sustaining, and customer-sustaining categories provide powerful insights into why facilities like the two pen factories, which have identical total physical outputs, could have drastically divergent cost structures. Both Simple Factory and Complex Factory have the same quantity of unit-level activities since they have the same physical output of 1 million pens per year. They also likely have the same level of facility-sustaining expenses (assuming that all nonmanufacturing costs occur outside the factories). But Complex Factory requires far more resources than Simple Factory to perform its additional batch and product-sustaining activities required to produce its thousands of products, ranging from low-volume, specialty products to high-volume blue and black pens.

ACTIVITIES AND BUSINESS PROCESSES

Activities can also be grouped together into higher-level business processes as shown in the standard activity dictionary of the chapter appendix. Some designers want to organize their entire ABC system around business processes, ignoring the finer detail available from an activity perspective. The problem is that a business process, like procurement, might be too heterogeneous to accumulate costs that then must be driven to products, services, or customers by a single cost driver. For example, activities within the procurement function could include ordering materials, scheduling delivery of materials, receiving materials, inspecting materials, moving materials, storing materials, negotiating with and selecting vendors, and paying vendor invoices. Each activity may require a different cost driver. If all the activities were aggregated, only a single cost driver, say number of purchase orders, would have to be selected for driving all procurement process costs to materials. Such an aggregation would fail to identify differences in the activities required for ordering different types of materials, from different vendors, using different ordering relationships. Activities with unique cost drivers are the basic unit of analysis for ABC systems. They capture the diversity of use by individual products, services, and customers that create the demand for the activities.

Activities, the basic cost collection units for ABC systems, can still be aggregated so that managers can see the total cost of performing a business process. Each activity can be coded, enabling costs to be accumulated and reported by business processes. For example, activities such as ordering materials, scheduling delivery of materials, receiving materials, inspecting materials, moving materials, storing materials, negotiating with and selecting vendors, and paying vendor invoices would be aggregated into a *procurement* process. Understanding costs at the aggregate business process level facilitates internal and external benchmarking. Managers can compare the cost of performing the same business process (e.g., procurement, order entry) at different plants or across different organizational units to identify where to study particularly efficient practices or to improve particularly inefficient processes.

ACTIVITY ATTRIBUTES

The activity cost hierarchy and business process coding are examples of *activity attributes*. Attributes are coding schemes associated with each activity that facilitate reporting of activity costs. Consider an activity dictionary with 125 entries. Activity attributes enable the activity cost information to be reported at higher levels of aggregation than does tabulating or charting data for 125 individual activities. One report could show the activity expenses and percentages within each level of the activity cost hierarchy; e.g., what percentage of expenses are in unit-level, batch-level, and product-sustaining activities. Another report could show activity expenses and percentages by, say, 12 business processes.

A particularly powerful attribute would be the degree of short-term variability of the activity cost.[7] Such an attribute would enable short-term marginal costs to be incorporated and reported within an ABC framework. At the simplest level, this attribute could be coded as an F-V variable. Consider an activity for which virtually all the resource expenses would stay the same even if the quantity performed of this activity fluctuated up or down by 2% or 10% each period. The activity costs would be considered fixed with respect to short-term variation in demand, and would be labeled with an F. Another activity, however, such as *supply energy to machines,* would be considered variable with short-term fluctuations in use. This activity would be labeled with a V. If all activities are coded in this manner, managers would have a good overview about the percentage of short-term variable and fixed costs in their operations. Such information provides insight about the degree of operating leverage in the facility. And since activity costs are linked and remain visible at the individual product, service, and customer level, managers would be able to quickly and easily see what components of assigned costs will vary, in the short run, with changes in production and sales volume and which will likely remain relatively the same. This information can be useful for detailed production scheduling, pricing of incremental orders, and other such short-term decisions.

A more complex coding of cost variability would recognize the length of time for resource expenses to adjust to actual activity levels. On a scale of one to five, a "one" would represent resources, such as energy to operate machines, whose supply adjusts almost immediately to changes in demand; a "five" would represent a resource such as a unique, special-purpose machine, whose supply is already determined, and which cannot be sold or eliminated even if demand for the machine were to disappear entirely. Within these extremes, resources coded with a "two" would represent personnel who can be shifted to other responsibilities over a period of several weeks or months, a "three" represents such resources as engineers and managers, where the supply adjustment could require up to a year, and a "four" would represent plant and equipment, where the supply adjusts over a period of several years. Such a coding system would give managers the ability to make decisions over various time horizons and see what portion of total expenses can be influenced over these time horizons by their decisions. Thus, ABC systems, with a simple attribute field, can easily accommodate, in fact expand upon, traditional Stage II cost systems' classification of short-term variable and short-term fixed costs.

Additional activity attributes could also be defined. For example, the location where an activity is performed or the person primarily responsible for the activity could be identified. That would permit sorting of activity expense data by place and by person.

Many firms rank activities according to their value or efficiency of performance. These coding schemes can vary from simple dichotomous ones such as value-added/non-value-added or necessary/unnecessary to more complex schemes using a 5- or 10-point classification scheme. We will illustrate such activity codings in Chapter 8, when we discuss operational activity-based management.

In summary, at the end of the second phase of building an ABC model, the organization knows expenses characterized by activities performed. Through appropriately selected attribute fields, it can view activity expenses from various perspectives, including cost hierarchy, business process, degree of variability, and degree of efficiency. At this stage, organizations already have new information that can be used for a range of activity and process improvement actions. But before turning to how ABC information can be used, let's continue with the construction of the first full ABC model. In the next two steps, activity costs are driven down to cost objects such as products, services, and customers.

Step 3. Identify the Organization's Products, Services, and Customers

Steps 1 and 2 for building an ABC model identify the activities being performed and the cost of performing those activities. Why is the organization performing activities in the first place? The answer, of course, is that the organization needs activities to design, build, and deliver products and services to its customers. Therefore, the ABC project team identifies all the organization's products, services, and customers. Initially, since we are analyzing the indirect and support costs of manufacturing facilities, we will focus here on driving costs to products, deferring the assignment of activity costs to customers and services to Chapters 10 and 12.

Step 3 is simple but important. Many practitioners of activity-based costing skip it and focus only on how to make activities and processes more efficient. They have not asked themselves whether these activities or processes are worth doing. Is their organization getting paid adequately for performing these activities? Answering that question requires that activity costs be linked to the products, services, and customers who are the ultimate beneficiaries of the organization's activities. Addressing this issue leads naturally to the fourth and final step in building an ABC model.

Step 4. Select Activity Cost Drivers That Link Activity Costs to the Organization's Products, Services, and Customers

The linkage between activities and cost objects, such as products, services, and customers, is accomplished by using activity cost drivers. An activity cost driver is a quantitative measure of the output of an activity. For example:

ACTIVITY	ACTIVITY COST DRIVER
Run Machines	Machine Hours
Set Up Machines	Setups or Setup Hours
Schedule Production Jobs	Production Runs
Receive Materials	Material Receipts
Support Existing Products	Number of Products
Introduce New Products	Number of New Products Introduced
Maintain Machines	Maintenance Hours
Modify Product Characteristics	Engineering Change Notices

SELECTING ACTIVITY COST DRIVERS

The selection of an activity cost driver reflects a subjective trade-off between accuracy and the cost of measurement. Because of the large number of potential activity-to-output linkages, designers attempt to economize on the number of different activity cost drivers. For example, all activities triggered by the same event can use the same activity cost driver: number of production runs. For instance, the activities of *preparing production orders, scheduling production runs, performing part inspections,* and *moving materials* can all use *number of production runs* as the activity cost driver. ABC system designers can choose from three different types of activity cost drivers: transaction, duration, and intensity (or direct charging).

Transaction drivers, such as the numbers of setups, receipts, and products supported, count how often an activity is performed. Transaction drivers can be used when all outputs make essentially the same demands on the activity. For example, scheduling a production run, processing a purchase order, or maintaining a unique part number may take the same time and effort independent of which product is being scheduled, which material is being purchased, or which part is being supported in the system.

Transaction drivers are the least expensive type of cost driver but can be the least accurate since they assume that the same quantity of resources is required every time an activity is performed; that is, the activity is homogeneous across products. For example, the use of a transaction driver like the number of setups assumes that all setups take the same time to perform. For many activities, the variation in use by individual cost objects is small enough that a transaction driver will do for assigning activity expenses to the cost object. If, however, the amount of resources required to perform the activity varies considerably, from product to product, more accurate and more expensive cost drivers are needed.

Duration drivers represent the amount of time required to perform an activity. Duration drivers should be used when significant variation exists in the amount of activity required for different outputs. For example, simple products may require only 10–15 minutes to set up, while complex, high-precision products may require six hours for setup. Using a transaction driver, like number of setups, will overcost the resources required to set up simple products and will undercost the resources required for complex products. To avoid this distortion, ABC designers use a duration driver, like setup hours, to assign the cost of setups to individual products.

Duration drivers include setup hours, inspection hours, and direct labor hours. For materials movement, distance moved can be considered a duration driver; distance is a proxy for the time taken to move materials from one point to another. In general, duration drivers are more accurate than transaction drivers, but they are more expensive to implement since the model requires an estimate of the duration each time an activity is performed.[8] With a transaction driver (number of setups), the designer only needs to know how many times a product was set up, information that should be readily available from the production-scheduling system. Knowing the setup time for each product is an additional, and more costly, piece of information. Some companies estimate duration by constructing an index based on the complexity of the output being handled. The index is a function of the complexity of the product or customer processed by the activity, assuming that complexity influences the time required to perform the activity. The choice between a duration and a transaction driver is, as always, one of economics, balancing the benefits of increased accuracy against the costs of increased measurement.

For some activities, however, even duration drivers may not be sufficiently accurate. *Intensity drivers* directly charge for the resources used each time an activity is performed. Continuing with our setup example, a particularly complex product may require special setup and quality control people, as well as special gauging and test equipment each time the machine is set up. A duration driver, like setup cost per hour, assumes that all hours are equally costly, but does not reflect extra personnel, especially skilled personnel, and expensive equipment that may be required on some setups but not others. In these cases, activity costs may have to be charged directly to the output, based on work orders or other records that accumulate the activity expenses incurred for that output.

Intensity drivers are the most accurate activity cost drivers but are the most expensive to implement. They should be used only when the resources associated with performing an activity are both expensive and variable each time that activity is performed.

A choice among a transaction, duration, or direct-charging (intensity) cost driver can be made for almost any activity. For example, for preparing engineering change notices (ECNs) to upgrade and support existing products, we could use:

- Cost per engineering change notice (assumes every ECN consumes the same quantity and cost of resources),
- Cost per engineering change hour used for an individual product (allows for ECNs to use different amounts of time to perform but assumes every engineering hour costs the same), or
- Cost of engineering resources actually used (number of engineering hours, price per hour of engineers used, plus cost of equipment such as engineering workstations) on the job.

Similarly for a sales activity, like support existing customers, we could use either a transaction, duration, or intensity driver; for example,

- Cost per customer (assumes all customers cost the same),
- Cost per customer hour (assumes different customers use different amounts of sales resource time, but each hour of support time costs the same), or
- Actual cost per customer (actual or estimated time and specific resources committed to specific customers).

The activity cost driver should match the level of the cost hierarchy of its associated activity. For example, the cost of unit-level activities (such as machining surfaces) should be driven to products and customers using unit-level activity drivers (such as machine hours), and the cost of batch-level activities (set up machines) should be driven to products and customers using batch-level activity drivers (number of setups, setup hours). Neglect of such matching guarantees that product and customer costs will be distorted. For example, using unit-based cost drivers (machine hours) for non-unit-based activities (set up machines) leads to the distortions inherent in traditional cost systems, high-volume and complex products are overcosted and low-volume, simple products are undercosted. Driving product-sustaining costs using batch-level drivers will cause products that use more than the average level of batch activities to be overcosted and those with less than average use of batch activities to be undercosted.

COMPLEXITY INDEXES

Often, ABC analysts, rather than actually record the time and resources required for an individual product or customer, may simulate an intensity driver with a weighted index approach. They ask individuals to estimate the relative difficulty of performing the task for one type of product/customer or another. A standard product/customer may get a weight of one, a medium complexity product/customer can get a weight of three to five, and a particularly complex (demanding) product/customer can get a weight of, say, ten. In this way, the variation in demands for an activity among products and customers can be captured without an overly complex measurement system. Again, it is important to make an appropriate trade-off between accuracy and the cost of measurement. The goal is to be approximately right; for many purposes, transaction drivers or estimates of relative difficulty may well do for estimating resource consumption by individual products, services, and customers.

The use of weighted index drivers shows how designers economize in selecting cost drivers. They can use a weighted transaction driver in place of a more expensive duration driver, or a weighted duration driver to emulate a more costly intensity driver. For example, identifying long and short setups enables simple and complex setups to be differentially costed. Alternatively, designers can reflect differences in complexity by defining separate activities. For example, instead of using a duration driver for the setup, they could split the setup activity into two distinct activities: setups for manual machines and setups for numeric control (NC) machines. They can then use a simple transaction driver—such as number of setups—for both activities. The driver rate for the more complex NC setups will, of course, be higher than the rate for the setups on the simpler manual machines.

Activity cost drivers are the central innovation of activity-based cost systems but they are also, as we have noted, the most costly aspects of ABC systems. Often project teams get carried away with the potential capabilities of an activity-based cost system to capture accurately the economics of their operations. The teams see diversity and complexity everywhere and design systems with upward of 500 activities. But in selecting and measuring the activity cost drivers for such a system, reality takes hold. Assuming that each different activity requires a different activity cost driver,[9] and that the organization has, say, 5,000 individual products and customers (not an atypically low number for many organizations), the analyst must be able to enter up to 2,500,000 pieces of information (500 × 5,000). This is why most ABC systems settle down, for product- and customer-costing purposes, to no more than 30–50 activity cost drivers, most of which can be accessed and traced to individual products and customers relatively simply in the existing information system.[10]

Activity-Based Costing: Worth the Price?

Originally, when many people heard the term "activity-based costing," they thought that accountants were just rearranging the deck chairs on the *Titanic* rather than abandoning a fundamentally flawed approach. Apparently, the failings of traditional cost systems were so pervasive that anything that alleged to perform product costing evoked an image of arbitrary allocations, unrelated to actual operations and experience. Asking many operating managers to free-associate about "costing" generates responses like irrelevant, useless, distorted, arbitrary, and "something done by accountants for accountants." Thus, activity-based costing, which is clearly a more complicated and expensive costing approach, can appear to be doing something not very useful in a more complex and expensive way. Obviously, we believe this view of ABC is very wrong. If we had to reintroduce ABC, perhaps we would not include the word "costing" in its title.[11]

Aside from semantic opportunities lost, is ABC merely a more complex and expensive way to allocate costs? No. An activity-based cost system can use its cost assignments to track down underlying economic events. For example, setup costs are assigned based on setups performed for individual products. Product support costs can be traced back to work performed to maintain products. And customer administration costs can be traced back to handling customer orders, responding to customer requests, and marketing existing and new products to particular customers. ABC systems do use many *estimates*. For example, a system may use a transaction driver to approximate the resources used each time an activity is performed rather than a detailed cost collection (direct charging or intensity driver) for each event occurrence. Or the system may estimate the cost of a machine hour by averaging acquisition costs, maintenance costs, and operating costs of the machine over some period of time. But these estimates are made, not because actual costs are impossible to trace to particular events, but because the cost of doing so seems too great vis-à-vis its value or benefits.

In principle, if more accurate cost attribution is desired, the ABC designer can install a more precise (and more expensive) measurement system and the task would be accomplished. So one should not confuse the extensive use of estimates in an ABC cost model, which is a design judgment made on a cost/benefit basis, from arbitrary allocations, which are not included in a properly designed ABC system. When arbitrary allocations are used, no cause-and-effect relationship can be established between the cost object to which the cost has been assigned and the resources whose cost has been assigned. In an ABC system, every cost assignment to an activity, or a product, service, or customer, should be transparent and traceable, via cause-and-effect relationships, to the demand for resources by the cost object (whether an activity, product, service, or customer).

Where to Apply Activity-Based Cost Systems

When will activity-based cost systems have the greatest impact? Or, asking this question another way, where should an organization look initially to demonstrate the potential benefits from installing an activity-based cost system? There are two simple rules that guide the search for high-potential ABC applications:

1. The Willie Sutton rule.[12] Look for areas with large expenses in indirect and support resources, especially when these expenses have been growing. Operations where almost all expenses are direct labor and direct materials, which can already be directly traced to individual products by traditional costing systems, may not need ABC systems. In effect,

if organizational activities are all at the unit level (virtually no batch or product-sustaining activities), ABC systems and traditional cost systems will likely give very similar economic signals.

2. The high-diversity rule. Look for a situation where there is a large variety in products, customers, or processes. For example, consider a facility that produces mature and newly introduced products, standard and custom products, high-volume and low-volume products. Or consider a marketing and sales organization that services customers who order high-volume, standard products with few special demands as well as customers who order in small volumes, special volumes, and require large quantities of presales and postsales technical support.

Not all organizations fall within the Willie Sutton rule. Take the example of an early Apple Computer factory that had been designed for automatic, high-efficiency assembly operations. The factory did no component or parts fabrication, no subassembly operations, only final assembly. As a result, more than 90% of the factory expenses were for purchased parts, equipment, and a small amount of direct labor. In this case, direct charging for labor, materials, and machine time can be done well by a Stage II traditional cost system. The indirect and support expenses were extremely small, since the factory had been designed for focused, unit-level operations. The Willie Sutton rule would have led Apple ABC designers to focus on product development, marketing, distribution, and selling expenses, not on factory overhead.

The high-diversity rule is violated by Simple Factory, making only a single product, blue pens.[13] When a factory produces only a single product, all its manufacturing expenses are easily attributable to that product. Simple Factory does not need an ABC system, or any system, to calculate its product costs. The original product mix at Siemens Electric Motor Works also violated the high-diversity rule.[14] The factory formerly produced a limited number of standard electric motors in high volumes. As the product mix shifted to include custom motors, the plant became highly diversified and adopted activity-based costing to implement its new strategy of supplying customers with specialized motors in low volumes as well as standard motors in high volumes.

Even in highly focused factories, however, where product costing is not a major concern, some organizations have still benefited from building ABC models to highlight their underlying process costs. For example, an early ABC implementation occurred in a defense factory that made only a single product: a complex weapon system consisting of tens of thousands of parts. The plant's management team wanted an ABC model so that it could understand better the costs of all the activities and processes used to produce the weapon system. Thus, the diversity of processes was sufficient to create a demand for a more accurate attribution of costs, in this case to activities and processes, that an ABC model could provide.

As another example, the initial ABC implementations of the Vitamins and Fine Chemical Division of F. Hoffmann-La Roche focused on installing one-off stand-alone models at individual manufacturing sites. The high indirect and support costs (the Willie Sutton rule) were driven down only to the activity level, not to the product level. This approach accomplished two important goals. First, it signaled that ABC was meant as a management tool, not a new accounting or costing methodology for products. Second, the analysis at the activity and business process level revealed immediate insights for reengineering and operational improvement activities (the subject of Chapter 8). The actions taken, based on these initial insights, led to quick and valuable benefits (cost savings of between 20% and 30% at each site), which were highly visible to management at all levels of the organization. Only in a second implementation phase, when the reengineering and operational improvement activities were completed and the organization was already familiar with ABC principles, were activity costs linked to products.

ABC: The Accuracy/Cost Trade-off

The goal of a properly constructed ABC system is not the most accurate cost system. Consider a target (see *Exhibit* 6-7), where the bull's-eye represents the actual cost of resources used each time a product is made, a service delivered, and a customer served.[15] To hit the bull's-eye each time requires an enormously expensive ABC system. But a relatively simple ABC system—perhaps including 30–50 activities and using good estimates and many transaction drivers, with few intensity drivers or direct charging—should enable an organization to hit consistently the outer and middle rings of the target; that is, activity and process costs will be accurate to within 5% or 10%. Stage II cost systems, in contrast, virtually never even hit the target, or even the wall on which the target is mounted, because of their highly distorted costs. The goal should be to have the best cost system, one that balances the cost of errors made from inaccurate estimates with the cost of measurement (see *Exhibit* 6-8).

Stage II cost systems may be inexpensive to operate but they create large distortions in the cost of activities, processes, products, services,

Exhibit 6-7   Cost Accuracy Target

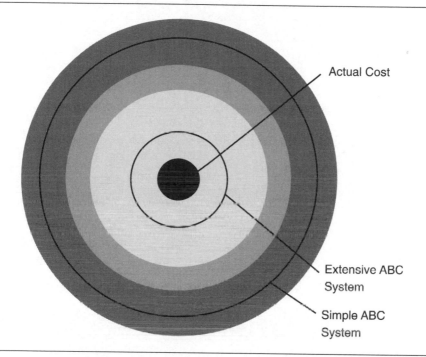

Actual Cost

Extensive ABC System

Simple ABC System

and customers. Consequently, managers may make serious mistakes in decisions taken based on this information; that is, there is a high cost of errors. But attempting to build an ABC system with 1,000 or more activities and directly charging actual resource costs to each activity performed for each product, service, and customer would lead to an enormously expensive system. The cost of operating such a system would greatly exceed the benefits in terms of improved decisions made with this slightly more accurate information.

Exhibit 6-8 indicates why activity-based cost systems only emerged in the mid-1980s. For many decades prior to the 1980s, the errors made by traditional systems were small. Companies had relatively narrow product lines so the distortions from producing high- and low-volume products and standard and customized products in the same facility did not occur. Also, many processes were labor intense and the costs of direct labor were well measured and assigned with traditional costing systems. As organizations automated their processes, greatly reducing or even eliminating direct labor, and introduced more variety into their product lines, they required much higher levels of batch and product-sustaining activi-

Exhibit 6-8 Activity-Based Costing: Designing the Optimal ABC System

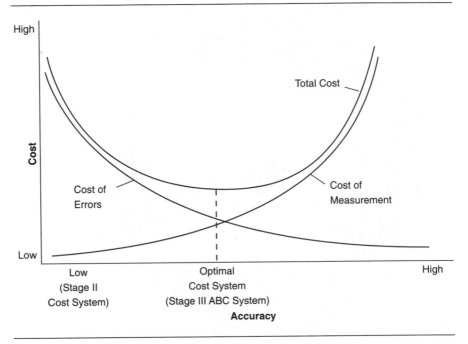

ties. Thus, as the cost of batch and product-sustaining activities increased, relative to the cost of unit-level activities, errors from traditional costing systems increased. Furthermore, as competition became more vigorous and more global, the costs of poor decisions—based on distorted information—became much higher. All these factors combined to shift the cost of the error curve upward.

Simultaneously, the continuous and rapid evolution in information technology greatly reduced the cost of measurement. The advent of automatic, remote data entry, new computerized systems for production scheduling, customer order processing, inventory management, engineering design, and many other organizational activities greatly increased the supply of data on current operations. And advances in microcomputers, and distributed computing like client-server systems, made the cost of collecting, processing, and reporting information plummet. The combination of a rapidly rising *cost-of-errors* curve with a rapidly falling *cost-of-measurement* curve led to the optimal cost system's becoming a more accurate, activity-based, cost system.

Using Activity-Based Cost Systems for Financial Reporting

Activity-based cost systems assign manufacturing expenses to products in a more comprehensive and transparent manner than traditional cost systems. So why not scrap Stage II cost systems entirely and use the ABC system to also value inventory in periodic financial statements? In principle, of course, an activity-based cost system can easily serve the financial reporting purpose. There are problems with using ABC systems too soon for this purpose, however, since financial statements must withstand the scrutiny of auditors and tax authorities. This scrutiny typically imposes more severe demands on the cost system for consistency, objectivity, and uniformity than those required for purely managerial purposes. For companies on LIFO, such a switch could trigger a loss of LIFO reserves, and lead to an immediate tax liability.

As noted, Stage III ABC systems should provide managers with a reasonably accurate economic map of the costs of their activities and business processes, and the cost and profitability of the organization's products, services, and customers. To construct such a map, ABC systems depend on much subjective judgment and many estimates. These skills are not normally required of financial accountants, particularly those on less than familiar terms with modern production, marketing, and management processes. Also, ABC systems must be built location by location. They are not embedded in a software program that can be rolled out easily to all manufacturing facilities. Each site must systematically verify the completeness of its activity dictionary, the appropriateness of activity cost drivers, the availability of information about these drivers, and the mapping from resource expenses to activities, and then to individual products. And, for sure, the first ABC model, while likely to be far more accurate than the existing traditional costing model, is still only a first approximation of what the model will look like after several years of feedback, learning, and adaptation.

Organizations typically iterate back and forth between model complexity and measurement cost, as described above, until they feel they are about at the optimal point, balancing the cost of measurement with the benefits from a more detailed and accurate system. As organizations experiment with and update their ABC models, and extend their applicability from initial pilot sites to company-wide implementation, they often prefer to use their existing (Stage II) cost system for external reporting purposes. Otherwise, they might find that a small but growing percentage of facilities are using ABC information for external reporting while the remainder continue to use the traditional standard cost system. Also, as a factory switches over to using its ABC system for financial reporting, the managers of that system may feel less free to continue updating the structure of the system to respond to new information or changes in the production process. Such innovation could risk a consistency qualification from auditors if the changes are deemed major enough to pass a materiality threshold.

In addition, financial reporting requirements may differ from the principles companies may wish to follow with their ABC product- and customer-costing system. Some expenses that managers want to apply to products may not be permissible to allocate to products for inventory valuation. Conversely, financial-reporting regulations may require the allocation of some expenses (such as facility-sustaining ones) to products that managers may prefer not to assign to those products in their ABC system.

Rather than complicate even more what is already a challenging implementation process, it seems only prudent not to burden it with the constraints imposed by external regulatory authorities. That is why we recommend a period (Stage III) of experimentation, learning, and innovation for newly installed ABC systems, while retaining the existing (or simplified) Stage II cost system for external reporting purposes. In Chapter 13, we describe enhancements to Stage III ABC systems that provide the foundation for Stage IV, where these systems become integrated into the financial reporting and budgeting processes of organizations.

Summary

Stage II cost systems, using only unit-level cost drivers such as direct labor hours, direct labor dollars, machine hours, and units produced, cannot capture the economics of complex, multiproduct production processes. In an attempt to capture some simple aspects of production economics, these systems may distinguish between short-term variable expenses—the expenses expected to change as one more or one less unit is produced—and short-term fixed expenses. Given improvements in production processes and guaranteed payments to employees, a diminishing share of total manufacturing expenses are classified as variable, leaving a large and growing percentage of costs classified as fixed and their causality unanalyzed by the Stage II cost system. Further, because Stage II cost systems must also value inventory for financial reporting purposes, many organizational expenses—including marketing, selling, distribution, and general overhead—are not traced to any cost objects, whether products, services, customers, or organizational units.

Activity-based cost systems provide more accurate cost information about business activities and processes, and of the products, services, and customers served by these processes. ABC systems focus on organizational activities as the key element for analyzing cost behavior by linking organizational spending on resources to the activities and business processes performed by these resources. Activity cost drivers, collected from diverse corporate information systems, then drive activity costs to the products, services, and customers that create the demand for (or are benefiting from) the organizational activities. These procedures produce good estimates of the unit cost and the amount of the activities and resources deployed for individual products, services, and customers. How to use and interpret this more accurate information is the subject of the next several chapters.

Appendix: ABC Activity and Process Dictionary

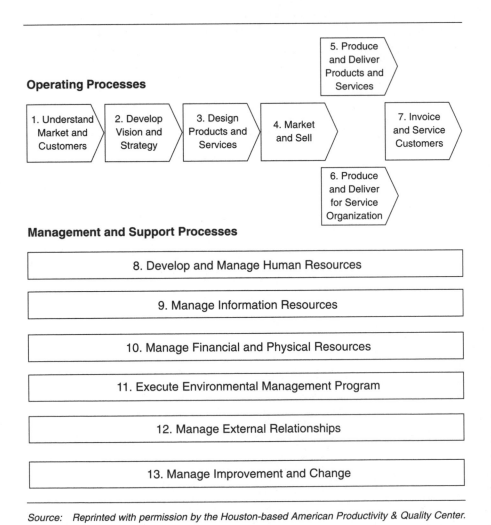

Operating Processes

1. Understand Market and Customers
2. Develop Vision and Strategy
3. Design Products and Services
4. Market and Sell
5. Produce and Deliver Products and Services
6. Produce and Deliver for Service Organization
7. Invoice and Service Customers

Management and Support Processes

8. Develop and Manage Human Resources

9. Manage Information Resources

10. Manage Financial and Physical Resources

11. Execute Environmental Management Program

12. Manage External Relationships

13. Manage Improvement and Change

Source: *Reprinted with permission by the Houston-based American Productivity & Quality Center.*

Operating Processes

1. Understand Market and Customers
   - 1.1 Determine customer needs and wants
   - 1.2 Measure customer satisfaction
   - 1.3 Monitor changes in market or customer expectations
2. Develop Vision and Strategy
   - 2.1 Monitor the external environment
   - 2.2 Define the business concept and organizational strategy
   - 2.3 Design the organizational structure and relationships between organizational units
   - 2.4 Develop and set organizational goals
3. Design Products and Services
   - 3.1 Develop new product/service concept and plans
   - 3.2 Design, build, and evaluate prototype products or services
   - 3.3 Refine existing products/services
   - 3.4 Test effectiveness of new or revised products or services
   - 3.5 Prepare for production
   - 3.6 Manage the product/service development process
4. Market and Sell
   - 4.1 Market products or services to relevant customer segments
   - 4.2 Process customer orders
5. Produce and Deliver Products and Services
   - 5.1 Plan for and acquire necessary resources
   - 5.2 Convert resources or inputs into products
   - 5.3 Deliver products
   - 5.4 Manage production and delivery process
6. Produce and Deliver for Service Organization
   - 6.1 Plan for and acquire necessary resources
   - 6.2 Develop human resource skills
   - 6.3 Deliver service to customer
   - 6.4 Ensure quality of service
7. Invoice and Service Customers
   - 7.1 Bill the customer
   - 7.2 Provide after-sales service
   - 7.3 Respond to customer inquiries

Management and Support Processes

8. Develop and Manage Human Resources
   - 8.1 Create and manage human resource strategy
   - 8.2 Cascade strategy to work level
   - 8.3 Manage deployment of personnel
   - 8.4 Develop and train employees
   - 8.5 Manage employee performance, reward, and recognition
   - 8.6 Ensure employee well-being and satisfaction
   - 8.7 Ensure employee involvement

8.8 Manage labor/management relationships
8.9 Develop Human Resource Information Systems (HRIS)
9. Manage Information Resources
   9.1 Plan for information resources management
   9.2 Develop and deploy enterprise support systems
   9.3 Implement systems security and controls
   9.4 Manage information storage and retrieval
   9.5 Manage facilities and network operations
   9.6 Manage information services
   9.7 Facilitate information sharing and communication
   9.8 Evaluate and audit information quality
10. Manage Financial and Physical Resources
   10.1 Manage financial resources
   10.2 Process finance and accounting transactions
   10.3 Report information
   10.4 Conduct internal audits
   10.5 Manage the tax function
   10.6 Manage physical resources
11. Execute Environmental Management Program
   11.1 Formulate environmental management strategy
   11.2 Ensure compliance with regulations
   11.3 Train and educate employees
   11.4 Implement pollution prevention program
   11.5 Manage remediation efforts
   11.6 Implement emergency response program
   11.7 Manage government, agency and public relations
   11.8 Manage acquisition/divestiture environmental issues
   11.9 Develop and manage environmental information system
   11.10 Monitor environmental management program
12. Manage External Relationships
   12.1 Communicate with shareholders
   12.2 Manage government relationships
   12.3 Build lender relationships
   12.4 Develop public relations program
   12.5 Interface with board of directors
   12.6 Develop community relations
   12.7 Manage legal and ethical issues
13. Manage Improvement and Change
   13.1 Measure organizational performance
   13.2 Conduct quality assessments
   13.3 Benchmark performance
   13.4 Improve processes and systems
   13.5 Implement TQM

Source: KPMG Peat Marwick LLP. Reprinted by permission.

7

Measuring the Cost of Resource Capacity

Virtually all Stage III activity-based cost systems start by estimating activity cost driver rates from historical data. But ABC should not be thought of solely as an historical accounting or general ledger system. ABC systems should be used proactively to estimate the costs of activities that will be performed in current and future periods. This enables decisions to be made that can influence future cost incurrence, not just better assign past costs. For this purpose, even Stage III ABC systems can use activity cost driver rates that are calculated using budgeted expense data for upcoming periods.

In addition to using budgeted expense information, the rates should also reflect the practical capacity of the resources supplied. Measuring, creating, and managing unused capacity are the heart of activity-based costing. One can view the entire ABC approach as giving managers insights about the existence, creation, and deployment of capacity, both used and unused. In this chapter, we show how to incorporate both budgeted and capacity information in ABC models.

Historical ABC

As a simple example of the use of historical data in an ABC model, consider an activity *handle customer order.* The interview and survey procedures described in Chapter 6 enable ABC analysts to review historical data for the most recent period (e.g., quarter, half-year, or year) and estimate the quantity of organizational expenses that can be traced to the resources (people, systems, facilities) used to process customer orders. Suppose the traced expenses equal $250,000. Next, the analysts select an activity cost driver for this activity, *number of customer orders,* and review historical records to determine the quantity of this activity cost driver in the most recent period. Say this number is 3,500 orders. The historical cost driver rate is then estimated as $71.43 per order ($250,000 in expenses divided by the 3,500 orders). This rate is used to calculate the cost and profitability of individual orders and customers during the estimation (historical) period. This historical method is objective and relatively simple to implement.

Such a calculation, while much more accurate and revealing than traditional costing systems about the cost of resources required by individual products and customers, is not quite as useful or correct as it should be. The historical cost driver rates have two major limitations. First, the actual cost driver rate is not calculated until after the period is over. One can readily imagine the following statement from a manager to an ABC cost analyst: "You are still acting as accountants. You're standing in the back of the boat giving me an extremely accurate picture of the boat's wake. I need a system that helps me to navigate to the future, to help tell me what I should be doing, not just reporting more accurately about where I have been." Managers will not want to wait until the end of the period to obtain cost driver rates for calculating product and customer costs and profitability.

Second, the accuracy of the cost driver rate is compromised if the capacity of the resources supplied to perform the activity were not fully used during the period. If the organization had the capacity to handle 4,000 customer orders during the period, not just the 3,500 that were processed actually, the correct cost driver rate is considerably less than the $71.43 calculated from historical data. The $71.43 rate includes both the cost of resources used to handle each customer order as well as the cost of resources that were supplied *but were not used* during the period.

Both these limitations need to be overcome if ABC systems are to be used proactively. Ideally, managers should use the ABC information to make better decisions about current and future processes, products, and customers, not just to reflect on the past.

Why Estimate ABC Models with Historical (Actual) Expenses?

It is, however, reasonable for Stage III ABC models to be estimated initially with historical data as virtually all companies have done. By closely analyzing the commitment of resources to activities during a recent period, the ABC project team can determine the actual distribution of effort in the organization in a reasonably objective and defensible manner. The team can use recent experience to anchor discussions with managers, supervisors, and employees about principal activities performed and the commitment of resources to these activities.

Further, the initial ABC analysis will often reveal inefficient business processes, unprofitable products, unprofitable customers, poor supplier relationships, and badly designed products. Since these results are based on historical data they represent actual operations, not hypothetical or potential results. The ABC model shows how the organization actually performed in a recent period with wasteful processes, and products and customers that required resources whose costs exceeded revenues earned. Unless managers planned for such inefficient processes and unprofitable products and customers, the ABC model has given managers new information about defects in operations.

By analyzing past data to affect the future, ABC is much like a formal TQM program. In TQM, employees study historical data (past defects) to learn about the root causes of the defects. After determining the root causes for the principal sources of defects, employees suggest and implement corrective actions so that the defects are eliminated and do not recur.

Similarly, the ABC analysis of past costs of activities, products, and customers usually reveals why certain activities are unexpectedly costly and why specific products and customers are highly unprofitable, while others are quite profitable. Employees and managers can then study the root causes and take corrective actions to reduce or eliminate inefficiencies and transform unprofitable products and customers into profitable ones.

History matters. As the famous philosopher George Santayana stated, "Those who fail to study history are condemned to repeat it." Patterns repeat. The circumstances that led in a past period to a costly activity or an unprofitable product, customer, or service are likely to be the same in the current period. ABC's clear picture of past operations should be used to stimulate thinking about how to avoid similarly adverse results in the current and future periods by changing decisions about product design, pricing, customer and supplier relationships, and process improvements. But ABC need not be limited to decisions based on historical cost and quantity data. Managers have even greater leverage for influencing current and future activities when they use future-oriented data in their ABC model.

Viewing the Future: ABC with Budgeted Expenses

Once the basic structure of an ABC model has been determined, it need not be restricted to driving actual historical expenses to activities, products, and customers. One can use, as inputs to an ABC model, the budgeted expenses for resources in the upcoming period. In this way, activity cost driver rates will be a function of anticipated expenses. This enables cost driver rates to be calculated in advance, at the beginning of a period, so that managers can use this information, in real time, when making decisions about products and customers.

Continuing our numerical example, assume that for an upcoming period, that the budgeted expenses of resources for performing the *handle customer order* activity is $280,000. And suppose the expected number of customer orders during the period is 4,000 orders. The ABC model using budgeted data calculates a cost driver rate of $70 per order based on budgeted expenses and activity levels. This amount ($70) will be charged to every customer order received during the period. Managers can use this information to establish reference points for pricing and order acceptance during the period, and to make decisions about minimum order size. They do not have to wait until the end of the period to learn how much it costs to handle an individual order.

Once the period has ended, financial analysts can easily reconcile the actual results of the period with the expected or budgeted expenses. Assume that actual spending turned out to be $273,600 and that 3,800 orders were actually handled. Using the standard cost driver rate of $70 per order, a total of $266,000 would be charged to the orders received during the period.[1] To reconcile among budgeted ($280,000), assigned ($266,000), and actual ($273,600) expenses for the period, the analyst must judge whether expenses, in the short run, are more likely to be variable or fixed with respect to changes in activity levels. It would be reasonable to assume that most of the resources performing indirect and support activities in organizations are fixed expenses in the short run. People are hired and come to work each day to perform activities. Facilities for them have already been acquired and provided, as have supporting resources such as information technology hardware and software, supervisors, and telecommunications. Therefore, even when the organization realizes a 5% reduction in activity levels (actual orders of 3,800 are 5% below the expected number of 4,000), the expected expenses for the period will still be $280,000. With the assumption that resource expenses are fixed in the short run, the difference between actual and budgeted expenses represents a spending variance—in this case $6,400, favorable—implying that the organization spent less to perform this activity than it had budgeted for. The difference between costs assigned to products ($266,000) and the budgeted expenses ($280,000) represents an unfavorable volume variance of $14,000. This volume variance comes from processing 200 fewer orders than anticipated, at a standard cost of $70 per order. The complete reconciliation between budgeted and actual expenses is shown below:

	Expense	Activity Level	Cost Driver Rate
Budgeted	$280,000	4,000 orders	$70/order
Actual	$273,600	3,800 orders	n/a

($6,400)
Spending Variance

Actial
$273,000 cost

Budgeted
$280,000 cost

$14,000 Volume Variance
Expected Orders – Actual Orders
200 @ $70

Order Expenses Charged to Product
$266,000
(3,800 orders @ $70)

Continuing this process, ABC models can estimate resource expenses even farther into the future than the next budgeted period. Past or current operations may represent quite inefficient activities. In many companies, TQM or reengineering initiatives are under way to reduce or eliminate inefficiencies in activities and processes (these will be discussed in Chapter 8). If managers can estimate the quantity and cost of inefficiencies, they can exclude these costs from the data used to estimate activity expenses. With this procedure, the expenses used to estimate activity cost driver rates and then assigned to products and customers will represent the costs of efficient operations. Managers can bid for business, price products, negotiate supplier and customer relationships, and design products based on expected efficient operating procedures to be achieved in the future. For example, if managers estimate that 15% of the expenses in the *handle customer order* activity can be eliminated by process improvements, the budgeted cost of this activity will be estimated at $238,000, with a corresponding reduction in the activity cost driver rate for this activity. Any deviation between actual expenses and budgeted expenses can be assigned to the department responsible for managing the excess costs out of this activity. By basing forecasted activity expenses on efficient operations, managers will be using their ABC model as a target-costing mechanism.[2]

Working with budgeted rather than historical expenses overcomes one of the objections raised by many managers. They now have a cost model to forecast the future, not just explain the past. We must still cope with the second limitation. Even working with budgeted data, the forecasted activity volume may be well below the quantity that could be handled by the resources supplied to perform this activity. In our example, the $70 activity cost driver rate may include expenses of both used and unused resources, at a forecasted activity level of 4,000 customer orders.

Measuring the Cost of Capacity Resources

If managers use forecasted activity levels (such as those 4,000 orders) to calculate cost driver rates, they risk launching a death spiral in their organization. Suppose, as we have assumed, that the resources supplied to perform most indirect and support activities are fixed in the short run. If activity levels decline—perhaps because of a general slowdown in economic activity or loss of a major customer—the activity cost driver rate will increase (a simple arithmetic calculation since expenses, the numerator of the calculation, remain the same while the cost driver quantity, the denominator, declines). If the now higher cost driver rate is used for pricing, discounting, and order acceptance decisions, the company may set a higher reference price for taking business to offset the higher cost driver rate. But such an action could lead to even lower activity levels if customers balk at the company's attempt to recover excess capacity at their expense. If these lower activity levels are then fed back into the cost driver rate calculation, an even higher cost driver rate gets calculated the next period, reinforcing the vicious cycle of losing more business and recalculating higher cost driver rates.

The use of forecasted activity levels not only risks a death spiral; the calculation is conceptually incorrect. If, as we have assumed, the resources supplied to perform an activity, such as *handle customer order,* are essentially fixed in the short run, we need to obtain an additional and very important piece of information: how many customer orders could be handled during the period by the resources supplied? This new information represents the practical capacity of the resources for this activity, the largest number of customer orders that could be handled without creating unusual delays, forcing overtime work, or requiring additional resources to be supplied. Suppose, for purposes of illustration, that the practical capacity for this activity is 5,000 customer orders per period.[3] In this case, the correct cost driver rate is $56 per order, not the $70 per order calculated using the forecasted activity volume. Why is $56 "more correct" than $70?

Managers, through past or recent budgeting decisions, have authorized a supply of resources expected to cost $280,000 for performing the *handle customer order* activity. What does this mean? They have obtained a capacity to handle 5,000 customer orders. Assuming that each customer order requires approximately the same resources to handle (if not, the ABC model should use a duration or intensity driver, or a weighted index of order complexity as discussed in Chapter 6), about $56 of resources are used each time an order is handled. This number represents the basic efficiency of the order-handling processes. If, in a period, only 4,000 orders are received, the efficiency of the activity should remain about the same since only $56 of resources are required per order. The people and other resources needed to perform this process do not suddenly become less efficient ($70 per order) just because fewer orders come in. The lower number of orders received means that not all the resources supplied during the period are expected to be used. Because of the contracts and commitments (explicit and implicit) made to the resources performing this activity, the supply of resources cannot be lowered in the short run in response to the expected lower activity level (that's what we mean by a fixed cost). Alternatively, managers may want to retain the current level of resource supply in order to handle higher expected order volumes in the future.

In either case, the cost driver rate should reflect the underlying efficiency of the process—the cost of handling each customer order—and this efficiency is measured better by recognizing the capacity of the resources being supplied. The numerator in an activity cost driver rate calculation represents the costs of supplying resource capacity to do work. The denominator should match the numerator by representing the quantity of work the resources can perform.[4]

The Fundamental Equation of Activity-Based Costing

The basic principle represented by the capacity-based approach is simple yet profound. And the calculations are remarkably simple and transparent. When the practical capacity is used to calculate activity cost driver rates, the organization has an additional line item in its periodic financial reports—the budgeted cost of unused capacity. In our numerical example, the organization expects to have 1,000 fewer orders than it could potentially handle with the resources supplied. At a cost driver rate of $56 per order, the budgeted unused capacity equals $56,000. The details of the calculation and the reconciliation to the same actual outcomes as in the previous section are shown below.

	Expense	Activity Level	Cost Driver Rate
Practical Capacity	$280,000	5,000 orders	$56/order
Budgeted	$280,000	4,000 orders	n/a
Actual	$273,600	3,800 orders	n/a

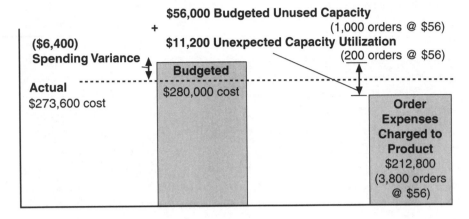

These calculations are based on the following fundamental equation:

Cost of Resources Supplied		Cost of Resources Used		Cost of Unused Capacity
	=		+	

Financial systems—whether general ledger systems that measure expenses actually being incurred or budgeting systems that measure expenses expected to be incurred—measure the left-hand side of this equation. They measure the amount of organizational expenses incurred to make resources available for productive use. This is an important measurement and one that needs to continue to be made by any current or future system. It represents the heart of systems for financial reporting and for operational control (see discussion in Chapters 3–5) by measuring (or forecasting) the actual spending by the organization. But such a measurement, by itself, is inadequate for measuring the costs of resources required to actually perform work.

ABC systems rectify this limitation by measuring the first term on the right-hand side of the equation. ABC systems measure the cost of resources used (or, alternatively, the resource costs of activities performed) for individual products, services, and customers. The difference between the resources supplied and the resources actually used during a period represents the unused capacity of resources for the period.[5]

Confusion About Activity-Based Costing

The distinction between the cost of resources supplied and the cost of resources used is critical for clearing up many people's confusion about ABC systems. Some observers have claimed, incorrectly, that activity-based costing assumes that almost all organizational costs are variable.[6] These observers' general understanding of a variable cost is one that changes with respect to a particular decision such as to take on an additional order. People who interpret ABC systems as predicting that taking on an additional order would cause organizational spending to rise by $56 (in the above example) completely misunderstand the fundamental concept of activity-based costing.

Eli Goldratt, in his Theory of Constraints,[7] has this limited concept of a variable cost exactly right. In most organizations, the only variable costs—those where spending would change based on accepting or rejecting an individual order—are the materials costs associated with the incremental order (and perhaps the energy cost to operate machines to produce the order). For most service organizations, the variable costs of an additional customer or an additional transaction are even lower, perhaps close to zero. One would hardly need to develop a new costing approach built around activities, cost drivers, and linkages to individual products and customers to estimate such short-run variable costs "more accurately."

Some people believe that using the ABC cost hierarchy means that at least unit-level costs are synonymous with short-term variable costs. This is also incorrect. Obviously, many unit-level expenses are related to providing machine capacity and would be traced to products using a unit-level driver like machine hours. But apart from a few, and minor, resource elements such as power and consumable supplies, most expenses driven to products by machine hours would be incurred whether the machine operated one more hour or not. Similarly, most if not all expenses driven to products via direct labor hours or direct labor dollars (two widely used unit-level drivers) are not short-term variable costs. Today many companies have guaranteed work weeks for their front-line employee or treat them comparably to salaried employees. Therefore, almost all employees will get paid, whether or not they are fully occupied during the day or the week.[8] Only if employees are paid on a piece-work basis, or only for the hours during which they actually work, would direct labor and supporting expenses be considered variable costs. That is why we agree with the Theory of Constraints claim that materials expenses are the primary short-term variable cost in organizations today. Activity-based cost systems were never intended to measure such short-run cost behavior (though, as discussed in Chapter 6, such behavior can be accommodated in an ABC analysis by a coding of activity cost elements).

Committed and Flexible Resources

Organizations contract to supply most of their resources, especially those other than materials, energy, and other services purchased from external vendors, before they are actually used.[9] The organization makes a commitment or actual cash outlay to acquire such resources that will be used for current and future activities. We refer to these resources as *committed resources*. As examples of committed resources, the organization acquires buildings and equipment that will supply a capacity for work for several periods into the future. Such a transaction leads to an expense being recognized in each period of the useful life of the resource. The expense of supplying this resource is incurred, each period, independent of how much of the resource is used. As another example, the organization can enter into an explicit contract to obtain the services from a resource for several periods in the future. It can lease buildings and equipment, and guarantee access to energy or key materials through take-or-pay contracts. Again, the amount of the cash payment and associated expenses are independent of the actual quantity of usage of the resource in any period.

Perhaps the most important example is when an organization enters into implicit contracts (and occasionally explicit ones, especially with top executives or a unionized workforce) to maintain employment levels despite short-term downturns in activity levels. Engineers, purchasing managers, production supervisors, sales and marketing managers, and the salaried workforce remain on the payroll even when the short-term demand for their services may have declined. The spending and accrued expenses for such employees are constant, independent of the quantity of work performed by the employees.

In each case, the organization acquires units of service capacity before the actual demands for the service are realized. Consequently, the expenses of supplying the service capacity from these resources are incurred whether the resources are used or not. This independence in the short-run supply and expenses of these resources has led many to label these expenses as fixed costs.[10]

From this perspective, variable costs represent only those resources, typically acquired from outside suppliers, that the organization can acquire just as needed. We refer to such resources as "flexible resources"; they include materials, energy, telecommunications services, temporary workers hired on a daily basis, employees paid on a piece-work basis, and overtime that is authorized as needed. For these resources, the organization acquires only what it needs to meet short-term demands so the cost of acquiring these resources equals the cost of using the resources. Such resources have no unused capacity; whatever is supplied is used, or conversely, whatever is needed is supplied.

Activity-based systems differ from traditional cost systems by estimating the costs of all resources, both flexible and committed, used by activities and products. ABC systems recognize that almost all organizational costs (other than those of flexible resources) are not variable in the short run just because demand fluctuates. Rather, committed costs become variable costs over longer time periods via a two-step procedure. First, demands for the resources supplied can change because of shifts in activity levels. For batch and product-sustaining resources, the activity levels change because of changes in variety and complexity. In the second step, the organization changes the supply of committed resources, either up or down, to meet the new level in demand for the activities performed by these resources.

When the capacity of existing resources is exceeded, the pain is obvious through shortages, increased pace of activity, delays, or poor-quality work. Such shortages can occur on machines, the usual case that comes to mind, but the ABC approach makes clear that such shortages can occur for resources performing support activities such as designing, scheduling, ordering, maintaining, and handling products and customers. Companies, facing such shortages, move to the second step of making committed costs variable: They spend more to increase the supply of resources and relieve the bottleneck.

Demands for resources can also decline. Should the demands for batch and product-sustaining resources decrease because of managers' actions, little immediate spending improvement will be noticed. Even for many unit-level resources, like machine and labor capacity, a reduced demand for work from these resources will not lead to spending decreases. The reduced demand for organizational resources will *lower the cost of resources used* (by products, services, and customers) but this decrease will be offset by an equivalent *increase in the cost of unused capacity.*

For committed costs to become variable in the downward direction—after the demand for the supplied resources has decreased, creating unused capacity—the organization must manage the unused capacity of these resources out of the system. At that point, and only at that point, will the costs of resources supplied start to decrease. Thus what makes a resource cost variable in a downward direction is not inherent in the nature of the resource; it is a function of management decisions—first to reduce the demands for the resource and, second, to lower the spending on the resource.[11]

This is why we stated, at the outset of this chapter, that measuring and managing used and unused capacity is the central focus of activity-based costing. Even actions taken to improve the efficiency of activities (to be discussed in Chapter 8) require an understanding of how unused capacity is created and then managed. Let's continue our example of the *handle customer order* activity. In our numerical example, the organization supplies resources costing $280,000 to perform this activity, and the practical capacity of these resources is handling 5,000 customer orders per month.

Suppose that a continuous (TQM) or discontinuous (reengineering) improvement initiative is launched to reduce waste and non-value-added tasks in processing customer orders. Perhaps even a modest technology investment, such as electronic data interchange (EDI), is made to help employees be more productive. Such initiatives typically result in expanding the capacity to perform work (since the amount of time and resources devoted to nonproductive or non-value-added work will be sharply reduced or eliminated). In such a case, the practical capacity will rise, say, to 7,000 customer orders per month. But expenses will remain the same; they may even rise slightly if any technology investments are made. People have been hired; they continue to come to work; they have desks, computers, and telephones; they continue to take coffee breaks, vacations, and sick leave; and they accumulate time to pensions.

Has the cost of handling customer orders been reduced by the TQM or reengineering initiative? Absolutely! Previously, the cost of handling a customer order required $56 of resources; after the initiative, a customer order can be handled with only $40 of resources ($280,000/7,000), perhaps a little higher to cover any new technology investment. But suppose that only 4,000 orders are expected the next period. How much should managers expect to *spend* next period on resources devoted to handling customer orders?[12] The answer, of course, is $280,000. If business activity goes as planned, the expenses assigned to the actual orders received will decrease to $160,000 (4,000 @ $40) from the previous level of $196,000. This will signal that the order handling cost has been reduced because of the TQM/reengineering initiative. But the cost of unused capacity will rise to $120,000 (3,000 @ $40) since all the resources previously supplied are still being paid for.

Thus, for initiatives designed to improve the efficiency of activities to yield improvements in spending, managers must plan to eliminate or redeploy the additional unused resource capacity they have created. The example clearly shows that applying TQM or reengineering to resources already in excess of the supply required to perform the forecasted level of activities will produce even more excess capacity. ABC systems can signal those resources that are currently at, or expected to soon reach, capacity constraints. Improvement initiatives can then be focused on the activities performed by these constraining resources. Alternatively, the ABC systems will signal where unused capacity already exists in the organization, or that will be created after improvement activities or decisions about products, services, and customers. Such a signal tells managers they must eliminate the unused capacity. Unused capacity can be eliminated in only two ways:

1. Spending reductions by reducing the supply of resources for performing the activity, or
2. Revenue increases by increasing the quantity of activities demanded for the resources to perform.

Often, however, organizations cannot do anything about unused capacity. They keep existing resources in place, although the demands for the activities performed by the resources have diminished substantially. And they fail to find new activities that could be handled, without incremental expenses, by the resources already in place. In this case, and only in this case, will the organizations not benefit from their decisions. But the failure to capture benefits from operational or strategic decisions is not because costs are intrinsically fixed. Rather, the failure occurs because managers are unwilling or unable to exploit the unused capacity they have created.

The costs of these resources are only fixed if managers cannot or do not exploit the opportunities of the unused capacity they helped create.

A final example should drive home this point even further. A pharmaceutical company conducted an initial ABC study and found, as expected, that many of its products, especially those produced and sold in small-order quantities, were unprofitable. The company had previously used a direct costing system, in which only materials cost was considered a product cost. The company was located in a country where laying off employees was extremely expensive and time-consuming. Also, the pharmaceutical workers were highly skilled so that if laid off, they could be hired rapidly by other companies and it could take up to two years to train newly hired employees to the same skill levels. Thus organizational treatment of all labor and machinery as fixed costs seemed plausible. When confronted with the losses incurred in many products, managers naturally responded: "If we drop the unprofitable products, revenues will go away immediately. But most of the costs [labor and equipment] will remain."

This is not only a normal response; it is the correct response. On the margin, managers could be encouraged to persuade customers to focus their orders on fewer products or to order in larger quantities, but no drastic action to drop unprofitable products or customers was warranted since the creation of unused capacity could not be translated into spending reductions.

Shortly thereafter, the ABC consultant learned that the company was contemplating a new investment project costing about $75 million (a large amount for a company with about $500 million in annual sales). The consultant inquired about the rationale for the new investment, and was told that increased worldwide sales exceeded existing capacity and that a new facility had to be added to handle the growing demand. At that point, the consultant inquired about the unprofitable products. When many products, on a fully costed ABC basis, are unprofitable, the organization knows that they are not paying for the capacity already being supplied: people, support resources, equipment, and facilities. The consultant asked whether the company would build the new facility just to produce the unprofitable products. The answer, of course, was no. And that was exactly the message from the ABC system. The company then initiated an ongoing process to outsource and prune its product line so that its scarce manufacturing capacity would not be used for unprofitable products.

Often, if not always, the cheapest source of new capacity is that freed up by contracting out the production of unprofitable products or the sales to unprofitable customers. If the company is not willing to hire an additional salesperson to service currently unprofitable customers, or an additional production control person to handle currently unprofitable products, or an additional purchasing person to order materials for unprofitable products, it can certainly contemplate shifting the resources already being supplied from unprofitable to profitable uses. In a capacity-constrained situation, ABC gives companies the information to outsource or eliminate unprofitable products and customers and replace them with profitable ones. The capacity made available through operational and strategic decisions based on activity-based costing information (see Chapters 8–11) is likely a much cheaper source of new supply than the capacity created by hiring additional employees, purchasing additional equipment, or building additional facilities. That is why we characterize ABC as a system for identifying, measuring, creating, and managing capacity. Understanding the subtle interplay between the actions taken with ABC information and capacity management is our central message.

From an ABC Resource Usage Model to Decisions About Resource Supply

As a model of resource usage, not spending, activity-based cost systems are not designed for automatic decision making. ABC identifies the relationship between revenues generated and resources consumed. However, it does not identify the relationship between changes in resources used and changes in resources supplied.

Making decisions based solely upon resource usage (the ABC system) is problematic because there is no guarantee that the spending to supply resources will be aligned with the new levels of resources demanded in the near future. For example, if a decision is made to reduce inspections by 10%, no economic benefit will be achieved unless the resources supplied to perform inspection, which are no longer needed, are eliminated or redeployed to higher-revenue uses. Consequently, before making decisions based on an ABC model, managers should analyze the resource supply implications of such decisions.

With the insights gained from the ABC model, managers can do special studies to determine the resource supply implications of their upcoming decisions. For example, consider a decision about whether to maintain the existing product mix, or to eliminate a subset of the products. The ABC model identifies a number of products whose resource consumption is higher than the revenues they generate (that is, they are losers). Managers' attempts to redesign the products or improve production processes to make the products profitable have failed. Careful analysis of the customers that buy these products indicates that none is major and that nearly all of them can use substitutes without any inconvenience. These are the products on which special studies should be performed to determine how much current expenses can be reduced by eliminating some or all of the losers.

To repeat, the ABC resource usage model identifies the decrease in resource usage that will occur if the unprofitable products are dropped. It does not, however, indicate if the firm can take advantage of this reduction by decreasing the resources supplied. Managers must perform special studies to determine when the reduction in resource demands—for example, dropping the right mix of products—enables enough resources to be redeployed so that the cost savings exceed the revenue losses. At that time, managers are confident that they can drop products, eliminate the resources currently supplied, and have the resulting cost savings produce a profit increase for the company. We will discuss the role of what-if analysis to implement such special studies in Chapter 15.

The ABC resource usage model produces, at relatively low cost, an economic map of the enterprise. Performing special studies between decisions about products (or customers) and spending changes (because of changes in resources supplied) without the initial ABC model is a difficult and expensive search. There are too many possibilities to consider. For example, managers at a company that produces a narrow range of products, say only 100, are contemplating whether to eliminate a subset of these products (a simple, binary, go/no go decision for each product). In an exhaustive and unguided search through all the possible combinations of products that could be dropped, the managers would have to evaluate 2^{100} possible decisions, a number beyond the collective computational power of all the computers on the planet, running for the lifetime of the solar system. The ABC model reduces the dimensionality of managers' search problems; it guides managers to the special studies that will have the most promising opportunities for profit improvement.

Measuring Capacity

We have illustrated the calculation of activity cost driver rates with practical capacity using a simple numerical example. In practice, there are many complications in measuring practical capacity.[13] Several major research studies have focused exclusively on the measurement and management of capacity.[14] Here, we discuss a few of the complications and provide rules-of-thumb for coping with them.

What Is Practical Capacity?

Practical capacity can be studied analytically in some depth or estimated somewhat arbitrarily. The arbitrary estimate approach assumes that practical capacity is a specified percentage, say 80% or 85%, of theoretical capacity. That is, if an employee or machine normally can work 40 hours per week, practical capacity could be assumed to be 32 hours per week, allowing 20% of personnel time for breaks, arrival and departure, and communication unrelated to actual work performance, and 20% of machine time for downtime for maintenance, repair, and scheduling fluctuations.

For a simple but less arbitrary approach, the analyst can review the time series of past activity levels. For example, look at the number of customer orders handled over the past 12 or 24 months and identify the month with the maximum number of orders. Check whether the work was handled without excessive delays, poor quality, overtime, or stressed employees. If not, as a starting point, one can use that maximum number as the estimate of the capacity of the resources performing that activity. As with all ABC design decisions, the analysis is not greatly sensitive to small errors in estimating parameters. It is better to make a reasonable estimate of capacity and use that number as the denominator volume in calculating the activity cost driver rate than to introduce arbitrary fluctuations by using last period's actual or next period's expected activity level.

The analytic approach starts with theoretical capacity and then subtracts time required for maintenance, repairs, startups, and shutdowns. It can also incorporate an amount of time held in reserve for protective or surge capacity, which allows the plant or a piece of equipment to respond to short-term fluctuations in demand, or disruptions within the factory, without sacrificing output. Having some protective capacity allows the facility to continue to meet customer demands despite short-term unexpected delays of materials (either from external vendors or from upstream production processes), or when short-term surges in demand occur.

A complication occurs when surge or protective capacity must be supplied for particular customers. For example, the plant may have two types of customers: the first provides steady, predictable demand; the second has demand that is erratic and unpredictable but that must be met with short lead times when it occurs. In this case, the plant must hold protective capacity for the second type of customers, but would need little to no surge capacity if all its customers were of the first type. It would be reasonable to assign the cost of protective and surge capacity only to the second type of customers—the ones creating the demand for that capacity—and not assign any of the costs of the capacity held in reserve to the first type of customers.

Most of the complications with measuring practical capacity occur for physical rather than for human resources. Human resources are more flexible. They can either be assigned to alternative tasks or be taken off the payroll if they are not redeployable. Also, human resources come in small increments—one person at a time. Since many of the cost assignments in ABC systems relate to activities performed by human resources, the measurement of practical capacity should not be that difficult for those resources. In what follows we briefly comment on several issues that arise with measuring the capacity of equipment resources.

For example, suppose the unused capacity arises from the lumpiness of asset acquisition. A company wants a machine to process 800,000 units per year, but the smallest machine with this minimum capacity produces 1,000,000 units per year. So the company acquires a machine with a practical capacity of 1,000,000 units per year, but because of demand constraints or constraining resources elsewhere in the production process will only produce a maximum of 800,000 units per year. If the machine acquisition was justified in the full knowledge that a maximum output of 800,000 units per year would be produced, the practical capacity is 800,000, not 1,000,000. Should external demand be higher than anticipated, or if internal bottlenecks elsewhere in the plant are relieved, so that output climbs, unexpectedly, to 900,000 units per year, the denominator volume can, of course, be reset to the higher figure.

A variation on this theme occurs when a machine is acquired whose annual cost (rental or amortization of purchase cost plus operating cost) is, say, $120,000 per year. Demand is expected to build over time, starting with a low value of 100,000 units the first year, 200,000 units in year two, and reaching 400,000 units in year three and thereafter. The naive approach would estimate the first-year cost at $1.20 per unit, the second-year cost at $0.60 per unit, and the third-year cost at $0.30 per unit. These calculations suggest that the machine is four times more efficient in year three than in year one, when, in fact, its efficiency is identical for the three years. Only the volume of business is changing, not the efficiency of the machine. Two approaches seem more plausible. The first would use the practical capacity (400,000 units per year) as the denominator volume so that machine costs would be $0.30, independent of which year a unit was produced. The unused capacity of $90,000 in year one was anticipated in the capital budgeting decision. It could be charged either to the investment account or written off as unused capacity, but it should not affect the signal about the cost of the resources used (25% of capacity) by year one production.

Alternatively, the operating costs over the lifetime of the equipment could be assigned to anticipated lifetime production (sum of production units in years one, two, three, up through the maximum economic life of the equipment). This also produces a constant cost per unit produced, independent of which year production of the unit occurs, but does not lead to an unused capacity amount in any year (unless actual production is less than anticipated).

This principle extends not only to equipment cost but also to quality of service. Suppose a communications company has two types of customers. The first type is satisfied with low speed, moderate quality voice transmission. The second requires high speed, very high-quality communication capable of excellent voice communications and high-speed data or video transmission. Rather than supply two different and parallel communications channels, the company finds it cheaper to build the higher-quality, but more expensive, channel required to attract the second type of customer. Both customers use the same system, but if an average unit cost is assigned to both types of customers, the first is being costed out for a higher-quality service than it is willing to pay. The decision to invest in the more expensive channel was justified by the preferences of the second type of customer and the decision of the communications company to offer a high-quality, high-bandwidth channel to that customer cohort.

In this case, one could estimate the costs to be assigned to the first customer type by a simple mental or modeling experiment. How much would it have cost to construct a vanilla-type network (low-speed, low-bandwidth communication), assuming that all the customers were type one? The unit cost of providing a vanilla network is a reasonable cost assignment to type one customers. The extra cost to build the network with high-speed, high-quality features and service can all be attributed to type two customers. So although both customers use the same network, the less demanding customers are assigned only the costs associated with delivering the desired value proposition to them, and the demanding type two customers bear the incremental costs of providing the capacity to deliver the more complex value proposition to them. The ability to assign costs differentially to different types of customers hinges on being able to distinguish among the different service levels required by diverse customer segments. But such knowledge is usually available so such distinctions can be made and the relevant costs estimated.

Differential costs can even occur with materials. As an example, a refinery was purchasing a high-grade (sweet) crude oil because only such an input would produce a high-quality intermediate product needed for a specific product (lubricants) in a downstream refinery operation. The refinery was paying, say, a $3/barrel premium, for the sweet oil relative to the cheaper sour crude that would satisfy the needs of all other products produced at the refinery. Under the existing plant costing system, the gasoline, heating oil, and jet fuel produced at this refinery was 10–20% more expensive than the outputs produced at other company refineries in the United States, a difference largely explained by raw materials purchase costs. As this plant performed its ABC study, recognizing that the $3/barrel premium paid for all crude oil purchased should be assigned to the lubricants that created the demand for the high-grade crude was one of the most important innovations and contributions of the study. It placed the plant in a far more competitive situation versus its sister plants that did not produce the lubricants.

The extension to seasonal capacity is now straightforward. Consider two demand periods during the year (or week, or day): peak and slack. The cost of providing capacity is constant throughout the period. The simplistic costing approach would show a lower cost in the peak period since its period cost would be divided by the high (peak) volume, while the demand in the slack period would seem expensive since its (same) period cost would be divided by the low (slack) demand. This result runs counter to any economic intuition. The provision of extra resources is associated with peak period demand, not slack period demand.

The counterpart of the vanilla network in the communications example is the level of resources that would have to be provided throughout the period to satisfy the demand in the slack period alone. The cost of the extra resources required to handle the peak demand would then be assigned entirely to the production of products during the peak demand period. That is, production in the peak demand period must pay for not only the costs of capacity resources it uses but also the cost of capacity resources supplied, but not used, during the slack demand period.

Assignment of Unused Capacity Costs

When activity cost driver rates are based on practical capacity, the cost of unused capacity is not assigned down to individual products or customers.[15] But the cost of unused capacity should not be ignored; it remains someone's or some department's responsibility. As with the judgment about how to measure practical capacity, the best guidance for assigning unused capacity can be obtained by identifying the decision that led to creation of the excess capacity.

One can think about the assignment of unused capacity costs using the *rational customer rule*. This rule states that unused capacity costs should only be assigned to a customer if that customer, acting rationally under a cost plus contract, would accept that cost. For example, a customer that orders on a predictable, regular basis, without making any changes, would not accept the cost of any unused capacity. Nothing in the way the customer acts requires its supplier to maintain unused capacity. But, consider a customer that insists on perfect service but whose demands are difficult to forecast, or that continually modifies the volume and timing of orders. The supplier, in order to maintain service to this customer, requires some degree of reserve capacity to meet these unpredictable demands. In this situation, a rational customer should recognize that its behavior leads to some unused capacity for its supplier and accept an assignment of the unused capacity costs.

If a rational customer does not accept the cost of the unused capacity, one can look back to the individual who authorized the acquisition of the capacity. For example, if the capacity was acquired to meet anticipated demands from a particular customer or a particular market segment, the costs of unused capacity because of lower than expected demands can be assigned to the person or organizational unit responsible for that customer or segment. Such an assignment should be done on a lump-sum basis (e.g., as a sustaining, not a unit-level, expense) so as not to distort the unit cost of meeting demands from that customer or segment.

If the unused capacity relates to a product line, say when certain production resources are dedicated to individual product lines, the cost of unused capacity is assigned to the individual in charge of the product line where demand failed to materialize. It should not be treated as a general cost, to be shared across all product lines. Nor should the product-line unused capacity be allocated down to individual products. That could cause some products to appear unprofitable, risking the launch of a death spiral by repricing or dropping products.

As another example, suppose division management knew in advance that resource supply would exceed resource demand, but wanted to retain existing resources for future growth and expansion. Then the cost of unused capacity could be assigned to the division deciding to retain unused capacity. In making such assignment of unused capacity costs, the objective is to trace the costs at the level in the organization where the decisions are made that could affect the supply of capacity resources and the demand for those resources. The lump-sum assignment of unused capacity costs provides valuable feedback to managers on their supply and demand decisions.

ABC and the Theory of Constraints

Eli Goldratt, the creator of the Theory of Constraints, argues forcefully against assigning any capacity costs to products, except perhaps to bottleneck or constraining machines.[16] In TOC, only three variables are relevant: throughput, measured as cash received from sales less materials costs;[17] operating expenses, all organizational expenses other than materials costs; and inventory, measured as assets acquired (facilities, equipment, and materials) but not yet converted to cash. The goal, also the title of Goldratt's best-selling novel that popularized TOC in the mid-1980s, is to maximize throughput while attempting to keep steady or preferably reduce operating expense and inventory. In this view, operating expenses are unrelated to decisions made about products sold and customers served; some would call them fixed costs. TOC, which in its deterministic version is linear programming with only a single binding constraint, is persuasive and logically correct given the problem it set out to solve. This problem is how to maximize throughput when the organization has a fixed supply of resources, when its expenses and spending for the next period—other than for materials—has already been determined, when its products have already been designed, when its prices have been set, and when its customer orders have been received. The solution is to maximize the throughput processed by the bottleneck or constraining resource. This is an elegantly simple yet powerful conclusion, but, of course, one that has existed for decades. Even more complex production scheduling problems with multiple constraints have been solvable since George Dantzig developed the simplex algorithm for linear programming problems in the 1940s.

In the linear programming and TOC world assumed by Goldratt, a world where operating expenses are assumed to be independent of product mix and customer decisions, there should be no attempt to assign operating expenses to individual products and customers. That is why Goldratt is so scornful of traditional cost accounting[18] as well as what he perceives to be attempts to rehabilitate cost accounting by introducing activity-based costing. And given the assumptions of linear programming models and TOC, such skepticism, or even scorn, is absolutely correct.

But let's consider the empirical validity of the assumption that operating expenses are indeed fixed costs. First the assumption raises the interesting question about how operating expenses reached their current level. Why does the Complex Pen factory (described in Chapter 6) have much higher operating expenses than the Simple Pen factory? Why does an organization have monthly operating expenses of, say, $200 million instead of $10 million? If operating expenses are fixed, why are they not fixed at a low rather than a high level? The dynamics of how operating expenses reached a level of $200 million per month, but are now fixed independent of future decisions about products and customers, are not addressed in the TOC world.

Second, the assumption that operating expenses are fixed, independent of product volume, mix, and complexity implies that all organizations in the same industry and the same line of business should have the same level of operating expenses. The assumption is that some minimum set of resources—people, facilities, and equipment—is required to provide the capacity to operate. Once such resources are provided, however, they can handle all varieties of demands for products and customers. If the supply of resources varies because of differential demands by products and customers, then the cost of supplying such resources cannot be a fixed cost. Empirical evidence suggests that the assumption that all organizations have the same operating expenses, independent of product and customer volume and mix is wrong. If anything, operating expenses seem variable with size, or, in the case of some companies, even supervariable; they have grown faster than sales.

If the assumption that operating expenses are fixed was even close to being valid, as demand has grown over past decades, the level of operating expenses would be trivially small relative to sales. Assume that operating expenses were fixed at a given level of sales, and that sales have increased by a factor of 5 or 10. Were operating expenses to be fixed, their ratio to sales would be only 10–20% of their initial level, a conclusion in sharp conflict with the real world of virtually all organizations.

We do not say that the assumptions underlying TOC are invalid. They are an excellent approximation of reality for the problem TOC has been designed to solve: short-term product mix and scheduling of bottleneck resources. This is a problem for which ABC provides little insights since during such a short period, all organizational expenses, other than materials and energy, are precommitted. The relevant costs for short-term production optimization are short-term variable costs, and such information can be approximated by materials expenses or, somewhat better, by the GPK variable cost systems described in Chapter 3. ABC plays little role for short-term production scheduling decisions, or decisions about whether to accept one-time incremental orders that do not have externality effects with other products or customers.[19]

ABC's contribution is to identify how demands by activities performed for products, services, and customers lead to the organization supplying resources to perform the demanded activities. ABC systems give managers signals about which products and customers are generating revenues in excess of resource costs, and which products and customers require resources more costly than the revenues generated from the resources current uses. ABC also enables managers to anticipate how changes in activity management, process performance, product mix, product design characteristics, and customer relationships will affect the future demands for resources. They can then forecast both where new bottlenecks for resources will develop in the future as well as to identify resources whose current and future supply will likely exceed the future demands for the capabilities they provide. They can also iterate back and forth between decisions that affect the demands for resources with decisions to increase or decrease the supply of resources.

ABC provides a dynamic theory of constraints, enabling managers to make better decisions today in light of their impact on future resource constraints. ABC models also allow managers to decrease operating expenses of resources in excess supply, without the risk or without reducing the supply of a resource below a level that it becomes a constraint to current or future production.

Much of the mechanics of linking decisions taken today with resources to be provided in the future occurs when activity-based costing is integrated into the organization's budgeting processes. We will discuss this topic in more detail in Chapter 15.

TOC and ABC are not in conflict. In fact, they complement each other beautifully, with TOC providing short-term optimization to maximize short-term profits (when operating in a constrained production environment) and ABC providing the instrumentation for dynamic optimization of resource supply, product design and mix, pricing, and supplier and customer relationships for long-term profitability.[20] The now central feature of ABC theory—distinguishing the current supply of resources from the usage of resources, and identifying resources operating at capacity levels as well as those for which significant unused capacity exists—is entirely compatible with concepts underlying TOC. Both TOC and ABC have the same goal: to maximize organizational profits. TOC operates to enhance profitability within existing resources and constraints, and existing products and customer relations. ABC examines the economics of existing resource supply, product design, pricing and mix, and customer profitability, and provides the map by which the existing economics can be enhanced for the future.

Summary

An organization's initial ABC systems almost always calculate historical activity cost driver rates, based on last period's expenses for resources actually supplied and realized (actual) quantities of cost drivers. But ABC should not be thought of as an historical accounting or general ledger system. It can and should be used proactively to estimate the costs of activities that will be performed in current and future periods. ABC enables decisions to be made that can influence future cost incurrence, not just better assign past costs. For this purpose, activity cost driver rates should be calculated using budgeted expense data for the forthcoming period.

Besides being based on budgeted expense information, the rates should be calculated using the practical capacity of the resources supplied. This enables the activity cost driver rates to represent the underlying efficiency of the activity, as measured by the cost of resources required to perform one unit of the activity. In addition to giving a more accurate estimate of the activity cost driver rate, the use of practical capacity enables ABC to distinguish between the cost of resources used during the period versus the cost of unused resources. This distinction provides a powerful signal for management as it contemplates decisions about process improvement, products, customers, and investments in new capacity. We turn to such decisions in the next four chapters.

8

Activity-Based Management:
Operational Applications

In Chapters 6 and 7, we described the construction of an activity-based cost model. The ABC model provides managers with a more accurate economic map of organizational spending and activities. How can managers benefit from this information?

Activity-based management, or ABM, refers to the entire set of actions that can be taken, on a better informed basis, with activity-based cost information. With ABM, the organization accomplishes its outcomes with fewer demands on organizational resources; that is, the organization can achieve the same outcomes (e.g., revenues) at a lower total cost (lower spending on organizational resources). ABM accomplishes its objective through two complementary applications, which we call *operational* and *strategic* ABM.

Operational activity-based management encompasses the actions that increase efficiency, lower costs, and enhance asset utilization—in short, the actions required to do things right. Operational ABM takes the demand for organizational activities as given, and attempts to meet this demand with fewer organizational resources. In other words, operational ABM attempts either to increase capacity or to lower the spending (i.e., reduce the cost driver rates of activities), so that fewer physical, human, and working capital resources are required to generate the revenues. The benefits from operational ABM can be measured by reduced costs, higher revenues (through better resource utilization), and cost avoidance (because the expanded capacity of existing resources obviates the need for additional investments in capital and people).

Strategic ABM—doing the right things—attempts to alter the demand for activities to increase profitability while assuming, as a first approximation, that activity efficiency remains constant. For example, the organization may be operating at a point where the revenues being earned from a particular product, service, or customer are less than the cost of generating those revenues. Strategic ABM encompasses shifting the mix of demand for activities away from such unprofitable applications, by reducing the cost driver quantities demanded by unprofitable activities. The ABC model also signals where individual products, services, and customers appear to be highly profitable. This information can be used by marketing and sales managers to explore whether demand for those highly profitable products, services, and customers can be expanded to generate incremental revenues that exceed their incremental costs. Thus, with strategic ABM, managers shift the activity mix toward more profitable uses. Strategic ABM also includes decisions about product design, product development, and supplier relationships that reduce the demand for organizational activities.

Obviously, operational and strategic decisions are not mutually exclusive. Organizations will get the greatest benefit when they both reduce the resources required to perform a given quantity of activities and, simultaneously, shift the activity mix to more profitable processes, products, services, and customers. But before launching an ABC analysis, managers should attempt to identify where they expect to obtain their near-term benefits. The design of an ABC system can vary, depending on the intended application. Strategic systems may require relatively few activities (typically 20–60) while operational ABM systems often require several hundred activities to provide a finer view of the processes that underlie production and customer service.

ABC: The Organizational Cost Function

It is also important to recognize the limitations of activity-based management as well as its opportunities. To make many decisions, an organization needs a broader information base than mere knowledge of its cost structure. In particular, an organization needs understanding of how to create and grow revenues, that is, the drivers of customer demand. Marketing people estimate how multiple factors, such as price, functionality, features, and convenience, create demand for the organization's products and services.

One should think of ABC as providing the organization with information about the cost of supplying quantities of demanded products and services to customers. To maximize total profits, however, managers need to combine their knowledge of the ABC cost curve with the organizational demand curve—what creates and drives revenues.[1] Thus, to get maximum benefits from the strategic component of ABM, managers must combine the cost driver knowledge from their ABC model with information from their marketing and sales organizations on customer and market demand—that is, the organization's demand or revenue curve.[2]

In this chapter, we present various aspects of operational ABM: improving the efficiency and reducing the resources to perform activities. In subsequent chapters, we present strategic ABM: focusing the organization on the most profitable uses of its resources.

Operational ABM

Organizations today are currently deploying many performance improvement programs. The initial impetus for these programs came from the shock of learning about the efficient practices used by many leading Japanese manufacturing companies, especially those in the automotive, heavy transportation, electronic, and semiconductor industries. Total quality management programs of one kind or another have, by now, been adopted by most Western companies.[3] Later, in the 1980s, companies adopted time-based competition ideas as well.[4] In general, these initiatives have been referred to as continuous improvement programs.

Reengineering launched another wave of improvement programs.[5] We characterize reengineering and transformation efforts as discontinuous improvement.[6] These programs are deployed when existing processes are so badly designed that improvement by a sequence of incremental (continuous) steps will not lead to the dramatic breakthroughs in process performance that often becomes possible when a completely new approach is taken. Reengineering also yields substantial benefits even when operating processes have been optimized within existing functions and departments. Such a reengineering initiative enables a process to be optimized across multiple functions and departments, an opportunity that becomes highly visible with an operational ABM approach. Reengineering in its purest and most radical form urges employees and managers to redesign important business processes from the ground up, with a view to achieving large multiples of (discontinuous) performance improvement.

Although the actual practice of total quality improvement differs considerably from reengineering improvement, we have seen activity-based cost information used in a similar fashion for both types of efforts. Therefore, we will describe the role for operational ABM for both continuous and discontinuous improvement programs. In general, operational ABM is used with TQM and reengineering to:

1. Develop the business case
2. Establish priorities
3. Provide cost justification
4. Track the benefits
5. Measure performance for ongoing improvement

Develop the Business Case

Managers may be unaware of the many available opportunities for cost reduction and improved efficiency of activities and processes. Industrial engineers have focused for decades on improving front-line manufacturing and service operations within existing departments. But, until recently, they have not attempted to improve support activities and processes or cross-functional activities and business processes. When spending on support activities and processes was small relative to front-line operations, and operations and business processes were simple to understand, such a priority was undoubtedly correct. In today's organizations, however, an increasing proportion of organizational expenses is associated with indirect and support activities, and the same activity or business process is affected by the actions taken in many different departments and functions.

And even in repetitive manufacturing and service operations, industrial engineers, until about 1980, focused on making production operations more efficient, not on quality improvements. They installed inspection stations, and deployed inspection and quality control personnel to detect problems and to recycle defective items to rework areas. Each stage—of inspection, detection, and rework—could be done very efficiently but the engineers did not question whether it might be better to do the job entirely differently, for example, by training personnel and improving processes so that defective items would not be produced at all, thereby eliminating the need for most inspection and rework.

As part of the ABC analysis, the ABC project team can classify quality-related activities using the well-established cost-of-quality framework: prevention, appraisal, internal failure, and external failure.[7] The theory is that if organizations concentrate more on prevention activities, expenditures for detecting failures, and repairing them (either internally or, worse, after they have been detected by customers) will be significantly reduced.[8] Thus certain activity expenses can be classified as being associated with prevention, appraisal, internal failure, or external failure. If such a classification is made, as relevant, for each activity, the ABC model will automatically provide existing patterns of organizational spending across these four quality categories.

Beyond identifying costs associated with producing and repairing nonconforming products and services, the ABC project team, when it collects information about organizational activities and processes (see Chapter 6), can usually detect when the activities and processes are done inefficiently or poorly. The cross-functional and cross-departmental perspective of an ABC model highlights when an activity involves extensive handoffs from one department to another, and when an activity is highly fragmented, involving people from several different departments performing various or even the same aspects of the activity.

For example, *Exhibit 8-1* shows the expenses associated with the activity *respond to customer requests*. Total spending on this activity was about $117,000 for the most recent six-month period. Plant managers were not surprised that $38,000 was spent by the customer service department. That was one of the principal functions of that department. What surprised them was how much of this activity was also being performed by people in six other departments. Apparently, customers, when they did not, or could not, get the response they desired from the customer service department, called personnel in other departments. Although managers vaguely knew about this, they were unaware of how much of people's time in the other departments was actually spent on this activity.

An ABC project team, in order to identify opportunities for process improvements, can specify, for each activity, an attribute field that summarizes the team's assessment of the activity's efficiency. Alternatively, analysts can classify whether an activity adds value for meeting customer expectations. We will focus here on the efficiency classification and treat the features and limitations of the value-added/non-value-added classification in the chapter appendix.

On the efficiency dimension, a highly repetitive production or service activity, one that has been under continued scrutiny of industrial engineers for decades, is likely quite efficient. At the other extreme, an activity that is highly fragmented, involves extensive handoffs between individuals and departments, and has never been studied for improvement would be rated highly inefficient. The ABC project team can define an attribute field to

Exhibit 8-1 Costs of the Activity *Respond to Customer Requests*

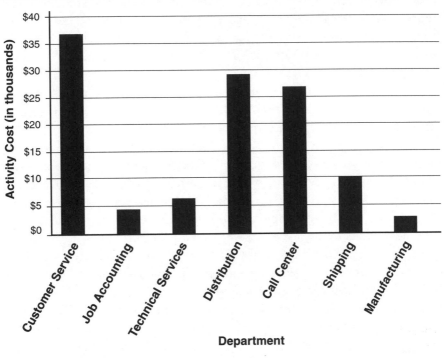

Source: R. S. Kaplan and N. Klein, "Activity-Based Management at Stream International," Case 9-196-134 (Boston: Harvard Business School, 1996), 11. Reprinted by permission of Harvard Business School.

summarize an activity's efficiency. The team can use a simple scale, say one to five, that summarizes their judgment about the current efficiency of the activity:

1. Highly efficient, little (< 5%) apparent opportunity for improvement
2. Modestly efficient, some (5–15%) opportunity for improvement
3. Average efficiency, good opportunities (15–25%) for improvement
4. Inefficient, major opportunities (25–50%) for improvement
5. Highly inefficient, perhaps should not be done at all; 50–100% opportunity for improvement

After the activity analysis, the data can be sorted using this attribute field to reveal how much of organizational spending occurs in the five categories. Similarly, if the cost-of-quality activity information is coded into an attribute field, a data sort will reveal the amount of organizational spending in the four quality categories. This summary reveals how much existing spending occurs in inefficient activities, and in defect-detection and correction activities. For managers who are still skeptical about the potential benefits of TQM and reengineering programs, such information can persuade them to launch change initiatives. The activity data will show that while TQM and reengineering may be expensive programs, the organization is already paying a high price, every operating day, for inefficiency and poor-quality production. To paraphrase an old Henry Ford axiom, "If you need TQM and reengineering, and don't deploy them, you pay for them without getting them."

The operational ABC system can also provide a base for benchmarking, both internally and externally. The use of a standard activity dictionary and data collection process across plants and companies enables the same activity to be compared across organizational units. Awareness that activity costs are out of line with those of other organizational units can highlight where a unit should be focusing its process improvements.[9]

In summary, the first benefit from an activity analysis occurs from classifying activity expenses by opportunities for cost improvement. The improvements arise either by designing entirely new processes or by improving the quality and performance of existing ones. The activity classification enables managers to see how much of their current operating expenses occur in inefficient and low-quality processes. Used in this way, ABC information provides the front-end insight and motivation for launching continuous and discontinuous improvement programs.

Establish Priorities

Many organizations already have gotten religion for TQM or reengineering programs. They, therefore, do not need the additional data about current spending on inefficient and low-quality activities, obtained during the first step of operational ABM, to become committed to the improvement programs. But without the information from an activity analysis, managers may not focus their improvement programs on the activities and business processes with the highest potential payoff. For example, many organizations have empowered their employees and work teams to continuously improve or reengineer their processes. And these decentralized employee work teams may accomplish remarkable improvements in their local processes, but without noticeable impact on total organizational spending. Making a process improvement of 50%, or even 100% (by eliminating the need to even perform the activity) in an activity that consumes less than 0.01% of organizational expenses will produce an imperceptible benefit to the organization's bottom line.

The scarcest resource in an organization is a manager's time. Managers, to conserve this resource, must follow the Willie Sutton rule and go where the money is. Rather than disperse employee improvement initiatives across isolated and low-impact processes, managers can direct employee efforts to improving activities and processes where the opportunity for substantial cost reduction is highest. The ABC model identifies where those opportunities exist. Managers can then use this information to set priorities for TQM and reengineering programs which, if successful, will deliver substantial and quantifiable financial benefits to the organization. ABC information is not the ongoing operational tool for such improvement activities. For that, employees need direct feedback on quality, yield, and cycle time improvements, as well as information on cost reduction received through the kaizen costing and pseudo-profit center systems discussed in Chapter 5. The ABC model provides the front-end guidance for deciding where all those initiatives should be launched.

The linkage, between ABC and financial systems specifically designed for feedback on learning and improvement, is another example of the two different managerial roles for cost systems introduced in Chapter 2. ABC systems cannot provide local, timely feedback to ongoing improvement initiatives. But this type of local feedback does not draw the big picture about where such improvement efforts should be concentrated for maximum impact. The two systems are complementary and mutually reinforcing. They are not substitutes or competitors, nor can both roles be done well with a single cost system.

Provide Cost Justification

In the early stages of the total quality management movement, managers were told that "quality was free."[10] While initially skeptical that producing fewer defective items could be accomplished without increasing costs, both Japanese and U.S. companies with TQM programs soon were convinced that they previously had been operating at highly inefficient production points. Front-end TQM expenditures incurred by having employees focus on process improvement, robust product designs, and ongoing problem-solving and prevention activities were quickly and amply repaid with lower costs for appraisal, repair, rework, and scrap.

Once the early rewards from picking low-hanging fruit have been achieved, however, further improvements are not always free. That is, to get to pick the next level up, someone may have to buy a ladder. Also, the original definition of quality for TQM programs was "conformance to specifications." Success was measured by producing each item and delivering each service in accordance with the specifications established for that product and service. Once operations and delivery processes had been stabilized to produce consistent output, in conformance with specifications, the quality stakes were raised. The definition of quality shifted from conforming to specifications to meeting customer expectations. If targeted customers' expectations for product or service delivery performance exceeded previously established specifications, the specifications would have to be raised. Even the most ardent TQM advocates do not argue that achieving higher levels of *performance* versus adhering to *conformance* could be achieved at zero cost.

And reengineering cannot deliver on its promises for breakthrough improvements in cost and performance without substantial front-end investments. Reengineering programs are not inexpensive; they usually involve heavy commitments to external and/or internal consultants to identify and facilitate the program, employee involvement to design and implement new processes, and spending on new technology, particularly the information technology required to provide the infrastructure for the new processes. Many organizations may be understandably reluctant to launch such major and expensive initiatives on faith alone. They usually want to see a benefits case to justify the heavy commitments of time, energy, and financial resources required for a successful reengineering effort.

To illustrate the role that activity-based costing can play at the front end of a process improvement initiative, take the case of a producer of personal computer software manuals and documentation.[11] During the 1980s, the large majority of the plant's business had been devoted to a single large customer, IBM. During the early 1990s, IBM's demand for software documentation decreased, but, fortunately, other personal computer manufacturers, software companies like Microsoft and Intuit, and producers of video games and CD-ROMs, became important customers of the plant's output. The production facility, however, had been optimized in the 1980s for a single large customer and was not well configured for the more diverse products it now produced. In particular, storage at the main factory was fully devoted to work-in-process and finished goods for IBM products, so finished goods products for all other customers had to be shipped to rented warehouse space, several miles away. Furthermore, items often stayed in that warehouse only a few days before being shipped.

The plant manager turned to activity-based costing to help him understand the economics of the new competitive environment. The first stage of the plant's ABC project, a period of about three months, was devoted to developing an activity dictionary for the plant—choosing 159 activities for the initial model, and, by interviews and surveys, mapping indirect plant expenses to the 159 activities. At the conclusion of this stage, the project team had identified the cost of performing each of the 159 activities.

Before having the ABC project move to the next phase, collecting cost driver information and driving activity costs to products and customers, the plant manager announced to his six direct reports that in two weeks they would meet to discuss the implications of this initial analysis. As the plant manager said when he launched the ABC project: "We were throwing resources at problems, relying on our instincts to tell us what was worth doing. I needed to know what kinds of process changes mattered most, and how much should I be willing to spend."[12]

He directed each manager, including himself, to examine the initial activity cost information and, with this information, suggest a cost-savings or process-improving project. The managers came to the meeting with excellent suggestions, some well grounded in the data, others based on rough estimates about the savings opportunities.

One of the more detailed proposals addressed the management of work-in-process and finished goods inventory (see documentation in *Exhibit 8-2*, pages 147–149). The proposal included archiving or destroying WIP inventory that had not been accessed for more than 12 months, transferring the slow-moving IBM inventory to less-expensive long-term storage, and reconfiguring the main production facility so that finished goods could be stored at the end of the production line until they were shipped to customers within a few days. This proposal would produce much faster customer response times, virtually eliminate the several truck-load movements each day between the production facility and the auxiliary warehouse, and greatly reduce the demand for warehouse space.

The manager who suggested the inventory management improvement project said she knew for many months that the existing process was both obsolete and highly inefficient. But to change the process required a front-end investment of nearly $600,000—to install new finished-goods shelves in the factory for the high-turnover items and streamlined shipping docks. Until the cost data from the activity analysis became available, the only visible cost from the existing process was the approximately $200,000 to truck finished goods to the warehouse. This was not sufficient to justify

Exhibit 8-2 ABM Project: Manage Work-in-Process and Finished Goods Inventory Space

	Problems
1.	We currently have too much inactive inventory stored in the South Street plant, and too much active inventory being shipped to Elmore Street, stored for a week or two, and then sent back to South Street to be shipped to the customer.
2.	We haven't known true cost of storage.
3.	The vast majority of WIP inventory is never shipped. Storage costs outweigh potential for use.
	Action Steps
1.	Eliminate WIP inventory. • Define process to store inventory. • Kill all parts with no known use.
2.	Exchange warehouses. • Install automated FG handling in the South Street plant. • Move active loads to the South Street plant. • Keep all inactive loads at Elmore Street. • Press clients to remove inventory or pay higher storage costs. • Redesign South Street for minimum movement layout. • Elminate outside warehouse (1,001 loads).

the cost of installing the new inventory-handling process. But the ABC activity analysis revealed that the organization was currently spending more than $1,200,000 on the process, and that the reengineered process would save more than $800,000 per year (without counting the benefits from faster customer response times). The activity cost data made the project highly attractive. In fact, as the project was analyzed in greater detail, the annual savings increased to $1,200,000 annually, a six-month payback.

This abbreviated case description illustrates all three types of benefits from operational ABM already discussed. First, the initial activity analysis identified large amounts of spending on inefficient operations. Senior plant managers then proposed several independent and different projects where TQM, process improvement, or reengineering could have a major impact. Second, with the opportunities for cost savings, the managers could set

Exhibit 8-2   continued

What Do We Know Today?

Load Movement Indirect Expense = $1,412,048 annually
Managing Inventory Expense = $ 447,600 annually
Physical Facility Expense = $ 614,758 annually
(see below for breakdown by activity)

Related Annual Expense—Managing Inventory

Item #	Description	People	Expense	Total
Load Movement Expense				
5.2.3.1	Find Material to Be Moved	$212,542	$227,103	$ 439,645
5.2.3.3	Move WIP	58,754	68,473	126,227
5.2.3.4	Move FG within Plant	111,552	193,093	304,644
	Move to/from Elmore Street	81,174	77,077	158,251
5.2.3.5.4	Move Material to/from Outside	24,595	88,017	112,611
5.2.3.8	Material Equipment Cost/(Depreciation/Rent)	—	269,670	269,670
	Total	**$488,616**	**$923,432**	**$1,412,048**
Managing Inventory Expense				
5.6.2.2	Managing WIP	$110,621	$ 65,023	$175,824
5.6.2.3	Managing Finished Goods	108,669	163,136	271,836
	Total	**$219,290**	**$228,159**	**$447,660**

Physical Facility Expense	Square Feet	$/Square Foot	Total
Elmore Street Warehouse Rent	80,630	$3.00	$241,890
Elmore Street Energy, Insurance, Taxes			76,400
WIP Rent—All Areas	45,630	2.54	115,287
FG Rent—Rack Aisles Only	50,512	2.54	128,381
Outside Warehouse			52,800
Total			**$614,758**

Total Annualized Expense	$2,474,466

priorities about which project should be done first. All the projects had merit, but because the lean plant management team had only limited time for new initiatives, it could rank order the proposed projects so that the ones with the largest impact and achievable in the shortest time would be done first. And, third, although the most desirable project came with an upfront price tag of $580,000, the managers agreed that the rapid payback from documented cost savings more than justified this project.

This case also illustrates several other important points about managing an ABC project. At first glance, driving expenses to 159 activities seems

Exhibit 8-2   continued

Potential Benefit = $808,291
(see below for benefit by activity)

Potential Benefit $—Load Storage

---

1. Store All Active Loads in CSS

$318,290	Annual Savings with Elmore Street Warehouse
(115,000)	Rent 35,000 Square Feet for Long-Term Storage
(75,000)	Moving Expense Admin./Loads
$128,290	

---

2. Load Movement Improvement

$158,251	Load Movement to Elmore
112,611	Move to/from Outside Storage
91,393	Move FG within Plant—30%
38,135	Move WIP within Plant—30%
87,929	Find Material—20%
26,926	Equipment Savings of 10%
$515,286	

---

3. Manage WIP Improvement

$43,956	25% Improvement

---

4. Manage FG Improvement

$67,959	25% Improvement

---

5. Eliminate Outside Warehouses

$52,800

Total Annualized Potential—$808,291

Associated Costs of Implementation
Provide Direct and Immediate Payback

Demolition and rack erection	$ 25,000
New production office	150,000
Electric, air, and data connections	65,000
Equipment for parcel and pick/pack	230,900
Consultant fees	72,400
System hardware (M.A.U., controller, and token rings)	25,000
Pallet flow racks for freight staging	15,000
Total	**$583,300**

Source: R. S. Kaplan and N. Klein, "Activity-Based Management at Stream International," Case 9-196-134 (Boston: Harvard Business School, 1996), 18–21. Reprinted by permission of Harvard Business School.

to require building a complex and expensive model. But, as discussed in Chapter 6, the most difficult and expensive elements of an ABC model are developing the activity cost driver information for each activity and measuring the quantity of each activity cost driver for each product and customer. The initial phase of an ABC project, however, which maps resource costs to activities, is not that difficult, time-consuming, or expensive. If the organization knows that operational ABM is one of the goals of the project, it makes sense to collect activity data in enough detail so that the costs of doing microprocesses (see the four- and five-digit activity data used in Exhibit 8-2 to justify the new project) become visible. Process improvement, redesign, and reengineering will usually be facilitated by having activity cost information at a quite disaggregated level. As the project moves to the next phase, the high number (159) of disaggregated activities can be grouped together. As a rule, all activities that use the same activity cost driver can be grouped into a single activity without any distortion of product and customer cost information. This rule, plus concentrating on those activities that amount to 95% or 98% of total costs, will allow the data collection on activity cost drivers and model building—for linking activity costs to products and customers—to proceed with, say, 20–30 higher-level activities.

The initial effort to develop costs at the activity and business process level also provides an invaluable learning experience for the organization. Creating a cross-functional, cross-departmental map of activities brings together, usually for the first time, employees from different organizational units who are involved in the same process. This experience enables them to understand the linkages between their functions and departments, and facilitates the subsequent reengineering and business process improvement initiatives.

A second message in this case is the importance of getting a near-term win from the project. The plant manager did not wait until a complete ABC model, with detailed product cost and customer profitability, had been developed. He shared the ABC model with senior plant management early—three months into the process—and developed a plan of action that everyone could see would produce short-term benefits. This action plan was tangible proof of the benefits emanating from ABC. The cost savings it revealed also, in effect, paid for the initial development of the ABC model. It also bought time and resources for the next phase of the project. While managers reengineered the inventory management process, the ABC project team continued to collect activity cost driver information and used the drivers to link activity costs to individual products and customers. Thus, by the time the process improvement project had been completed, plant management would be ready to review product and customer profitability information and contemplate strategic ABM opportunities.

In summary, the first three aspects of operational ABM—identifying process improvement opportunities, setting priorities for these opportunities, and committing resources to realize the benefits—can be done early in an ABC project. These steps provide relatively easy, near-term visible wins without involving people outside the production or operations organization (such as marketing, sales, or engineering). It is not surprising, therefore, that for many organizations, ABM is synonymous with operational improvements.

Track the Benefits

Assume that operational ABM actions have been taken—TQM, process redesign, or reengineering—based on the initial activity cost information as described above. Many organizations, however, never fully realize the benefits from these actions. They improve or change processes, enabling the same output to be achieved with much fewer organizational resources, but they never redeploy or eliminate the resources no longer needed. In effect, the organizations have created excess capacity through their operational ABM actions (see Chapter 7), but they haven't eliminated the excess capacity they created. So organizational expenses remain the same.

The ABC model provides information about resource elements (general ledger expense code, assets, and full-time equivalent [FTE] personnel) assigned to an activity. By periodically refreshing and updating the basic ABC model, the organization can reestimate the resources (expenses, assets, and FTEs) deployed for performing activities and business processes. In this way it can verify whether the operational improvements are yielding actual benefits in terms of reducing resource capacity: fewer assets, fewer people, and lower spending required for the activity. The periodic ABC models provide tangible, documented feedback whether benefits have been achieved from previous operational improvements, and signal when anticipated benefits have yet to be realized.

Some modification of the activity dictionary may be required if activities have been eliminated as a result of reengineering, or additional activities introduced because of new products or customer demands. The activity dictionary, interview protocols, and survey forms already exist. The ABC project team is already trained, and employees are familiar with how to respond to questions relating to their activities. In general, refreshing the ABC model and obtaining ex post tracking of benefits should be relatively inexpensive.

Measure Performance for Ongoing Improvement

The final aspect of operational ABM links to ongoing and continuous improvement. We have emphasized that Stage III ABC models are not an effective means for operational control, learning, and improvement. That is why we described the performance measurement and new operational control systems, like kaizen costing and pseudo-profit centers, in Chapters 4 and 5. These systems are explicitly designed to provide frequent feedback to employees and managers for their learning and improvement activities. Nor should an ABC system serve, in Stage III, for periodic reporting of actual versus budgeted costs. We will show, in Chapter 14, how Stage IV ABC systems can be integrated with periodic financial reporting systems.

Nevertheless, even Stage III ABC systems can provide some benefits for ongoing process improvement. They need not be limited to the front end of project identification and selection, and the back end of benefits tracking.

The Cost Management Systems Program of an industry group, CAM-I, developed a generic illustration of an activity-based costing model that added a dimension for performance improvement.[13] The CAM-I model introduced a process view as a horizontal axis at the activity level (see *Exhibit 8-3*). The process view introduces a different type of cost driver, which we shall call a "process driver." Process drivers help explain the quantity of resources, and hence the cost, required to perform an activity. Recall that activity cost drivers (the cost drivers used in the vertical dimension to assign activity costs to products) measure the quantity of activities demanded by individual products. Process drivers relate to the efficiency of performing the activity. Any activity could have several process drivers associated with it. Take, for example, an activity such as processing materials through a machine. If incoming materials are out of specifications, or just inside specifications, more time and rework may be required to convert them to finished goods. So the quality of incoming materials is one process driver. Another process driver of this activity might be the training and skill levels of employees associated with the process.

Consider the situation of Maxwell Appliance Controls, a manufacturer of electromechanical control devices such as thermostats, relays, timers, and switches.[14] After performing its activity analysis, the ABC project team identified the process drivers of major activities and derived behavior-

Exhibit 8-3 CAM-I Basic ABC Model

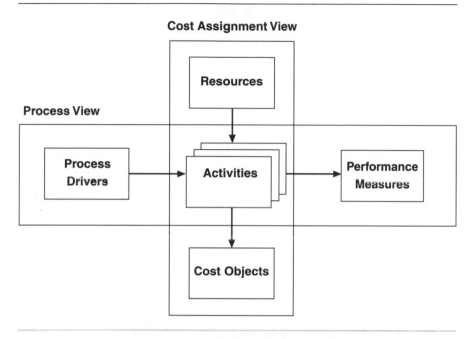

Source: Adapted from The CAM-I Glossary of Activity-Based Management, edited by Norm Raffish and Peter B.B. Turney (Arlington, Texas: CAM-I, 1991).

based measures that could be used to focus employees' continuous improvement activities. Examples are shown below:

ACTIVITY	ROOT CAUSE	PROCESS DRIVERS
Materials handling	Product line lengths Discontinuous operations	Assembly line feet per line Number of stop points per line Average distance between operations Number of areas containing > 4 hours of inventory
Setups	Difficult setups Inflexible machinery	Average setup time Number of setups > 10 minutes Number of different dies
Parts administration	Stockkeeping practices	Number of parts per product line Number of purchase orders
Product redesign	New parts; new processes	Number of new parts introduced Number of unique parts

The identification of process drivers helped the employees understand the linkages between measures they could influence and the overall company goals to reduce costs and improve quality. Merely directing employees to reduce the cost of an activity or an activity cost driver rate required them to guess at what actions would reduce the cost. Instead, employees were told to concentrate on improving the process driver measurements. If the employees succeeded, the cost, quality, and responsiveness of the associated activities would improve.

Some advocates of this approach use a sports metaphor as an illustration. Telling people how to keep score in tennis and then ordering them to win matches won't do it! Matches are won not by showing people the score (the outcome measure), but by instruction and training in the fundamentals (forehands, backhands, serves, volleys, and lobs; i.e., the process drivers required to play good tennis). The advocates claim that if players concentrate on improving the fundamental measures—the process drivers—the score should take care of itself. The finance manager at Maxwell commented on the impact of showing employees the playbook metrics (his term for process drivers):

> We wanted to highlight the choices that create costs. These measures were a simple feedback mechanism to help everyone understand what triggers an activity so that they could minimize the resources consumed to perform that activity. This enabled everyone—from engineers to line workers—to get better at reducing costs without focusing on the cost itself. Talking about "costs" always seemed to make operations people squirm, but the ABC information was invaluable to get senior-level managers to agree that the playbook metrics would be effective motivators. ABC allowed us to quantify the cost that could be saved by reducing the number of parts, the number of operations, or the number of production stop points.[15]

Of course, Maxwell's use of process drivers reminds us of the hierarchical control system of the scientific management movement. It assumes that managers and engineers (or consultants) are better than front-line employees at identifying the underlying drivers of cost, quality, and responsiveness. This philosophy is quite different from that used in kaizen costing and pseudo-profit centers (see Chapter 5) where managers trained front-line employees to understand cost and quality and encouraged them to find innovative ways of improving process performance. Also, as we discussed in the preceding chapter, many process improvements create unused capacity but don't automatically lead to lower costs. So focusing only on the process drivers and not on cost savings realized may lead to a disconnect between measured operational improvements and realized benefits.

Some companies have worked directly with employees, asking them to identify the process drivers. Employee work teams use storyboarding to visually represent information about the team, its tasks, and the activities it affects. The teams develop performance measures to guide their day-to-day improvement efforts. The goal is to improve quality and reduce the cost and time required to perform activities. The ABC model provides the cost input into these activity-improving tasks.[16]

Focusing ABC systems on process drivers and continuous improvement of local activities and processes is certainly an element of operational ABM and can lead to gradual improvements of individual activities and processes. But it is not clear that such incremental, local improvement is where employee energies are best applied. Setting priorities for improvement of local processes is best performed within the framework of the Balanced Scorecard (BSC).[17] The BSC approach to performance improvement identifies and highlights processes that are most critical for strategic success. It identifies those processes not only for their potential for cost reduction, but also for their ability to meet targeted customer expectations. With the Balanced Scorecard, managers usually see that excelling at entirely new processes may be more important for successful strategy implementation than making gradual cost improvements in existing processes. Perhaps the best use of ABC information for local process improvement occurs *after* those processes have been identified by a high-level strategic implementation process, such as constructing the organizational Balanced Scorecard, as most critical for organizational success.

Alternatively, the strategic ABM approach, described in subsequent chapters, will highlight the quantity and cost of activity cost drivers used by products and customers. Strategic ABM will often identify where process improvements will be most critical for lowering the cost of producing vital products or serving valued customers. Defining process drivers for those processes will then focus employee efforts on improvements most crucial for organizational success.

In short, managers can define process drivers for activities that will indicate where employees should direct their attention to improve the efficiency, quality, and responsiveness of existing local processes. Whether supplying such information is better than allowing employees to identify for themselves where the most promising opportunities are for process improvement depends on who has better insights about where these opportunities are likely to be: managers or front-line employees. Also, managers need to determine, before defining process drivers as performance measures, whether they want a lot of local process improvement, or radical process improvement of a limited set of processes that have been identified, such as through the Balanced Scorecard management system or from a strategic ABM analysis, as being the most critical for the organization's long-term success.

Summary

Operational activity-based management enables managers to achieve short-term and highly visible successes from their Stage III ABC system. Opportunities for transformation, reengineering, and continuous process improvements are quickly identified and quantified (though, depending on the magnitude of the projects, the benefit stream may take some time to be realized). A simple coding of activities in a partial ABC model, one that links only resource costs to activities, identifies the opportunities for such improvement initiatives and helps set priorities for attacking the most inefficient and least value-adding activities. Often such improvement initiatives can be quite costly. The partial ABC model provides the benefits case for launching the initiatives by revealing how much is spent each period by continuing to operate inefficiently. Many improvement projects turn out to be self-funding, with even substantial front-end costs being rapidly repaid by more efficient and responsive processes. Subsequent ABC models can track whether anticipated benefits have been achieved in the transformed processes. And process drivers can be defined to direct employee attention for ongoing, continuous improvement of the transformed/reengineered processes. In the following chapters, we move to strategic activity-based management where companies can reap the benefits of a full ABC model, by driving activity costs down to individual products, services, and customers.

Appendix: Value- and Non-Value-Added Activities

As part of the initial phase of an operational ABM project, many firms rank their activities with a simple dichotomous variable identifying whether an activity is value-added or non-value-added. The definition of what constitutes a value-added activity varies considerably; some common definitions include an activity that adds value in the eyes of the customer, or that is being performed as efficiently as possible, or that supports the primary objective of producing outputs. For example, in the finance group, the activities required to produce the firm's annual report might be viewed as value-added.

Managers use such a value-ranking scheme to focus their cost reduction programs. Reducing resources devoted to performing activities that do not create value for customers lessens the risk of accidentally reducing the perceived functionality of the output. Some activities are quite easy to classify with this scheme. For example, machining a part for a product and delivering the service to the customer are generally considered value-added activities. Conversely, reconciling an incorrect invoice, moving materials around a poorly designed factory floor, and repairing defective products are generally considered non-value-added activities since if the original design or production process had been done well, the need for these activities would not have arisen. In effect, the non-value-added activities represent activities that customers should not normally be paying for.

Unfortunately, there are several problems with simplistic value-added/non-value-added classification schemes. First, under careful scrutiny, people usually cannot consistently define what constitutes a value or a non value-added activity. Apart from the extreme examples illustrated above, take an activity like *setting up machines*. Most advocates of value-added coding schemes instinctively classify setups as a non-value-added activity. We point out that without setups, the plant can only produce a single product, like blue pens. If the customer values customized or diverse products, changing machines from one product variety to another creates value for the customer. At that point the value-added proponent blurts out, "But you want to do the setup as quickly as possible, since the customer does not value long setup times." We respond by saying isn't this true, as well, for machining the product. Doesn't the customer prefer this (value-added) machining process to be done as quickly as possible? The discussion then turns to how efficiently the process is currently being performed, which is exactly the classification scheme we describe in Chapter 8, and is completely independent of whether we classify the activity as value-added or non-value-added. The dollars saved by improving the efficiency of a value-added activity are just as valuable as the dollars saved by improving the efficiency of a non-value-added activity. We have checked with bankers to determine the validity of this proposal. They have confirmed that the dollars deposited from value-added activity cost reductions are counted just like dollars deposited from non-value-added activity cost reductions.

Advocates of identifying and eliminating non-value-added activities claim that they can be eliminated without reducing the value of the product or service provided to the customer. For example, the customer does not explicitly get value from the company having large work-in-process (WIP) inventory so managerial efforts to reduce WIP should save money without reducing the value delivered to the customer. In contrast, attempting to save money on value-adding activities, such as switching from a four-bolt to a three-bolt mounting system, may matter a great deal since it could reduce the functionality of the product for the customer. But this distinction is not entirely valid. If managers' attempts to reduce WIP inventory lead to stockouts, the failure to deliver on time will be highly visible to the customer and decrease the value of the delivered product. Conversely, perhaps the customer may value having fewer bolts since that will facilitate maintenance and replacement. So it is possible to enhance customer value by reducing the quantity of what initially appears to be a value-added activity. The company's attempt to classify value-added and non-value-added activities does not provide clear guidance about the best opportunities for cost reduction activities.

Another major difficulty with the value-added/non-value-added activity descriptor is employee reaction. In general, employees get annoyed when informed they are performing a non-value-added activity. And their annoyance is fully justified. After all, they did not choose to perform this activity.

They were told by higher-level managers to do the job. We have noted, on more than an isolated set of projects, that considerable resistance to ABC implementations arises because of extensive publicity of the non-value-added activities uncovered by the project team. Since the concept itself does not have enormous validity (see preceding paragraphs) and can easily be replaced by a much more robust concept—the opportunity for cost reduction and process improvement—the rationale for using a simplistic value-added coding scheme eludes us.

Perhaps proponents of the value-added/non-value-added coding scheme believe it is easier to reduce the cost of non-value-added activities than of value-added ones. After all, industrial engineering resources have concentrated on direct labor reduction, automation, and increasing the speed with which machines can operate, all improvements aimed at value-added activities. Therefore, many indirect and support activities that do not directly or obviously benefit end-users may have received virtually no industrial engineering attention, and may still be performed inefficiently. As with quality improvements, initial implementations may pick off some low-hanging fruit identifying and eliminating activities that clearly provide no benefit to customers. But once this initial surge of simple activity redesign and elimination has occurred, opportunities for cost reduction can occur in either direct production, product design, and customer service activities as well as in indirect and support activities.

One company did expand beyond a simple two-category value-added classification into a four-category value-added coding scheme:

1. An activity required to produce the product or improve the process; the activity cannot, on a cost justification basis, be improved, simplified, or reduced in scope at this time.
2. An activity required to produce the product or improve the process; the activity can be cost justifiably improved, simplified, or reduced in scope.
3. An activity not required to produce the product or improve the process; the activity can be eventually eliminated by changing a process or a company procedure.
4. An activity not required to produce the product or improve the process; the activity can be eliminated in the short run by changing a process or a company procedure.

Such a scheme avoids the pejorative overtones of a value-added/non-value-added classification and directs managers' and employees' process-improvement energies to category three and category four activities.

9

Strategic Activity-Based Management: Product Mix and Pricing

In Chapter 8, we described operational activity-based management: using an ABC model to motivate and track improvements in the efficiency with which organizational resources are used to perform activities and business processes. In this chapter, we introduce strategic activity-based management: modifying the demand for organizational activities to enhance profitability. Strategic ABM works by shifting the mix of activities away from costly and unprofitable applications to more profitable ones. Strategic ABM encompasses decisions made about:

- Product mix and pricing
- Customer relationships
- Supplier selection and relationships
- Product design and development

Many ABM practitioners focus only on operational ABM. They are leaving an important weapon unfired when they ignore strategic ABM. Often, individual products, services, and customers demand a complex mix of expensive activities for which the business unit is not adequately compensated under current pricing and volume arrangements. Managers must understand the existence and frequency of such unprofitable demands so they can take actions to ensure that they are more adequately compensated. Alternatively, managers can shift the mix to less costly activities. The demand for activities ultimately arises from decisions about individual products, services, and customers. Managers also need to understand how decisions made at this level affect the quantity and the cost of organizational activities. In this chapter, we discuss decisions made about existing products. In subsequent chapters, we discuss the customer, supplier, and product design components of strategic ABM.

ABC Product Profitability: The Whale Curve

Product costing was the first application of strategic activity-based costing. Distortions made by traditional costing systems, particularly those that relied on direct labor to allocate indirect and support costs to products, led several companies in the early to mid-1980s to use activity-based costing to assign overhead costs more accurately to products.[1] By defining and using a broader set of activities and cost drivers, particularly batch and product-sustaining activities (see Chapter 6), ABC gave a very different picture of product cost from that derived either from traditional full costing, direct-labor-based systems, or direct- (or marginal-) costing systems, which assumed that no relationship existed between product mix and volume and the demand for indirect and support resources. For example, *Exhibit 9-1* shows the cumulative sales volume versus cumulative number of products for a typical full-line producer.

Exhibit 9-1   Cumulative Sales

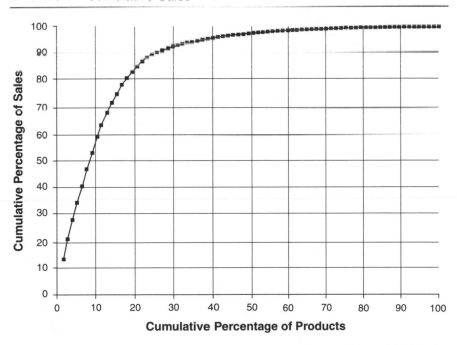

Source: Data from Jane Montgomery and Robin Cooper, "Schrader Bellows (D-1)," Case 1-186-053 (Boston: Harvard Business School, 1985).

The exhibit shows the normal 20-80 rule associated with business activities: the highest-volume 20% of products generate about 80% of sales. More revealing, however, is the 60-99 rule: the highest-volume 60% of products generate 99% of sales. Or, looking at the curve from the other direction, the lowest-volume 40% of products generate a cumulative total of 1% of sales. Traditional direct, labor-costing systems generally report, however, that all these low-volume products are profitable since pricing is based on a normal markup over standard costs.[2]

In contrast, an ABC analysis will generally show that after assigning accurately the cost of activities such as setup, purchasing, quality assurance, inventory management, and product support, many products are extremely unprofitable. For example, *Exhibit 9-2* shows a typical ABC finding: cumulative profitability is plotted against products, where the products are ranked on the horizontal axis from the most profitable to the least profitable.[3] The most profitable 20% of products can generate about 300% of profits. The remaining 80% of products either are break-even or loss items, and collectively lose 200% of profits, leaving the division with its 100% of profits. This curve happens so frequently in ABC analysis that it has been given a name, the "whale curve." The height or hump of the whale indicates the profits earned by the business unit's

Exhibit 9-2 Cumulative Profitability

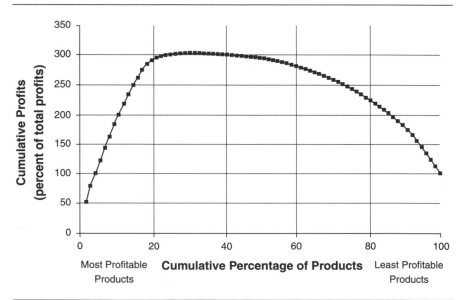

Source: Data from Jane Montgomery and Robin Cooper, "Schrader Bellows (D-1)," Case 1-186-053 (Boston: Harvard Business School, 1985).

most profitable products. The remaining products, break-even and loss, bring total profits down to sea level.

An alternative, and even more revealing, display of the whale curve is shown in *Exhibit 9-3* where cumulative profits are plotted against cumulative sales volume of individual products; the products in Exhibit 9-3 are again ranked on the horizontal axis from the most profitable to the least profitable. The exhibit shows that the profitable products (about 20% of the product line) generate 85% of sales and 300% of the unit's profits. The remaining products generate 15% of sales and lose 200% of the unit's profits.

Another interesting aspect of Exhibit 9-3 is that, for the profitable 20% of products, the plot of cumulative profits versus cumulative sales is approximately a straight line. The slope of this line represents the profit margin earned per dollar of sales for these products. In effect, these mostly high-volume products are sold in reasonably competitive markets where the price is set to earn a normal return. The costs of these high-volume products are relatively unchanged by the shift from traditional to activity-based costing (the ABC-assigned costs for these products will decrease, but usually by less than 10%). Therefore, their traditional and activity-based profit margins are not grossly different.

Exhibit 9-3 Cumulative Profitability vs. Cumulative Sales Volume

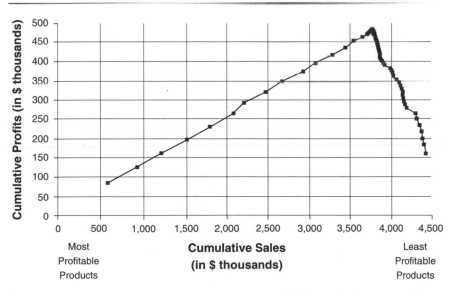

Source: Data from Jane Montgomery and Robin Cooper, "Schrader Bellows (D-1)," Case 1-186-053 (Boston: Harvard Business School, 1985).

The low-volume products, in contrast, tend to be unique, customized products. The company relies on its traditional standard costing system to set prices for these products since often no competitive product exists. The company may even set the apparent profit margin somewhat higher to reflect the lack of competition. But, because the company's standard cost system severely underestimates the cost of designing, producing, sustaining, and delivering these low-volume, custom products, the higher margins fail by substantial amounts to cover the cost of resources used for these products. The ABC costs are often more than 100% higher than the costs assigned to these products by the existing Stage II cost system.

Exhibits 9-1 to 9-3 are reproduced in virtually every activity-based cost system built for business units that meet the two rules cited in Chapter 6: 1) Willie Sutton rule: large expenses in indirect and support resources and 2) High-diversity rule: diversity in products, customers, and processes.

Companies, operating for decades with either traditional standard cost systems or direct (marginal) costing systems, overproliferate their product lines and overcustomize their product offerings. They fail to see how decisions on product variety and complexity inevitably lead to much higher expenses in the indirect and support resources required to implement a full-line product strategy.

Even leading Japanese manufacturers have not been immune to the adverse consequences of excessive variety. For example:

> *Japanese buyers of the Nissan Stanza can choose from nearly 200 variations with different engines, bodies, tires, and transmissions. The company has sold fewer than a dozen units of some combinations. . . . Nissan is trying to save money by cutting back on the number of variations it is offering, even if it means sacrificing market share. And it is trying to use the same parts in more models. Right now there are about 70 kinds of steering wheels used in its automobiles, when far fewer would do.*
>
> *The Japanese "lean production" system, first developed by Toyota, involves rapid introduction of models, a flexible manufacturing system that can make many kinds of cars on the same assembly line, low inventories and long-term relationships with suppliers. But now manufacturers are starting to cut the number of products they offer, slow the pace at which they bring out products, reduce their reliance on low prices as a marketing strategy, keep larger inventories, and loosen historic bonds with suppliers.*[4]

And Japanese electronics companies also suffered from excess part and product proliferation:

Sony eliminated several models' sizes of televisions, and Mitsubishi is cutting back on its 30 different varieties of fax machines. . . . Japanese electronics will eliminate 25 models of video-cassette recorders and 10 models of televisions. Matsushita is re-thinking the philosophy of its founder who declared that products should be "as cheap and readily available as tap water." Now the company is scaling back from its 220 types of televisions and 62 types of VCRs, recognizing that only 10% sold well.

Consumer product manufacturers are also retrenching. Kao, Japan's P&G, has trimmed its product line from a high of more than 600 offerings in 1989 to slightly more than 550 in 1992. Its main rival, Lion, has announced plans to reduce its product line by 30%.[5]

Lacking activity-based cost models that identify the high costs of product variety and proliferation, even excellent companies can introduce and sustain far more products than are economically warranted. The company's whale curve indicates the need for it to address the issue of whether customers truly value the wide range of products it currently provides.

Product-Related Actions

Managers or students, when they first encounter a whale curve of total profitability, often suggest that the company can work less hard by producing only a small fraction of existing products. By retaining the profitable 80–85% of existing sales, the business unit can see profits double or triple by eliminating the loss products. On reflection, the respondents see several fallacies with this line of reasoning. First, many existing customers may want to buy from a full-line producer. While the business unit may earn the bulk of its profits from selling higher-volume standard products, like vanilla and chocolate, it must also offer its customers the occasional small quantity of specialty flavors, like butter-pecan fudge swirl, that are more expensive to design and produce.

Second, many of the expenses assigned to products by the ABC analysis will remain, in the short run, even were the products to be dropped. In this case, the revenues will disappear immediately, but most of the costs (other than materials) will likely still be incurred. If no further actions are taken, the remaining expenses could be (incorrectly) spread back to the remaining products, causing many of them to now look unprofitable.[6] Should these be dropped, the business unit is now well along into a death spiral.

Clearly, for strategic ABM to be effective, it must cope with these legitimate concerns. In fact, managers have a wide choice of actions to modify their whale curves, and increase the profitability of their product lines:

- Reprice products
- Substitute products
- Redesign products
- Improve production processes
- Change operating policies and strategy
- Invest in flexible technology
- Eliminate products

And, as suggested in the ordering of this list, dropping unprofitable products should be, perhaps, the last possible action to be contemplated. In the rest of this chapter, we will take a closer look at these potential actions.

Reprice Products

Some companies have little discretion in product pricing. Their high-volume products are sold in highly competitive markets, where it is difficult to differentiate the product along quality or functionality dimensions, and where customers find it easy to switch suppliers to obtain the lowest price. For these situations, repricing products in response to an ABC analysis may not be a viable option. These companies must look elsewhere to improve the profitability of their products, for example, to redesign, substitution, process improvement, or deletion.

Many companies, however, have discovered they have considerable discretion in adjusting prices, particularly on their highly customized products—the ones making up the bulk of the right-hand side of the whale curve. Pricing strategies for products not sold in competitive markets are often derived either from standard markups over standard costs (as calculated from a traditional, unit-based costing system) or from extrapolation from prices charged for existing, physically similar products. For example, prices for high-volume blue and black pens are established by competitive market forces. Specialty products, like fuchsia and lavender pens, which appear similar and follow a similar production process, will be priced about the same as standard blue and black pens, perhaps a little higher because of their unusual features. Missing from this analysis, however, are the much higher costs for product development, product enhancement, purchasing, receiving, inspection, setup, and maintenance resources required for specialty colors. Often, for a customer, the item is a small fraction of its total costs (the cost of purchasing specialty pens for writing wedding invitations is less than 0.01% of the total cost of the wedding) and the customer may be willing to pay a considerable price premium for the high quality, reliable supply, and unique functionality of that product. After an initial ABC analysis, companies have frequently been able to sustain price increases of 25–50% for their specialty, customized products.

As a specific numerical example, consider a product with the following characteristics:

Number of Units Ordered	100
Material Cost per Unit	$12.40
Direct Labor Time per Unit Produced	0.6 hours
Direct Labor Rate	$20/hour
Machine Hours per Unit Produced	0.8 hours
Number of Components	10
Number of Production Runs*	6
Average Setup Time per Production Run	3 hours
Number of Shipments	1
Engineering Design and Process Time	20 hours

*The large number of runs is required to machine several unique components before assembly into the final product.

The existing cost system applies overhead costs using only labor and machine hours (two unit-level drivers). The rates are 200% of direct labor costs and $70 per machine hour. The calculated cost per unit is:

Materials	$ 12.40
Direct Labor	12.00
Overhead Applied on Direct Labor	24.00
Overhead Applied on Machine Hours	56.00
Total Costs per Unit	**$104.40**

For an order of 100 units, the total costs would be estimated at $10,440. If the company wants a 35% markup over manufacturing costs, it would quote a price of $14,094.

The activity-based cost analysis could reveal the following activities and activity cost driver rates:

ACTIVITY	ACTIVITY COST DRIVER RATE
Direct Labor Processing	$50/hour
Machine Processing	$60/hour
Purchase and Receive Components	$150/purchase order
Schedule Production Orders and Perform First Item Inspection	$200/production run
Set Up Machines	$80/setup hour
Process Customer Orders: Negotiate, Package, Ship, Invoice, Collect	$100/customer order
Perform Engineering Design and Support	$75/engineering hour

The ABC cost buildup for the product is:

COST		AMOUNT
Materials	(12.40 * 100)	$1,240
Direct Labor	(0.6 * 50 * 100)	3,000
Machining	(0.8 * 60 * 100)	4,800
Unit-Level Expenses		**$9,040**
Acquiring Materials	(10 * 150)	$1,500
Production Runs	(6 * 200)	1,200
Set Up Machines	(6 * 3 * 80)	1,440
Process Customer Order	(1 * 100)	100
Batch-Level Expenses		**$4,240**
Engineering Support	(20 * 75)	$1,500
Product-Sustaining Expenses		**$1,500**
Total Product Expenses		**$14,780**

Here, even if the company gets the business at the 35% markup over the full costs calculated by its traditional cost system, the revenues for the 100-unit order would be less than the (ABC) costs of all the resources required to fulfill the order. The complex low-volume product (containing six components, each requiring its own production run), demands a disproportionate amount of resources for performing batch and product-sustaining activities. Low-volume products, with many specialty components, place high demands on an organization's support resources.

Conversely, if the costs of the low-volume specialty products have been correctly assigned, the costs of high-volume standard products will decrease. Costs of mature products may drop by 5–8%. While such a cost reduction may appear minimal, the high-volume mature products are typically sold in competitive markets, where margin increases of 3–5% are extremely hard to generate. In reality, these products may already be earning the higher margins, once the expenses of resources not being used for them are not assigned to them. In this situation, companies can bid more aggressively to increase the sales of these profitable products even more. Managers now see that increased production of these products involves only increases in unit-level expenses, but none in batch, product-sustaining, and facility-sustaining expenses. For example, a John Deere components plant, after its initial ABC analysis, successfully bid to produce two high-volume products, on a subcontract basis, for a General Motors plant.[7] Deere dedicated 12 of its most productive, automated machines in a highly efficient cellular arrangement to produce the two parts on a continuous flow basis. One may question why GM would outsource these two high-volume parts. The answer, of course, is that GM's decision was based on its internal (traditional) costing system, a system that allocated large amounts of factory overhead to the two products because of their high direct labor and machine-hour content.

Measuring product profitability for strategic ABM is entirely consistent with competitive strategy considerations. In the early 1980s, Michael Porter pointed out that companies have two generic strategies that can be successful: low-cost and differentiated.[8] His framework has been elaborated upon in recent years; for example, to identify several differentiation strategies, like product leadership or customer service.[9] But Porter's basic point remains valid. Some companies succeed by offering high-volume products at the lowest possible price. Most companies, however, wish to break out of the price-driven, commodity segment of their industry and offer products with unique functionality and/or superior customer service. In this way they can earn price premiums over the commodity-like blue and black pen (or vanilla and chocolate) products.

Initially, companies gain apparent benefits from a differentiation strategy. Newly introduced, customized, and more functional products can earn a price premium over standard, mature commodity products. And customers are willing to pay, modestly, for improved service and features. But to make a differentiation strategy successful, companies must do better than earn price premiums for their customized products and services. As Porter pointed out more than a decade ago: "Differentiation leads to superior performance if the price premium achieved exceeds any added costs of being unique. . . . A differentiator must always seek ways of differentiating that lead to a price premium greater than the cost of differentiating. A differentiator cannot ignore its cost position, because its premium prices will be nullified by a markedly inferior cost position."[10] Companies that follow a differentiated strategy but use a traditional Stage II standard costing system, or, worse, use a direct or marginal costing system, cannot estimate the incremental costs of achieving differentiation. They will be seduced by the apparently higher profit margins reported by their standard or direct cost system into believing that their differentiation strategy is being implemented successfully. And, even more perversely, as we saw in the pen factory example of Chapter 6, many of the higher costs associated with the differentiation strategy are shifted, by a Stage II standard cost system, to the company's high-volume standard products—since they still constitute the bulk of the unit's labor and machine hours, and materials purchases. Therefore, the profitability of these standard products will seemingly erode, further confirming the apparent success of the differentiation strategy. As the plant increases its product diversity, indirect and support expenses will begin to explode—to handle the increased variety and complexity—and the organization finds itself in a "differentiation" death spiral, triggered by the increasing diversity of its products.

Companies with a differentiation strategy require an activity-based cost system to measure accurately the costs of increased variety and customization. They will then be able to see whether customers are willing to pay higher prices to compensate the business unit for its higher costs. Of course, if the company is able to differentiate its products and services without incurring a cost penalty, this capability will be identified by the ABC system, and the company does not have to seek price premiums for its unique features and services.[11]

Substitute Products

An alternative to raising prices on low-volume, customized products is to substitute existing, lower-cost alternatives. In many instances, customers are relatively indifferent to certain aspects of product variety that impose high costs on the producer. They may want a lavender pen, but a purple pen that is already produced in moderate-to-high volume may be good enough if it can be purchased at a significantly lower price.

Pricing and product substitution are complementary. Marketing and sales representatives can give the customer the choice between paying a higher price for exactly the right functionality, or obtaining a lower price by accepting relaxed product specifications. Using the information from an ABC analysis, marketing and sales representatives can have intelligent, fact-based discussions with customers to determine their trade-off among functionality, uniqueness, and price charged. Some sales representatives have notebook computers with installed ABC models so that they can conduct real-time discussions with customers about the trade-offs between product variety and price.

Product innovation and variety are important and valued. Activity-based costing should not be construed as discouraging business units from continually attempting to meet customer needs with new and varied products. But ABC does provide a discipline to ensure that the value customers receive from new and different products more than offsets the costs of offering these products. If the value is not higher, customer preferences, including a sensitivity to price, may be satisfied better by existing products, not new varieties. Also, many products may be at the end (or beyond the end) of their useful life cycle. Products now known to be "dogs" started life as enthusiastic and hopeful "puppies." Companies need to discipline their product breadth by substituting more popular existing products for those that never fulfilled their expectations when launched or that have outlived their usefulness and value to customers.

Redesign Products

Many products are expensive because of poor product designs. Without an activity-based cost system to guide their product design and product development decisions, engineers ignore many of the costs of component and product variety and process complexity. They design products for functionality and do not consider the costs of adding new and unique components, new vendors, and complex production process requirements. The best opportunities for lowering product costs through excellent design occur when the products are first designed. We will discuss this option at some length in Chapter 11. Occasionally, however, the ABC analysis will reveal design aspects—a particularly expensive or complex component or a complex process specification that adds little to product performance and functionality—that can be eliminated or modified even for existing products. Redesigning products is an attractive option since it will usually be invisible to customers and the company will not have to reprice or substitute another product.

Often, however, the options for redesigning existing products may be limited. The division manager of an electronic controls company reflected:

> *One appliance manufacturer used a basic system for all its models and the cost of supplying the product for this single system turned out lower than we had thought. A second manufacturer, however, had proliferated its designs, requiring us to develop and offer more products for them. I now see that this led to much more engineering and support costs. If I had understood this better, we could have cut the cost of our basic product and also raised the price for the newly designed variants to discourage the customer from switching to the new devices. It's probably too late now; we're locked into the current pricing structure and we've already added the support and engineering staff to handle the different devices.*[12]

The manager realized that the time to discuss the cost of developing and supporting the new devices was early in the design cycle. By the time the devices had been designed and prices negotiated, it was too late to reverse earlier decisions. In Chapter 11 we discuss the opportunity to influence future manufacturing costs during the product design and development stage.

Improve Production Processes

We have already discussed operational ABM, involving continuous and discontinuous process improvement. This analysis was triggered by measuring and analyzing cost behavior at the activity and business process level. But opportunities for process improvement can also be determined by careful examination of ABC costs calculated at the product level.

Traditional product costing (with Stage II cost systems) of complex products relies on a *bill of materials* that identifies all the components and subassemblies of the final product. The cost system then adds the cost of labor and overhead associated with the product. For example, a Stage II product cost buildup (shown earlier in the chapter) identified materials, labor, labor overhead, and machine overhead as the only elements of total product cost. An engineer or accountant looking at this product buildup would see some obvious ways to reduce product costs:

- Lower materials purchase prices
- Lower direct labor cost
- Lower machine-related costs

In fact, exactly such actions have been taken for decades. Managers searched for cheaper suppliers, wherever they happened to be, purchased materials and components in bulk to obtain volume discounts, built automated warehouses to house and move the materials purchased and delivered in bulk, and deployed extensive inventory control and scheduling resources to arrange for delivery and to expedite items that were delivered late from unreliable suppliers. Companies spent thousands of dollars on industrial engineering studies to reduce a product's direct labor content by tenths of hours; they automated processes whenever possible and shifted labor-intense processes to low-wage countries. Managers invested in expensive, inflexible, high-speed machines to reduce machine time per unit. These machines, however, were difficult and expensive to change over from one product variety to another. Also, industrial engineers encouraged workers to run existing machines at higher and higher speeds, risking poor-quality products, unexpected breakdowns, and high maintenance and repair costs.

All these actions appeared sensible when viewed through the lens of the materials, labor, and machine-hour costs highlighted by traditional costing systems. These systems encouraged managers to spend heavily to reduce their *unit-level* costs of materials, labor, and machine time, but doing so produced an enormous escalation in *batch* and *product-level* expenses.

An ABC cost system does, of course, retain the bill of materials structure. But it adds a new dimension, a *bill of activities*. For example, recall the ABC bill of activities for the same product (see page 168). Rather than show indirect costs as overhead, the ABC analysis reveals the costs of activities performed for this product, in this case scheduling and handling production orders, setup, acquiring materials, setting up machines, and engineering support for the product. This bill of activities suggests a whole additional set of actions that can lead to lowering the costs assigned to this product.

The insights from a bill of activities, as well as an analysis of the costs of products in the right-hand tail of the whale curve in Exhibits 9-2 and 9-3, stimulate process improvements. The high cost for many of these products may be caused by long and complex setups on existing equipment and complex material flows. As in operational ABM (Chapter 8), understanding activity costs at the individual product level focuses attention on where process improvements can be particularly valuable.

Think about an industrial engineer who has attended a seminar on JIT techniques. He returns to his factory committed to a major program to reduce setup times. While some improvement can be accomplished through simple process changes, additional improvements may require investments in new fixtures and equipment modifications to facilitate rapid changeovers. Imagine the conversation about such an initiative with a plant controller intimately familiar with the plant's traditional cost system that measures and accounts only for direct materials, direct labor, and labor- and machine-related overhead.

Controller: *How was the conference?*

IE: *Terrific, this just-in-time will really improve our operations. I can hardly wait to start.*

Contr: *Go to it. Good luck.*

IE: *Oh, there is one small thing. I will need to spend some money on training and education, and also on new fixtures and modifications to our existing equipment to achieve single-minute-exchange-of-dies [SMED].*

Contr: *Hmmm. That may require an increment in our operating budget; perhaps a new capital authorization request. But these should be straightforward. What's the benefit case? I see that materials are a big part of product costs. Will your project reduce our materials cost?*

IE: *No, we will have the same materials. The project will enable us to switch over faster from one product variant to another.*

Contr: *No savings in materials costs. OK. Will your project enable us to reduce the direct labor required to produce a part?*

IE: *No, the basic production process remains the same. But by reducing setup times we can move faster from one product to another.*

Contr: *Ok, no savings in direct materials, no savings in direct labor, and no savings in direct labor overhead. I see that machine hours are costly for these products. Will your project enable the machines to run faster?*

IE: *(exasperated) No, the damn machines will run at the same speed as before, we will still need as much direct labor for the product as we did before, and we still need the same materials for the product. But JIT will enable us to improve the velocity with which products move through the plant.*

Contr: *Velocity, velocity? Where does it say on our cost sheets that velocity is a cost driver? You engineers keep finding new gimmicks and toys that just add to our overhead costs and don't do anything to reduce our identifiable costs.*

Clearly, traditional cost systems' focus on unit-level traceable costs (direct materials, direct labor, machine hours, and the overhead allocated by these unit-level drivers) provides a difficult environment to capture the cost savings from JIT procedures. The costs from slow velocity—long setup times, many inventory accumulation points, and extensive material movements—are certainly substantial. But they are invisible because they are buried in large, highly aggregated overhead pools.

The ABC bill of activities reveals a radically different picture. It indicates the large expenses associated with long setup times, the obvious targets for cost reduction and cost avoidance with implementation of JIT procedures. Such savings, however, do not come for free.

Think about the time required by the average driver to change a flat tire. By the time he or she has found the jack, read the instruction manual, replaced the tire, and returned to the driver's seat, 60–75 minutes have passed.

How long does it take for a driver to change not one, but two tires, in the midst of the Indianapolis 500 race? Perhaps 10–15 seconds. How can the same process be done with twice the productivity (two tires versus one changed) in less than 0.5% of the time? Obviously, the process improvement comes from a combination of:

- *Technology and Capital:* the race car and its wheel have been designed to facilitate rapid changeovers; even with penalties for added weight, the car includes a hydraulic system that enables it to be raised instantly by connecting an air hose to an external valve; the wheels are attached to the car with only a single lug nut. The mechanics are also equipped with special equipment to remove and retighten the lug nut at high speed.
- *Training:* the driver has a highly trained team to change the tires. The team has practiced the changeover many times so that it performs the task very efficiently.
- *Preparation:* the team does not wait until the racing car appears in the pit, then discovers that the driver wants two tires changed, and thereupon issues a request to the stock room for two replacement tires. The team has the two replacement tires standing ready so that they can be bolted on to the car immediately.

Clearly, the technology, specially trained changeover team, and preparation require that some expenses be incurred. But the benefit case is so clear that the investments are readily made. Similarly, the high costs associated with long, inefficient setups, high levels of WIP inventory, and tortuous materials flow paths become readily identified in an ABC analysis. The ABC map of product economics highlights the inefficient processes and provides the financial justification for investing in improved processes and fixtures. Managers can see clearly how they are already incurring high costs for the current, inefficient operations. The business case for JIT and other continuous improvement initiatives to improve batch-level processes such as setup and material movement, even if the initiatives require some front-end spending, becomes clear and defensible.[13]

In addition, the high level of product-sustaining costs for products identifies cost-saving opportunities for design-for-manufacturing initiatives: redesign products to use fewer and more common components and customize products with standard components and modules as late in the production process as possible.

The bill of activities shown in *Exhibit 9-4* shows a similar story. The activities and business processes performed for the customized product are a much higher percentage of total product costs than for the similar, but standard and high-volume product. Large opportunities for cost savings exist if the activity and business process costs can be reduced for the customized product.

Change Operating Policies and Strategy

Several companies, in view of Toyota's goal of "efficient lot sizes of one," made arbitrary reductions in their batch sizes and allowable inventory levels. This led to many low-volume runs and more frequent shipments to customers. Subsequently, with the insight from an initial ABC model, the companies realized that their cost structure had increased substantially because of the increased number of batch-level activities. A little knowledge is a dangerous thing. In effect, these companies heard only part of the Toyota story. Efficient lot sizes of one are the *result* of success in reducing the cost of batch-level activities, not the driver of the cost reduction. Without any fundamental improvement in performing batch-level activities, frequent changeovers not only raised batch-level expenses, they also consumed valuable equipment capacity. The ABC model pointed out that blind adherence to fashionable management slogans, without making basic improvements in the underlying business processes, will raise, not lower, costs.[14]

Exhibit 9-4   Revised Product Costs: Two Sample Products

	STANDARD PRODUCT D28X3		CUSTOM PRODUCT D28Y4	
	Total	Per Unit	Total	Per Unit
Units	4,256,027		799,262	
Average Sales Price	$2.36		$1.53	
Revenues	10,029,796	$2.36	1,220,626	$ 1.53
Direct Materials	1,508,455	0.35	265,955	0.33
Direct Labor	1,047,043	0.25	188,689	0.24
Contribution Margin	7,474,298	1.76	765,982	0.96
Principal Processes				
Production	1,994,694	0.47	540,849	0.68
Nonproduction				
Customer Administration	83,774	0.02	24,835	0.03
Procurement	98,630	0.02	19,514	0.02
Production Management	193,585	0.05	45,838	0.06
Quality Control	157,898	0.04	49,078	0.06
Production Tooling	99,090	0.02	62,279	0.08
Maintenance	739	0.00	93	0.00
Warehousing	23,914	0.01	4,121	0.01
Total Nonproduction	657,630	0.15	205,758	0.26
Total Principal	2,652,324	0.62	746,607	0.93
Change Processes				
Internal Changes	2,889	0.00	4,626	0.01
External Changes	177	0.00	2,444	0.00
Total Change Processes	3,066	0.00	7,070	0.01
Support Processes				
G&A and Finance	-134,122	-0.03	-14,273	-0.02
Human Resources	111,315	0.03	14,952	0.02
Environmental and Safety	81,436	0.02	17,016	0.02
Total Support Processes	58,629	0.01	17,695	0.02
Total Indirect Expenses	2,714,019	0.64	771,372	0.97
Production Income Before Taxes	$4,760,279	$1.12	$ - 5,390	$ - 0.01

Source: Adapted from R. S. Kaplan, "Maxwell Appliance Controls," Case 9-192-058 (Boston: Harvard Business School, 1992), 23. Reprinted by permission of Harvard Business School.

In addition to its ability to set priorities and highlight the benefits of continuous improvement initiatives, the ABC bill of activities and associated classification by cost hierarchy provide a powerful connection to contemporary developments in operations management. The focused factory concept described by Skinner in the early 1970s, and later elaborated on by Hayes and Wheelwright,[15] can now be understood as advocating that the production of high-volume products (lots of unit-level activities, few batch and product-sustaining ones) be separated from the production of low-volume, customized products (few unit-level activities, lots of batch and product-sustaining activities). The focused factory approach recommends that high-volume products should be produced in facilities optimized to perform unit-level activities efficiently. Such facilities, however, may be quite inefficient for performing batch and product-sustaining activities. Therefore, low-volume, high-variety products should be produced in facilities that perform batch and product-sustaining activities highly efficiently—such as a job shop, with skilled operators and general purpose equipment—but that may be quite inefficient for unit-level activities. The unit-level activities are more expensive in the job shop since a higher quantity and quality of direct labor is required to operate the general purpose machines, and the general purpose machines run slower than the specialized, highly automated production equipment. But for the small-run sizes of new and customized products, the much lower batch and product-sustaining expenses in a job-shop environment more than compensate for the somewhat higher unit-level labor costs and machine run times.

Invest in Flexible Technology

Jaikumar's work on flexible manufacturing systems (FMSs)[16] articulates how advanced manufacturing technologies can break through the Skinner-Hayes-Wheelwright trade-off between mass-production efficiency and flexibility. The capabilities of FMS, and other information-intense production technologies, such as computer-aided design (CAD), computer-aided engineering (CAE), and computer-aided software engineering (CASE), can be viewed as greatly reducing the cost of performing activities such as changing over production from one product to another, scheduling production runs, inspecting products, moving materials, and designing products while retaining the efficiencies of high-speed automated production. Thus, the business case for investing in these advanced (and expensive) manufacturing technologies can now be justified by appealing to the reduction in costs currently incurred for performing batch and product-sustaining activities with conventional manufacturing technology.[17] These costs, however, are visible only if the organization has developed an ABC system for explicitly measuring them. These large and now visible batch and product-sustaining costs become the prime targets for elimination with new investments in computer-integrated manufacturing technology.

Eliminate Products

We have illustrated a wide variety of actions that managers can take to transform unprofitable products into profitable ones. If none of these actions is feasible or economically justified, managers may have to confront the final solution—kill unprofitable products.

Marketing and sales personnel may object to dropping unprofitable products, even when no other action is feasible to make them profitable. They argue that these products are complementary to other products that are profitable. That is, in order to sell tankloads of chocolate and vanilla, the company must be prepared to occasionally sell half pints of butter pecan fudge swirl. Clearly, such an argument is based on the products' demand curves, not their cost curves. ABC, as a cost-estimating model, says nothing about product demand curves, so one cannot respond to such objections with the logic and evidence contained in an ABC model. Financial managers should not attempt to second-guess marketing and sales experts about customer preferences.

Rather than engage in an unproductive debate on the issue, it may suffice for financial managers to assign the loss from unprofitable products to the appropriate responsibility—say a product manager, or customer representative—and allow that person to manage the mix of profitable and unprofitable products to maximize total profitability. One can make small shifts in the incentive structure, by awarding commissions and incentive pay based on profitability, not sales. Or, even simpler, allow unprofitable products to continue to be produced, marketed, and sold but not count their sales in salespersons' quotas and incentive pay. Hence, if the unprofitable products do increase total profitability, sales reps can continue to sell them; but if they do not contribute to total profitability, the incentive to continue selling them is greatly reduced.

Summary

The product-related actions described in this chapter, if implemented successfully, will reduce the resources required to produce products. Pricing and explicit product substitution will shift the mix from difficult-to-produce products to simple-to-produce ones. Redesign, process improvement, focused manufacturing facilities, and new technology will enable the same products to be produced with fewer organizational resources. And eliminating products clearly implies that fewer resources are required for the remaining products. In order for the organization to capture the benefits from these actions, however, it must eliminate the spending associated with the resources no longer needed.

Most, if not all, of the batch and product-sustaining expenses are associated with committed resources (recall the discussion in Chapter 7), whose supply is determined in advance of demand. Therefore, they will not be variable costs as conventionally defined. Performing one less setup, ordering one less batch of materials, moving one less load of materials, and executing one fewer engineering change notice will not result in any automatic reduction in spending. The totality of product-related actions discussed in this chapter will create additional unused capacity. Benefits will accrue only when managers take action to eliminate the unused capacity created (as discussed in Chapter 7). That is why activity-based management and capacity management are so intimately intertwined.

10

Strategic Activity-Based Management: Customers

The strategic ABM analysis in Chapter 9 concentrated on the traditional domain of cost accounting—assigning manufacturing and factory costs to products. With the more accurate ABC product-cost information, managers could take a variety of actions to improve product profitability. Organizations are now performing more comprehensive activity-based cost analyses. They are extending the domain of analysis, beyond manufacturing and factory costs, by getting below the gross margin line to items like marketing, selling, and administrative expenses. Analysis reveals that many demands for organizational resources arise not only from products but also from customers and distribution and delivery channels.

By tracing activity costs to customers, and to distribution and delivery channels, managers have even more opportunities to improve their organizations' profitability. The opportunities include:

- Protecting existing highly profitable customers;
- Repricing expensive services, based on cost-to-serve;
- Discounting, if necessary, to gain business with low cost-to-serve customers;
- Negotiating win-win relationships that lower cost-to-serve with cooperative customers;
- Conceding permanent loss customers to competitors; and
- Attempting to capture high-profit customers from competitors.

These actions should enable managers with good (ABC) instrumentation to dramatically improve their profitability, especially in industries where their competitors do not understand the economics of their customer relationships.

Selling, Marketing, Distribution, and Administrative Expenses: Fixed, Variable, or "Supervariable"?

Some people have argued against trying to assign selling, marketing, distribution, and administrative (SMDA) expenses to cost objects like customers or marketing channels. They claim that such expenses are fixed costs and, therefore, any assignment to individual customers would be arbitrary and misleading.

Many companies, however, have SMDA expenses that are a significantly higher percentage of sales today than they were, say, 30 years ago. Suppose, for example, that their SMDA expenses are now, say, 22% of sales. Most managers, extrapolating from the experience of their own organizations, would say that SMDA expenses were lower decades ago, say, 15–20% of sales. If they have been tracking general worldwide economic growth, they also would recognize that over the past three decades real sales volumes have likely increased at least threefold. But if SMDA expenses were truly a fixed cost, and sales volumes have tripled, SMDA expenses should be only one-third as high a percentage of sales—say, 5–7%—as they were 30 years ago. That's the definition of a fixed cost, one that stays constant even as sales volume increases or decreases. If SMDA expenses were merely a variable cost, one that increases in proportion with sales volume, they should have remained as a constant percentage of sales; that is, 15–20% of sales. In most situations, however, SMDA expenses have become an *increasing* percentage of sales. They are not fixed costs. They are not even variable costs. These are *supervariable* costs, costs that are rising faster than sales volume.

For an expense category to be treated as fixed, it should remain constant (in absolute amount), independent of production and sales levels. If the absolute value of the expense does not stay constant as volume increases, it makes little sense to treat the expense category as a fixed cost. An alternative and complementary approach is to scan the industry. If an expense is fixed, every company in the industry should have the same absolute expense level. For the smallest company, the expense will be a high percentage of total costs; for the largest company, the expense will be an extremely small percentage of total costs. If, however, the expense category represents about the same percentage of total costs, independent of size, the expense is more accurately described as variable.

A final test on this fixed versus variable cost issue is the Rule of One. Skeptics, when confronted with the evidence of costs increasing proportionally with or faster than sales, often ask, "How are you going to allocate the cost of the CEO to all the products and customers? Don't you need one CEO regardless of production and sales volume?" The response is, of course, to admit that any allocation of the CEO's expense to individual products or customers would indeed be arbitrary. This expense is an excellent example of a *corporate-sustaining expense,* one that is required for each corporation, independent of production and sales activity.[1] And sustaining expenses should not be allocated to individual units supported by the resource. But most departments, other than the CEO's office, have more than one unit of a resource: they consist of more than one salesperson, accounts receivable clerk, human resource person, security guard, market researcher, economist, or financial analyst. The Rule of One states that as long as a department or resource category (e.g., a collection of similar machines) has more than one resource unit, the supply of these resources must be determined by the demand for work from that department or resource category that one resource unit alone cannot handle. It is this demand for work that is the logical basis for cost assignment.

Should people argue that the costs of a multiresource organizational unit are fixed, and therefore not assignable to activities or cost objects, ask a simple question: "OK, we agree that it may be a fixed cost, but why not do the work of that department with a single person? After all, it's better to have a fixed cost that is low rather than one that is high." The answer is always, there is too much work for a single person to do. Understanding the nature of demand for work from that department, which requires 5, 7, or 13 people to perform, will lead to the articulation of activities performed by that resource, as well as the basis (cost driver) for assigning the costs of the resources in that department to the activities and cost objects that are creating a demand for that work. So an ABC analysis should not be concerned with assigning the cost of a single resource unit.[2] But once a department has multiple units of a resource (several people, several pieces of equipment), clearly analysis will reveal the nature of the activities and cost effects that are creating demands for work by this department and the basis for assigning its cost.

Having established that SMDA expenses are neither fixed nor likely subject to the Rule of One, we can now show how the assignment of these expenses can reveal dramatic opportunities for profit improvement.

Customer-Based ABM: The Case of Kanthal

An early and influential example of customer-focused ABC analysis was the case of Kanthal, a Swedish heating wire manufacturer.[3] Kanthal's president was concerned about the growth of selling and administrative expenses which accounted for 34% of total expenses. The senior managers understood well that the increase in variety and complexity of their business operations had led to the demand for more indirect and support personnel. As the chief financial officer remarked: "One hundred years ago we had one bookkeeper for every 10 blacksmiths but today we have eight bookkeepers for every three blacksmiths."[4] Two factors contributed to this shift: 1) productivity improvements and automation of the direct labor workforce, and 2) the increased complexity of and inattention to administrative processes.

Kanthal's managers analyzed their administrative expenses and found they could capture much of the behavior of customer-related costs through a simple expansion of their existing system. They added two new cost drivers: number of orders for nonstocked products and number of orders.

Kanthal had more than 15,000 product varieties. It operated with the 20-80 rule: since 20% of the products represented 80% of sales, these products were produced and stocked on a normal basis. When an order came for one of the 80% nonstocked items, the company performed a special job order to meet the request. The first cost driver represented the additional cost of ordering materials and scheduling production for nonstocked items. The second cost driver represented the normal expenses associated with any customer order such as pricing, scheduling delivery, invoicing, and collecting. Kanthal estimated the cost driver rate for these two newly identified activities and linked them to orders placed by individual customers. The format for calculating the profitability of an order for a nonstocked product is:

Sales Price	SEK **10,000**
Manufacturing and Selling Costs Proportional to Volume	5,600
Margin on Volume-related Costs	**4,400**
Order Cost	1,000
Nonstocked Item Manufacturing Cost	2,000
Operating Profit	**1,400**

This calculation reveals that a low-volume order, say for SEK (Swedish krona) 2,500, could only be profitable if it were for a standard, stocked item. Otherwise, the SEK 2,000 cost of handling a nonstocked item would overwhelm any manufacturing margin on the product. Conversely, for a large order, say SEK 100,000, the company would be virtually indifferent to whether it was for a stocked or a nonstocked item since the SEK 2,000 cost of processing an order for a nonstocked item was only 2% of invoicing value.

The Kanthal project team accumulated, for each customer, the profit and loss figures from each individual order placed by that customer. The analysis (see *Exhibit 10-1*) revealed that the company had a few extremely profitable customers, many customers that made a small profit, broke even, or lost a little money, and a few extremely unprofitable customers (see Customers #198, #199, and #200).

The graph of cumulative profits by customer showed the familiar whale curve (see *Exhibit 10-2*): the most profitable 20% of customers generated 225% of total profits, the middle 70% of customers about broke even, and the least profitable 10% of customers lost 125% of total profits, leaving the company with its 100% of total profits.

Most surprising, initially, to Kanthal was that the two most unprofitable customers were in the top three of sales volume. Upon reflection, this result was not that surprising. A company cannot lose large amounts of money with a single small customer. Only a large customer, working in a particularly perverse way, could be this unprofitable. Other customer based ABC analyses have yielded very similar conclusions. Large custom-

Exhibit 10-1   Kanthal Individual Customer Profitability

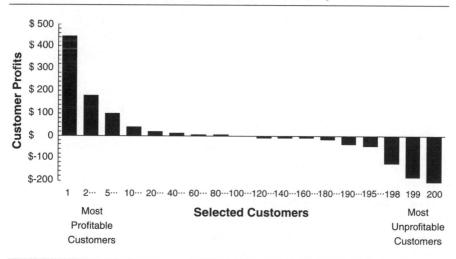

Source: R. S. Kaplan, "Kanthal (A)," Case 9-190-002 (Boston: Harvard Business School, 1989), 13. Reprinted by permission of Harvard Business School.

Exhibit 10-2 Kanthal Cumulative Customer Profitability

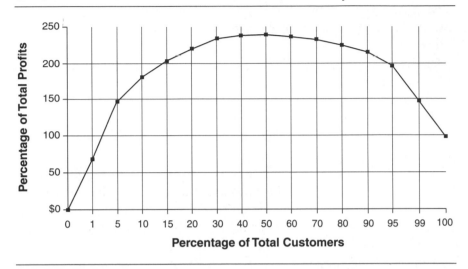

Source: Adapted from R. S. Kaplan, "Kanthal (A)," Case 9-190-002 (Boston: Harvard Business School Press, 1989), 14. Reprinted by permission of Harvard Business School.

ers tend to be either the most profitable or the least profitable of the entire customer base. It would be unusual for a large customer to be in the middle of the total profitability rankings.

Kanthal's senior management knew that it did not want to fire these two large-loss customers. Customer relationships are valuable, and difficult to win back once relinquished or dissipated.[5] The managers used the ABC information to understand the sources of losses with these key customers. The bill of activities for them revealed the nature of the problem for each and the opportunity for remedial action.

Customer #199's losses were caused by an extremely large number of small orders. Kanthal did not realize that the customer had moved to just-in-time ordering from its suppliers. Kanthal had been treating each order as a separate event, and deploying standard administrative procedures to handle it. Kanthal could have informed Customer #199 that JIT may be fine in Japan, but not appropriate for Sweden; that, in the future, it should place only a few orders for large quantities of material, not hundreds of orders for small quantities of material to be delivered just-in-time. Or Kanthal could have imposed a surcharge on each small order to compensate it for the administrative expenses incurred in processing the order. Kanthal, however, realized that this important customer was under great cost pressure from excellent global competitors and had moved to JIT operations to gain substantial operating efficiencies. Attempts to undo its costumer's JIT operations or to increase the price for JIT service were not likely to be successful.

Now that it understood the nature of the problem, Kanthal developed a creative solution. It told the customer how much Kanthal valued its business and relationship over the years. And as a gesture of appreciation for this business, Kanthal presented the customer with a gift—a computer terminal that would be wired directly into Kanthal's information system. Since the customer now preferred to order frequently, Kanthal wanted to make that task as simple as possible. The customer could monitor Kanthal's finished-goods inventory levels and production schedule. It could place orders that would be processed automatically. Pricing would be agreed on in advance; no salesperson would call on the customer and the customer's purchasing staff would not have to call anyone at Kanthal. All communication, including payment, would be done electronically. Kanthal's selling and administrative expenses, especially for routine orders of standard products, for this key customer would be sharply reduced, as would the customer's cost of purchasing from Kanthal. Kanthal used its ABC customer-profitability information to create a win-win solution for both parties. Of course, in a revised ABC calculation, Kanthal would not assign the standard order-processing cost for business done with Customer #199 because this activity was now handled with a very different and much lower cost process.

Kanthal's solution to this problem illustrates the interaction between the strategic and the operational aspects of activity-based management. The strategic aspect (customer profitability) identified a major problem, a large unprofitable JIT customer. The operational aspect resolved the problem, decreasing the costs of the activities performed in a way that benefited both Kanthal and its important customer.

Customer #200 represented a different challenge. It was a large multinational company using Kanthal as a backup supplier. Any time this customer needed a large amount of a standard product, it went to its primary supplier. When it asked this supplier for a small volume of a specialty product, the prime supplier generally demurred, claiming that it was not good at producing small lots of unusual varieties, and suggesting that the customer turn to Kanthal to supply this order. Managers occasionally ask, "How do I know when I have a distorted and obsolete cost system?" Any time you receive business referrals from a competitor, you can be reasonably assured you have such a system. The referral indicates that your competitor knows that the order will be particularly costly to fulfill.

By shifting the order to Kanthal, it keeps its own costs down (so that it can continue to be the prime supplier for high-volume standard products) while driving up Kanthal's cost structure (making it a less effective competitor for high-volume, profitable orders). Customer #200 was such a large company that even as a backup supplier it was Kanthal's third largest customer.

With its new understanding of Customer #200's behavior, Kanthal developed a carefully crafted solution. It again went to the customer, reaffirmed how much it valued its business, but indicated that it could not continue to do business with the customer as before. Kanthal shared with the customer the ABC analysis, which showed the implications of producing only small orders for nonstocked products. Kanthal offered a new pricing structure in which high-volume orders of standard (stocked) products would get a discount, up to 10%, while small orders for nonstocked items would have price premiums, up to 60%, added to them. Kanthal structured its discount and surcharge schedule so that any order received would be profitable for it. The results of the new relationship were immediate. In the following year, Customer #200 gave Kanthal the same sales volume (measured in Swedish krona) of business; but it ordered half as many times, and with 50% less variety of products. As a result, in one year this customer moved from being the most unprofitable to one of Kanthal's most profitable customers.

To summarize, Kanthal applied operational ABM with Customer #199: the number of times the activity (customer ordering) was performed remained constant, but the quantity of resources consumed by each activity was greatly reduced (through information technology). For Customer #200, Kanthal used only the strategic aspect of ABM. It did not change the resources consumed by each ordering activity, but it did reduce the number of order-related activities that were performed.

As Kanthal implemented specific pricing and order-handling arrangements across its entire customer base, the demands on its administrative, selling, and support resources decreased. In the next year, the company enjoyed a 20% sales increase. Much of the increase came from general worldwide economic growth, but up to a third was attributable to sales revenue increases from its new strategies derived from its ABC model. And Kanthal handled the sales increase with *fewer* administrative resources.[6] The ABM actions reduced the demand for administrative resources, thereby creating some unused capacity. Some of this capacity was eliminated by shifting people from administration to sales and production positions. But the remaining unused capacity was available to handle the increased sales volume. For once, these resources really did represent fixed, not variable or supervariable, costs. Since the incremental sales volume could be handled by administrative and sales resources already in place, the gross margin from any increase in sales (45%) became the net operating margin. All the gross margin benefits flowed to the bottom line; none of it was consumed in additional sales, administrative, and other support resources.

We have examined the Kanthal case at some length because the story is representative of what many companies have done—with strategic ABM—to modify their relationships with customers. They have transformed unprofitable customers into profitable ones through targeted negotiations: on price, on product mix and variety, on delivery terms, and distribution and payment arrangements. In addition, the Kanthal example shows how customers can influence production costs, not just selling and administrative costs. One of the two new drivers in Kanthal's ABC system, *number of orders for nonstocked products,* related to batch-level production costs at the company. Customer behavior and demand can strongly influence manufacturing costs (and operating costs in service industries, as we will see in Chapter 12). This causes customer costing to become even more important than product costing.

Hidden Loss and Hidden Profit Customers

As another example, a U.S. consumer goods manufacturer analyzed its warehousing costs. It was spending $2.8 million on one activity, *pick, stage, and load cases.* With an annual activity volume of about 70 million cases, its average handling cost per case was $0.04. A more careful activity analysis revealed that it was using six different packaging options for its customers; two of the options, *full-pallet* (63%) and *layer and case* (34%), represented 97% of the orders. The activity analysis revealed that $600,000 of expenses were associated with full-pallet loadings and $2 million were associated with the layer and case option. The cost driver rates for these two options were, therefore, $0.015 and $ 0.080, respectively. The company, however, had been setting its price for all its customers based on an average cost of $0.040 per case. One large retailer had been requesting that 60% of its deliveries use the layer and case option, so that only 40% used the standard full-pallet option. The manufacturer could now see that the cost to serve this important customer averaged $0.054 per case, and that the incremental price charged for this service was below cost on 60% of the shipments to this customer.

As did Kanthal, the company went to the customer and shared this data with it, indicating that it would be pleased to continue with the layer and case option, but that pricing must be a function of the type of delivery requested. The customer proceeded to examine its own activities and discovered, unexpectedly, that its cost for handling deliveries with the layer and case option were higher because of higher than average breakage and special handling. The customer agreed to shift to 100% full-pallet shipments, enabling the ABC analysis, as it did with Kanthal, to produce a win-win solution, in which both the company and its customer would realize cost savings.

Kanthal's U.S. operation encountered an analogous situation with its largest and most important customer, GE Appliance Division (GEAD). Kanthal's ABC analysis revealed exceptionally high costs of serving GEAD. A normal customer order cost a total of $150, but orders from GEAD, because of many changes, rescheduling, and expediting, cost in excess of $600. The president of Kanthal U.S. faced a dilemma. How could a small subsidiary of a foreign-based company negotiate with a giant and sophisticated multinational company? The president adopted an open-book policy revealing the high costs of serving GEAD and suggested that all the GEAD changes were not only a cost to Kanthal but probably a cost to GEAD as well. The GEAD managers did their own internal study and confirmed the president's speculation: their changes were the consequences of internal inefficiencies that had not been previously identified. Kanthal soon signed the largest contract in the company's history with GEAD that incorporated two ABM principles: a minimum order size and a surcharge for any change made to an existing order.[7]

These examples are indicative of the powerful opportunities for transforming customer relationships with fact-based discussions. Activity-based costing enables managers to identify the characteristics that cause some customers to be more expensive or less expensive to serve. Kanthal referred to these extremes as the hidden loss and the hidden profit customers (see *Exhibit 10-3*). The losses and profits were hidden because either no attempt was made to assign marketing, selling, technical, and administrative costs to individual customers, or else the assignment was done arbitrarily, using sales dollars rather than the actual cost drivers.[8] *Exhibit 10-4* shows the characteristics of hidden cost (high cost-to-serve) and hidden profit (low cost-to-serve) customers.

All companies can generally recognize customers that exhibit some or all of the high cost-to-serve characteristics. Occasionally companies are fortunate to enjoy low cost-to-serve customers as well. The only downside

Exhibit 10-3 Hidden Profit and Hidden Cost Customers

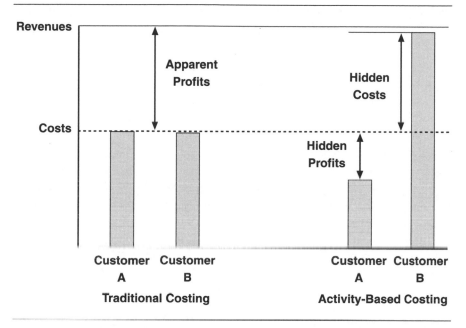

Source. Adapted from R. S. Kaplan, "Kanthal (A)," Case 0-190-002 (Boston: Harvard Business School Press, 1989), 8. Reprinted by permission of Harvard Business School.

Exhibit 10-4 Characteristics of High and Low Cost-to-Serve Customers

HIGH COST-TO-SERVE CUSTOMERS	LOW COST-TO-SERVE CUSTOMERS
Order Custom Products	Order Standard Products
Small Order Quantities	High Order Quantities
Unpredictable Order Arrivals	Predictable Order Arrivals
Customized Delivery	Standard Delivery
Change Delivery Requirements	No Changes in Delivery Requirements
Manual Processing	Electronic Processing (EDI)
Large Amounts of Presales Support (Marketing, Technical, and Sales Resources)	Little to No Presales Support (Standard Pricing and Ordering)
Large Amounts of Postsales Support (Installation, Training, Warranty, Field Service)	No Postsales Support
Require Company to Hold Inventory	Replenish as Produced
Pay Slowly (High Accounts Receivable)	Pay on Time

of having a low cost-to-serve customer comes when the customer itself realizes that its behavior reduces costs to its supplier, and demands low prices (high discounts from list price) in exchange.

Wal-Mart, in particular, has from its inception leveraged its unique purchasing characteristics to negotiate exceptionally favorable terms with suppliers. Sam Walton, Wal-Mart's founder and long-time CEO, would even go to giant multinational companies like Procter & Gamble and AT&T with something like the following (though hypothetical) pitch:

We like your products and want to carry them in our store. But we don't want a lot of variety; we want a large package and a small package (or a white phone and a gray phone) for each category we carry. Don't send us a lot of marketing people, we've already made up our mind which of your products we want to carry. And we don't want to have to place orders through your sales force. We will connect you to our point-of-sale terminals in all our stores. Your job is to monitor the rate of sales, and keep our distribution centers adequately replenished based on consumer takeaway. Don't bother us with special deals and promotions. We want standard products, continually replenished, at everyday low prices.

Hearing this, marketing executives thought they had just gone to heaven. They had never met a customer that would be so easy to support and serve. They were certainly prepared to offer an attractive discount to Mr. Walton for such an arrangement. But they never got to offer a discount, since Mr. Walton had already decided what he was prepared to pay, and this was far less than the marketing executives had ever contemplated offering. The executives objected, indicated their sincere interest in working with an enterprising growing retailer but were not prepared to offer goods at such a substantial discount, where their company might lose money. Mr. Walton would respond:

The price I am prepared to pay is fair based on your costs of serving me. The high gross margins you are accustomed to earning on your products are necessary to pay for all the marketing, technical, selling, and administrative resources required by your normal customers. But you are not going to need these resources for me, the way I am prepared to work with you. I don't want to pay for resources I don't use. Collect revenues from your other customers. They should be the ones to pay for those resources since they're using those resources.

In the end, as the suppliers conducted their own ABC analyses, they could see the truth of this claim.

Managing High and Low Cost-to-Serve Customers

Companies can view their customers through the lens of a simple 2×2 diagram (see *Exhibit 10-5*). The vertical axis shows the net margin earned from sales to the customer. The net margin equals net price, after all sales discounts and allowances, less manufacturing cost (as measured by an ABC product-costing model). The horizontal axis shows the cost of serving the customer, including order-related costs plus the specific customer-sustaining marketing, technical, selling, and administrative expenses, as measured by an ABC customer-costing model of these expenses.

This diagram shows that companies can enjoy profitable customers in different ways. A customer such as Wal-Mart would be at the lower left-hand corner of the curve: demanding low prices, so net margins will be low, but also working with its suppliers so that the cost-to-serve is also low. High cost-to-serve (hidden cost) customers, exhibiting characteristics in the left-hand column of Exhibit 10-4, can also be profitable (they would be located in the upper right-hand corner of Exhibit 10-5), if the net margins earned on sales to these customers more than compensate the company for the cost of all the resources deployed for them. In effect, Exhibit 10-5 is an alternative to Porter's admonition not to attempt to

Exhibit 10-5 Customer Profitability

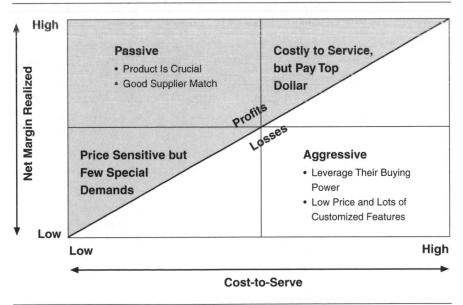

Source: Adapted from B. P. Shapiro, V. K. Rangan, R. T. Moriarty, and E. B. Ross, "Manage Customers for Profits (Not Just Sales)," Harvard Business Review (September–October 1987), 104. Reprinted by permission of Harvard Business Review.

be simultaneous low-cost and differentiated. Perhaps, an ABC system enables a company to offer low-cost service to Wal-Mart-type customers, and special services to those customers that value unique functionality, features, and extensive customer service. The trick has always been to be profitable with both types. A customer-based ABC model gives companies a new capability to offer and price out differentiated services to customers, based on their individual needs and preferences, in order to be both a low-cost and a differentiated supplier—and to make money with both types of service. Increasingly, companies are going to menu-based pricing where the cost to the customer is determined not only by the volume and mix of products purchased but also by the method of delivering to and serving the customer. Menu-based pricing is based on the cost-to-serve calculated by the company's activity-based costing model.[9]

Occasionally, a company may count its blessings by observing that several of its customers are in the upper left-hand quadrant: high margins and low cost-to-serve. These customers should be cherished and protected. They could be vulnerable to competitive inroads, so managers should be prepared to offer modest discounts and incentives, or special services, to retain the loyalty of these hidden profit customers if a competitor threatens.

The most challenging set of customers is found in the lower right-hand corner: low margins and high cost-to-serve. This is where Kanthal found Customers #199 and #200, and GE Appliance Division. As we discussed, Kanthal and other companies can use the bill of activities in the net margin and cost-to-serve ABC calculations to modify relationships with such customers and move them in a northwest direction, toward breakeven and profitability. For example, the bill of activities may reveal that some of the company's internal processes are quite costly and inefficient, which leads to high manufacturing costs or high costs-to-serve. The first action should be to improve the performance of those critical processes; i.e., reduce the cost of activities associated with serving these customers. The bill of activities may also show that high cost-to-serve is caused by customer-ordering patterns: unpredictability, changes, excessive frequency, customized products, nonstandard logistics and delivery requirements, large demands on technical and sales personnel. The company can share this information with the customer, indicate the costs associated with such actions and encourage the customer to work with the company in a less costly manner; that is, reduce the number of activities demanded by the customer. Both improvement of internal activities and business processes and better coordination between the company and its customers will lower the cost-to-serve, thereby moving the company in a westerly direction on Exhibit 10-5.

Alternatively, if the customer is not able or willing to shift its buying and delivery patterns to lower operating costs, the company can augment its revenues, for example, by modifying its pricing arrangements: lowering the discounts it is prepared to grant, and pricing for special services and features. A McKinsey study revealed that managers are often unaware about the actual net price they receive from customers.[10] For example, *Exhibit 10-6* shows the price waterfall from list price to actual realized price. Every element of discounts and allowances constitutes a leakage of revenue to the customer. Yet typically, these items are reported in separate account codes and not accumulated together by customer and order. As a result, many of these discounts and allowances are not linked to actual performance by the customer, or to the economics of the relationship with the customer.

The study also revealed that the same or similar items sell for a wide variety of prices to different customers and different industry groups. Price bands (the difference between the highest and lowest priced transactions) of 60–70% with some in excess of 200% were reported. Perhaps these price variations could be justified by differences in the cost to serve the different customers in the different industries. But, more likely, the

Exhibit 10-6 In the Pocket Price Waterfall, Each Element Represents a Revenue Leak

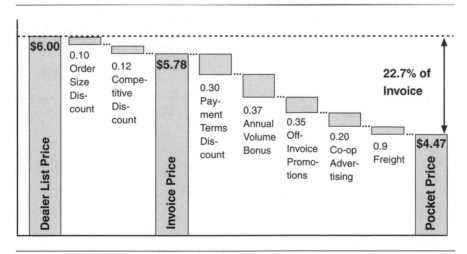

Source: Michael V. Marn and Robert L. Rosiello, "Managing Price, Gaining Profit," Harvard Business Review (September–October 1992), 86. Reprinted by permission of Harvard Business Review.

variation in prices and discounts, as in the price waterfall, is random, caused by the bargaining power or skill of the customer, not by the economics of serving the different customers.[11] ABM can help the company identify when price variations are unrelated to the economics of its relation with the customer.

As a specific example of an unmanaged discount policy, one supplier of plastics did an analysis of the total ABC cost-to-serve (including manufacturing costs) versus discounts from list prices for several customers in the appliance industry (see *Exhibit 10-7*). The results showed that discounts were unrelated to the cost-to-serve. Several customers, in the lower right-hand section of Exhibit 10-7—some large though others quite small—received high discounts although they were high also cost-to-serve. Some companies, however, received low discounts although they were relatively low cost-to-serve. This evidence indicates that without an ABC model of cost-to-serve, many companies' pricing and discounting policies

Exhibit 10-7 Discounting Appears to Be a Function of Factors Other Than Cost-to-Serve

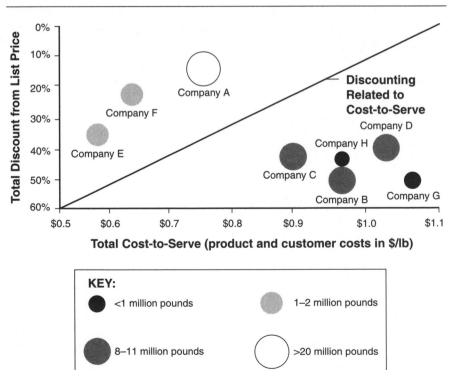

will likely be unrelated to the cost of supplying individual customers.[12] Marketing managers can use the information about the economics of the customer relationships, as revealed in Exhibits 10-5 or 10-7, to have fact-based discussions with customers. They can link discounts to specific customer actions that lower the company's cost-to-serve.

As managers reprice and manage discounts better on their product and service offerings, as Kanthal did with Customer #200, they move unprofitable customers northward on Exhibit 10-5. Margins increase to compensate the company for high cost-to-serve customers.

Cost-to-Serve for Distribution and Retailing

Cost-to-serve pricing now occurs in the vendor to supermarket retailing supply chain. In 1995, Procter & Gamble announced a new price incentive intended to influence the trade to adopt more efficient practices in logistics and promotions. Wholesalers and retail distributors that partner with Procter & Gamble in eliminating inefficiencies in the distribution stream will pay lower prices on P&G products.

Primary features of the P&G initiatives are:

- Efficient ordering and billing: Customers will be able to automate all orders and billing using EDI, which will improve speed and accuracy, reducing the need for manual intervention.
- Efficient delivery: Retailers will be rewarded for picking up backhaul loads on schedule and for unloading P&G deliveries in two hours or less. P&G will also begin using its Chep pallet-pool system [pallets that it already is using for transport in the manufacturing process] for all its shipments except for a few paper items.
- Efficient promotion: P&G will streamline its offerings of display-ready unit loads from its current level of more than 400 options down to 100 choices that reflect the company's biggest brands and best-selling stockkeeping units.
- Comarketing: The company will build on its existing account-customized direct-mail marketing programs by offering a custom-published family magazine that can be configured and distributed to meet retailers' marketing objectives.
- Activity-based costing: The company makes intensive use of ABC techniques to identify the per case cost of inefficient industry practices, and the amounts that can be saved by improving those practices.

P&G stated:

> One of the real objectives was to reduce complexities that we had built into
> our own systems. We were averaging 27,000 manual interventions monthly
> in our order and invoice process, or 31% of orders. We have now reduced
> that in one year to 5,000 per month or less than 6% of orders
>
> Last year we were implementing something like 55 pricing changes per
> day with 100 brands. Those changes were in large part promotion-related.
> Multiply that by 17 different pricing brackets and the complexity was enor-
> mous.[13]

P&G expected that the total savings from these cost-cutting initiatives
could be as much as $50 million. According to an industry study, delivery
and receiving efficiencies represent more than $2.5 billion annually in
potential cost savings to the industry.[14]

Pillsbury, facing the same competitive environment as P&G, is also using
its ABC model to restructure relationships with customers.[15] Pillsbury is
using the information, from its ABC customer and store-level profit and
loss statements to develop menu-based pricing schemes. Pillsbury charges
more for special services that some customers want but others do not. It
has developed a base level of service that all customers receive, plus service-
based pricing for specially desired initiatives like category management,
modular pallets for promotions, direct store delivery, cross-docking, one-
way pallets, and other delivery options that save the retailer money. Or,
rather than charging extra for these services, the company negotiates with
the retailer to pass on the savings to consumers by lowering the prices
on Pillsbury products and by special merchandising and promotion of
our products. A senior VP of sales noted: "To make these partnerships
work, both companies will require activity-based cost systems to keep
track of cost incurrence and cost savings. It won't work if retailers continue
to peanut-butter[16] their operating expenses across all suppliers."

Managing Unprofitable Customers

Pricing initiatives and process improvements, either by the company or
jointly with its customers, are often successful in transforming customers
from unprofitable to profitable, moving them out of the lower right-hand
quadrant of Exhibit 10-5. What about the unprofitable customers that
remain in that quadrant? Should the company consider firing them?

Not yet!

Some of the currently unprofitable customers in the lower right-hand quadrant of Exhibit 10-5 may be relatively new to the company. Considerable expense (now accurately traced to these new customers) may have been incurred to attract them as customers. Furthermore, the customers may be testing the new supplier by only giving it a small portion of their total business, and that in relatively demanding applications, so that they can assess how well the new supplier can perform. The company (the new supplier) hopes to grow these customers into long-term profitable relationships. For these new customers, the initial losses revealed by the cost-to-serve ABC model can be considered part of the investment in obtaining new customers. This initial investment will, the company hopes, be repaid in higher volume and more profitable mix of business in subsequent years.[17] So companies will certainly not want to fire new but unprofitable customers; they will want to track them to ensure that such customers migrate in a northwesterly direction on Exhibit 10-5 in subsequent periods, reaching profitability through some combination of higher volumes, higher margins, and lower costs-to-serve.

Other unprofitable customers in the lower right-hand quadrant of Exhibit 10-5 may give the company benefits that cannot be quantified by the ABC cost-to-serve model. For example, some companies are prestigious to have as customers because they are known to be demanding of their suppliers for quality and performance. In effect, as an ongoing supplier to such customers, the company has gained benefits that it can leverage with other customers. The losses reported on Exhibit 10-5 by the ABC model then become considered an element in advertising or promotion costs. They represent the price of establishing the company's reputation and credibility. As in any discretionary expense, of course, such losses should be monitored and managed. It would be even more desirable to establish reputation and credibility at a negative cost, by finding ways to transform the currently unprofitable relationship with the prestigious customer into a profitable one.

Another difficult-to-quantify benefit from certain customers is the opportunity for learning. Japanese companies, like Toyota, Nissan, and Honda, that established manufacturing presence in the United States have demanded performance from U.S.-based suppliers that is comparable to what they enjoy from their Japanese-owned suppliers. Many U.S. suppliers found it quite costly to meet the stringent requirements for quality, delivery times, and flexibility from their new Japanese customers. If they were to understand the full costs they are incurring to provide such stringent performance, they likely would find these customers to be unprofitable, especially initially. Some of these losses could be rationalized as using currently excess capacity that would otherwise go unused. A more compelling justification, however, is that the working relationships with such customers also provide a learning opportunity; demanding customers are prepared to work with their new suppliers and show them how new management processes, equipment, and technology will enable them to satisfy customer demands without incurring excessive cost penalties. Thus, the initial losses incurred in satisfying these customers can be viewed as the cost of education about new manufacturing and logistics processes that could be beneficially deployed to all of its customers in the future.

Firing Customers

Let us now summarize the customer component of strategic ABM. We have analyzed the net margins and cost-to-serve of all our customers. We celebrate having profitable customers, both low cost-to-serve and those high cost-to-serve. We have established protective measures in case competitors attempt to win business from our most profitable customers. For many of those initially found to be unprofitable, we have transformed them to profitable customers by improving internal processes, negotiating improved ordering and delivery relationships, reducing discounts if not accompanied by reduced cost-to-serve, and establishing menu-based pricing for special services and features. Other unprofitable customers were recently acquired. We will watch them for profitability progress in subsequent periods. Still others were important for our strategy either because they give us prestige by association, or because they help us learn to improve our internal processes.

Suppose, however, that a customer falls into none of these categories. Such a customer is not profitable, resists all our attempts to transform the unprofitable relationship into a profitable one, is not a new customer, and the only thing we have learned from 10–15 years of working with this customer is that we do not want another 10–15 years just like the past. We have now reached the point of considering firing the customer. But we still might not have to take such a drastic action. We can, perhaps, let the customer fire itself, by refusing to grant discounts and reducing or eliminating marketing and technical support.

What can the company do with its technical and marketing people formerly deployed for incorrigibly unprofitable customers? In the short run, these people are still on the payroll so their expenses still accrue to the company. The answer is obvious once one returns to the insights found in Exhibit 10-5. Why not analyze the characteristics of the most profitable customers, the ones in the upper left-hand quadrant: high margins and low cost-to-serve. Our company likely has excellent and valued products and services for these customers. By understanding the characteristics of such customers—industry, location, size, strategy—we may be able to identify companies with similar characteristics that are not existing customers. Our marketing, selling, and technical resources can be deployed in an attempt to win their business and loyalty. If successful, we may capture a high, lifetime profitability customer from a competitor that, lacking an ABC model of its own, may not realize how profitable such a customer might be. Even better, if the competitor wishes to retaliate by capturing one of our existing customers, we have an excellent set of disgruntled customers—the ones that remain in the lower right-hand quadrant, currently unserved and undiscounted—that would be delighted to switch to a new supplier.

Summary

Managers often ask: "Can I benefit from strategic ABM when my company is the only one attempting to manage based on accurate customer profitability information? How can I reconfigure pricing and service relationships when others in the industry are not guided by the same analytic insights?" The answer, of course, is that when we have even a rough economic map of our customer profitability, and our competitors don't, we have enormous opportunities for profit improvement. We have shown, in this chapter, the wide variety of actions managers can take to transform unprofitable customers into profitable ones through initiatives on pricing, technology, ordering, and distribution.

A company with a Stage III ABC system geared to customer profitability can target discounts and value-added services based on actual cost-to-serve. These actions should provide such companies with significant competitive advantages, especially when their competitors continue to follow the signals from their Stage II cost systems, which makes them vulnerable to the targeted actions taken by informed companies.

11

Strategic Activity-Based Management: Supplier Relationships and Product Development

In this chapter we extend strategic ABM back in the value chain, to suppliers and to product designers and developers. Chapter 9 dealt with decisions about internal manufacturing and operating processes that are at the center of a company's value chain. Chapter 10 moved forward in the value chain, describing actions that improve the profitability of customer relationships. Here we consider two additional categories of decisions in strategic ABM: managing supplier relationships to lower the costs of acquiring purchased materials, and informing product design and development decisions to lower the costs of manufacturing new products before they reach the production stage. These kinds of actions reduce costs *prior* to the company initiating its own conversion, selling, and distribution processes.

When applied to supplier relationships, strategic ABM helps companies select and evaluate suppliers based on total cost, not just on purchase price alone. Perhaps the biggest opportunity for cost reduction, however, arises when products are first designed. Most operational and strategic ABM actions work to reduce the costs and improve the profitability of existing products, customers, and supplier relationships. The potential for cost reduction for new products may be even more dramatic. As noted in Chapter 1, 80% or more of manufacturing costs are determined during the product design and development stages.[1] The challenge is to provide product designers excellent predictive cost information at a time when they have the greatest opportunity to influence costs.

Stage II cost systems, as we have discussed, focus on the costs of direct materials, direct labor, and machine-processing time. Consequently, with information from a traditional costing system, designers can make decisions that ignore the costs of using unique versus common parts, new versus existing vendors, and simple versus complex production processes. Stage II systems also overestimate the cost of using any driver that has been used to allocate overhead costs to products. Such distortions lead designers to overinvest in reducing new products' consumption of direct labor, machine hours, or any other cost allocation base. Many companies now use their Stage III ABC systems primarily to provide better information to product engineers and designers to help lower the total manufacturing costs of new products.

We start by exploring the role for ABC in managing supplier relationships, and then move to the even more important role for ABC, to inform decisions made by product designers and product development engineers.

Supplier Relationships

Historically, relationships with suppliers have been conducted in an arm's-length adversarial mode. Purchasing managers were told to obtain the lowest possible price. For example, the major U.S. automobile companies would not enter into long-term relationships with their suppliers. Every six months, they would put their steel demand out for bid and all the steel companies would compete to win the business by offering the lowest price for the next six-month period.

This continual spot-market contracting based on price was entirely consistent with a traditional standard costing view of the world. Managers and industrial engineers established standards for materials prices and materials usage. Production managers and workers were held accountable for meeting the quantity or usage standards and purchasing managers were held accountable for meeting or improving upon the price standards. The performance of purchasing managers was evaluated by *purchase price variances* that were unfavorable if the actual price exceeded the standard price, and favorable if the actual price was less than the standard price. Purchasing managers soon figured out how to reduce the risk of unfavorable variances—by purchasing:

- In bulk quantities, earning volume discounts;
- From marginal suppliers whose quality, reliability, and delivery performance were less than outstanding;
- From distant domestic suppliers, especially if freight costs were not traced to individual shipments, that offered slightly lower prices;

- From suppliers in low-wage countries;
- From suppliers with low overhead because of their underinvestment in technology and systems; and
- From suppliers with limited engineering and technical resources.

Such actions could indeed lower purchase prices, the metric used to evaluate performance, but lead to much higher costs for the procurement activities listed in *Exhibit 11-1*.

The cost of all these activities can be appropriately identified in a Stage III ABC system. In Stage II systems, however, the cost of resources performing these activities are buried in large overhead pools and allocated to products using unit-level drivers. Consequently, companies with Stage II systems cannot distinguish between suppliers and components that create a high demand for internal procurement activities and those that make minimal demands on the organization's procurement resources.

Again, leading Japanese companies surprised Western companies with a paradigm shift in supplier relationships. Japanese automotive, electronics, computer, and optical firms (and many others) chose to work with many fewer suppliers, established long-term relationships with suppliers—even to the extent of equity investments in key suppliers—and engaged suppliers in relationships directed at lowering the company's total cost of acquiring materials. These practices led to the just-in-time purchasing where suppliers delivered small batches of items directly to the company's production process just before they were needed.

Exhibit 11-1 Procurement Activities

Receive materials
Inspect materials
Return materials
Move materials
Store materials
Scrap obsolete materials
Scrap and rework products because of (undetected) defective incoming materials
Order materials
Delay production because of late deliveries
Expedite materials to avoid shutdowns because of late-arriving materials
Design, engineer, and determine materials specifications (using internal engineering resources, not suppliers' engineers)
Pay for materials

In the 1970s and 1980s, Western companies built elaborate, automated warehouses to store their incoming raw materials. One midwest U.S. company proudly took a visiting Japanese management and engineering group on a tour of its newly constructed automated warehouse. The warehouse used many robots and extensive computer technology to place items into inventory, maintain accurate inventory records, and pick the inventory when needed by the nearby factory. The visitors were very impressed with this technological accomplishment but, when questioned about their reactions, overcame their normal reticence to say, "Why did you build a palace to house waste?" To the Japanese, acquiring large amounts of inventory well in advance of need, was wasteful.

In contrast, a first-time visitor to a Toyota assembly plant watched in amazement as a supplier's truck pulled up to the factory but was denied entry by the automated gate. The driver had not lost his entry card. Quite the opposite. The electronic reader at the gate had recognized the driver and his load. The plant's computer, monitoring the flow of production in the plant, however, knew that the production process was not ready for this load of material. The driver had showed up too early and the plant had no space to store incoming materials. The driver waited until the relevant production processes were ready for the materials. Then the gate opened, the driver drove onto the plant floor, and delivered the materials directly to the workstations where they were immediately used.

Many Western companies initially misunderstood JIT. They thought JIT meant that suppliers held large quantities of inventory until the company was ready to use it; the large inventory ensured that stockouts did not occur. This, however, only shifted cost from the assembler to the supplier, but did not lower the total cost of operating the supply system. Japanese JIT linked suppliers' processes with those of the assemblers so that suppliers could produce and deliver the desired goods directly to the manufacturing process when needed, without the supplier holding finished goods inventory or the assembler holding raw materials inventory. Such practices require, of course, near-zero defect production. Assemblers do not inspect materials before they enter their production processes and suppliers have little leeway to inspect and rework defective items before shipping them to the assembler.

Beyond the direct linkage of production processes between them and their suppliers, companies are now looking to suppliers to assist in the design and engineering of the incoming materials. Japanese target costing and value engineering require high-intensity involvement of supplier engineering resources to develop ways to expand the functionality, raise the quality, and lower the cost of materials and components.[2] When companies can look to their suppliers to provide technological expertise and assistance, they not only improve their processes and the quality of their products, they can lower their own internal cost of engineering.

Choosing Low-Cost, Not Low-Price, Suppliers

All these developments explain why suppliers cannot be chosen solely on the basis of low price and why purchasing managers cannot be evaluated by their ability to avoid unfavorable purchase price variances. The best suppliers are those that can deliver at the lowest total cost, not the lowest price. Is purchase price still important? Of course, but purchase price is only one component of the total cost of acquiring materials. The total cost of acquiring materials, referred to by many companies as the *total cost of ownership,* includes purchase price plus the cost of all the procurement-related activities listed earlier. For example, one study revealed that total ownership costs can be many times higher than the purchase price (see *Exhibit 11-2a* and *Exhibit 11-2b*). An "ideal supplier" enables a company to avoid many of these costs by delivering items:

- using electronic data interchange
- with no defects
- requiring no inspection
- just-in-time
- directly to the manufacturing process
- using internal (supplier) engineering resources
- with no invoice
- using electronic funds transfer (EFT) payment

Some companies have gone even further by eliminating their purchasing function for certain items entirely. They have invited suppliers to place a member of their own staff at the factory site; that person is responsible for ordering and managing the flow of incoming materials (including any local storage) before releasing the materials to the production process as needed.

How can companies choose and evaluate suppliers based on low total cost, not low price? A traditional standard cost system will, at best, report net purchase price from a supplier. Only an activity-based cost system enables a company to understand the total costs of working with an individual supplier. Items purchased from an ideal supplier

Exhibit 11-2a Total Ownership Costs Compared to Purchase Price:
Integrated Circuits

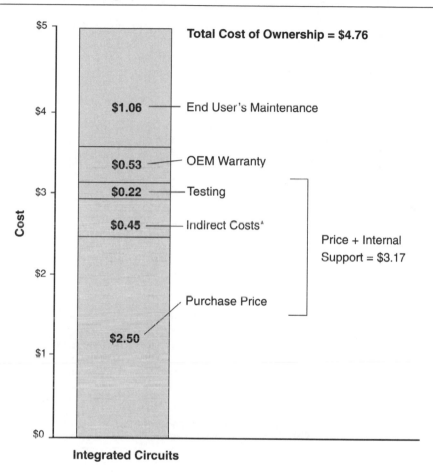

Total Cost of Ownership = $4.76

$1.06 —— End User's Maintenance

$0.53 —— OEM Warranty

$0.22 —— Testing

$0.45 —— Indirect Costs*

Price + Internal Support = $3.17

Purchase Price

$2.50

Integrated Circuits

Source: Data from Exhibit 1 of C. D. Ittner and L. P. Carr, "Measuring the Cost of Ownership,"
Journal of Cost Management *(Fall 1992), 42–51.*
*Indirect includes cost of Inspection, Warehousing, Insurance, Handling, Transportation, and
Purchasing activities.

may have a somewhat higher purchase price but will be assigned no other purchasing costs. Conversely, a low-price supplier that cannot meet any of the requirements described above will have many other costs assigned to its items. The activity-based costs of supplier-related activities enables a company to have fact-based discussions on how it wishes to work with suppliers and how cost savings can be shared between supplier and customer.[3]

Exhibit 11-2b Total Ownership Costs Compared to Purchase Price:
Connectors

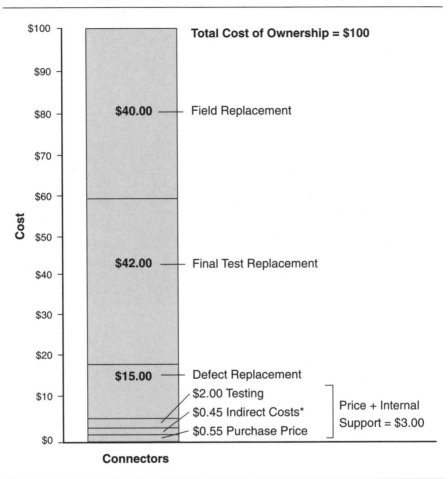

Source: Data from Exhibit 1 of C. D. Ittner and L. P. Carr, "Measuring the Cost of Ownership,"
Journal of Cost Management *(Fall 1992), 42–51.*
*Indirect includes cost of Inspection, Warehousing, Insurance, Handling, Transportation, and
Purchasing activities.

Chrysler has worked with its suppliers to develop ABC models of the
supply chain relationships so both can learn how their product-design
decisions affect the manufacturing costs of the other party. The understanding enables both parties to make better decisions to reduce total
manufacturing costs throughout the supply chain.[4] Other companies, such
as Northrup, Texas Instruments, McDonnell Douglas, Black & Decker,

and Digital Equipment, have developed elaborate supplier-rating systems that explicitly incorporate the total cost of ownership.[5] The cost of ownership information allows strategic partnerships to be developed between buyers and their suppliers. The relationships are no longer evaluated by traditional performance measures like purchase price variances; they reflect, in addition to purchase price, costs that measure delivery, quality, flexibility, and service performance.

Vendor-Sustaining Costs

We can now link the ABC cost hierarchy (see discussion in Chapter 6) to the costing of supplier relationships. Other than the purchase price itself, only a very limited number of purchasing costs are unit-related. Some costs, such as those associated with ordering, receiving, inspecting, moving, and paying for materials, are batch-related. Other costs are product sustaining, the costs of designing and maintaining specifications on individual materials and components.[6] And the supplier perspective gives us a new category since some costs are *vendor-sustaining*. These are the costs associated with a given vendor that are independent of the quantity and variety of items ordered. Such costs include ongoing discussions between the parties about the company's product plans, delivery requirements, and production plans; maintaining files on vendor characteristics and performance; and periodic evaluations of vendor performance. Companies have discovered that, because of vendor-sustaining costs, they may have too many vendors. They are now attempting to shrink the number so they can work more effectively and more efficiently with fewer vendors.

For example, the Pillsbury company had developed an extremely complex system of vendors and sourcing arrangements for its more than $500 million of raw materials purchases. The system encompassed:

- More than 1,200 different materials specifications (recently reduced from nearly 2,000);
- 260 different vendors (recently reduced from more than 400);
- Complex recipes and ingredient specifications;
- Arm's-length, price-sensitive relationships with vendors; and
- Virtually no technology or information integration with vendors.

The company believed that by shrinking its vendor base even further, and leveraging its relationships with the remaining vendors, it could reduce its purchasing costs by 8% and accomplish significant reductions in working capital as well.[7] Furthermore, streamlining supplier relationships would benefit consumers, by permitting more on-shelf availability of fresher goods.

A close company-vendor relationship may also facilitate the development of simultaneous engineering techniques where a company and its vendors work on their respective portions of product design at the same time. Simultaneous engineering makes any design problems relating to vendor-supplied components visible much earlier in the design process. This enables the company and its vendor to make more fundamental changes to the product's design to correct the problem. Activity-based cost models of supplier relationships facilitate the forging of long-term relationships with fewer and more competent suppliers so that costs can be lowered and quality and responsiveness increased throughout the supply chain.

Product Design and Engineering

We have already noted the great leverage obtained from influencing manufacturing costs during the product design and development stages. When product designers and engineers had only the distorted cost signals from Stage II cost systems, they often made decisions that led to unexpectedly high indirect and support costs.

For example, electronic instrument companies, like Hewlett-Packard and Tektronix, found themselves in the mid-1980s drowning in part numbers. Every time a new instrument was designed, the engineers started with a new component list. Cost savings from using standard parts, already ordered in high volumes for existing products, were invisible to product designers. Once these companies built activity-based cost systems, they could see the extremely high costs associated with ordering and maintaining excessive numbers of different components.[8]

Financial managers at a food processing company, one of the leading producers of canned soups, wondered why their operating margins were significantly below those of the most efficient companies in the industry. The search soon turned to excessive variety and SKU (stockkeeping unit) proliferation, a situation comparable to those of companies discussed in Chapter 9. As the managers probed more deeply, they discovered that similar overproliferation occurred in the components used in their products. As a specific example, the company had 17 different specifications for diced carrots. Each time a soup requiring diced carrots had been developed, the designer had chosen a different specification. The problems with such a policy could not be detected by any standard costing system since the raw materials cost would be about the same for any of the 17 specifications. But ignored were the high costs of ordering, processing, handling, storing, and just keeping track of 17 different sizes of diced carrots. Perhaps some soup mavens could distinguish among several of these varieties, but the company found it could immediately reduce the number of varieties to 7 without compromising the functionality or value of the finished product to consumers.

Product designers at a lamp supplier to one of the U.S. Big 3 auto manufacturers had designed different lamp assemblies for each individual model in a product line. Some assemblies required not only multiple colors to be brought together in an injection molding machine, but also the careful alignment of moving parts to produce a complex one-part, curved shape. Large quantities of quality assurance and process engineering resources were required each time a batch of lamps was produced. Production was slow and scrap levels for each complex part were high. Yet because of the large number of different lamp assemblies required, production runs were short so that the very high costs required with each setup only produced a relatively small number of finished units.[9] By the time the massive inefficiencies from scrapped parts and high setup costs were discovered, it was too late to redesign the lamps so that fewer different varieties could meet the needs of the many models, or to simplify the specifications so that parts could be produced with fewer engineering and quality assurance personnel and less scrap.

At Euclid Engineering, another automobile component manufacturer, the product designers had taken to heart the new approaches to design for manufacturability. They attempted to follow a recommendation to reduce the number of parts required to achieve a desired functionality. Unfortunately, their decisions were still informed by the company's Stage II direct-labor overhead allocation system. Consequently, they strove to design products with few parts and that required little to no direct labor. For example, they designed a new door panel that required only a single component. Euclid, however, had to purchase a $1 million piece of equipment to fabricate this component. After its initial ABC system had been developed, the company realized that it had overlooked a far less expensive solution. The same functionality could have been achieved by bolting together two simpler parts, both of which could have been fabricated on existing equipment. Direct labor may be expensive, but the quantity of direct labor required to bolt together two parts would have been far cheaper than the cost of the new equipment and managing the production of the one complex component. Without an ABC system, Euclid's product designers did not make the appropriate trade-offs between technology costs and potential labor savings.

As another example, consider the standard costs associated with seven different products shown in *Exhibit 11-3*. The cost pattern shown in Exhibit 11-3 is generally consistent with our ABC intuition. The cost of high-volume products decreases with the more accurate ABC system, while the cost of the low-volume products increases, which corresponds to the higher batch and product-sustaining expenses associated with low-volume production. In particular, for Product #3, the ABC support expenses are nearly 10 times higher than the company's traditional costing system had reported. This sharp increase occurred because almost all of this low-volume product's components were unique so that all the batch and product-sustaining expenses associated with them were attributed to the product.

The nonintuitive aspect of Exhibit 11-3 occurs with Product #7. It has the second-lowest volume product in the mix, and yet its cost decreases under ABC. Why? Upon closer examination, it turned out that this product used components that were already being produced in large batch sizes for the two high-volume products, #1 and #6. Product #7 had no unique components. Consequently, the only operation done specially for this

Exhibit 11-3   Activity-Based Costing Changes Product Profitability

PRODUCT NUMBER	ANNUAL VOLUME (units)	MANUFACTURING OVERHEAD PER UNIT			GROSS MARGIN	
		OLD SYSTEM	NEW SYSTEM	PERCENTAGE DIFFERENCE	OLD SYSTEM	NEW SYSTEM
1	43,562	$5.44	$ 4.76	−12.5%	41%	46%
2	500	6.15	12.86	+109.0	30	−24
3	53	7.30	77.64	+964.0	47	−258
4	2,079	8.88	19.76	+123.0	26	−32
5	5,670	7.58	15.17	+100.0	39	2
6	11,196	5.34	5.26	−1.5	41	41
7	423	5.92	4.39	−26.0	31	43

Source: Adapted from Robin Cooper and Robert S. Kaplan, "Measure Costs Right: Make the Right Decisions," Harvard Business Review (September–October 1988), 101. Reprinted by permission of Harvard Business Review.

Note: Students of this case have estimated the appropriate overhead charge on valve 3 (listed at $77.64 per unit) to be as low as $64 and as high as $84. Whatever the exact figure, the difference between this activity-based cost and the original estimate ($7.30 per unit) suggests that the current labor-based system is seriously flawed.

product was final assembly, and assembly operations are flexible and not highly sensitive to volume. In effect, Product #7 was like a blue pen with a black cap. Not many people ordered such a strange combination of components. But since blue pens and black pens were already being produced in high volumes, the additional effort required to put a black cap on a blue pen was minimal. The ABC system had revealed that customizing a product at the final stage of production, when all components have already been acquired or fabricated for high volume products, is quite inexpensive. In contrast, customizing a product with unique processes at all production stages is extremely expensive.

We sometimes describe this phenomenon as the McDonald's versus Wendy's approach. McDonald's offers a limited product line, fewer than a dozen different types of hamburgers. It achieves high economies by continually mass-producing its narrow product line. One of the authors loves Big Macs but is highly allergic to cheese. When he asks for a Big Mac without the cheese, he is initially told to find another supplier. If he persists, he is told to wait while they customize the production of his unique request. On good days, the wait is no more than 30 minutes.

Wendy's, in contrast, offers its customers 256 varieties of hamburgers. And its production process for this broad product line is so flexible that patrons can call in their order to a squawk box as they enter the parking lot and have the order waiting by the time they arrive at the pick up window. How is this accomplished? Wendy's produces the core ingredient for its product, the hamburger, on a continuous basis so that a "hot and juicy" hamburger is always ready for the next customer. Customization occurs with a choice of eight different toppings on the hamburger. When the production employee receives the next customer's order, he or she grabs a hamburger off the grill, slaps on up to eight different toppings, wraps up the finished product, and places it in the takeout bag. Since $2^8 = 256$, Wendy's can offer 256 different combinations to each of its basic products (single, double, and triple burgers) with minimal impact on its fundamental production process.

Traditional costing systems ignore the enormous cost savings and efficiencies of final-stage assembly processes and high-volume common components. The information from ABC systems, such as that shown in Exhibit 11-3, informs product designers of the potential benefits from efficient design, as well as the high costs associated with producing low-volume final products with components and production processes dedicated for that one application alone.

ABM for Product Design

Electronic assembly companies like Hewlett-Packard and Tektronix used their initial ABC models to enhance the design decisions of their product engineers. By understanding batch and product-sustaining costs, engineers could incorporate the economics of using existing parts, especially those ordered and used in high volumes, into their design decisions. As a simple example, suppose a resistance of 2.2K ohms was required in a circuit. Under the old system, the designer would specify that a resistor of that amount be used, even if it meant the use of a new component that would not be used in any other circuit for any other product. Alternatively, if 1K and 0.1K resistors were already being purchased and used in extremely large quantities, the same functionality could be obtained by stringing together two 1K resistors and two 0.1K resistors in series. The materials purchasing prices of the four components would likely be higher than the unit purchase price of one 2.2K resistor (even controlling for the high-volume orders for standard resistors versus the higher unit price for a low-volume order), and the placement costs for four components would undoubtedly be higher than for a single component. But these cost disadvantages may be more than offset by the high ordering, receiving, storage, and handling costs of the unique, low-volume component. The correct balance between satisfying functionality with four common parts versus one unique part cannot be determined a priori. Designers need a comprehensive cost model to balance the trade-offs involved.

The use of common versus unique parts often creates interesting trade-offs. For example, after mastering the ABC cost model of a farm equipment production process, a product engineer came up with an unusual proposal for a new product line with 12 different models. He suggested that by paying more for materials and machining, the company could reduce factory and corporate overhead.

His bosses were initially skeptical about how such a trade-off could be accomplished. The engineer said:

> Our normal practice is to select designs that accomplish product functionality with minimized materials and processing costs. This leads us to customizing our designs for each of the 12 different application segments.
>
> If I understand the message from the ABC model, we might do better to use one design across all 12 models as much as possible. For example, why not use one set of wheels, a set that satisfies the most demanding requirements for the 12 tractors? For the 11 less-demanding models, these wheels will be over-specified, providing more functionality than required,

and incurring higher costs for higher-grade materials and longer machining times. But even with higher materials and machining costs, we will be doing one production run rather than 12, ordering materials and parts for one set of wheels, not 12, and designing and maintaining only one set of specifications for wheels, not 12.

And if these savings in design, ordering, setup, and product maintenance are not high enough, think about our savings and those of our dealers in field inventory. With 12 different sets of wheels, our dealers will have to stock all 12. With my proposal, only one set of wheels has to be carried either by our field support organization or our dealers.

This product engineer was a good ABC student. He understood how ABC information can be used across the entire value chain—from product design and development, through purchasing and manufacturing, and out to logistics and distribution—to reduce the total costs of production and support, not just the obvious costs of direct materials, labor, and machining.

Choosing Activity Cost Drivers for Product Design: Accuracy versus Influencing Behavior

Using ABC to influence product design decisions requires a balance between two important objectives. The first is the normal ABC objective: provide relatively accurate information about the economics of a product's manufacturing and service costs. The second is to provide information that product engineers can understand and use in their design decisions.

For the second objective, consider a choice between two alternative activity cost drivers used in electronic printed circuit manufacture: insertion hours and number of insertions. If each insertion process of a certain type (say through-hole insertion, or surface mount) takes the same amount of time for all components, the two drivers will report identical product costs. But most engineers understand number of insertions a lot easier than insertion hours since number of insertions is identical to the number of components in their circuit design. Therefore, the driver *number of insertions* will send a clear message that every additional component adds manufacturing cost, whereas the driver *insertion hours* requires that engineers will likely have to convert back to number of insertions to know how they can reduce product costs.

Because the choice of an activity cost driver sends such a powerful message to product designers, managers must consider the behavior they could be encouraging. For example, a traditional standard cost system, focused on direct materials and direct labor cost, told engineers that they should reduce the cost of purchased materials. This led product designers to proliferate the number of components to find the most cost-effective solution for each decision, and for purchasing staff to search among a large number of vendors for the cheapest source. So, as we have already noted, companies found themselves supporting a huge number of different components and a very large vendor base.

To avoid this situation, some companies chose a new cost driver, *number of different part numbers*. This was a clear message to engineers to attempt to increase the use of common components. Further, if the cost per part number is assigned to individual products and models by dividing this component-sustaining expense by the volume of the part used, this driver encourages engineers to reduce part proliferation and to increase parts commonality.

Some electronics companies, in their early applications of ABC to product design, implemented extremely simple systems with only a few activity cost drivers. Their objective was to load most expenses on those drivers, such as number of part numbers, and thus pressure engineers to design products using already existing components and to avoid adding new components.[10] However, when product engineers developed new designs that had very low reported costs according to the simplistic ABC system, more experienced engineers could see that the new designs would actually be quite expensive. The outcome of these poor "low-cost" designs was either a loss of faith in the system on the part of the engineers and eventual demise of the system or a redesign of the system to make it more accurate. By adding additional drivers to their ABC systems, companies increased the accuracy of information and restored the engineers' faith in the system.

The explicit behavior modification approach may be called for when managers already know what the best near-term solution is, such as reduce part count or decrease the number of vendors. In this case, the managers are using the ABC system to reinforce decisions already taken, not to inform the decisions. Once the previous inefficient behavior driven by the inadequacies of the previous Stage II cost system has been mitigated, we advocate that managers opt for accuracy over their perceived need to influence engineers' and purchasing department's behavior in a particular way. The desire for accuracy, however, must still be balanced by having a system that enables engineers to understand the impact of their decisions on the required quantity of activity cost drivers.

Many firms resolve this trade-off by starting with a system that is sufficiently accurate that designers will not lose faith in it in the near future, but sufficiently simple that the product engineers can understand it immediately. As the engineers gain experience with the system and begin to understand its limitations, more activity cost drivers are added. This iterative design process continues until the system has reached sufficient sophistication that there are diminishing returns to accuracy from adding new drivers, and increasing risks that engineers will have problems using it.[11]

ABC and Target Costing

Early on, Japanese manufacturers noticed the powerful leverage of excellent product designs on manufacturing costs. Many Japanese companies use target costing to motivate product engineers to select designs that can be produced at low cost.[12] At the heart of target costing is a very simple syllogism:

1. Let the marketplace determine the selling price of the future product,
2. Subtract from this selling price the profit margin that you want to generate, and
3. This figure yields the target cost at which the product must be manufactured.

In target costing, the cost of a new product is no longer an *outcome of* the product design process; it becomes an *input into* the process. The multifunctional product design team has to design a product with the functionality and quality that the customer demands, and which can be manufactured at a target cost that enables the company to earn a desired profit. We provide a brief overview of target costing in the appendix to this chapter.

Japanese target-costing processes focus on savings in materials, labor, assembly, and machining costs, the unit-level cost drivers prominently featured in traditional Stage II cost systems. Therefore, target costing can function effectively even with Stage II cost systems, an observation consistent with Japanese companies being slow adopters of activity-based costing. But as the focus of target costing extends beyond direct manufacturing costs to include supplier, distribution, and customer relationships, the capabilities of a total or ABC cost model should enable an integration between ABC and target costing.

By integrating activity-based and target costing, designers can make trade offs between direct and indirect costs that are impossible with only target costing or with a combination of target and traditional costing.

With such integration, companies have their best chance to develop products that can be produced at low cost while still offering the functionality and quality that customers demand. The target-costing system enables product designers to reduce the direct unit-level costs by focusing attention on new products' material, labor, and assembly costs. At the same time, the designers manage indirect and support costs with an activity-based costing system that reports activity cost driver rates they can use to make cost-benefit trade-offs between indirect and direct costs. For example, to maintain a component in the firm's bill of material might cost $500 a year. Reducing component count by 30 components will, therefore, save $15,000 per year. This savings might allow unit costs to increase to enhance functionality while keeping total costs unchanged (so that target cost is still achieved) by obtaining offsetting savings in batch and product-sustaining expenses.

Some Western companies are already using their ABC model for target-costing purposes. For example, an electronics assembler of data communication devices incorporated its manufacturing ABC model into its target-costing process.[13] Initially it used the insights from the model for two target-costing purposes: selection of electronic components and packaging materials.

The ABC model replaced an obsolete direct labor-costing model. It provided product engineers with information on the cost of placing different types of components: manual insertion, through-hole insertion, and surface mount. The model revealed order of magnitude differences between these different placement technologies. Product engineers could now make economically informed decisions, using different types and combinations of components, that balanced the purchase price, the functionality, and the placement cost of alternative designs. And these decisions were being made when the products were being designed, when the opportunity to have a major impact on ultimate product cost was the greatest.

A similar method of analysis led to significant savings in packaging for products. Previously, each final product had a unique package. This led, inevitably, to the need to purchase, receive, and store a large number of different package types. The high costs and inefficiencies associated with the proliferation of containers had been invisible in the company's old system. The company discovered that by using the same package for many different final products, it could contract its vendor base, order packages in larger quantities to get reductions in purchase price, and greatly simplify its ordering, receiving, and storage processes for packaging materials.

Activity-based product design highlights the interplay between the cost assignment (strategic) and process (operational) views of ABC. The cost assignment view identifies products, current and future, that require aggressive cost reduction in their design stage. During the product design phase, process drivers, such as number and type of components, can be changed relatively easily. The process view identifies the drivers that have the most impact upon future activity costs. With ABC information, product designers can ensure that the products will consume fewer of the process drivers, thereby enabling products to be manufactured with low indirect and support costs.

In general, activity-based costing works very compatibly with target costing. The ABC system gives product designers and developers a model of manufacturing support costs that enables them to balance the functionality and quality of the final product with economics-based decisions about component selection and design characteristics.

Activity Analysis of Product Design and Development

One final application of activity-based analysis to product development occurs in the cost of the design and development process itself. We discussed, earlier in this chapter, Euclid Engineering's use of its initial ABC study to inform product engineers' design decisions on the trade-off between simple and complex components. Euclid's managers also discovered that the company was spending more in launching new products than on direct labor expenses to produce existing products. Product development and launch expenses were 10% of expenses, whereas direct labor costs were only 9%. Of course, in the previous direct labor cost system, all attention had been focused on reducing direct labor costs (hence the decision to design one very complex part that required no direct labor for assembly). Product development and launch costs were blended into the factory overhead rate applied to products based on direct labor cost. Now Euclid's managers realized that they had a major cost reduction opportunity by attacking the product launch cost directly.

They shared the data of high launch costs with the product designers, many of whom were industrial artists, and the product engineers, and solicited their suggestions about how they might all work together to reduce launch costs. Euclid's customers, the Big 3 automobile companies, had become increasingly concerned about their suppliers' high development costs and were less willing to reimburse them fully for these outlays. In the past, few employees working in the design and development process had seen the total costs associated with product launch.

Fortunately, a strong atmosphere of trust and cooperation existed between the product design/development people and Euclid management so that an innovative approach was soon forthcoming. Employees felt they could not attack the high development and launch costs unless they understood the underlying factors. First, the engineers designed a time card so they could record how much time each of them spent on different activities (see *Exhibit 11-4*) such as engineering models, customer requested changes, internally generated changes, and validation studies. Time spent on the expensive computer-aided design workstations was also recorded.

Not to be outdone, the studio designers developed a time card with 19 different activities, plus use of CAD terminals (see *Exhibit 11-5*). The designers and engineers felt that such detailed reports were required if they were to be able to influence the time and cost of the design phase.

Exhibit 11-4   Engineering Time Card: Product Development

Name _____ Social Security # _____ Week Ending _____

Project	Func	Mon	Tue	Wed	Thur	Fri	Sat	Total

Dept. _____

Function Code
Description

D = Unsold
      Development
E = Engineering
      Aids/Models
C = Customer
      Requested
V = Validation
P = PC Changes

Function Code
Suffix

2 = CAD-related
      activity

Source: Adapted from Robert S. Kaplan, "Euclid Engineering," Case 9-193-031 (Boston: Harvard Business School, 1992), 18. Reprinted by permission of Harvard Business School.

Exhibit 11-5 Design Department Time Card

Name _____   Social Security # _____   Week Ending _____

Description	Project	Func	Orig/ Chng	Area Code	Mon	Tue	Wed	Thurs	Fri	Sat	Total

Dept. _____

1 = Non-Cad Time
2 = CAD Time

A- Theme Molding
B- Engineering Clay Modeling
C- Prove-out Clay Model
D- Templating
E- Armature Prep
F- Layout
G- Communication
H- Mock-up Fabricator
I- Studio Show Prep
J- Casting/Lay-up
K- Modeling: Other (foam, cardboard)
L- Shipping & Handling
P- Programming NC
Q- Milling
S- Surfacing
T- Studio Eng-Sold
U- Studio Eng-Unsold
V- Studio Eng-Proactive Design
Z- Digitizing

1- CAD original intent
2- Manual original intent
3- CAD customer change
4- Manual customer change
5- CAD price change

Source: Adapted from Robert S. Kaplan, "Euclid Engineering," Case 9-193-031 (Boston: Harvard Business School, 1992), 19. Reprinted by permission of Harvard Business School.

The designers were now deciding on their own whether they needed to build expensive clay models for each new product development. Euclid's controller commented on the impact of this information:

> *The system helps all the people who must interface with a program to identify the cost and technical implications of a design decision well before the design becomes embedded into a technical drawing. This information provides better visibility for trade-offs in design decisions, and helps the product manager assign people to activities and to manage the individual activities. The launch teams now make trade-offs to lower total launch costs, such as by building prototypes without full tooling.*[14]

The new information on the cost of design activities also facilitated more meaningful dialogues with Euclid's customers. The more detailed breakdown of design and engineering activities enabled customers to see all the activities and associated costs that were being performed for them. They could now determine whether all the activities were really necessary, and often would request that some proposed activities not be done. The system also enabled Euclid to forecast the cost of any customer-proposed design changes. Previously Euclid would make the changes and then have a long arduous negotiation at the end of the project when it attempted to collect for the cost of these changes. Now, the engineers estimated the cost of implementing each customer-requested design change, and would not proceed with the change until the customer authorized the expenditure.

Euclid's experience is generalizable to many professional service organizations. Although the early applications of ABC have been in manufacturing environments with repetitive processes, the activity analysis at Euclid is an example of how activities can be tracked, measured, and costed even in environments where employees have considerable discretion in the allocation of their time and other resources. Even rough estimates of the cost of the elementary processes involved in a complete chain of delivering a service will provide insight and guidance about how to make the service more efficient and cost-effective for the customer. We turn, in the next chapter, to a more explicit treatment of the application of ABC to service environments.

Summary

Large opportunities for cost savings can come from upstream operations. By understanding the costs associated with ordering, receiving, inspecting, moving, storing, and paying for materials, companies can make better decisions in choosing the lowest total cost suppliers, not just the lowest price suppliers. An ABC model of the supplier relationship enables managers to work with their best vendors to search for ways to lower inventory levels and total supply chain costs, benefits that will avail both parties. The ABC model of the as-is supply chain cost provides the insights and justification for exploring such opportunities, and an ABC model constructed for the streamlined supply chain will identify the cost savings that can be shared across supplier and customer. The ABM actions from such supplier models will enable companies to lower their costs of acquiring and using purchased materials and services.

Moving upstream in time gives managers the best opportunities for cost reduction during product design and development. When design engineers have an accurate cost model, one that incorporates the cost of unique components, and of batch and product-sustaining activities, and when they work within a disciplined target costing process, they will be able to achieve desired functionality requirements at much lower total manufacturing costs. And understanding the cost of design and development activities enables the costs of these activities themselves to be managed and reduced.

Appendix: Target Costing

We describe contemporary target costing by decomposing the process into four major steps: market-driven costing, product-level target costing, component-level target costing, and chained target costing.[1]

Market-Driven Costing

The market-driven costing process starts by identifying the target selling price—the product's anticipated price when launched. This price must reflect the perceived value of the product in the eyes of the customer, the anticipated relative functionality and selling price of competitive offerings, and the firm's strategic objectives for the product.

Firms that undertake target costing typically have extensive market analysis procedures to identify what their customers want and how much they are willing to pay for it. Occasionally, however, a new product may not come from surveying potential customers. For example, the initial Xerox machine or Sony Walkman was not a product that customers were asking for. Once customers saw the implications of dry paper copying and how the Walkman could improve the quality of their commutes and exercise routines, however, the companies had extremely successful products. So there is a real skill to listening to the customer, but at the same time allowing for creativity in anticipating consumer preferences.

Managers, in setting the target market price, must also be cognizant of the prices of competitive products. If competitive products have higher functionality and quality, the target selling price will have to be lower than the competitors'. If the functionality and quality are higher, selling prices can either be equal to competitors' prices (thus increasing market share) or above these prices (thus increasing profits).

Finally, the firm's strategy for the future product influences its initial selling price. The firm might want to set a lower price to gain market share rapidly, or a higher price to increase overall long-term profitability and create an image of technical excellence.

After setting a target price, the market-driven costing process continues by establishing the target profit margin. For products that replace earlier generations, the margin will typically be the historical profit margins earned by the existing products. This historical margin is adjusted for two additional factors: any unusual costs at the front end (e.g., research and development) or back end (e.g., salvage or disposal) of the life cycle, plus revised profit objectives for the product line.

In the final step, managers calculate an allowable cost by subtracting the target profit margin from the target selling price. The allowable cost is the cost at which the product must be manufactured if it is to earn the target profit margin at the target selling price. The allowable cost is different from the target cost because the market-driven costing process has yet to take into account the capabilities of the firm and its suppliers. Therefore, there is no guarantee that the firm can design the product so that it can be manufactured at its allowable cost. The objective of the next process, product-level target costing, is to set target costs that are achievable.

Product-Level Target Costing

The product-level target-costing process starts with the current cost of the proposed product. This is the cost at which the firm could launch the new product today without undertaking any design changes or introducing any process improvements in existing manufacturing processes. The initial discrepancy between the current cost and the allowable cost gives the project team an estimate of the magnitude of the cost reduction opportunities it must identify to achieve the allowable cost.

The cost reduction objective is split into two portions, achievable and unachievable. The achievable portion, the target cost reduction objective, captures the level of cost reduction that the design teams believe they can achieve by expending considerable effort during the design process. Three engineering techniques typically play a critical role in achieving this objective: value engineering, quality function deployment, and design for manufacture and assembly. If product-level target costs are set properly, and the three engineering techniques effectively deployed, the target should be achieved about 80% of the time.

The unachievable portion of the cost reduction objective is called the strategic cost reduction challenge. Strategic cost reduction challenges identify how far the firm is from being competitive. The splitting of the cost reduction objective between the achievable and unachievable portions takes considerable skill. Setting product-level target costs that are too aggressive will result in unachievable target costs and eventual failure of the target-costing process. Setting too high a strategic cost reduction challenge leads to easily achieved target costs but a loss of competitive position.

The cardinal rule for target costing is that the target cost can never be violated. Applying the cardinal rule rigorously implies that even if engineers find a way to improve the functionality of a product, they can incorporate the improvement only if they can also identify how to offset any additional costs. The only exception occurs if the improved functionality allows the target selling price to be increased by an appropriate amount. If the design team cannot achieve the product-level target cost, the application of the cardinal rule requires the project be scrapped. It is the rigorous application of the cardinal rule that differentiates firms that truly apply target costing versus those that just perform the calculation of an allowable or target cost.

Component-Level Target Costing

In the component-level target-costing process, the design team establishes the target cost for every component in the future product. These component-level target costs establish the suppliers' selling prices. Therefore, via component-level target cost, target costing transmits the competitive pressure faced by the firm to its suppliers.

In the establishment of component-level target costs, products are typically broken down into their major functions. Major functions represent important performance capabilities that the product must have in order for it to perform its primary function. For example, the primary function of an automobile is to transport passengers from point A to point B. Some of the major functions such as the engine and transmission systems are required to achieve the basic objective; others such as the air conditioner and audio systems are required to augment the basic function. These major functions enable the passengers to be transported in comfort.

The chief engineer sets the target cost for the major functions. The engineer decides the theme of the product and that certain functions should be emphasized. For example, in order to give a car a sportier ride, the chief engineer might specify a larger high-performance engine. This decision means that a greater percentage of the total cost of the product will be spent on the engine than was spent in the previous generation.

However, under the cardinal rule, if the chief engineer spends more money on the engine, less can be spent on the other major functions. The sum of the costs of all the major functions has to be equal to the product-level target cost of the product (after taking into account the assembly and indirect manufacturing costs).

Once the major function target costs are established, the design team for each major function must find ways to design that function so that it can be produced at its target cost. The team breaks the major function down into its components and then distributes the major function-level target costs to component-level costs. Under the cardinal rule, the sum of the component-level target costs must equal that of the major function that contains them.

The component-level target costs establish the allowable selling prices of suppliers. The assembly companies do not want to squeeze the profits of their component suppliers to zero. They want to ensure that the entire supply chain is earning sufficient profits to remain viable while delivering low-cost products demanded by the customers. Therefore, they bring their major suppliers into the product design process as early as possible. The suppliers provide and receive inputs on how to reduce costs. The suppliers also estimate costs for each component. These estimates are imputed into the component-level target-costing process subject to the constraint of the cardinal rule.

Chained Target Costing

In today's highly competitive environments it is not enough to be the most efficient player; it is also necessary to be part of the most efficient supply chain. One of the major ways to achieve increased supply chain efficiency is through the use of chained target-costing systems. Target-costing systems are chained when the output of the buyer's target-costing system becomes the input to the supplier's target-costing system. The buyer's component-level target costs become the supplier's target selling prices. The supplier's target-costing system develops both product-level and component-level target costs, thus transmitting the buyer's competitive pressure to the supplier's product designers.

If the supplier's suppliers also use target costing, the chaining continues down the supply chain. Thus, chained target-costing systems can transmit the competitive pressure from the buyer down the supply chain, making the entire chain more efficient. The intense cost reduction pressure that is characteristic of target costing thus permeates the whole supply chain.

12

ABC in Service Industries

So far, we have articulated the development of activity-based costing and activity-based management in manufacturing settings. While ABC had its origins in manufacturing companies, many service organizations today are obtaining great benefits from this approach as well.

In practice, the actual construction of an ABC model is virtually identical for both types of companies. This should not be surprising since even in manufacturing firms, the ABC system focuses on the "service" component of the factory and company as a whole. In general, the ABC system in manufacturing companies retains the direct labor and direct materials elements of the company's Stage II manufacturing cost system.[1] The changes come when factory indirect and support expenses are analyzed. These expenses represent the cost of providing *services* to manufacturing operations; that is, ordering, scheduling, moving, setting up, designing, inspecting, training, and supporting—all service activities that enable products to be produced but that are not directly involved in actual production.

When we extend the ABC model outside the factory (see Chapters 10 and 11) to include the activities of marketing, sales, logistics, purchasing, and corporate staff, the service orientation of ABC becomes even more obvious. ABC, from its origins, has been service-oriented rather than production-oriented. Thus, its extension to organizations that provide only service does not involve any new principles.

Service companies have exactly the same managerial issues as manufacturing companies. They need activity-based costing to link the costs of the resources they supply to the revenues earned by the individual products and customers serviced by these resources. Only by understanding such linkage, and the interplay among pricing, features, customer usage, and process improvement can managers make good decisions about the customer segments it wishes to serve, the products it will offer to customers in those segments, the method of delivering the products and services to those customers, and, ultimately, the quantity and mix of resources it will supply to enable all this to happen. Because virtually all their operating expenses are fixed once resource supply has been committed, service organizations need the costing insights from ABC even more than manufacturing organizations.

Why then did ABC originate in manufacturing companies and not service organizations? One explanation is that manufacturing companies already had product costing systems to satisfy the inventory valuation requirements of financial reporting. Therefore, when those systems became disconnected with changes in products, customers, and business processes, managers could easily see the effects of making decisions with their distorted signals.

Most service companies, in contrast, had no statutory need to measure the costs of their products or customers.[2] They operated for decades without cost systems. They did not, of course, operate without financial systems. Service companies managed operations through budgetary control of responsibility centers. The companies were organized by functional departments, budgets were established for each department or responsibility center, and financial performance was measured and managed by comparing actual with budgeted results. In effect, service companies had their own version of operational control systems (see Chapter 3), though they didn't make much use of flexible budgeting since, as we discuss in further detail, almost all of a service company's costs come from resources committed in advance of use; that is, they are fixed costs in the short run. Thus, even though service companies were frequently as complex and diversified as manufacturing companies, managers knew neither the costs of the services they produced and delivered, nor the cost of serving their different types of customers.

For example, the manager of a supermarket may know how much is spent, by type of expenditure, at each retail store and at each warehouse. But the manager would not know the cost of receiving a case of canned vegetables from a supplier, storing it in a distribution center, transporting it to the retail outlet, and moving it to a shelf. Similarly, a bank president would know revenues and expenses by line item (interest revenue, fee income, retail bank expenses, data processing costs), but would not know the cost of various types of checking accounts or the costs to serve individual customers.

This lack of accurate information about products and customers was not a concern for many decades because most service companies operated in benign, noncompetitive markets. Many service companies have, until recently, been highly regulated. In Canada and Europe, railroads, airlines, and telecommunications were not even private companies; they were government-owned and -operated monopolies. In these noncompetitive environments, managers of service companies were not under great pressure to lower costs, improve the quality and efficiency of operations, introduce new products that made profits, or eliminate products and services that were incurring losses. Regulators set prices to cover the operating costs of inefficient companies. Laws prevented more efficient competitors from entering the markets in which regulated or government-owned service companies operated; and taxpayers subsidized any losses in government-operated companies.

Lacking strong competitive pressures, managers of service organizations had little demand for cost information about products, customers, and processes. Consequently, the financial systems in most service organizations were simple. They allowed managers to budget expenses by operating department, and to measure and monitor actual spending against these functional departmental budgets.

Changing Competitive Environment

During the last two decades of the twentieth century, however, the competitive environment for most service companies has become as challenging and demanding as for manufacturing firms. Since the 1970s the deregulation movement has completely changed the ground rules under which many service companies operate. Pricing, product mix, and geographic and competitive restrictions have been virtually eliminated in the financial services industry. Transportation companies can now enter and leave markets and determine the prices at which they offer services to customers. Telecommunications companies now compete aggressively on price, quality, and service. Health care reimbursement is shifting away from pure cost recovery schemes. Utility companies are crossing previously impermeable borders to compete across geographic regions. Even government monopolies such as the postal service are experiencing competition from private companies. For example, Federal Express and UPS offer overnight delivery of letters and packages; telecommunication companies allow documents to be sent via facsimile transmission; and the Internet and World Wide Web permit the transmission of mail, messages, and documents on international electronic networks. And the trend toward privatization that is now sweeping the world completely

changes the rules of the game for former government-operated companies. They must transform themselves into private, competitive entities.
Even local retail outlets, historically sheltered from national or global
pressures, are facing vigorous competition from new entrants—efficient
mass merchandisers of everything from food, toys, office supplies, and
home furnishings to pet supplies.

More than ever, managers of service companies require information to
improve the quality, timeliness, and efficiency of the activities they perform, and to understand accurately the cost and profitability of their
individual products, services, and customers.

Service Companies: A Complex Environment for Costing Products and Services

Service companies in general are ideal candidates for activity-based costing, even more than manufacturing companies. First, virtually all their
costs are indirect and appear to be fixed. Manufacturing companies could
at least trace important components (direct materials and direct labor) of
costs to individual products. Service companies have minimal to no direct
materials and much of their personnel provide indirect, not direct, support
to products and customers.[3] Probably because of their insulation from
strong competitive forces, most service companies did not deploy large
numbers of industrial engineers to study and standardize direct labor
operations for those employees who did provide direct service for products
and customers.[4] Consequently, service companies did not have a platform
for measurement of direct costs on which to erect systems for assigning
indirect costs to individual products and customers.

The large component of apparently fixed costs in service organizations
arises because, unlike manufacturing companies, they have virtually no
material costs, the prime source of short-term variable costs. Service companies must supply virtually all their resources in advance. The resources
provide the capacity to perform work for customers during each period.
Fluctuations in the demand by individual products and customers for the
activities performed during the period by these resources do not influence
short-term spending to supply the resources. In the proposal stage of an
ABC project, a bank executive asked why the bank needed to develop an
ABC system for assigning costs to products and customers. Shouldn't
decisions be based on marginal costs? The ABC consultant asked in return,
What do you think your marginal costs are for handling an extra transaction or an extra customer?

The answer, of course, is that the marginal cost (as conventionally defined—the increase in spending resulting from an incremental transaction or customer) is essentially zero. For example, a transaction at an ATM machine requires consumption of a small piece of paper to print the receipt, but no additional outlay. For a bank to add an additional customer may require a monthly statement to be mailed, involving the cost of the paper, an envelope, and a stamp, but little more. Carrying an extra passenger on an airplane requires an extra can of soda pop and bag of peanuts (for U.S. flights these days), and a very minor increase in fuel consumption, but nothing else. Treating one more patient in a hospital or health care facility may involve an incremental expenditure on pharmaceuticals and bandages. But for a telecommunications company, handling one more phone call from a customer, or one more data transfer, involves no incremental spending. Therefore, if service companies were to make decisions about products and customers based on short-term marginal costs, they would provide a full range of all products and services to all customers at prices that could range down to zero. But then, of course, the companies would get limited to no recovery of the costs of all the (fixed) resources that enabled the service to be delivered to the customer. Only by fully incorporating the capacity-based costing ideas articulated in Chapter 7 will service companies be able to measure and manage their cost structure, service offerings, and customer relationships.

For service companies, there is almost a complete separation between decisions to incur costs and the decisions by customers that generate revenues. Decisions to incur, or subtract, costs involve adding or contracting the supply of resources to provide service; for example:

- Adding a new city to an airline's route,
- Building another rail line or acquiring additional locomotives and freight cars by a railroad,
- Hiring additional physicians or adding operating room capacity for a hospital,
- Expanding the network for a telecommunications company, and
- Building additional branch or retail outlets for a bank or retailer.

Consumer decisions that generate revenues include:

- The size of monthly checking account balances,
- Length of long-distance phone calls placed,
- Number of passenger miles flown, and

• Number and type of health care procedures requested.

In manufacturing companies, the costs associated with meeting customer demands and the revenues associated with selling products to customers are linked by the direct costs of a product's materials and the direct labor and energy costs to produce it. Service companies have no such direct connection. All linkages between the costs of resources supplied and their use by individual products and customers must be inferred and estimated, a process identical to how ABC links indirect manufacturing resources to products. Also, a revenue-generating event—taking an airline flight, shipping a container by rail, obtaining medical treatment, completing a long-distance phone call, receiving a kilowatt of energy, and using a checking account for a month—makes demands on and requires the service output from many different organizational units in a service company.

Service companies are ideal for understanding why companies need different systems for operational control and for measuring the costs and profitability of products and customers (as discussed in Chapter 2). For short-term (daily, weekly, monthly) monitoring and control, service companies need an operational control system that provides feedback on expenses incurred in each of its organizational units, as well as other measures of performance such as quality and response times. Some service organizations have highly detailed systems for measuring expenses, line item by line item, in every one of thousands of different responsibility and cost centers. But knowing how much is being spent in such centers, by detailed type of expenditure, communicates nothing about how much it costs to process a single customer transaction that benefits from the resources provided in dozens of different organizational units.

For example, take the simple example of a telecommunications company responding to a customer request for a new connection. The process involves people from many different departments, including customer call desk, credit check, planning, dispatching, engineering, billing, and customer service. The cost of performing this basic service differs dramatically if the customer changes the order, complains about the outcome, fails the credit check, or wants additions to capacity. One cannot view this process from the perspective of cost control in responsibility centers. A Stage III activity-based cost system can measure the consumption of resources in diverse responsibility centers by individual products and customers, and by the activities and business processes that deliver the products to customers. Only the end-to-end process analysis from an ABC perspective reveals the cost of performing basic services for individual customers.

Demand for Product and Customer Costs by Service Companies

Why do service companies find it useful to understand the cost of activities, business processes, products, and customers? The demand for such cost information comes from three broad classes of managerial decisions:

- Managing products and customers,
- Configuring the customer service delivery chain, and
- Budgeting the organization's supply of resources.

We will discuss each of these applications in turn.

Managing Products and Customers

Service companies typically offer a highly diverse set of offerings. Retail banks have many different types of checking and savings accounts as well as many types of consumer and commercial loans; telecommunications companies offer many calling plans and provide local and long-distance service, plus voice, data, and video transmission capabilities; transportation companies offer service between a large number of origins and destinations (each of the enormous number of combinations can be viewed as a unique product); health care facilities obviously offer treatment for a wide variety of ailments and conditions; and retail establishments can stock tens of thousands of different items. Each product, with its unique characteristics, makes different demands on the organization's resources. Service companies must continually assess the economics of their product line variety, making decisions on pricing, quality, responsiveness, and introduction and discontinuance of individual products. The cost and profitability of individual products are vital to such decisions.

For example, a telecommunications company can offer point-to-point capacity either with a dedicated private circuit or by a secure ISDN line. The private circuit is expensive to install and maintain, requiring a dedicated sales and engineering force and specialized maintenance. An ISDN line could provide similar quality of service but at much lower cost since ISDN lines already exist in much of the network and are serviced and maintained by standard engineering and maintenance teams. By understanding the significant differences in total cost structure between private dedicated lines and shared ISDN lines, the company could price its services so that customers with high demand for point-to-point traffic could be satisfied by existing, and much lower-cost, ISDN capacity.

But beyond product-related decisions, service companies must focus on customer economics far more than manufacturing companies. Consider a manufacturing company producing a standard widget. It can calculate the cost of producing the widget without regard to how its customers use the widget; the manufacturing costs are "customer independent." Only the costs of marketing, selling, order handling, delivery, and service of the widget might be customer-specific. For service companies, in contrast, even the basic operating costs of a standard product are determined by customer behavior.

Take a standard product like a checking account. As we will see, it is relatively straightforward—using ABC methods—to calculate all the costs associated with such an account. And the revenues, including interest earned on monthly balances and service fees, are also simple to attribute to this product. The analysis will reveal whether such a product is profitable or unprofitable. Such a total or average look, however, will hide the enormous variation in profitability of this product across customers.

One customer may maintain a high cash balance in his checking account and make very few deposits or withdrawals. This customer generates high revenues and imposes few demands on the bank's resources. Another customer may manage her checking account balance very closely, keeping only the minimum amount on hand, and make many withdrawals and deposits. Her checking account may be highly unprofitable under current pricing arrangements. Service companies need to identify the differential profitability of individual customers, even those using standard products. Using the framework developed in earlier chapters, the service company can determine and control the *efficiency* of its internal activities, but it is the customer who almost completely determines the *quantity* of demands for the operating activities.

Alert readers will note another important limitation of the analysis. In addition to a standard checking account, the customer may have a savings account, a credit card, a mortgage, and a personal loan. Therefore, before taking drastic action with a customer with an unprofitable checking account, the managers should understand all the relationships between the bank and that customer, and act on the total relationship profitability, not just the profitability of a single product. On the commercial side, a bank may break even or lose money (after an appropriate risk-adjusted cost of capital is applied) on a corporate loan but since the loan may establish a relationship between the bank and the corporation, the bank may make enough profit on trust services, corporate money management, and merchant-banking services that the total relationship is highly profitable.[5] But a marginal borrower that uses no other commercial or merchant banking services is a prime candidate for repricing, aggressive marketing activities, or deletion (if all other attempts to generate a profitable relationship fail).

Other customers may appear unprofitable because they have been recently acquired. Many service companies invest considerable resources in marketing campaigns to attract new customers. Because of the high cost of acquiring new customers, and the time required to establish a broad and deep relationship (such as across multiple product offerings), new customers may seem unprofitable.[6] Service companies need to distinguish the economics of newly acquired customers from long-time customers.[7] Thus, in addition to recognizing cross-sectional variation of customer demands, they must also forecast the longitudinal variation of customer demands over time to obtain total life-cycle profitability. Activity-based cost systems will provide service companies with the fine detail required for intelligent management of customers, individually and over time.

Companies may find it difficult to target their offerings and modify the behavior at the individual customer level. Since many service companies have millions or tens of millions of customers, they must group customers into manageable market segments. Companies may have as few as three to five segments or, with sophisticated databases and consumer information, up to 100–200 segments. Rather than report and manage profitability at the individual customer level, service companies may prefer that their ABC systems calculate cost and profitability information at the segment level. As companies come to understand the characteristics and the preferences of these segments, they can decide which segments will be most profitable to target and retain, and which should be deemphasized. It may be impossible to serve all customer segments profitably. Companies, knowing their internal capabilities (or core competencies), can select the value propositions they wish to deliver to targeted segments that enable them to attract significant business from customers in these segments, and be highly profitable in all targeted segments. Unprofitable customers in untargeted segments are prime candidates to be "demarketed." The ABC system gives executives the information and confidence they need to follow a profitable segmentation strategy. As one bank CEO explained his motivation for developing an ABC system: "We were prepared to make bold, innovative decisions to enhance our profitability. But if you are going to be bold, you had better be sure your facts are correct."[8]

Configuring the Customer Service Delivery Chain

If service companies understand the preferences of customers in different segments, they can tailor their offerings and the method of delivery to satisfy the preferences. For example, one telecommunications company conducted a needs-based market segmentation study to identify the different demands and expectations of its more than 100,000 business customers. The project team did a survey on a representative sample of customers and grouped respondents into segments based on their similarity of scores among several factors, representing different service demands, and a number of independent attributes. Six segments emerged:

- Service-oriented performers
- Growth/cost-conscious
- High public contact
- Profit-focused
- Data trackers
- Status quo keepers

Details of the characteristics of businesses in these six segments appear in *Exhibit 12-1*.

The company realized, however, that the needs-based segment analysis provided only one important part of the economics of customer relationships. It also needed to understand its current costs of delivering products, services, and customer support if it were to develop efficient marketing and delivery channels to all its business segments. For this it turned to activity-based costing.

With the ABC information, the project team analyzed the attractiveness of the six business segments, and of the opportunity to reengineer business processes to improve performance on those processes valued by each segment. Using this analysis, the project team selected three of the six segments to be targeted for aggressive business development. For each targeted segment, the project team identified the value proposition—the products, services, relationship, and delivery mechanisms—that it would offer to customers in the segment. For example, one customized value proposition consisted of providing dedicated marketing and sales resources to individual customers as well as developing compensation policies that

Exhibit 12-1 Customer Segment Analysis

1. Service-Oriented Performers

- Above-average profit performers, larger companies
- Maintain close, personal ties with customers
- Hold high expectations for suppliers' performance
- Seek to leverage advantages from computing and telecommunications capabilities
- More likely to be wholesale and manufacturing industries

2. Growth/Cost-Conscious

- Key objectives include profitability and growth
- More likely to be in business, professional services, and financial institutions
- Want to identify customer needs and to satisfy them, and to seek out new customers
- Short-term success depends on low-cost operations
- Supplier relationships and inventory management less critical

3. High Public Contact

- Entrepreneurial, dislike bureaucracy
- More likely to be in retail and food and beverage industries
- Want dependable suppliers that provide timely and accurate information
- Provide high-quality service through easy access and frequent contact with customers
- Want to improve quality of products and services, and customer-buying experiences

6. Status Quo Keepers

- Bureaucratic, bottom-line (profits) oriented
- More likely to be in public works and transport and education
- Offer customers standardized, off-the-shelf products/services
- Customer contact often limited to reporting progress on work completed

Pie chart segments:
- 1. 19%
- 2. 15%
- 3. 13%
- 4. 21%
- 5. 18%
- 6. 14%

5. Data Trackers

- Want to track lots of data: receivables, payables, business performance, inventory levels, production
- More likely to be in construction, hospital/nursing homes, and government agencies
- Want to gain better use of computer and telecommunications technology
- Want to enhance employee capabilities
- Less sure about customer requirements and specifications
- Less interest in becoming low-cost producer or service provider

4. Profit-Focused

- Continually monitor operations, especially for profitability
- Smaller enterprises
- Emphasize smooth-running processes and effective internal communications
- Want easy, convenient transactions with suppliers, but not relationship-oriented

encouraged the sales representatives to develop strong relationships with these targeted customers. Another value proposition included offering stable, low-cost, and highly reliable standard services.

Previously the telecommunications company provided a full range of products and services to all business customers. Now it could see large variations in the needs and willingness to pay among its more than 100,000 customers. By targeting the needs of specific, attractive segments, the company could focus its limited marketing, product and service development, and customer support resources to capture the business from targeted segments, while still offering standard products, services, and support to its nontargeted customer base.

Health care is another service industry where insights from ABC analysis can have a profound impact on the quality and efficiency of delivering care. As a simple example, one ABC study revealed that performing kidney dialysis at home versus at the health care institution was far less costly than had been estimated by the hospital's (Stage II) cost system, which had been developed based on regulatory costing principles.[9] This finding helped the facility's managers make better informed decisions about the appropriate venue for the dialysis for each patient. Furthermore, the evidence of substantial unused capacity in health care facilities will have dramatic and surprising implications as to where patients can be treated at lowest cost.[10] Treating patients in existing facilities may be much lower-cost than had previously been believed, once the cost of unused capacity is separated from the cost of used capacity.

Because service organizations are so close to their customers, any decisions made about product offerings, features, price, and delivery must involve an interplay between customer preferences (such as that derived from the needs-based marketing study) and the cost of satisfying those preferences. Service companies will make the best decisions when they combine their activity-based cost analysis with reliable information about the attributes and features valued by customers in different market segments. In this way, they can select the segments they wish to target for growth and profitability, and customize their service offerings to these segments so that each one becomes individually profitable.

Budgeting the Organization's Supply of Resources

Finally, an accurate activity-based cost model, linking organizational spending to supply resource capabilities to the activities performed and then to the demands by individual products or customers, will facilitate decisions on the appropriate supply of resources. As described earlier in the chapter, service companies typically budget and manage their costs by responsibility centers. Without an ABC model, service company managers have no way of linking budgeting decisions that authorize the supply of resources for individual responsibility centers to the demands of products and customers, for the activities and services provided by these responsibility centers. They must set budgets in annual negotiations between responsibility center heads and the senior executive team. An ABC model, as we will discuss in Chapter 15, can be used as the foundation of an organization's budgeting process. In this way, decisions to authorize spending in responsibility centers become linked to outputs demanded from these units by the anticipated volume and mix of products and customers. The model enables the service company to supply resources for products and customers that contribute to long-run profitability and to identify where cost reduction may be required for critical processes in the service delivery chain.

Case Study: The Co-operative Bank

We will use the example of a medium-sized U.K. retail bank, The Co-operative Bank, to illustrate the development of an activity-based cost model in a service organization.[11] The bank formed a project team of 11 people from different areas of the bank. The team selected the most recent three-month period for which data was available. A review of the general ledger revealed 210 resource cost pools divided into three broad categories:

OPERATIONAL STAFF (85)	INFRASTRUCTURE (85)	MISCELLANEOUS (40)
Personal Network Staff	Personal Network	Outsourced Processing Fees
Processing Centers Staff	Visa Card Administration	Stationery Costs
Personal Accounts Opening	Processing Centers	Personal Checkbooks
	ATM Network	Visa Card Statements

The ABC team then spent eight weeks in operational areas, identifying and mapping activities on brown paper. It concluded by selecting 235 principal activities performed at the bank such as:

- Open customer accounts
- Maintain customer accounts
- Accept checks
- Process transactions
- Close accounts
- Handle customer queries
- Issue checkbooks
- Market and sell products
- Make money market transfers
- Perform Visa transactions
- Perform ATM transactions
- Encode data
- Train personnel

- Process loan applications
- Manage risk
- Recover money
- Prepare management reports
- Prepare financial statements

With resource pools specified and a dictionary of 235 activities defined, the team went to each area of the bank and through interviews, surveys, and time sheets assigned resource costs to the individual activities.

Next the ABC team traced the costs of each activity to the different bank products using activity cost drivers for each activity (see *Exhibit 12-2* for activities and activity cost drivers for products in the personal sector). The project team identified approximately 50 products or groups of closely related products. Corporate products included business loans, corporate current accounts, and leases. Personal products included personal loans and advances, current accounts, and Visa accounts. Product

Exhibit 12-2 Bank Activities and Activity Cost Drivers

ACTIVITY	ACTIVITY COST DRIVER
Provide ATM Service	ATM Transactions
Clear Debit Items	Debits Processed
Check Branch Operations for Debit Items	Branch Counter Debits
Issue Personal Checkbooks	Checkbooks Issued
Clear Credit Items	Credits Processed
Ensure Lending Control and Security	Interventions
Handle Customer Inquiries	Duration of Telephone Calls
Execute Marketing and Sales Activity Strategies	Accounts Opened
Do Computer Processing	Computer Transactions
Prepare Statements and Mail	Statements Issued
Advise on Investments and Insurance	Duration (Minutes, Hours) of Advice Provided
Process Visa Transactions	Visa Transactions
Issue Visa Statements	Visa Statements Issued
Open/Close Accounts	Accounts Opened/Closed
Administer Mortgages	Mortgages Maintained

Source: Adapted from Srikant Datar and Robert S. Kaplan, "The Co-operative Bank," Case 9-195-196 (Boston: Harvard Business School, 1995), 16. Reprinted by permission of Harvard Business School.

costs were calculated by determining the quantity of each activity cost driver used by each product, multiplying these quantities by the associated activity cost driver rate, and summing across all the activities used by the individual products. (See *Exhibit 12-3* for the activity and product costs for personal banking products.)

Not all operating expenses were assigned to banking products. Several resource pools, such as accounting, finance, strategy, planning, and human resource management were considered as business-sustaining, in that they supported the organization as a whole. These sustaining costs, which were not allocated to products, amounted to about 15% of total operating expenses.[12]

The team could now calculate product profitability by subtracting the cost of all activities supporting a particular product from the net interest revenue earned from each product plus the fees derived for performing various services for customers. The interest revenue calculation used a transfer interest rate based on an appropriate market rate.

As in all ABC studies, the graph of cumulative profitability produced a whale curve (see *Exhibit 12-4*). Half the products generated all the profits; some of the products were much more profitable than anticipated, while several, previously thought to be strong profit contributors, turned out to be unprofitable. The results, which were still to be confirmed by collecting and analyzing data from subsequent periods, immediately stimulated a range of new strategic thinking about product promotion, product deletion, and even some discontinuous process improvements—such as outsourcing the ATM network, computer operations, and even the check clearing department—which, managers could now see, were not competitive with the efficiencies enjoyed by much larger banks that could capture significant economies-of-scale for these activities.

The project team took the ABC analysis to its next logical step, by segmenting the customer base and determining the profits earned by each customer segment with each product or natural grouping of products. This study revealed that up to half of all current accounts, particularly those with low balances, were unprofitable. Visa accounts also exhibited wide variation in customer profitability, with the most profitable customers having large unpaid balances that generated interest income, and many credit-card transactions, generating high processing fees. The marketing department was redirecting its resources to attract more customers whose behavior would be profitable for the bank and to deepen relationships even further with already profitable customers.

Exhibit 12-3 Matrix of Activity Resources Used by Persona Sector Products

ACTIVITY	TOTAL	CURRENT ACCOUNT PLUS (1)	PERSONAL LOANS (2)	MORTGAGES (3)	VISA CLASSIC (4)	VISA AFFINITIES (5)	VISA GOLD (6)	HANDYLOAN/ FASTLINE (7)	DEPOSIT PRODUCTS (8)
								PRODUCTS	
Provide ATM Services	£ 462,914	£ 403,360	£ 0	0	£ 25,410	£ 7,729	£ 15,447	£ 921	£ 10,047
Clear Debit Items	980,154	921,643	0	0	33,792	10,397	14,296	0	26
Check Branch Operations for Debit Items	668,341	487,796	1,770	0	90,131	35,775	44,617	6,151	2,101
Issue Personal Checkbooks	252,663	252,663	0	0	0	0	0	0	0
Clear Credit Items	212,565	91,982	4	0	53,731	20,381	45,284	1,149	34
Check Branch Operations for Credit Items	529,397	506,273	0	0	3,131	103	807	0	19,083
Ensure Lending Control and Security	1,345,149	532,918	61,501	20,825	540,563	6,809	143,906	5,387	3,240
Handle Customer Inquiries	1,166,487	850,569	97,014	324	107,052	14,749	57,630	5,959	33,190
Handle Customer Correspondence	638,622	462,178	64,409	970	56,701	2,439	23,598	6,332	21,995
Execute Marketing and Sales Strategies	2,073,943	673,641	815,211	0	202,552	54,000	197,334	41,210	89,995
Do Computer Processing	1,536,705	1,215,933	113,403	0	31,292	11,317	19,256	38,131	107,373
Prepare Statements and Mail	431,685	336,094	19,179	56	15,241	1,433	49,277	4,430	5,965
Process Visa Transactions	1,174,207	223,320	18,672	0	468,257	177,895	270,904	15,159	0
Issue Visa Statements	443,107	0	0	0	235,406	94,017	113,684	0	0
Open/Maintain Handyloans	846,806	0	0	0	0	0	0	846,806	0
Open and Close Accounts	427,751	188,373	104,346	0	51,505	1,078	35,397	11,934	35,118
Administer Mortgages	182,255	10,596	17,117	121,907	0	1,631	0	0	30,974
Total Activity Costs	£13,372,721	£7,157,339	£1,342,626	£144,092	£1,914,764	£439,753	£1,031,437	£983,569	£359,141

Source: Adapted from Srikant Datar and Robert S. Kaplan, "The Co-operative Bank." Case 9-195-196 (Boston: Harvard Business School, 1995), 17. Reprinted by permission of Harvard Business School.

Note: Numbers disguised to maintain confidentiality.

Exhibit 12-4   Co-op Bank Cumulative Product Profitability

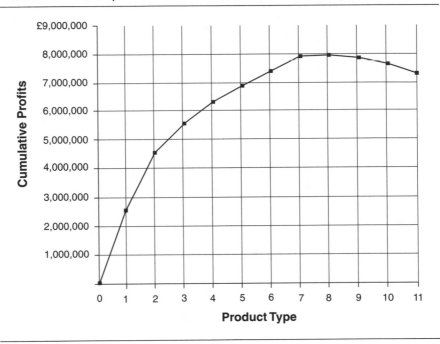

In summary, the bank's ABC model stimulated a full range of operational and strategic ABM actions, once the senior managers had a clear, understandable, and defensible picture of the economics of their operations.

Case Study: Telecommunications Company

A major telecommunications company launched its ABC project as part of a major transformation program designed to convert it from a highly regulated provider of common services in a protected domestic market to a leading global competitor of telecommunication and information products and services. This company's ABC model encompassed 500 resource pools, 700 activities, and 360 cost objects (products, lines-of-business, customer segments). As with the telecommunications company described earlier in the chapter, this ABC project was accompanied by a needs-based marketing study that grouped customers into relatively homogeneous (with respect to demand for telecommunications products and services) segments, and identified the value propositions that the company could deliver to attract and retain customers in each segment. It developed a sample population of 10,000 customers, and identified, for each customer, information on monthly bill, payment method, and local (customer-site) equipment used. By knowing the cost of each transaction, the company could produce an annual profit and loss for each of the 10,000 customers. This information is now being used to manage customers by market segments, with customized pricing, product mix, and servicing policies designed to lead to profitable operations in each market segment.

Case Study: Government Agencies

Activity-based costing is now being applied to government agencies.[13] The U.S. Veterans Affairs Department has identified the cost of the 10 activities performed to process death benefits and uses this information to monitor and improve the underlying cost structure for performing this function. The U.S. Immigration and Naturalization Service (INS) uses its ABC cost information to set fees for all its outputs, including administering citizenship exams and issuing permanent work permits (green cards). The INS also now estimates the fees to charge for new services based on the ABC cost breakdowns for performing similar or related services.[14]

The U.S. Internal Revenue Service has conducted an activity-based analysis of its operations. Previously, like all service companies, it had budgeted in exquisite detail, line-item expenses for salaries and benefits, facilities, occupancy, computing, and telecommunications. But it had no idea how much it cost to conduct various types of audits—individual accounts, corporate accounts, partnerships, tax shelters, etc. Nor could expenses be aligned with the individual activities and processes performed by operating units, to process returns, receipts, and refund disbursements. Consequently, the organization had no idea about inefficiencies and non-value-added activities being performed, and had no guidance for aligning its resources to alternative uses.

The ABC models highlighted major opportunities for process improvements. They revealed that the cost of handling electronically filed returns were far lower than for manual returns, an insight that stimulated the agency to encourage taxpayers to shift to electronic filing. The alignment of returns (revenues generated from audit activities) with the cost of alternative types of audits also permitted district managers to make more cost-effective assignments of their audit staff to the different programs.

Some programs yielded less than $1 in returns for each $1 spent in audit activity while others generated more than $10 in returns per audit dollar spent (the IRS version of the whale curve).[15]

Perhaps the most innovative application of ABC to government agencies is in making decisions about privatization. A good example is the City of Indianapolis, where Mayor Stephen Goldsmith was elected on a platform of privatization. The mayor wanted to make government smaller, to make it more responsive, and to make its managers think about value— the cost and quality of services delivered to its customers, the citizens.

Upon assuming office in 1992, Mayor Goldsmith asked for information about the current cost of government-supplied services. He wanted to be sure that privatization would result in lower costs to taxpayers: "Introducing competition and privatization to government services requires real cost information. You can't compete out if you are using fake money."[16] He found, however, that no cost information was available about the cost of city services. Programs were not linked to dollars. The new head of the Department of Transportation asked the senior managers for a list of their current activities and their cost.

It seemed like these were simple questions. But we couldn't begin to answer them. We didn't have any relevant data and we had no costing system. No one had ever focused on what they did, on how much it cost to do whatever it was they did, and, certainly, on whether whatever they were doing was being done effectively or efficiently.[17]

The Indianapolis senior managers formed a project team, which included several representatives from the unionized workforce and the non-unionized management team, to do an activity-based costing study. The study proceeded just as a private sector study would. An activity dictionary consisting of 35 activities was constructed and departmental expenses were mapped to each activity. In addition to the direct costs of departmental employees, supervisors, materials, and equipment, the project team also assigned fixed assets (office furniture and computers) and indirect support costs to the activities. The mayor wanted to have his departments compete against the private sector and these calculations would put city services on a more level playing field with private sector companies. The calculation also included the cost of unused equipment, a controversial decision. The cost of unused equipment ranged up to 10% of total costs for some city services because, under the previous budgeting system, all departments attempted to maximize the resources they could control.

The city workers liked having all vehicles available, just in case. The ABC project team talked with the workers about only having equipment that they needed on a regular and routine basis; that for the few times each year they needed the backup equipment, it would be cheaper to rent than to maintain the stand-by reserve capacity. Also, they might get better utilization by acquiring multiple-use equipment since many of the crews did not need a different vehicle for each use. The team explained how departments could realize savings by sharing their equipment and vehicles with each other. Until they had the results of the ABC analysis, however, the team couldn't generate any enthusiasm in individuals or departments to voluntarily give up or share vehicles.

The first estimate of more than $400 per ton for filling potholes provoked enormous interest. Prior to activity-based costing, employees and managers only thought about the number of hours per day that employees spent filling potholes. Nobody ever thought about unproductive time, excess equipment, real estate, inventory, or overhead, including management. Now, the employees could look at a specific pothole-filling team and see how many take-home vehicles had been allocated to it, what its annual supplies budget was, and its costs for rent and maintenance of both facilities and vehicles. People hadn't realized all the costs that got buried in a pothole with the asphalt. In many cases, employees' hourly wages were only 20% of the fully loaded cost. Before ABC, management might have placed that number at 80–90% of the cost.

When confronted with the evidence, and in anticipation of the upcoming competitive bidding process, senior management and line employees suddenly developed the same desire: How could they reduce or eliminate costs? They began to scrutinize the cost to maintain a vehicle, which was done in another division, because the inefficiencies in the equipment maintenance group and its expensive oil changes were hitting the union employees' and DOT's bottom-line cost of fixing potholes. Management and the union sat down and worked together to reduce costs (operational ABM). They determined that they didn't have to go out with a five- or six-man repair crew, plus a supervisor, if they could do the job safely with a three- or four-man self-managed crew. They realized that they didn't need 36 supervisors when there were only 75 hourly employees out on the streets. The city managers dismissed half the supervisors, most of whom had been political appointees.

Every line item on the ABC report was closely examined and there was tremendous pressure on support groups to justify their expense. The union reconfigured its approach to filling potholes by reducing manpower on each team and changing the type and amount of equipment used. A union supervisor described the process:

> *I move around quite a bit. I just take my laptop loaded with the ABC model out to a work site and say, "OK, suppose we get rid of that single-axle dump, delete that extra mixer off there, take that truck driver off, now look what it would cost you to do a ton a day." The guys know that the next time they show up on a job they better have those improvements made or they'll lose a bid to the private sector and be out of a job.*
>
> *We also got some benefits by doing multiple tasks with the same resources. While the patching crew was waiting for the asphalt to be picked up and delivered to the pothole, I had them doing other jobs, like sweeping a bridge or picking up limbs. Those were all activities in the ABC model so we could charge their time to those tasks. This way our people are kept busy doing useful tasks, and the pothole-filling activity is not charged for unproductive time.*[18]

By eliminating half the supervisors, changing the crew assignments for filling potholes, from eight down to four or six, and gaining efficiencies in the use and assignment of trucks, the union team realized significant cost reductions. It recalculated the costs, based on actual current practice, and saw a 35% cost reduction. In the subsequent bidding against the private sector, the municipal workers easily won the competition.

The city also invited the union to bid on several large capital projects. The union, after looking at the work involved, decided that it should concentrate on work that was closer to its core competencies. In addition, there were several unskilled tasks like picking up trash on the side of the road that city employees didn't like doing and for which their high wages made them noncompetitive against private sector alternatives. The union was willing to let this work be privatized as well. The union wanted to concentrate on the tasks that leveraged the skills and experience of its people.

By the end of 1995, after nearly four years of using operational and strategic ABM to make city services more competitive, the City of Indianapolis had become remarkably more cost effective. Total city employment had dropped from 4,675 to 3,650, with the decrease almost completely accomplished by a 40% reduction in non-public-safety employees, from 2,425 to 1,484.

The city conducted 66 competitive bidding projects, involving more than $500 million during the four-year period. Each competition pitted activity-based cost estimates from the public sector against the private sector bids. The private sector won the majority (37) of the bids, typically the larger competitions, both the terms of dollars involved and length of contract. The private sector was more successful in contracts involving complex technical issues such as wastewater treatment and advanced technology such as information technology services. City employees won the bulk of their 29 bids for labor-intensive contracts such as for street repairs, pothole filling, and crack sealing, where they could leverage their experience, skills, and existing capital equipment.

City planners identified the cost savings already achieved from the competitions at nearly $80 million, and identified an additional $150 million in contractually committed savings to be realized over the next few years. With the introduction of ABC-based competition, city budgets declined for four consecutive years, and the 1996 budget was about $90 million less than if the previous 8% per year trend in city spending had been allowed to continue for another four years (see *Exhibit 12-5*). Even better, the cost savings were accompanied by improvements in service output. For example:

- Private contractors, in their first year of operations, towed 2,251 abandoned vehicles from city streets, compared to 947 towed in the previous year.
- A single city trash crew now serviced 1,200 homes per day, up from 680 before competition and the reengineering of their processes.

Mayor Stephen Goldsmith commented on the impact of the ABC-based competition:

Most of the line workers have now accepted the imperative of competition. It's a remarkably different language than what existed three or four years ago. Today we can tell them they are good people, they can compete and win. When the solid waste workers won a bid to extend their routes, and then came in under their bids, we shared some of the savings, checks of about $1,750 to each worker. It was a pretty remarkable event.

There's a sense of reality now. City employees have redesigned their tools and their teams to think in different ways, and they win. People who aren't competitive are moved out of their departments or eliminated. The ones that are left are convinced that they are good at what they do. They have a sense of pride that they are better than the private sector. That makes a big difference in their whole attitude towards work, the quality of the work

Exhibit 12-5 Public Sector Experience of the City of Indianapolis

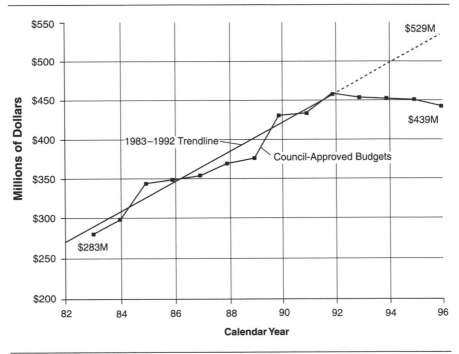

Source: R. S. Kaplan, "Indianapolis: Activity-Based Costing of City Services (B)," Case #9-196-117. (Boston: Harvard Business School, 1996). Reprinted by permission of Harvard Business School.

they do, and, frankly, how the rest of the citizens think today about their city workers.[19]

ABC is clearly not just a tool for the private sector. The Indianapolis experience is generalizable to almost all government-supplied services that pass the Yellow Pages test. This test, developed by the deputy mayor of Indianapolis, states: "If you can't find the service in the Yellow Pages, you shouldn't try to privatize it." The Yellow Pages test indicates the existence of private contractors prepared to offer the same or similar services as that currently provided by an internal government group. The Yellow Pages test precludes governments from putting their army and air force out for competitive bids, but it allows for competition in the provision of repairs, maintenance, depot management, food service, data processing, and financial services to the military services.

Summary

Applying ABC to service organizations requires a keen appreciation of costing for committed resources. One could observe service organizations and think that all their costs were fixed, independent of quantity and mix of usage. Such a naive view would preclude motivation for developing activity-based cost systems in such settings. But once one realizes, using the framework established in Chapter 7, that managers determine the supply of committed resources in anticipation of demands for services by products and customers, the rationale for linking resource usage to such demands becomes far more compelling. Managers need the information from an ABC model to make decisions about the products and services they wish to offer, the customer segments they wish to serve, the method of delivering the products and services to those customers, and the supply of resources required for their products, services, and customers. Managers will use the ABC information to develop products and services that can be delivered to customers at prices that cover the costs of resources used, thereby enabling them to serve customers in profitable relationships.

13

Extending Activity-Based Cost Systems

In previous chapters, we have described how organizations launch their activity-based costing programs. Managers develop cost models of critical organizational processes: manufacturing, service operations, marketing and selling, and product development. These Stage III ABC models are developed on historical data, with the information used to guide operational improvements and make better decisions about product pricing and mix, customer and supplier relationships, and product design. In most cases, organizations continue to use their existing (Stage II) financial and cost system to prepare financial reports to investors, creditors, regulators, and tax authorities.

What is the next step? What advances and enhancements can be made in activity-based cost systems to extend their usefulness, application, and impact? How can organizations move from their episodic Stage III systems, implemented opportunistically where initial benefits were expected to be the greatest, to wide-scale organizational implementation, where ABC systems become fully integrated into the ongoing management, reporting, and control systems? How should ABC systems interface with enterprise-wide systems from SAP, Oracle, PeopleSoft, Baan, and others? The answer to these questions becomes especially important as organizations install enterprise-wide systems that promise fully integrated information and control systems.

We believe the answers to these questions come in two parts. First, organizations extend the reach and applicability of their ABC systems beyond their initial applications to provide comprehensive assignment of organizational spending and expenses to products, services, customers, and organizational entities. Second, the information from ABC systems is integrated with other information systems, especially operational and strategic learning and improvement systems, and the organization's budgeting and reporting systems. In this chapter we discuss the extension of

ABC methodology to all organizational spending and expenses. In the following chapters, we provide recommendations for achieving a Stage IV system, when comprehensive ABC systems become integrated with enterprise-wide information systems.

Extending the reach of activity-based costing involves:

- Assigning business and corporate-level expenses;
- Assigning brand, product line, and channel support expenses;
- Distinguishing primary and secondary activities;
- Assigning assets: integrating ABC with economic value-added (EVA™); and
- Measuring life-cycle costs and profitability.

Assigning Business and Corporate-Level Expenses

Initial activity-based cost models are usually built for repetitive operations directly involved with products and customers. Once expenses for manufacturing, service operations, product development, and direct customer administration and support have been analyzed, managers can see how all resource expenses, within their unit, can be traced using the cause-and-effect relationships of activity cost drivers to the cost objects (products, services, and customers) that benefit from or create the demand for the resources. They naturally ask why the ABC methodology couldn't be extended to assign, on a more rational and transparent basis, the cost of corporate- and division-level resources. It can be.

Typically, companies treat corporate support costs as discretionary expenses. Lacking good measures of the output from corporate support departments and of the use of corporate-level services by operating units, senior executives authorize the spending in these departments in the budgeting process. As a consequence, the authorization is based on the power and negotiating ability of managers of corporate support departments and the senior executive team. And when times get tough, and executives need to cut expenses, corporate and divisional support departments provide the most convenient targets, largely because the output of such departments is not nearly as tangible and quantifiable as the output of production, service delivery, customer support, and product development departments. Often such cuts are not sustainable since the loss in services from support departments eventually shows up as an inability to perform certain critical processes, and the departments are allowed to rehire personnel to restore their capabilities.

As we discussed in Chapter 7, on measuring costs of capacity, sustainable cost reductions in resource spending must come in two steps. First, reduce the demands for the resources, either by improving the efficiency and productivity of the work performed by the resources (operational ABM) or by reducing the demands for the services provided by the resources (strategic ABM). This step creates unused capacity in the resources, which can then be safely eliminated in the second step, by 1) reducing the authorized supply of the resources, 2) redeploying the resources elsewhere, or 3) finding new and more profitable ways to use them.

As an example of how this fundamental approach can be applied to corporate support departments, consider an early ABC application (1985) by the Weyerhaeuser Company.[1] Company executives were concerned about their limited ability to budget for and control corporate overhead costs. They wanted to provide incentives for corporate-level departments to become more efficient and responsive to profit-center managers. They also wanted to provide signals to these profit-center managers about the cost of the corporate support services they were using. Weyerhaeuser adopted a charge-back system in which corporate-level department costs were first assigned to the different activities they performed, and then attributed down to local profit centers through appropriately selected activity cost drivers.

A good example of the system occurred in the Financial Services Department (FSD), a staff unit in the corporate controller's department that was responsible for centralized accounting functions, including:

- Consolidations,
- General accounting,
- Salaried payroll,
- Accounts payable,
- Accounts receivable, and
- Invoicing.

An activity analysis revealed one or more activities within each of these functions as well as the associated activity cost driver, as shown in *Exhibit 13-1*.

We can illustrate the operation and theory of this system by examining, in more detail, the accounts receivable function identified in Exhibit 13-1. This function draws upon two types of resources—information systems and people—to perform two activities: receiving, recording, and

Exhibit 13-1   Activity Analysis and Activity Cost Drivers for Weyerhaeuser's Financial Services Department

FSD FUNCTION AND MAJOR ACTIVITIES	ACTIVITY COST DRIVER
Consolidation and Data Base Administration	
Prepare and Develop Reports	$/hour
Administer Data Bases	$/report
General Accounting	
Analytic and Clerical Support	$/hour
Systems	$/report
Salaried Payroll	
Issue Checks, Maintain Files	$/paycheck
Accounts Payable	
Micrographics	$/hour
Control and Support	$/document
Accounts Payable: Paper Division	$/invoice
Accounts Payable: Corporate	$/invoice
Accounts Receivable	
Process Cash Receipts	$/invoice
Maintain Customer File	$/customer
Invoicing	
Mill Sales Coding	$/transaction
Domestic Invoicing	$/invoice
Export Documentation	$/document

depositing cash receipts; and maintaining customer files (name, address, credit rating, payment history, outstanding invoices).

The activity cost driver for receiving cash was weighted, at one extreme, for customers whose receipts required extensive manual work to record and deposit versus, at the other extreme, those customers whose payments may have been received and processed electronically. As a first approximation, the cost of maintaining a customer file was independent of the volume and dollar value of payments made by the customer, hence the assumption of a constant cost per customer.

Consider, now, two paper divisions of the company, both of which had $200 million in annual sales. Under the previous system, in which corporate overhead was allocated proportional to sales, both divisions would have received the same allocation for the accounts receivable function (and for every other corporate-supplied service). But suppose that Division 1 sold to relatively few, large wholesale accounts, say 100 customers doing an average of $2,000,000 per year with Weyerhaeuser and paying invoices monthly (12 per year). And suppose Division 2 sold to many small retail accounts, say 10,000 customers (each buying about $20,000 of goods per year, placing orders on average three times a year). Without even controlling for the greater public availability of credit information for the large wholesale customers versus the many small retail customers, nor for the probable greater use of electronic information technology and lower error rates of the larger versus the smaller customers, just the sheer transactional volume indicates that Division 2 is making about 25 times more demand than Division 1 on the accounts receivable function, as measured by number of cash receipts, and about 100 times more demand, as measured by number of customers. Thus the charge-outs to the two divisions should not be equal; they should differ by a factor of between 25 and 100.

Such a charge-out system has several desirable characteristics. The supplying department—Financial Services Department—has incentives to perform its work more efficiently. The functions performed by most corporate overhead departments pass the Yellow Pages test, described at the end of Chapter 12. The identical function could be provided by alternative, and more focused, suppliers of this service. For the company to continue to perform the service itself, the internal department must either be lower cost or offer unique quality and functionality not available from outside vendors. While the ABC charge-out system may not measure quality, timeliness, and functionality, it does provide the cost measurement input for an outsourcing decision.

The cost signal also allows the internal service to contemplate selling its services externally. The information systems department at Weyerhaeuser began to sell some unused capacity to external users to reduce the costs that would have to be assigned to it (as an early ABC application, the company had not yet realized the benefits of basing its activity-based costs on practical capacity) and because it learned that the cost of supplying services (including that of capacity resources) was below the revenues it could earn; that is, the department could begin to act as a profit center, not a discretionary expense center.

Even if Weyerhaeuser did not want its internal service departments to be full-fledged profit centers, it could still use the ABC information to treat them as pseudo-profit centers, like Olympus did for its purchasing department (see Chapter 5). In this way, the economic signals from the

ABC system are the basis for promoting a continuous improvement philosophy within corporate staff departments.

In the charge-back system, the consuming departments get an indication about the cost of the services they use. Under the previous (Stage II) system, the cost of corporate-level services was allocated arbitrarily based on sales dollars. The only way a consuming department could reduce the corporate charge was to reduce their sales revenues, not an attractive option either to the department or the company. Consuming departments can now modify their demands for centrally supplied services: they can simplify the reports they receive, establish more efficient links with suppliers and customers so that billing, invoicing, paying, and collecting can be done electronically rather than manually, and negotiate with customers on pricing and minimum order size to better reflect the economics of the relationship. For example, Division 1 now recognizes that the cost of serving its few large customers, at least for invoicing and collecting, is significantly lower than previously reported, and Division 2 is informed about the high costs for invoicing and collecting from its myriad small retail customers.

Not all corporate staff activities may be charged back to operating divisions. For instance, certain activities relating to preparing external financial statements for shareholders and tax authorities have to be performed, independent of the number of operating divisions, and the volume and mix of business done in these divisions. The costs of such activities could be considered *corporate-sustaining expenses*. These costs can be differentiated from those caused by audit and tax work done for individual business units. The portion of the overall costs that is driven by the volume and complexity of work triggered by individual business units should be assigned to those units using appropriate cost drivers.

Some people have objected to ABC assignments of corporate expenses to operating units. They argue that such costs are fixed, so that any assignment would be arbitrary and not meaningful. There are two fallacies with this argument. First, the assignments are not arbitrary; they are based on an underlying cause-and-effect relationship between the demands for work by the operating divisions and the generation of costs by the corporate functions. Second, they are meaningful because many of these costs can be managed. Return to the Rule of One, first introduced in Chapter 10. As long as a corporate-level department contains more than one person, there is some demand for work from that department that one person cannot handle by herself. If an analysis of what creates work for the resources in the department leads to violation of the Rule of One, the analyst will be able to determine an appropriate basis and destination for assigning the resource costs of the department. Such expenses should not be parked in an unassigned sustaining category.

When someone claims that a department or activity is corporate-sustaining and cannot be causally attributed, via cost drivers, to operating departments, try to find out why the department is the size it is. What causes a department to require 12 people and $500,000 per year of computing resources to do its work versus 1 person with a $5,000 computer. Often, but not always, the answer to this question will reveal the driver that explains the magnitude of work for the activity, and this driver then establishes a cause-and-effect linkage to characteristics of operating departments. Such a cause-and-effect driver becomes the basis for assigning the costs of performing work at the corporate level to the operating department. Over time, if operating departments reduce their demands for the services provided by corporate-level support departments (step 1 to reduce so-called fixed costs), the organization can shrink the size of these departments (step 2 that enables so-called fixed costs to be permanently cut) by reducing the resources supplied (e.g., people, computers, space) for that support department.

The basic insight for assigning corporate- or division-level expenses is the same as for using activity cost drivers for assigning factory-level expenses to activities and to products. Look for a quantitative measure(s) representing the output of the staff department. If a quantity measure cannot be identified, so that the only method for allocation is to use a percentage, say of sales, expenses, or assets, of operating departments, any assignment would be an arbitrary allocation, not an attribution based on a cause-and-effect relationship. Rather than make an arbitrary allocation using percentages, the ABC cost model should treat the expense at the sustaining level, and not attempt to drive it farther down the organization.

When Albert Einstein was a scholar at the Institute of Advanced Studies in Princeton, a graduate student asked him how he knew how simple to make his models. Einstein said that he always made his models as simple as he could, but no simpler.

Extending Einstein's answer to building cost models, an ABC model should always attempt to drive costs as far down in the organization as it can, but no farther. If an activity is truly sustaining at a given level, no meaningful driver can be found that captures a cause-and-effect relation between the activity and a cost object at the next level.

How do analysts know when they cannot drive a cost any farther? When no quantity measure exists for such an assignment, so that the only remaining method would be to use percentages unrelated to the supply of services to the next level of the organization. The Weyerhaeuser accounts receivable example does represent a corporate-level cost that could be driven down to individual divisions or even customers since the demand for the accounts receivable service can be linked, via cost drivers such as number of customers and number of cash receipts, to identifiable actions at the individual division and customer level. Many corporate staff expenses, however, such as preparing divisional financial statements, can be driven down to organizational units, but not to the volume and mix of products and customers within each organizational unit. Such expenses should be treated as sustaining expenses for each organizational unit—part of the cost of establishing, maintaining, and managing each unit. In this case, the profit of each organizational unit is calculated by subtracting the unit's sustaining costs from the net contribution margins earned by the volume and mix of business done in that unit. But little to no benefit, for decisions on operational improvements, pricing, product mix, and customer relationships, is gained from allocating a unit's sustaining expenses down to individual products, services, and customers.

Assigning Brand, Product Line, and Channel Support Expenses

The analysis of corporate-level expenses can also be applied to brand, product line, and channel expenses. Take the cost of managing a brand, such as Procter & Gamble's well-known detergent Tide. P&G spends considerable resources on a brand management team for Tide, for ongoing enhancements of the products that carry the Tide label, and for promotions and advertising of the brand name. Suppose that the company has 100 different SKUs that carry the Tide name, representing different package sizes, variations in color, and different formulations. How can the cost of brand management, product improvement, and brand advertising be assigned to each of the 100 different SKUs that carries the brand name? The answer, of course, is that it cannot be, unless a cause-and-effect relationship can be estimated between the quantity of brand management, support, and advertising expenses and some characteristics of individual SKUs. If most of these expenses were incurred, even if only one SKU carrying the Tide name existed, they should be considered *brand-sustaining,* and not allocated down to individual SKUs. This recommendation follows from the insight that no decision made about individual SKUs would affect the level of spending on Tide brand management, brand improvement, and brand advertising expenses. To the extent that this strong assumption is violated, because some spending at the brand level can be linked to decisions to introduce or promote individual SKUs, the analyst has a basis for assigning those traceable expenses to specific SKUs.

And continuing up the organizational hierarchy, Procter & Gamble markets several brands of detergent. Suppose that some expenses are incurred for a manager, and support staff, of the detergent sector. Suppose too that some expenses are incurred to improve the performance of all detergent brands, not just Tide. For example, product development may be done to improve the environmental characteristics of all detergent products, or to improve their cleaning effectiveness. Such expenses can be unambiguously attributed to the detergent product line—they are detergent *product line-sustaining,* and certainly not the costs of being in the toothpaste, potato chip, or paper diaper business—but any allocation to individual brands within the detergent product line would be arbitrary (see *Exhibit 13-2*). Arguably, product line-sustaining expenses are incurred independently of how many different detergent brands are offered as well as the volume and mix of sales within each brand. If such an assumption is not accurate, the violation of the assumption—that is, the relationship between product line spending and individual brand or SKU characteristics—provides the basis for assigning the cost below the product line-sustaining level.

A similar line of reasoning would reveal that some marketing expenses cannot be attributed to individual customers. For example, the costs of advertising in trade journals, attendance and promotions at trade conferences, and the administrative infrastructure dedicated to particular distribution channels, such as retail, wholesale, or electronic commerce, support the sales activity for all customers that purchase through that channel. Rather than arbitrarily allocate such *channel-sustaining* expenses down to individual customers within the channel, these expenses can be attributed to a higher level of the marketing hierarchy (the channel level, sitting above the customer level; see Exhibit 13-2), and used to determine channel profitability, but not individual customer profitability within that channel.

Hierarchies: A General Perspective

Exhibit 13-2 identifies three groups of hierarchies; for product lines, marketing and distribution channels, and location. We refer to costs incurred at any hierarchical level as sustaining costs at that level. Hierarchies identify the lowest level to which certain costs can meaningfully be assigned. They help identify the impact on resource consumption of adding

Exhibit 13-2 Activity-Based Profitability Map

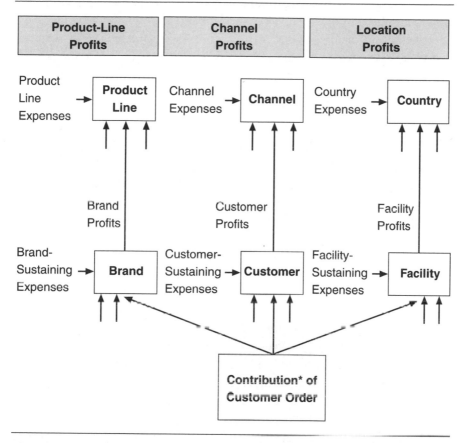

*Contribution equals price less unit and batch costs (from an ABC model) associated with the order.

or dropping items at each level of the hierarchy. For example, if the firm drops a brand, activities at the brand level and below will be affected, but activities done at higher levels, such as the product line level will be unaffected. Similarly, eliminating an object at one level of the hierarchy should cause all activities related to that object at lower levels of the hierarchy to disappear. For example, if a product is dropped, then all of the batch- and unit-level activities associated with that product will disappear. The identification of hierarchies allows managers to forecast the effect of decisions to add or drop objects such as products, brands, customers, and facilities.

This approach assumes there are no interactions across different groups of hierarchies. Such an assumption may be violated; for example, returning to the manufacturing cost hierarchy, if a product is dropped, all batch activities related to unique components for that product will automatically disappear. But activities related to components that are also used in other products may not disappear. If a common component is used in other products and only one batch of that component is produced in the period, the batch-level activities for that common component will remain. In this case, only the dropped product's share of the unit-level activities are eliminated.

The existence of common elements, whether they are components, products, customers, or facilities introduces another layer of complexity into estimating the effect of changing the object mix produced or served by the firm.[2] For example, in Exhibit 13-2, how does dropping a brand affect customers? Presumably, revenues will decrease to the extent that the customers do not switch their purchases to alternative brands made by the company. But the customer-sustaining expenses should remain the same since, by assumption, those expenses are independent of the volume and mix purchased by the customer. Only if a customer were buying nothing but that single brand from the company, and could not be switched to another brand, would the customer-sustaining expenses be affected by the decision to drop the brand. Similarly, dropping a single customer or group of customers will affect the sales of products and brands, but should not affect the product- and brand-sustaining expenses, unless these customers were the only ones purchasing those products and brands.

These conditions for interactions across different categories of sustaining expenses (brand- versus customer-sustaining) are sufficiently rare that the profitability branches captured by Exhibit 13-2 seem to represent useful ways for viewing the underlying profitability structure of the organization. Managers can use the Exhibit 13-2 profitability map to make decisions at individual hierarchical levels with minimal impact on other portions of the profitability map.

Of course, second-order effects can still occur. Dropping a product or brand could cause a currently profitable customer to become unprofitable because of lower volume of sales to that customer; and dropping a group of customers could cause currently profitable products or brands to become unprofitable. Exhibit 13-2 gives a first-order approximation as to where the company is making or losing money. Managers can review the objects (such as products, customers, brands, or facilities) that are highly profitable or unprofitable and adjust their strategies accordingly. But as in the resource usage/resource supply decisions discussed in Chapter 7, studies should be made to explore the impact of such decisions on the profitability of other objects and on overall resource supply. The ABC profitability map focuses managers on profit and loss opportunities, but does not obviate the need for special studies assessing interactive effects and potential impact on resource supply.

Distinguishing Primary and Secondary Activities

The introduction to ABC in Chapter 6 assumed that all the activities performed by the support departments directly benefited either products or customers. This enabled the costs of such activities to be linked to products and customers through activity cost drivers. As we have noted, many support or service departments in companies do not directly support the production of products or delivery of services to customers. These departments provide support to other departments, many themselves service and support departments, as well as to production departments or activities that directly benefit products. For example, a human resource or a payroll department provides services to both production and support departments throughout the organization. Or resources, often considered *facility-sustaining*, provide space, heat, light, and air-conditioning throughout the plant to both production areas and support areas. How can the expenses of these resources be assigned, and do they all eventually find their way to final products?

To illustrate how to handle this situation, assume that a company has two production departments, one production support department, and several general support departments, including plant administration, factory support, security, buildings and grounds, information systems, and human resources. Analysis of the activities provided by the various support departments reveals three principal activities:

- Provide space for people, machines, materials, and products;
- Provide CPU cycles of information processing; and
- Provide employee support (training, advice, etc.).

The resource expenses from various support departments assigned to the activity *provide space* include building depreciation, insurance, and taxes; and the expenses of heat, light, air-conditioning, security, internal housekeeping, and maintenance of the grounds outside the factory. The output from this activity is square feet of usable floor space.[3] The cost of this activity would then be assigned to the space occupied by production departments (a primary activity), the space used by the production support department (another primary activity); and the space used by the information systems equipment and people, and the human resource department (secondary activities). After assigning out the cost of the *provide space* activity, the costs of the IS and HR departments will include not only their own traceable department costs but also the assignment of occupancy costs. The HR department costs associated with the activity *support employees* has, as its cost driver, the number of employees.[4] Since the IS department has a significant number of employees, it would receive a cost assignment from HR that would include its pro rata share of HR expenses, which in turn would include an occupancy charge for HR personnel it received from the *provide space* activity. Thus, two of the secondary activities, *provide space* and *support employees,* would assign some of their expenses to primary activities, and some to other secondary activities like *provide CPU cycles.* At the final round, the costs in the *provide CPU cycles* activity (which include space and HR costs) would be assigned to production departments and other primary activities, based on the number of CPU cycles used by each activity. So, the expenses of secondary activities will ripple through and eventually find their way to primary activities where they can be assigned to products, services, and customers via activity cost drivers.[5]

This assignment of secondary activities to primary activities (which may be done through other secondary activities) often permits expenses, previously classified as sustaining, to be driven down to activities that directly benefit products and customers. Why is this important to do? Isn't this moving ABC toward cost allocation and away from its initial premise, to understand direct cause-and-effect relationships about the costs of resources required by individual products and customers? Not at all! If operational and strategic ABM decrease the resources required for primary activities, products, and customers, excess capacity will be realized not only in the primary activities but also in the secondary activities that support them. Therefore, if managers want to exploit fully the excess capacity they have created by reducing organizational spending on unused capacity, they need to look at resources (space, personnel [FTEs], and equipment) for secondary as well as primary activities. The ABC model that links secondary with primary activities provides the road map for such spending reduction opportunities. But to understand the opportunity for short- versus long-term cost reduction, ABC analysts may wish to identify which assigned costs come from primary and which from secondary activities.

Assigning Assets: Integrating ABC with Economic Value-Added (EVA™)

Recently, managers have been encouraged to maximize net profits, after controlling for costs of capital employed. This encouragement has come from the advocates of shareholder value analysis,[6] cash flow return on investment,[7] and economic value-added (EVA).[8] Such analysis is performed at the level of the corporation, a division, or a strategic business unit, where the assets or capital employed can be reliably measured. If organizations are judged on such metrics, they may wish to assign not just operating expenses but assets down to individual activities, products, and customers. For the greatest leverage to increase EVA may come from taking decisions not at the SBU or corporate level, but at the level of the activities and products. It is simple to extend activity-based costing to the assignment of assets as well as operating expenses. After all, many expenditures, such as for plant and equipment and to acquire materials, are temporarily classified as assets before they flow through the income statement as expenses. Many assets represent expenditures on their way to becoming expenses.

We can illustrate the integration of ABC and EVA with a simple example. Take an SBU with the income statement shown in *Exhibit 13-3*.

This statement reveals a marginally profitable SBU, with a net operating margin of 9% of sales. After assigning a cost of capital of 12% to the net assets employed, this SBU has destroyed economic value during the year; that is, its earnings are below the cost of capital employed to generate the earnings.

Exhibit 13-3 Divisional EVA™ Income Statement

	INCOME STATEMENT	(%)
Sales	$1,000,000	100
CGS	480,000	48
Gross Margin	520,000	52
Selling Expenses	210,000	21
Distribution Expenses	116,000	12
Administrative Expenses	108,000	11
Operating Profit	86,000	9
Capital Employed	840,000	84
Capital Charged @ 12%	100,800	10
Economic Value-Added	$ (14,800)	−1

Executives' initial reaction to a negative EVA operating unit is to search for ways to raise margins (through price increases and cost cutting) or increase asset intensity. They may instruct the SBU managers to cut selling expenses or administrative expenses as a percentage of sales, raise prices across the board, cut production support expenses, and demand lower inventory levels and accounts receivable in their attempt to increase reported EVA. But such across-the-board actions, designed to cut fat and waste, may also cut into muscle and bone. Consider the situation where the SBU consists of two distinct product lines. One product line is well established, runs on efficient, focused production processes, and is sold to customers with whom the SBU has long-standing relationships. The other product line, developed to enter new customer markets, is a highly customized business with many product variants and short production runs as well as heavy marketing and selling expenses to service existing customers and reach new ones. An activity-based cost analysis permits the product line income statements shown in *Exhibit 13-4*.

The ABC financial report in Exhibit 13-4 shows the danger from the meat cleaver approach to cost cutting. No problem exists for Product Line 1. Its efficient processes and loyal customer base enable it to earn high gross and operating margins. Any attempt to cut costs further or raise prices may seriously compromise this highly attractive segment. The SBU's profitability and EVA problems arise from Product Line 2, which exhibits the characteristics of hidden loss products (the right-hand side of the product profitability whale curve) and hidden loss customers (lower

Exhibit 13-4 Applying ABC to EVA™ Analysis

	TRADITIONAL INCOME STATEMENT	(%)	PRODUCT LINE 1 INCOME STATEMENT	(%)	PRODUCT LINE 2 INCOME STATEMENT	(%)
Sales	$1,000,000	100	$600,000	100	$ 400,000	100
CGS	480,000	48	240,000	40	240,000	60
Gross Margin	**520,000**	**52**	**360,000**	**60**	**160,000**	**40**
Selling Expenses	210,000	21	90,000	15	120,000	30
Distribution Expenses	116,000	12	36,000	6	80,000	20
Administrative Expenses	108,000	11	48,000	8	60,000	15
Operating Profit	**86,000**	**9**	**186,000**	**31**	**(100,000)**	**−25**
Capital Employed	840,000	84	420,000	70	420,000	105
Capital Charged @ 12%	100,800	10	50,400	8	50,400	13
Economic Value-Added	**$ (14,800)**	**−1**	**$135,600**	**23**	**$(150,400)**	**−38**

right-hand quadrant of Exhibit 10-5). Managers' attention should not be focused on across-the-board spending reductions, but on specific actions to restore the profitability of Product Line 2.

The connection of ABC to EVA appears in the bottom section of Exhibit 13-4. The EVA analysis reinforces the message beyond the profitability analysis alone. It points managers to a range of opportunities to improve both margins *and* asset intensity for Product Line 2. The ABC analysis of assets employed reveals that Product Line 1 requires only $0.70 of assets per dollar of sales, whereas Product Line 2 requires $1.05 per dollar of sales. This differential arises because Product Line 1's managers have established close relationships with a few suppliers so raw materials shipments are generally made on a just-in-time basis; the predictable demand pattern for these products enables machines to operate near capacity levels (so they have little to no unused capacity); and dedicated efficient and JIT production processes enable this product line to be produced with much lower work-in-process and finished goods inventory levels. Further, its excellent customer relationships keep accounts receivable to a minimum. Product Line 2, in contrast, requires $1.05 of assets per dollar of sales because it uses high inventory levels at all production processes, has extensive setups and idle time on machines, and its customers pay slowly. Thus, there is a large differential—13% of sales versus 8% for Product Line 1—in the EVA capital charges applied to the two product lines.

Driving EVA from a divisional or SBU level down to activities, products, and customers gives managers far more leverage to increase total EVA for the unit. Instead of a shotgun approach applied to all expenses, assets, products, and customers, managers can devise rifle-like solutions customized to the particular activities and to individual products or customers that have negative EVAs. For example, at one printing company, an analysis of the paper acquisition process revealed that purchased paper stayed in inventory an average of more than 60 days. About $18 million of paper was in inventory (enough to go around the world 14 times), with $9.5 million of it more than 30 days old. It occupied 225,000 square feet of storage space at a cost (operating plus capital) of $750,000 per year. Once the company saw the data, it launched a reengineering effort to reduce paper inventory to less than 30 days, leading to annual operating and capital cost savings of $1.8 million annually.

The assignment of many assets to individual products should be straightforward. Some assets, like inventory, are already directly attributable to individual products. Dedicated assets, such as specialized production equipment, tooling, and test equipment, can be assigned to the narrow range of products that use these resources. Other assets, such as general purpose equipment, may be used by a wide range of products. In this case, the asset assignment can be done with the same cost drivers—machine hours—used to drive the operating expenses (depreciation, maintenance, power) of the equipment to individual products. The Stern-Stewart methodology for EVA also encourages companies to capitalize many expenditures—research and development, marketing, and promotion—and amortize them over a specified useful life.[9] The assignment of such intangible assets to individual products should be obvious.

As with operating expenses, not all asset assignments should be made to individual products. Some assets can be causally attributed to individual customer behavior. A common example of a customer-specific asset is accounts receivable. Another is that some customers may require their suppliers to hold specific inventory for them. In such cases, the asset (inventory) may be better attributed to the customer, not to the product. Also, the company may have purchased specific equipment, done specific research and product and process development, or developed specific software for an individual customer or identifiable segment of customers. The capitalized value of these intangible assets can then be attributed to specific customers or segments.

For example, a software fulfillment company identified the following capital costs associated with one of its customers, Innovative Software, with $22 million in revenue:

	Q1 1996 CAPITAL CHARGE	PERCENTAGE OF REVENUE
Current Assets		
Accounts Receivable	$ 672,000	3.1%
Raw Materials Inventory	269,000	1.2
Finished Goods Inventory	75,000	0.3
Work-in-Process Inventory	28,000	0.1
Total Current Assets	**$1,044,000**	**4.7%**
Current Liabilities		
Accrued Payroll Expenses	$ (12,000)	−0.1%
Accounts Payable	(135,000)	−0.6
Total Current Liabilities	**$ (147,000)**	**−0.7%**
Productive Assets	**$ 405,000**	**1.8%**
Total Capital Charges	**$1,302,000**	**5.9%**

The high capital costs were caused by the customer requiring the company to purchase raw materials based on a medium-term sales forecast, the customer taking an average of 77 days to pay its invoices, and the commitment of expensive machines for producing manuals and CD-ROMs for the customer's products. The company now had specific facts about the high capital costs incurred with Innovative Software and it used them to negotiate new pricing, inventory management, and accounts receivable arrangements. The company's division director commented: "This tool helps us make our operations more efficient and allows us to focus on product lines and customers who create wealth. This business model will not only create value for our shareholders, it will also make us stronger in the market place."[10]

As another example, this time outside manufacturing, commercial banks offer different types of facilities[11] for their commercial customers. Traditional ABC analysis would identify the profitability of such arrangements by attributing interest revenue, fee income, interest expense, and operating expenses to the individual loans and customers. But different types of lending arrangements require different amounts of risk-adjusted bank equity to be reserved against the facility. The EVA loan and customer profitability analysis must reflect:

1. The capital required to support the particular type of facility sold to a particular customer,
2. The extent to which the individual customer draws upon the facility, and
3. The risk-adjusted cost of capital for the facility.[12]

The integration between ABC and EVA seems natural. Both ABC and EVA were developed to solve a distortion in the financial reporting of a company's economics. ABC corrected the arbitrary allocations of factory overhead to products and the failure to assign other indirect expenses to products and customers. EVA corrected the financial accounting failure of calculating company profits without recognizing the cost of capital as an economic expense (as in the example in Exhibit 13-3, where a division shows an accounting profit while failing to earn a return sufficient to repay its use of capital employed). Using both, managers obtain a clearer economic map of profitability and losses, and can direct their attention and specific actions—through operational and strategic ABM—to operations where economic losses are incurred, and be highly sensitive about retaining, protecting, and expanding economically profitable operations.

Asset Measurement

When valuing and assigning assets, particularly long-lived assets like plant and equipment, managers may ask whether they should use the book values, as reported in financial statements, or perhaps more current (and, theoretically, preferable) values such as replacement, market, or fair values. Neither ABC nor EVA depends upon the particular valuation method used. The principal innovation for both techniques deals more with associating the *quantity* of assets to individual divisions, products, and customers. The pricing of the assets is a separate decision, independent of asset assignment methodology, but still one that must be made.

We have found that most managers and employees have a limited capacity to internalize radical new measurement approaches. If, at the same time that ABC and EVA are introduced, the company also shifts from historical cost to current cost in its asset valuation methodology, managers will find it difficult to separate out the effects from the multiple innovations. We prefer that managers turn one dial at a time and get comfortable with the new setting; this conservatism is consistent with our wing-walking metaphor in Chapter 2. Once managers have become comfortable with an integrated ABC/EVA approach, and it has become imbedded in the way they think about their organizational economics, they can contemplate refinements like some form of market-value asset valuation.

Occasionally, a manager also questions whether the cost of capital for plant and equipment isn't already reflected in the depreciation charge. The answer is no. Depreciation reflects the return *of* capital; is the organization getting back the money that it has invested in the asset? The interest charge against assets measures the return *on* capital; the additional return the asset must generate to compensate owners for the length of time their capital has been invested in the asset. Think about a mortgage. Depreciation is analogous to the repayment of the principal component in the monthly payment. The EVA cost of capital is analogous to the interest expense in the monthly payment. All bankers want to get their money back (depreciation) and earn a return on the money advanced for the mortgage loan (the EVA cost of capital).

Measuring Life-Cycle Costs and Profitability

We have already observed that many products and customers in their early years will appear unprofitable, particularly if their introduction is accompanied by heavy front-end expenses. Also, initial production and sales volumes are likely to be low for new products and customers so that revenues earned will not be sufficient to cover initial year batch-, product-, and customer-specific expenses. In fact, the profitability of new products is even lower than reported in their initial years. In addition to any operating losses, many product-specific expenses, such as product design and development (see Chapter 11), may have been incurred even before the initial year of production. In Stage II systems, the costs of launching new products and acquiring new customers are spread (peanut-buttered) across all existing products and customers. In ABC systems, these front-end expenses are assigned to the new products and customers that are the specific beneficiaries of launch and acquisition activities.

Some managers express concern with the more accurate assignment of launch and development expenses to products because they feel that seeing how unprofitable new products can be will deter the organization from continuing to launch new products. We do not find this a compelling objection. If current year product development and launch expenses are peanut-buttered across all existing products so as not to "burden" the new products, the organization encounters two types of distortions. First, the profitability of existing products is depressed downward, perhaps triggering inappropriate decisions on pricing, outsourcing, or product discontinuance. Second, the company fails to see the costs of the new product development and launch process. By reporting the high costs associated with development and launch, greater visibility is provided for improving these processes (operational ABM), a signal consistent with recommendations made by leading technology and operations management scholars.[13] Similarly, if companies, particularly service companies, see the actual high costs of acquiring new customers, they may reassess their strategies and processes used to acquire new customers. In all these cases, the ABC report of unprofitable new products and customers helps managers focus on critical processes and avoids the fallout from bad decisions using distorted cost information.

When product development, product launch, and customer acquisition costs are high, rather than looking at product and customer profitability on a year-by-year basis, managers should look at a report of lifetime profitability of individual products and customers. Ex post, it is easy to prepare lifetime product and customer profitability reports. They require only two spreadsheets: one for products and one for customers. The rows on the spreadsheet represent individual products; the columns represent individual years. Each year the ABC product and customer profit or loss is entered into the appropriate spreadsheet cell. Such a report makes it easy to calculate breakeven times, a key measure for new product launches.[14] The breakeven time measures how long it takes a new product (or a new customer) to repay its front-end expenditures and initial operating period losses. The report also highlights when products have reached the end of their profitable life cycle. At that point, declining sales volume and prices that have been lowered to meet competition or stimulate demand for the mature product are no longer sufficient to repay annual product-sustaining expenses and the batch costs associated with small-lot production.

The ABC customer profitability analysis could also be used prospectively (anticipating the discussion of what-if ABC models in Chapter 15). Before launching major marketing campaigns, managers could assess how much they are willing to spend to acquire customers with certain characteristics based on the volume of business expected to be done with these newly acquired customers and—the ABC part—the specific ongoing costs of serving those customers.[15]

Activity-based costing also applies to the end of a product's life cycle. Environmental laws in many North American and European countries are enforcing responsibility for product take-back costs; companies that produce products will be responsible for the recycling or disposal of the product after customers are finished with it.[16] Similarly, companies dismantling or abandoning large production facilities are responsible for any environmental cleanup costs at the site. Companies that wish to minimize such costs will want to recognize and to consider environmental costs during product and process design stages. As with manufacturing costs, the greatest influence on environmental costs occurs during product and process development stages.

To minimize environmental costs, companies must first understand the magnitude of the costs, and the specific products and processes that contribute to total environmental costs. Most companies don't even know their total environmental costs. One study revealed several cases where actual environmental costs were three to four times higher than management estimates.[17] A comprehensive ABC model will help companies identify all the activities and the total resource costs related to preventing and remediating expected environmental damage. The ABC model can then link current environmental costs to the specific products and processes requiring environmental intervention. As with differentiating between the costs of launching new products versus sustaining existing products, current environmental costs must be correctly attributed to both existing products and past products. If the cost system assigns the current costs for remediating discontinued products to current products, it will introduce considerable distortion into the economics of production of existing products. And the converse is also true. Failing to recognize, in today's production costs, the costs of future disposal, recycling, and remediation will underestimate the total costs of producing today's products.

Applying ABC to environmental costs requires no new principles; the motivation and approach are identical to that already articulated for assigning production costs to products, marketing costs to customers, and assets to products and customers for an EVA calculation. Not all products have the same degree of environmental hazard or toxicity. Nor are all products equally costly to dispose of or recycle. Therefore, as analysts analyze environmentally related activities, they can identify cost drivers and product consumption patterns that permit a good attribution of environmental costs to individual products.[18] To the extent that some environmental costs are traced to specific processes, all the products converted by these processes will be assigned a share of the process-specific environmental costs.

The visibility of assigning, via ABC, current environmental costs to existing and past products will highlight the opportunity to influence the potential environmental costs of future products during product design and process development stages. For examples, aluminum cans are more expensive to produce initially but recycled cans enable new cans to be produced at much lower costs. Kodak now recovers and reuses 97% of the solvents used in film production; the reuse of the solvents is only one-seventh the cost of acquiring and then disposing, after one use, entirely new materials. The 3M company made a $60,000 investment to replace a solvent-based system with a water-based one, but saved $180,000 in pollution-abatement equipment and $15,000 per year in materials purchases.[19] Chapter 11 discussed the use of ABC models of manufacturing costs to influence product design and development decisions. Similarly, an ABC model of environmental expenses can inform product design and process selection decisions to reduce total life-cycle costs of products: materials acquisition, materials conversion, and materials disposal and recycling.

Summary

In this chapter we have extended the application of activity-based costing in new directions. We have indicated how many business- or corporate-level expenses, formerly treated as facility or business unit-sustaining, could be driven farther down the organizational hierarchy through the use of secondary and primary activities. We have proposed the use of a hierarchical profitability map to capture organizational expenses at the lowest possible activity level. The profitability map points managers to those areas where special attention should be devoted to brands, product lines, customers, distribution channels, facilities, and regions. We have shown how assets can be assigned to activities, products, and customers so that an economic value-added (EVA) calculation can be performed. Reporting EVA at the individual product and customer level provides an additional piece of information for managers and employees. They can work beyond increasing product and customer profitability to consider actions that will increase the asset intensity of products and customers, through lowered working capital levels and greater utilization of tangible and intangible assets. The individual product/customer EVA calculation will also signal to managers, in advance of committing assets to products and customers, that adequate returns be earned on the assets so committed.

Life-cycle costing enables product and customer profitability to be measured across their expected lifetimes, not just period by period. The lifetime perspective enables managers to make better decisions about product introduction, product design and development, customer acquisition, and, as we have discussed in the final section, the costs incurred after a product has been used. Environmental costs are growing in magnitude and importance at many organizations. Managers can benefit from better understanding the linkage between their total environmental expenses and decisions made about individual products and processes.

14

Stage IV: Integrating ABC with Enterprise-Wide Systems

Vision: Management reporting and control systems will be fully integrated, with a common set of information, entered once and accessible to all, supporting both internal and external reporting. The management systems will provide performance information for operational improvement and strategic learning, and accurate measurement of product and customer profitability.

Today, companies throughout the world have developed Stage III activity-based cost systems, and are using them to improve profitability through operational and strategic activity-based management. Typically, these ABC systems are retrospective. They are refreshed periodically, say annually or quarterly, based on operating performance during the most recent period.[1] The ABC systems usually reside on personal computers or PC networks, and depend on data downloaded from networks or floppy disks; some data may even require manual entry. In general, these ABC systems are an add-on to the organization's financial budgeting and reporting systems.

In parallel with the development of stand-alone, Stage III ABC systems, many companies are also investing in enterprise-wide systems. As noted in Chapter 1, an EWS can provide a company with an integrated set of operating, financial, and management systems. The EWS has a common data structure and a centralized, accessible data warehouse that permits data to be entered and accessed from anywhere in the world. Managers naturally would like to integrate their stand-alone ABC systems into their EWSs so that they can support fact-based decision making across a wide range of organizational activities. They also want the ABC systems to provide information about future operations, not just to report on the cost and profitability of past operations. This is the vision for Stage IV. In this chapter, we describe how companies can achieve these goals through integrated ABC and enterprise-wide systems.

Challenges of System Integration

Companies, in their initial attempts to integrate their PC-based Stage III ABC systems into their financial reporting systems, encountered problems with the sheer magnitude of data flows. These problems limited their ability to evolve to full Stage IV activity-based management.

But such data and information exchange problems still exist today for even their mature Stage III ABC systems. These systems require that data and information be transferred to them from numerous existing software packages such as the general ledger, the bill of materials, production scheduling, engineering, MRP (materials requirement planning), factory floor labor reporting, and sales and customer systems. But these transfers typically occur only annually or semiannually. In addition, there is infrequent and limited transfer of data and information from the ABC system back to the company's existing systems.[2]

The integrated, prospective reporting environment of Stage IV ABC systems demands much greater and more frequent data and information exchanges between the ABC system and existing systems. The flow from ABC back to existing systems reflects the greater integration of ABC information into the company's ongoing reporting systems. For example, activity-based budgets (see Chapter 15) can be used to set resource spending levels for the coming year, determine bonus levels, and establish transfer prices. Each of these applications requires that activity-based budgeting information be shared with other systems. The transfers become more frequent as the activity-based information is integrated into the mainstream management processes of the firm. Integrated ABC and performance measurement systems may require monthly, weekly, or even daily exchanges of information. Finally, the shift to prospective and what-if analysis often requires iterations between the ABC and the financial systems. For example, the ABC systems could be used to investigate the impact of different sales volumes on product and customer costs. In these analyses, the ABC-calculated product costs must be embedded into the system that forecasts sales, production, and profits. Several iterations might be required before the appropriate selling prices and product volumes are determined. These iterations require information to flow in both directions frequently. The demand for frequent and extensive information sharing is only intensified as companies respond to their highly competitive environment and launch operational effectiveness programs designed to produce a lean enterprise.

A few companies, recognizing the benefits for integrating their ABC systems with their ongoing reporting and information systems, have attempted to by-pass Stage III implementations. Instead of maintaining their Stage II financial system, with an ABC add-on, they scrapped their previous costing system entirely.[3] These companies now rely on their ABC systems, not only as an input to operational and strategic decision making, but also as the main cost reporting system. They are using prospective (not historical) activity cost driver rates to value inventory and as monthly feedback for performance measurement. These systems seem like Stage IV systems, in which ABC has become integrated and embedded in official systems and is used for financial reporting, product costing, and operational control. Unfortunately, the system's designers have made critical errors in applying ABC thinking, causing the reported information to be less useful than that obtainable from a well-designed Stage III system. As companies embed their ABC models within an integrated EWS framework, managers must make fundamental enhancements in their ABC and operational control systems if they are to have a valid, viable set of cost management systems.

A Failed Attempt to Go from Stage II Directly to Stage IV

Take the example of one electronics company. In 1990, its traditional direct-labor overhead costing system had become hopelessly obsolete, applying production overhead in highly automated processes at rates in excess of 500%. Managers believed that it would not be feasible to tinker with this system since labor-routing information in the MRP system was also out of date and needed a major overhaul. They decided to completely eliminate direct-labor reporting and maintenance of labor-routing information and move immediately to an activity-based costing system in which costs would be accumulated by production process and applied based on actual activity volumes in each process. Over a relatively short development period, they developed a system that collected costs in 15 production processes, and selected an appropriate activity cost driver for each activity (see examples below):

PRODUCTION PROCESS	ACTIVITY COST DRIVER
Surface Mount Technology	Placements
Pre-wave Hand Insertion	Parts Inserted
Functional Tests	Test Hours
Assembly	Parts Assembled
Post-wave Hand Insertion	Parts Inserted

Many costs could be directly assigned to each production process. The costs of indirect manufacturing departments, such as manufacturing management, training, and quality, were assigned with cost drivers that reflected the differential use of these departments by the individual production processes. General factory support departments, such as scheduling, planning, process engineering, test engineering, and shipping, were assigned to product groups based on monthly surveys of effort. After all expenses had been assigned to the 15 processes, the financial managers calculated a standard activity cost driver rate each year by dividing total budgeted expenses by the expected quantity of the cost driver for the upcoming year.

Improvements on this approach are obvious. First, the system relied almost entirely on unit-level drivers, and failed to reflect the cost of batch and product-level activities, an elementary component of any Stage III ABC system, as described in Chapter 6. Also, the system could have improved the assignment of costs between secondary and primary activities (as discussed in Chapter 13). Nevertheless, the basic structure of the new system was certainly an improvement on the previous direct-labor costing system.

One of the primary applications of this system was to influence decisions made by product design and development engineers (see Chapter 11). One product development engineer commented on the improvement in the quality of the information from the new system:

> We had been told to reduce costs by 10%, but the [old] cost system calculated product costs as materials and direct labor plus a burden rate in excess of 500% on direct labor. No one believed these numbers and it was hard to get the product design engineers' attention for cost reduction opportunities.
>
> Now, using the ABC methodology, we have the numbers that one SMT [surface mount technology] component costs $0.024 to place while an automatic [through-hole] insertion costs $0.08 and a postwave solder hand-insertion costs about $1. By knowing the differences in costs per insertion, we can work better with the product design engineers, encouraging them to replace components requiring hand assembly with SMT components. . . . We can also influence them to reduce the number of functional tests they specify if the tests are not really adding value to the process.[4]

If the system, with its annual calculation of cost driver rates, had been used to influence the design decisions for future products—a good Stage III strategic ABM application—it would have been, as the engineer said, a significant improvement over the Stage II system. The company used the system to value products for inventory valuation, thus accomplishing the financial reporting function of the obsolete cost system it replaced. But problems arose when financial managers thought they had developed a Stage IV system that could also be used for monthly reporting.[5]

Each period, the financial system accumulated actual expenses for each of the production and support departments. The system then calculated the *actual* monthly cost driver rate for each process by dividing the *actual* monthly expenses of that process by the *actual* quantity of the activity cost driver for the process. Managers posted monthly reports and charts of the cost driver rates throughout the plant to highlight the plant's continuous improvement efforts. Seemingly, the operational improvement and learning objectives (see Chapters 4 and 5) were also being met by the new activity-based cost system. If valid, the installed system would have represented a Stage IV system since it served all three cost measurement functions: valuing inventory for financial reporting, product costing, and operational learning and improvement.

In reality, however, the system fell short along several dimensions. Understanding in some detail the limitations of this system is vital before companies implement a Stage IV system. An integrated Stage IV system, particularly one installed on an EWS platform, will give companies the capability to access daily expenses for activities and process and daily quantities of activity cost drivers. Rather than waiting a month to get a report on actual cost driver rates, an integrated Stage IV system could calculate daily *actual* activity cost driver rates, providing even faster feedback to employees for their learning and improvement activities.

To paraphrase a former and almost impeached U.S. president, "It would be easy to do such a calculation, but it would be wrong." Actual activity cost driver (ACD) rates, whether calculated daily or monthly, are inappropriate to use for operational feedback and control. Nor should actual ACD rates be used for product and customer costing either. Three different sources of variation can cause actual ACD rates to fluctuate in the short term in ways that are unrelated to the underlying economics and productivity of activities and business processes:

1. Spending fluctuations
2. Volume fluctuations
3. Fluctuations in productivity and yields

These three sources of variations affect, respectively, the numerator, the denominator, and the ratio itself of the ACD rate calculation. Allowing these short-term fluctuations to affect calculated ACD rates will introduce errors when estimating the underlying rate, and mask underlying improvement, or deterioration, in activities and business processes. Managers who fail to understand such issues may set inappropriate priorities for process improvement initiatives and make incorrect decisions about products and customers.

Spending Fluctuations

Actual expenses in a period, the numerator of the ACD rate calculation, often reflects timing differentials related to when bills were paid (spending fluctuations) rather than how resources were used. Thus, reported expenses for a department or other operating unit in a period may be high because a batch of supplies were either paid for or received during the period, but are not used until a subsequent period.[6] Conversely, expenses may be low in a period when supplies are used but not replenished. These timing differences create a discrepancy between actual spending levels and the actual levels of resources used during the period.

Actual expenses also reflect the differential use of resources that are not supplied on a regular basis each period. Suppose a machine broke down unexpectedly and unusual repair expenses were incurred. This would raise the costs assigned to the production center and products in that period. Conversely, in a period when no maintenance and repairs were performed, the department would have unexpectedly lower expenses.

If such spending and usage fluctuations were allowed to flow through into daily or monthly activity cost driver rates, it would not be possible for employees and managers to distinguish between these temporary events and fundamental, sustainable improvements (or decrements) in efficiency and productivity. Even worse, were the daily or monthly actual cost driver rates allowed to flow into product and customer costs, managers would see erratic fluctuations in product and customer profitability that had no relation to the sustainable economics of producing products and serving customers.

For operational and strategic ABM, activity-based cost driver rates should reflect existing or expected activity efficiencies. That is why we argued, in Chapter 7, that the rates should not be calculated on historical expense data. The rates should use, in the numerator of the calculation, budgeted expense information. Presumably, budgeted data reflects managers' best estimates of the cost of resources required to perform a given quantity of activities. The budgeted information could also provide normalized estimates of the cost of activities whose timing is discretionary.

Take maintenance. Suppose, based on past experience and engineering studies, managers estimate that maintenance and overhaul must be performed after a machine has operated for 1,400 hours.[7] Assume that the machine is operated an average of 70 hours per week. Therefore, scheduled maintenance on the machine is performed every 20 weeks, or once every four months. Working directly from the actual recorded expenses, the financial system would report no maintenance expense for three months, leading to low actual activity cost driver rates during these months, and then a heavy expense in the fourth month when the actual maintenance is performed.[8]

Is the machine efficiency high in the three months when no maintenance is performed, and low in the month when the maintenance occurs? Are products produced during months when there is no maintenance less expensive than products produced during the month when maintenance is performed? Of course not. Basically the cost of maintaining the machine after 1,400 hours of use is a cost of operating the machine in every period, and in every hour, regardless of the time period in which the actual maintenance is performed. Every product that is processed on the machine, regardless of when it is produced, creates a little more demand for maintenance that must eventually be satisfied. As such, a normalized maintenance cost should be an element of cost for every product produced, not just the few products that happen to be produced in the period when maintenance is actually performed.

Should the actual amount of spending on maintenance be recorded and monitored? Absolutely. Managers of both the machining department and the maintenance department should monitor the actual frequency, quantity, and cost of maintenance activity. But such measurement and monitoring is part of the operational control system. Short-term fluctuations in spending on maintenance, or any other activity, should not flow into the activity-based costs of activities, processes, products, and customers. In practice, this problem rarely occurs in Stage III ABC systems since these systems covered periods of six or twelve months. For such long estimation periods, the impact of short-term fluctuations average out, and timing differences in expense recognition are small, relative to total expenses. But as the reporting period shrinks, distortions from fluctuations in spending will increase.

To reduce these distortions, activity-based cost driver rates should reflect budgeted or normalized costs for performing activities. Later in the chapter we discuss the connections and feedback between operational control systems and activity-based cost systems. For now, let us accept that the reporting for the two systems is different and that organizations need both systems. Attempts to incorporate short-term feedback on actual spending into activity cost driver rates will only distort and confuse efforts to improve operations and to make better decisions about activities, products, and customers.

Volume Fluctuations

The second problem with calculating actual activity cost driver rates relates to the denominator, the quantity of the activity cost driver rate. Consider a period (a month or, worse, a day) when demand is below normal. Almost all the expenses of resources supplied to perform the activity have been determined and committed in advance and will be incurred independent of the actual demands on the activity. Consequently, if actual activity cost driver quantities are used to calculate actual rates, the rates will increase when demands have been low and decrease when demands have been high. This is not rocket science. Nor does it require a degree in rocket science to realize that reporting a lower-than-normal activity cost driver rate during a period when demand is high is like Macy's taking credit for Christmas: "Wow, look at all the customers coming into the stores during December; we must have done something terrific to have attracted them."

We want activity cost driver rates to reflect the underlying efficiency of activities. This efficiency should be measured by the cost and quantity of resources used to perform each unit of activity demanded. Allowing cost driver rates to fluctuate with short-term variations in activity volume causes the activity cost driver rate to become a distorted signal about the efficiency and productivity of the activity. It also forces employees and managers to back out any volume effects, before getting to the root causes of any remaining unexpected variation. Why perform a calculation whose first-order effect is confusion and the second-order effect is creating a task to undo the calculation?

But a second, and perhaps even more serious, distortion comes from using actual cost driver quantities to calculate an actual rate. To recapitulate the argument we made in Chapter 7, the underlying efficiency of an activity is measured not by how much work we either expect to do in the upcoming period, or how much work was actually done in the past period, but by how much work *can* be done, given the resources supplied and their efficiency.[9] We dealt with this problem by recommending that ACD rates be calculated using practical capacity. This recommendation holds for both annual and daily ABC systems. The distortion caused by not following this recommendation, however, occurs only once a year for a Stage III annual ABC system; the distortion can occur 365 times a year if companies recalculate their ACD rates daily with a Stage IV integrated ABC system. Managers, with a system in which ACD rates fluctuate each day, week, or month with volume effects, will soon learn to assign the causes of all unfavorable fluctuations to volume effects, and will undoubtedly miss the more fundamental causes of decreasing efficiencies.

Fluctuations in Productivity and Yield

A third reason for not using actual cost driver rates relates to fluctuations in the efficiency of performing the activity itself, an error that affects the ratio of the ACD calculation. Deming emphasized that under proper statistical control, employees and managers should not react to normal statistical fluctuations. Process fluctuation around a mean or average value is normal, and people should assume that the mean value remains constant until they have sufficient data and evidence to reject the hypothesis. This statistical quality control principle also applies to activity-based costing. Managers should not introduce random fluctuation into estimates of an activity cost driver rate. But if they divide actual spending by actual quantities to calculate an actual cost driver rate, they violate this rule, by including normal statistical fluctuations into the calculated rate. While the impact of normal process variation on actual cost driver rates will likely be minor, relative to the distortions from using actual expenses and actual cost driver quantities, it is yet another reason for using a standard or budgeted cost driver rate, not an actual rate.

Companies, with Stage III ABC systems, aggregated their data over an extended time period. This reduced the impact of short-term fluctuations in productivity and yield. It is the shift to short time periods made possible by integrating ABC systems with enterprise-wide systems that leads to a potential significant problem.

These examples indicate that the time periods for estimating and reestimating activity cost driver rates should be chosen with care. Perhaps the periods can vary by activity and resource type. The period over which activity driver quantities are determined is a function of the frequency with which the activity is performed, the degree of statistical fluctuation in the efficiency and yield, and the ability to control for the effects of spending, usage, and productivity fluctuations. The period chosen should be long enough to capture a sufficient number of the performances of the activity to average out the fluctuations. If the degree of fluctuation is small, relatively few observations are required; if it is high, more observations and hence a longer time period are needed. Therefore, activities that are performed in high volume each day, and where spending fluctuations are easily controlled for, could be candidates for daily reporting and frequent updating. The costs of activities, like maintenance, which are performed infrequently, may not be updated for a year or even longer.

In summary, companies in Stage III typically use historical, postperiod data for their ABC systems. Cost estimates and assignment from such Stage III models are distorted by temporary spending fluctuations, timing differences in expense recognition, underutilization of resource capacity, fluctuations in activity volumes, and minor, temporary variations in underlying process efficiency. These errors exist but managers accept them because the activity cost driver estimates are still likely to be far more accurate than estimates from Stage II cost systems, which use only volume-based drivers. Also, many Stage III cost systems use aggregate data, estimated over three-, six-, or twelve-month periods, for which short-term fluctuations tend to average out. The only substantial error in estimating activity cost driver rates over these long periods of time comes from failure to reflect unused capacity costs.

With the advent of integrated, enterprise-wide systems, companies can move from semiannual or annual calculation of activity cost driver rates to monthly, weekly, and daily calculations. As the time period for estimation shrinks, all the temporary, nonrecurring, and timing factors become embedded in the activity cost driver rates, leading to fluctuations in these rates that are unrelated to the underlying efficiency and productivity of the activities. In effect, migrating a Stage III ABC system to an enterprise-wide environment, with daily rather than an annual calculation, will give managers distorted product cost and efficiency information every single day rather than just once a year (as in a traditional Stage II system). This is a good example where a higher quantity of more frequent data will actually provide less useful information to managers.

Differences Between ABC and Operational Learning and Improvement Systems

Before describing the migration to Stage IV integrated systems, let us review our journey so far. In Chapter 2, we described Stage I (broken) and Stage II (financial reporting-driven) cost systems. In particular, in Stage II, the cost system requirements are derived from financial reporting considerations (see *Exhibit 14-1*).

When the standard costs used for inventory valuation by the official financial reporting system are also used for managerial product costing, product costs are distorted by the simple, averaging procedures. Also, Stage II systems do not report on customer costs and profitability since financial requirements do not need any organizational costs to be assigned to customers. Using the variances from the financial reporting system for performance measurement leads to limited, delayed, and too highly aggregated signals for learning and improvement activities. Stage II operational control information is financial only and is supplied in the same cycle used to prepare financial statements.

Chapters 4–13 described the opportunities for Stage III cost systems (see *Exhibit 14-2*). Stage III requires separate systems for operational control and for product and customer costing, and both are likely to be separate from the official system still being used to prepare periodic financial reports. Chapters 4 and 5 described Stage III operational cost systems, specifically designed to help employees continually monitor and improve operations. These operational control systems are separate from the Stage III activity-based cost systems described in Chapters 6–13.

Operational control and ABC systems play important but different roles for managerial purposes. These dissimilar roles mean that the design characteristics of the two types of systems are also different. For example, operational control systems for learning and improvement should provide

Exhibit 14-1 Stage II: Financial Reporting Drives Managerial Systems

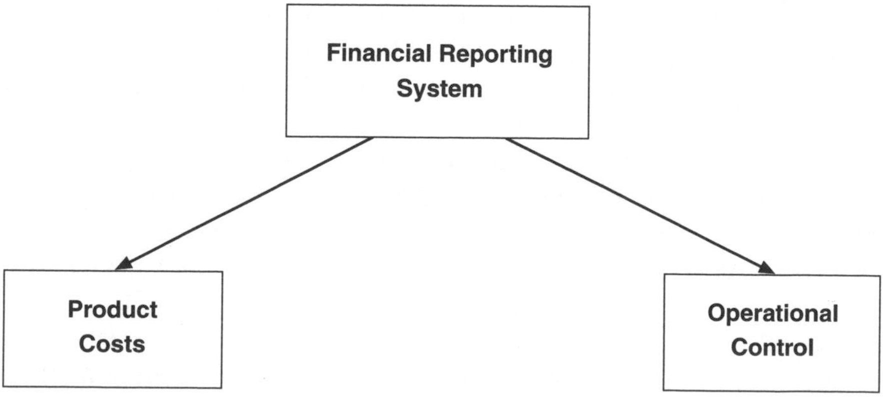

Exhibit 14-2 Stage III: ABC Systems Break the Linkage from Financial
Reporting Systems

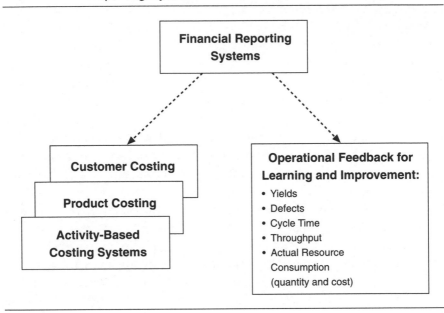

information, if not in real time, at least frequently enough for employees to get short-term feedback on process improvements. While ABC systems can also report in short intervals, monthly or weekly (see Chapter 7), their feedback reflects the demands for resources by products, services, and customers, not the efficiency with which the demands are met. By using standard rates for activity cost drivers, the ABC model assumes a standard level of efficiency associated with meeting demands.

The different characteristics of the ABC systems and operational control systems are summarized in *Exhibit 14-3*. By separating the two managerial systems, the functionality of each system can be developed and customized for its particular mission.

As this exhibit makes abundantly clear, the requirements for the two types of systems are so different that it would be impossible for a single system to perform both functions well. The power of Stage III allows organizations to experiment with new approaches that meet the requirements of the two functions as well as they can, without the added burden of integration and compatibility between the two new systems. By recognizing the distinct differences between the systems, managers can avoid the errors described earlier in this chapter made by the electronics com-

Exhibit 14-3 Comparison of Operational Control and ABC Systems

	OPERATIONAL CONTROL	ACTIVITY-BASED COSTING
Cost of Resources Used	Actual	Standard
Frequency of Updating	Continual	Periodic (Quarterly, Semiannual, or Annual)
Measurement Demands	Highly accurate	Estimates sufficient; more accuracy (duration and intensity drivers) when cost-justified
Scope of System	Responsibility center	Entire value chain: from suppliers and product development through operations, administration, customers, and postsales service
Focus of System	Resource spending: costs of resources supplied	Resource usage: costs of resources used
Cost Variability	Emphasis on short-term fixed and variable costs	Degree of variability identified via attributes but not a central feature; costs become variable as resource supply adjusts to resource demand
Applicability	Most useful in repetitive, predictable processes; less useful in highly discretionary and judgmental activities	Universally applicable: can adjust type of cost driver used (transaction, duration, and direct charging) to nature of underlying process
Complementary Systems	Nonfinancial measures (quality, cycle times)	Needs-based customer segment analysis; competitor and strategic information

pany, which used an ABC system—that failed to reflect capacity and resource usage concepts—as an operational control system to focus employee attention on reducing monthly cost driver rates. Adding roles to a satisfactory Stage III ABC system will compromise the functionality of the system for its main purpose: to calculate reasonably accurate costs for a complete set of organizational activities and processes, and of the products produced and customers served.

Stage III operational control and ABC systems are, of course, not unrelated. We have seen, in operational ABM, that the ABC system provides the front-end justification for strategic initiatives and improvement programs to reduce or eliminate inefficiencies in organizational activities.

Once such programs are launched, the operational learning and improvement system provides the continual measurement that helps employees improve activity efficiencies. A subsequent ABC model can identify whether the efficiency and the productivity have been captured through increased capacity and lower cost driver rates, and whether the additional capacity has been exploited either through a lower resource supply or by higher activity volumes being handled by the existing resources.

ABC and Periodic Reporting

In discouraging companies from using their ABC system as the primary mechanism for periodic reporting on efficiency and productivity, we do not wish to imply that activity-based cost information cannot be successfully integrated into monthly and quarterly financial reporting. In Chapter 7, we illustrated how the reconciliation between budgeted and actual expenses can be accomplished. To expand on the examples in Chapter 7, consider a more general situation in which resources to perform an activity are not totally committed in advance (i.e., fixed). Of the budgeted expenses of $280,000 for the period to perform the activity *handle customer order,* assume that $200,000 of that amount would be incurred even if no orders were received. These expenses represent the cost of resources such as facilities, equipment, technology, and salaried employees whose supply would not be diminished even if order volume fell drastically. The remaining $80,000 represent resources whose short-term supply (i.e., within the period of measurement) can be adjusted up or down, depending on need. They could represent the use of temporary workers, employees who could be reassigned, or the cost of purchased services—such as telecommunications or computing—whose supply is proportional to actual need.

To deal with this situation, of both a committed and a flexible resource supply, we develop a two-tiered activity cost driver rate. The first tier represents the cost of the capacity resources. This calculation follows the procedure already described in Chapter 7: divide the budgeted expenses ($200,000) by the *practical capacity* of work (5,000 customer orders) that can be handled by the budgeted supply of resources to obtain a cost driver rate of $40 per order. The second tier represents the cost of the flexible resources: divide the budgeted cost ($80,000) by the *expected* activity volume (4,000 customer orders) to obtain a cost driver rate of $20 per order. The total cost driver rate for this activity, $60 per order, is the sum of the two tiers.[10]

Suppose now that, as in the Chapter 7 example, the actual activity level for the period is 3,800 orders (200 less than expected), and that actual spending is $273,600. Then the period operating report looks like this:

	Expense	Activity Level	Cost Driver Rate
Committed Resources	$200,000	5,000 orders	$40/order
Flexible Resources	$80,000	4,000 orders	$20/order
Budgeted	$280,000	4,000 orders	$60/order
Actual	$273,600	3,800 orders	n/a

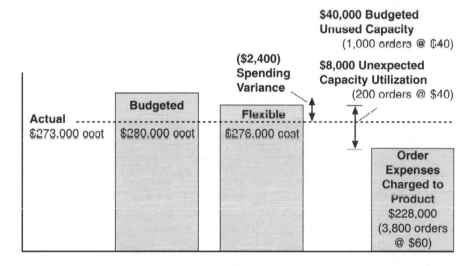

Here the flexible budget provides the linkage between changes in actual operating levels and changes in budgeted spending. This approach uses exactly the same philosophy as the Stage II standard costing/flexible budgeting systems described in Chapters 2 and 3. But the flexible budget/ABC approach allows activity cost driver rates to be based on the practical capacity of committed resources, while explicitly recognizing those resources whose supply can and should be adjusted within the period, to match the demand for the services from the resources. The activity cost driver rate ($60 per order) does not fluctuate with either actual spending ($273,600 versus the budgeted $280,000) or with differences between practical capacity and capacity expected to be used (5,000 versus 4,000 orders), nor with short-term unexpected variation in the quantity of demand for the activity (3,800 actual orders versus 4,000 expected orders).

This example clearly shows the distinction between using an ABC cost driver rate ($60 per order) for assigning resource costs to products and customers versus the operational control (or learning and improvement) objective to monitor short-term spending and efficiencies (explaining the difference between actual spending and the flexible budget calculated at actual activity volumes for each activity). The spending or efficiency variance can be analyzed in more detail, using traditional cost accounting practices to identify and highlight the source of variation reported during the period.[11]

Using standard activity cost driver rates, multiplied by actual quantities used of the cost driver, is suitable for assigning the costs of repetitive activities to products, services, and customers. Typically, the cost of such activities would be assigned using either a transactional (e.g., cost per order) or a duration (e.g., cost per hour of order-processing time) driver. Some expenses, however, are discretionary such as engineering support provided to products, and technical, marketing, and selling resources provided to individual customers. If these expenses are traced with direct charging, the actual costs of the effort supplied to support individual products, services, and customers can be directly assigned each period. Since the amount of such effort is somewhat discretionary, and can vary considerably from period to period, managers should not overreact to short-term variations in the reported cost and profitability of products and customers caused by assignment of discretionary expenses. When period-to-period demands in resources and effort supplied can fluctuate sharply, managers should consider the calculation of lifetime cost and profitability, as discussed in Chapter 11, to give a more comprehensive picture of the economics of products and customers.

ABC and Financial Reporting

As ABC systems become integrated into the mainstream reporting systems of the firm, managers will naturally ask whether the ABC system can be used to generate cost of goods sold and inventory valuations for financial reporting purposes. The answer is yes but with precautions.

The answer is yes because an activity attribute can be developed that identifies ABC costs that can be assigned to products but that cannot be assigned for financial reporting purposes. For example, the ABC cost might include the interest costs associated with the capital dedicated to that product. Conversely, the ABC system may not assign to products certain costs, such as facility-sustaining costs, that financial reporting requires be allocated to products. The first correction is trivial, requiring only an extra activity attribute field. The second correction, however, should be done by financial accountants outside the ABC system to avoid any confusion. They can pick an arbitrary cost driver, such as direct labor, conversion costs, or total ABC costs, to allocate costs required by GAAP but not traceable via cause-and-effect relationships from resources to activities to products.

The primary impetus to have the activity-based cost systems generate GAAP costs comes from concerns that, if the two systems are quite separate, they can report different profit figures. In this case, managers will be ambiguous about which system should be used to evaluate and reward their actions. Managers do try to maximize their reported performance, whatever measurement scheme is chosen. Unfortunately, the problem is not solved by using the ABC system to report GAAP costs. The addition of costs that are excluded by GAAP and the subtraction of costs that should be excluded by ABC principles mean that the two systems will likely always report different profits and balance sheets.

For example, take two products. Product A has a very high capital requirement and the associated interest is $100,000. In contrast, Product B has a very low capital requirement and its associated interest is $10,000. Product A has a low labor content and attracts a total of $5,000 in facility-sustaining costs while B, which has a high labor content, attracts $50,000. The two sets of reported profits are shown below:

ABC INCOME STATEMENT		
	PRODUCT A	**PRODUCT B**
Total Revenues	$800,000	$825,000
ABC Costs	600,000	600,000
ABC Profit	**$200,000**	**$225,000**

GAAP INCOME STATEMENT (reconciled from ABC Statement)		
Total Revenues	$800,000	$825,000
ABC Costs	600,000	600,000
Interest Costs	(100,000)	(10,000)
Facility Costs	5,000	50,000
GAAP Costs	505,000	640,000
GAAP Profit	**$295,000**	**$185,000**

In this example, the reconciliation between ABC and GAAP reverses the relative profitability of the two products. The ABC system reports higher profits for Product B while the GAAP system reports higher profits for Product A. If companies are to avoid confusion between the different requirements of ABC and GAAP systems, they must choose only one approach (obviously we recommend the ABC system) for internal reporting. They should have their accountants calculate GAAP cost of goods sold and inventory values only at the aggregate level of the income statement and balance sheet, and not decompose these calculations into individual product costs.

One hopeful sign may lead to a significant lessening of this problem. As companies move to the lean enterprise, drastically lowering their levels of inventory relative to cost of goods sold, accountants can use extremely simple methods, perhaps a simple markup over purchase price, for allocating costs to inventory. While the individual product costs calculated in this manner for external reporting (which should be inaccessible to managers anyway) will be wrong, the cost of goods sold and inventory valuations will be sufficiently accurate for financial reporting purposes, especially for companies with low inventories and stable product mixes.

Fungible Resources

Our capacity costing examples in Chapter 7 and earlier in this chapter have adopted a simplifying assumption. We have assumed a great deal of resource specificity; the resources supplied can perform only a single activity, *handle customer orders*. With this simplifying assumption, which may be met in practice for some activities, we could measure capacity at either the resource or the activity level.

In general, however, resources can perform multiple activities. For example, the same set of resources in the customer administration department might be called upon not only to handle customer orders, but also to maintain credit information on customers, handle customer complaints, measure customer satisfaction, and follow up with customers that pay their bills slowly. When resources can perform multiple activities, capacity must be measured at the resource level, not the activity level. Continuing the above example, the number of customer orders that could be handled in a period is not a unique number; the capacity for this activity depends upon all the other activity demands made on the resources supplied. If few complaints must be addressed during the period, many orders can be processed, but the time available to handle orders will be severely diminished during periods when there are many customer complaints, credit checks, and requests for customer satisfaction evaluations.

In this more general case, the costing can be handled well by estimating the practical capacity of the resources supplied. Capacity is generally measured by the hours of time available to perform a task. Even for machines, the basic measure is hours of machine time available for productive use. Alternative measures of capacity, such as number of units that can be processed, gallons and pounds of material that can be converted, or number of operations that can be performed, can be derived from the time-based capacity measure—by dividing the available time by the time per unit to process a product unit, convert a gallon or pound of material, or perform a standard operation.

We extend the numerical example in the previous section by assuming that resources, costing $560,000 per period, are supplied to perform three activities:

- Handle customer orders (the original activity in the numerical example),
- Process customer complaints, and
- Perform customer credit checks.

A Stage III ABC system would estimate the costs of these three activities by having analysts survey the people resources and estimate the percentage of their time spent (or expected to be spent) on these three activities. Suppose that these percentages are 70%, 10%, and 20%, respectively. We also find that the actual (or estimated) quantities of the respective activity cost drivers are:

- 7,000 customer orders
- 200 customer complaints
- 350 credit checks

The Stage III ABC system would perform the following calculations to assign the $560,000 resource cost to activities and to activity cost driver rates:

ACTIVITY	PERCENT	ASSIGNED COST	ACTIVITY COST DRIVER QUANTITY	ACTIVITY COST DRIVER RATE
Handle Orders	70%	$392,000	7,000	$ 56/order
Process Complaints	10	56,000	200	$280/complaint
Check Credit	20	112,000	350	$320/credit check
Total	100%	$560,000		

The activity cost driver rates would then be used to assign the expenses of these three activities to customers based on the number of orders handled, complaints processed, and credit checks performed for each customer. The three estimated rates, however, could be strongly influenced by the total demands and the mix of demands made on the customer administration resource. In addition, the calculation of rates requires that a new survey be performed each period to assess the distribution of effort across the three activities. This is a costly and perhaps tedious procedure.

For Stage IV ABC systems, we can consider a new procedure for assigning resource expenses to activities, one that explicitly incorporates the capacity of the resources supplied as well as the underlying efficiency with which individual activities are performed. You don't get something for nothing, however, and several new pieces of information will be required to implement the improved approach.

First, the ABC team must estimate the practical capacity of the resources supplied to perform the related activities. Suppose that the front-line people can supply 8,000 hours of useful work during the period.[12] Then the cost per hour supplied is $560,000/8,000 or $70 per hour.[13] Assume also that the $560,000 of expenses are committed for the upcoming period; they are not expected to vary based on the actual number of customer orders processed, complaints handled, or credit checks performed.

The second set of new information is the estimated (standard) time required to perform each activity. Of course, if the ABC model will use duration drivers to assign the costs of the three activities, this information will already be available (the length of time to handle a customer order, process a complaint, or perform a credit check).[14] Usually, however, organizations will use transactional drivers. Recall that one of the conditions for transactional drivers to be adequate is if the time required to perform each instance of the activity is approximately the same.[15] The new requirement is an estimate of the time needed to perform each instance of the activity, let us call it the unit time estimate. The unit times for each activity can then be multiplied by the $70 per hour cost of each hour to obtain the activity cost driver rate, as shown below:

ACTIVITY	UNIT TIME (hours)	ACTIVITY COST DRIVER RATE
Handle Customer Order	0.72	$ 50.40
Process Customer Complaint	3.60	$252.00
Perform Credit Check	4.11	$288.00

Notice that these rates are somewhat below those estimated with the Stage III ABC system. The reason for this discrepancy will be obvious once we estimate the hours actually used during the period.

ACTIVITY	UNIT TIME (hours)	QUANTITY	TOTAL HOURS
Handle Customer Order	0.72	7,000	5,040
Process Customer Complaint	3.60	200	720
Perform Credit Check	4.11	350	1,440
Total			7,200

The analysis reveals that only 90% of the practical capacity of the resources supplied during the period was used for productive work. The Stage III ABC system overestimated the costs of performing activities because its distribution of effort survey, while quite accurate—70%, 10%, and 20% of the productive work was the correct distribution across the three activities—incorporated both the costs of resource capacity used and those of unused resources. By specifying the unit times to perform each instance of the activity (or, at higher expense, using a duration driver to measure the actual length of time required to perform each instance of the activity), the organization gets both a more valid signal about the underlying efficiency of each activity and about any unused capacity or shortage of capacity in the resources supplied to perform the activity.

With estimates of the cost of resource supply, the practical capacity of the resources supplied, and the unit times for each activity performed by the resources, the reporting system becomes quite simple for each period. Suppose the quantity of activities shifts, in the subsequent period, to 7,100 orders handled, 220 customer complaints processed, and 310 credit checks performed. The costs of each of the three activities are assigned based on the standard rates, calculated at practical capacity: $50.40 per order, $252 per complaint, and $288 per credit check. This calculation can be performed in real time, as the quantity of demands becomes realized.

The period report is both simple and informative:

	NUMBER	UNIT TIMES	TOTAL TIME	COST ASSIGNED
Budgeted Expenses			8,000	$560,000
Activities:				
Handle Customer Orders	7,100	0.72	5,112	357,840
Process Complaints	220	3.60	792	55,440
Perform Credit Checks	310	4.11	1,275	89,280
Total			7,179	502,560
Unused Capacity			821	$ 57,440

The report reveals the estimated time spent on the three activities as well as the resource costs required to handle the activity demands. It also highlights the difference between capacity supplied (both quantity and cost) and the capacity used. Managers can review the $57,440 cost of the 821 hours of unused capacity and consider actions to reduce the supply of resources and the associated expense. Alternatively, since managers know how much unused capacity exists, resource by resource, as they contemplate new product introductions, expansion into new markets, or just shifts in product and customer mix, they can forecast how much of the increased business can be handled by existing capacity, and where capacity shortages are likely to arise that will require additional spending to handle the increased demands.

Stage IV: Integrating ABC and Operational Learning and Improvement Systems

In Stage IV (see *Exhibit 14-4*), we design and integrate activity-based cost systems and systems for operational learning and improvement. Each of these two systems has been customized, in Stage III, to meet the specific needs of managers for activity-based management and for monitoring and improving organizational activities and processes. In Stage IV, linkages and feedback loops between the two systems are established. The budgeting process identifies the practical capacity of the resources supplied to perform activities. The ABC-budgeting process also identifies the resources expected to vary with short-term fluctuations in activity volumes and develops a flexible budget for the supply and spending on these flexible resources. Finally, the Stage IV ABC system specifies estimates of the unit

Exhibit 14-4 Stage IV: ABC and Operational Systems Are Integrated

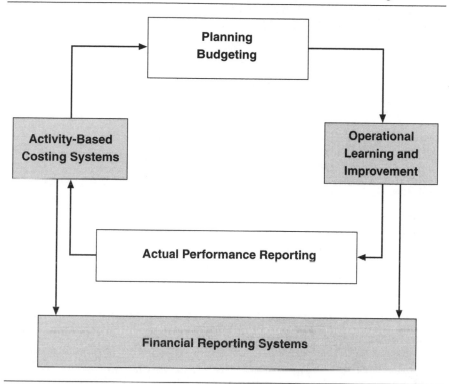

times required to perform different support activities. These estimates provide a standard that can be tested against actual practice.

Once the supply of resources has been determined for operating units, the operational learning and improvement system monitors actual supply and spending against the budgeted amounts. It also can monitor whether realized demands may be approaching the practical capacity of the committed resources. Such capacity monitoring may provide an early signal about potential bottlenecks. It may also provide feedback on the accuracy of the capacity estimates. If activity demands exceed the estimated capacity, without encountering delays and backlogs, the organization learns that the actual capacity of the resources to perform work is higher than previously estimated. This information can be fed back to the activity-based cost system to revise upward the rated practical capacity of the resources.

During the period, the operational learning and improvement system also monitors closely the efficiency and productivity of the resources. As organizational processes become more efficient and productive, the system should detect increases in the number of transactions that the existing resources can handle (capacity increases) or decreases in the standard unit times required to perform organizational activities (for example, to handle a customer order or to process a customer complaint). Stage IV operational learning and improvement systems track the two critical assumptions used to derive the cost of performing the activity: the resource costs of supplying an hour of time to perform the activity, and the actual time required to perform the activity. For example, recall (from Chapter 5) the disciplined process followed by Shionogi Pharmaceuticals to monitor and update its standards.

Stage IV operational control systems may incorporate expert systems[16] to detect when there has been a permanent shift in:

1. The capacity of the resources supplied,
2. The cost of supplying an hour of productive time on the resource, or
3. The efficiency (time required) in performing the activity.

When such a permanent shift has been detected, this information can be fed back to the ABC system to update the appropriate activity cost driver rate. In this way, the ABC system keeps current with permanent improvements made in organizational activities and processes.

The purpose of updating the driver rates is to draw attention to underlying changes in the economics of the business. Therefore, any reported changes should be sufficiently large to warrant updating the ABC model when observed. Otherwise, the changes can be made in conjunction with a periodic update done on a less frequent basis, say annually or semiannually.

In summary, activity cost driver rates can be determined from the budgetary system, or for companies like Shionogi, from the continually updated standards of a kaizen operational control system. The rates stay constant until managers have direct evidence (from their operational control system) about sustainable improvements or decrements in the efficiency with which the activity is performed, or the price of supplying resources to perform the activity. Daily and weekly monitoring of short-term trends in activity and process efficiency should be performed. But this monitoring, as in the company examples given in Chapter 5, should be done by the organization's operational learning and improvement system. The daily and weekly results recorded in a kaizen or pseudo-profit center system should not flow into the ABC system until permanent shifts in efficiency can be confirmed.

During the period, managers will use the information on standard cost driver rates for strategic ABM to make decisions about managing products, customers, and suppliers. At the end of each accounting period, information from the two systems can be brought together in an integrated report on organizational spending and expenses, activity costs, and the costs of individual products and customers. As emphasized earlier, the ABC report will highlight the quantity, standard cost, and profitability of demands made by activities, products, and customers. The operations report will highlight actual expenses, efficiency, quality, and responsiveness of organizational activities.

The vision for Stage IV systems, as shown in Exhibit 14-4, completely reverses the chain of causality in Stage II systems (see Exhibit 14-1). In Stage IV, when financial statements have to be prepared, the managerial information is sent to the finance group for massaging and processing. That group may remove cost assignments to products that are not permitted by regulations, and undo specific enhancements made for managerial purposes—such as using an EVA cost of capital to assign assets to activities, products, and customers—using market values rather than historic costs for some assets, and calculating activity cost driver rates based on targeted rather than current efficiencies. Stage IV companies have optimized their cost and performance monitoring systems for specific and identifiable managerial purposes. Financial reporting to external constituencies is important and must be done well, but it has been made an auxiliary function to the managerial cost and performance measurement systems.

Summary

The power of enterprise-wide systems will enable companies to achieve the Stage IV objective of integrated financial, cost, and performance measurement systems. But just installing an EWS does not guarantee a successful Stage IV system. Managers need a clear vision about the fundamental objectives of their management accounting systems. For example, frequent reports on actual resource consumption, quality, cycle times, and throughput are definitely desirable for the learning and improvement objectives of operational control systems. But managers will get distorted and confusing signals if the activity cost driver rates in their ABC systems are updated too frequently with available information on actual expenses and actual activity volumes. Exhibit 14-3 enumerates the many differences that must be retained if operational control and ABC are to be effective managerial systems.

We recommend that the ABC system calculate product and customer costs with standard activity cost driver rates and actual activity cost driver quantities. In parallel with the ABC system, the operational control system monitors the efficiency with which activities are performed and the actual prices of resources used to perform activities. When sustainable changes are detected, in activity efficiency, resource capacity, or the cost of resources supplied to perform activities, the operational control system can send a signal to the ABC system to update activity cost driver rates. Conversely, in a process to be explicated in greater detail in Chapter 15, managers will use their ABC system to establish the budget for supplying resources to perform activities. This spending budget becomes the baseline for monitoring spending, by the operational control system, in responsibility centers. Used in this way, the two systems retain their unique and valuable purposes and are integrated and compatible with each other. The data in both systems also becomes the basis for periodic financial reports (see Exhibit 14-4 for a representation of the integration among the three systems).

We have completed our blueprint for migrating to Stage IV integrated systems. We can now turn to a final set of topics to illustrate how companies can achieve substantial benefits from their integrated financial systems that were unavailable from Stage III stand-alone systems. In the final chapter, we show how activity-based costing can become the foundation for an organization's budgeting, decision-making, and transfer pricing processes.

15

Stage IV: Using ABC for Budgeting and Transfer Pricing

In Chapter 14, we discussed integrated Stage IV systems. When managers have access to such systems, they can use their ABC model to provide information for important, ongoing managerial processes, including budgeting, what-if analysis, and transfer pricing. By using ABC for budgeting, a practice we call "activity-based budgeting" (ABB), managers determine the supply of resources to operating units and responsibility centers based on the demands for activities they are expected to perform. Activity-based budgeting is an extremely important application; it is the process by which costs, previously thought to be fixed, are made variable.

What-if analysis enables managers to assess the consequences of major changes in product and customer mix. Transfer pricing allows current ABC information on production costs and capacity utilization to be incorporated into the operating, pricing, and selling decisions of decentralized organizational units.

The Impact of Activity-Based Budgeting

Until now, we have accepted, as given, the budgeted expenses for supplying resources to perform activities. In building an ABC model, we estimated appropriate activity costs and cost driver rates based on actual or budgeted costs and the capacity of supplied (budgeted) resources. We have talked about most of these expenses as being committed in advance (see Chapter 7), and noted that the supply and cost of these resources are not likely to vary much with short-term changes in activity demands.

The time has come to relax this assumption and treat the budgeted expenses as endogenous to activity-based management, not a decision made external to the ABC system. In fact, real sustainable payoffs from

ABC and ABM cannot occur unless they become embedded in the organization's budgeting process. Activity-based budgeting gives organizations the opportunity to authorize and control the resources they supply based on the anticipated demands for the activities performed by the resources.

Conventional budgeting practice is an iterative, negotiating process between heads of responsibility centers and senior executives. Responsibility center managers continually seek more resources while senior executives continually attempt to control increases in the spending authorized for their decentralized units. The result is that the budget for the next year builds on that of the previous year, plus or minus a few percent depending upon the outcome of the negotiations between senior executives and local management. Activity-based budgeting offers the opportunity for such discussions to be based more upon facts, and less upon power, influence, and negotiating ability. If the concept had not become discredited by poor theory and application in the Carter administration, we could refer to activity-based budgeting as *zero-based budgeting*.

If implemented successfully, activity-based budgeting demolishes conventional thinking about fixed and variable costs. Is it interesting to know how much more an organization will spend if, in the middle of the year, it should increase production from 2,000 units of a product to 2,001 units? Sure, it is of some interest, but, as we have repeatedly said, this narrow concept of a variable cost encompasses very few organizational resources. And the resources that are most variable, or flexible, within short periods of time represent mostly resources the organization purchases from outside suppliers: vendors from whom it purchases materials, utility companies from whom it purchases energy, manpower agencies from whom it purchases temporary, part-time workers, and individual labor suppliers from whom it purchases labor hours as needed or pays for on a piece-work basis.

Left unaddressed by conventional variable or marginal cost thinking is the entire organizational infrastructure of 1) personnel—front-line employees, engineers, salespersons, managers—with whom the organization has a long-term contractual commitment, 2) equipment and facilities, and 3) information systems supplying computing and telecommunications. Decisions to acquire new resources or to continue to maintain the current level of these committed resources are most likely made during the annual budgeting process. Once the authorization to acquire and maintain organizational resources has been made, the expenses of these resources appears fixed and unrelated to local, short-term decisions about product mix, pricing, and customer relationships. The time to make spending on these resources variable is during the budgeting process. Activity-based costing gives managers the information they need to acquire, supply, and maintain only those resources needed to perform the activities to be demanded in the future.

The Activity-Based Budgeting Process

Activity-based budgeting[1] is simply activity-based costing in reverse (see *Exhibit 15-1*). Recall that the ABC process starts from assigning resource expenses down to activities, and, via activity cost drivers, down to cost objects like products, services, and customers. Costs flow (on a conventional diagram) from north to south. In activity-based budgeting, the analysis flows from south to north. Activity-based budgeting follows the following sequence (see *Exhibit 15-2*):

1. Estimate next period's expected production and sales volumes by individual products and customers,
2. Forecast the demand for organizational activities,

Exhibit 15-1 ABB Reverses the Causal Relationships of an ABC Model

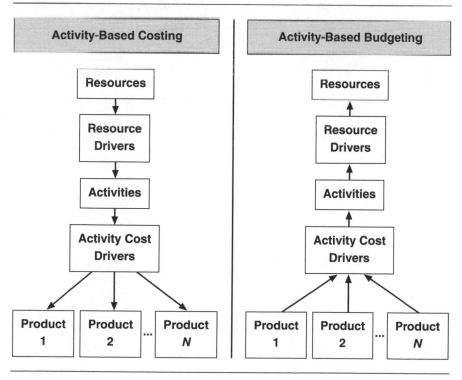

Exhibit 15-2 Activity-Based Budgeting Works from Products to Resources

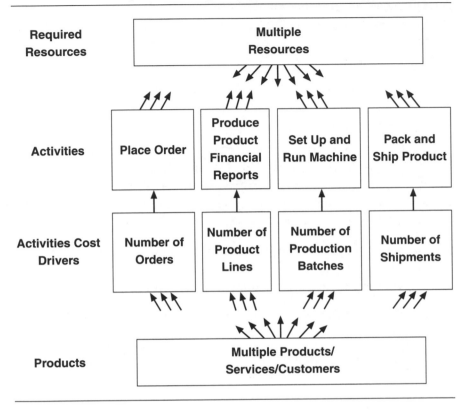

3. Calculate the resource demands to perform the organizational activities,
4. Determine the actual resource supply to meet the demands, and
5. Determine activity capacity.

Estimate Next Period's Production and Sales Volumes

The organization starts with estimates of expected production and sales volumes and mix.[2] The estimates include not only the products and services that will be sold, but also the individual customers (or customer types) expected to buy them. The estimates should include the total production of products and sales to customers, as well as details on the production and sales ordering processes. For example, the budget should include the number of production runs for each product, the frequency of materials orders and receipts, the number of customer orders, the method of shipment, and so on. (see *Exhibit 15-3*).

Exhibit 15-3 Estimates of Demand Are Required to Be More Specific

TODAY		TOMORROW		
Product A	$350,000	**Product A**		
		Product A-1	400 Units	4 Batches
Product B	$450,000	Product A-2	300 Units	1 Batch
		Product A-3	700 Units	10 Batches
Product C	$700,000			
		Product B		
		Product B-1	300 Units	5 Batches
		Product B-2	200 Units	2 Batches
		Product B-3	800 Units	6 Batches
		Product C		
		Product C-1	900 Units	12 Batches
		Product C-2	450 Units	5 Batches
		Product C-3	300 Units	7 Batches
		Product C-4	250 Units	2 Batches

Forecast the Demand for Organizational Activities

The budgeting exercise continues by forecasting the demand for organizational activities required to meet the forecasted volume and mix of products, services, and customers. This process should be identical to that used in conventional budgeting for calculating budgets for purchases of materials, the utilization of machines, and the supply of direct labor based on the forecasted production mix for the upcoming year. Activity-based budgeting extends the conventional exercise by forecasting the demands for all the indirect and support activities: ordering, receiving, and handling materials; processing customer orders, complaints, and requests for technical support; scheduling and setting up for production runs; and all other activities identified in the activity dictionary. The ABB exercise estimates the expected *quantity* for all activity cost drivers: how many setups, how many customer orders, how many engineering change notices, how many products and customers to support, and so on. Therefore, the budgeting team must now know both the volume of production and sales as well as how the production and sales volume will be achieved; that is, knowledge of the underlying processes that will be used to produce the products and services, and market, sell, and service customers. For example, *Exhibit 15-4* shows the calculation for the number of truck shipments, based on the total number of units to be shipped, and the average shipment size. Thus, starting from a forecast of product and customer demands, one obtains a forecast for the quantity of activities that must be performed during the next budgeting period.

Calculate the Resource Demands to Perform the Organizational Activities

With knowledge of the expected *quantity* of demands for activities, the budgeting team then estimates the resources that must be supplied to perform the demanded level of activities. The forecast of resource supply is based on an understanding of the underlying *efficiency* of performing activities. The team must know how many resources, and of what types, must be supplied to handle the demanded quantity of activities. For example, if the production schedule calls for 2,400 production runs, and each run requires a setup that averages 40 minutes, machine and personnel resources capable of performing 1,600 hours of setup activity must be supplied. If each production run requires 20 minutes of scheduling and

Exhibit 15-4 Quantify the Amount of Resources Required to Meet the Demand

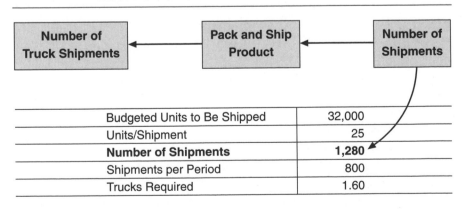

Budgeted Units to Be Shipped	32,000	
Units/Shipment	25	
Number of Shipments	**1,280**	
Shipments per Period	800	
Trucks Required	1.60	

Shipment Consumption Rate = 1 Truck/800 Shipments
= **0.00125 Trucks/Shipment**

quality assurance (QA) activities, 800 hours of scheduling and QA resources must be provided.

With fungible resources, those that support multiple activities, the total demand becomes the sum of the resource demands for all the activities performed by the fungible resources. For example, *Exhibit 15-5* shows how changes in the demand for resources by multiple activities accumulates into changes in the total demand for different resources.

Determine the Actual Resource Supply to Meet the Demands

In the next step, the budgeting process converts the demand for resources to perform activities (calculated in the third step) into an estimate of the total resources of each type that must be supplied. For simplicity, we start with the assumption that each activity consumes unique resources, deferring to later in this section the treatment of fungible resources. *Exhibit 15-6* shows how the demand (from Exhibit 15-4) for 1.6 truck shipments

Exhibit 15-5 Recognize Capacity Changes with Changes in Activity Levels

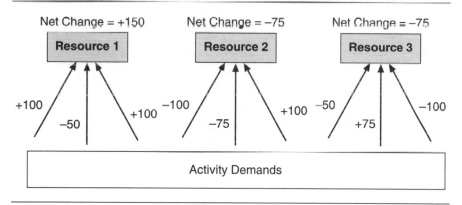

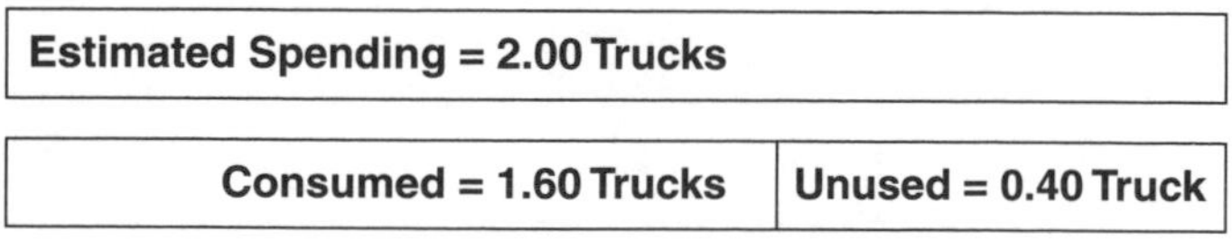

Exhibit 15-6 Recognize the Difference Between Spending and Consumption

per period translates into a required estimated resource supply of 2 truck-loads per period.

In general, each resource has a particular resource spending profile (see *Exhibit 15-7*). These profiles reveal how the supply of each resource changes with activity volume. The activity-based budgeting process uses three basic profiles: flexible, committed-fixed, and committed-step function.

For flexible resources (see *Exhibit 15-8*), such as energy used for machine operations or labor paid hourly or based on actual production, the supply can be matched closely to the demand for these resources. This profile leads to resource supply costs that are essentially linear with demand.

At the other extreme, for committed-fixed resources such as plant floor space, any demand that is less than the capacity of the committed resources can be met by the existing supply without additional spending.[3] Therefore, this profile shows no spending changes with demand (*Exhibit 15-9*).

In between these extremes, we have committed-step resources (see *Exhibit 15-10*) where the supply of the resource increases in definite steps as demand increases.[4]

The estimation of resource supply is undertaken for each resource used by an activity. In general, as shown in *Exhibit 15-11*, when multiple

Exhibit 15-7   Different Resources Have Different Spending Patterns

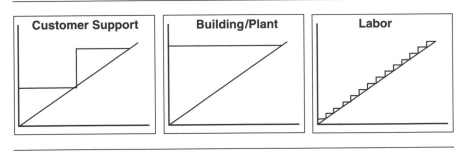

Exhibit 15-8   Spending Profile: Flexible Resources

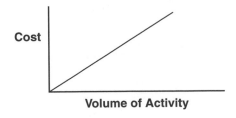

Exhibit 15-9   Spending Profile: Committed-Fixed Resources

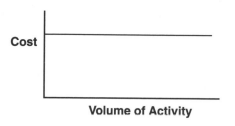

Exhibit 15-10   Spending Profile: Committed-Step Resources

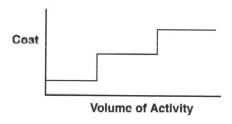

Exhibit 15-11   Understand the Spending Pattern of the Different Resources
That Provide the Activity

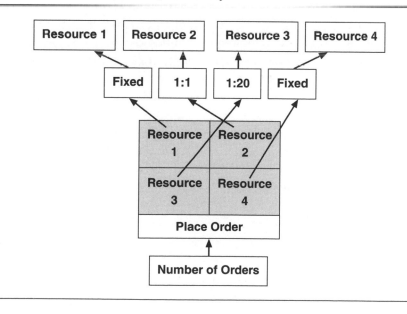

resources must be supplied to perform a given activity, the ABB model must estimate the relationship between the demands for activities and the derived demand for all the resources that must be supplied to perform that activity. Activity-based budgeting attempts to approximate future resource supply, not to try to model it perfectly. Users can always develop new profiles for their needs or adjust the predicted supply of the three basic resource types after the initial budgeting calculation.

Determine Activity Capacity

When all an activity's resources have been identified, the user can determine the practical capacity of the activity, which is the capacity of the resource that first constrains the ability of the firm to perform the activity. For example, suppose Activity A consumes two resources, R1 and R2. The predicted demand for Activity A is 100 units, which converts to a required supply of $220 and $360 of R1 and R2, respectively. Activity A uses $2 of R1 and $3 of R2 each time it is performed. Therefore, the activity driver rate for Activity A is $5 ($2 + $3) and the activity's practical capacity is 110 units (220/2). This practical capacity means that the predicted demand for 100 units of Activity A will result in unused capacity of 10 units (110 − 100) at a cost of $50 ($5 × 10), and a surplus capacity of R2 of $30 ($360 − [$3 × 110]). There is no unused capacity predicted for R1. Therefore, the total cost of unused capacity is $80.

This example shows that in activity-based budgeting, there are two forms of capacity, one at the activity level and the other at the resource level. When the resources are fungible, the unused capacity at the resource level requires a calculation for each activity that uses the resource. Say Activity B also consumes R2. The total demand for R2 is $500 ($300 for Activity A and $200 for Activity B). The resource supply profile requires a supply of R2 of $550. The practical capacity of Activity A consumes $330 of R2 and the practical capacity of Activity B consumes $210 of R2. Therefore, the unused capacity of R2 is now only $10 ($550 − [$330 + $210]). Nothing stops the fungible resource from setting the practical capacity of an activity. If the resource supply profile of R2 had been such that the level of R2 available for Activity A was below $330, R2 would have been the constraining resource, the practical capacity of Activity A would be lower, and surplus capacity would emerge for R1.

The concept of separate capacities at the resource and activity levels does not emerge in retrospective (Stage III) systems that assign resource costs based upon interviews about percentage of time required for different activities. Systems that use percentage estimates typically assume that 100% of the supplied resources are required to support practical capacity.[5] In prospective Stage IV systems, unused capacity can be identified at both the activity and resource levels.

Using Activity-Based Budgeting

Several modifications to the budgeting process are required as the company becomes more efficient (operational ABM) and, also, as it changes the demand for activities through strategic ABM. First, the costs of performing the activity can decrease and, second, an activity such as inspections or moving material may be performed less often. In our example, 100 units of Activity A were required. If the company becomes more efficient, or reduces the demand for this activity, the same output may be produced with Activity A being performed 90 times, not the 100 originally forecast. Also, the resources required each time Activity A is performed might only be $1.95 of R1 and $2.75 of R2 (less than the $2 and $3 previously needed). These two improvements can easily be reflected in the computation of resource supply, practical capacity of the activities, and resource capacity by changing the estimated requirement for activity cost driver quantities, and the changed relationship between activities performed and resources required for these activities. Including such improvements before they have been achieved obviously risks developing overly optimistic activity-based budgets. Consequently, any proposed improvements should be subjected to considerable scrutiny to ensure that they are plausible.[6]

Activity-based budgeting works, of course, in service organizations as well as in manufacturing ones. Once an ABC model has been developed for costing services and customers, running it south to north provides estimates of activity demand and associated resource requirements. At the conclusion of a south-to-north chain of reasoning, the budgeting team has a forecast of the total organizational resources that must be supplied to meet the forecasted volume and mix of products, services, and customers in the upcoming year.

Activity-based budgeting is most useful for resources performing repetitive activities, especially activities triggered by demands from products, services, and customers. In addition to this derived demand for the organizational resources performing repetitive activities, the budgeting team must also estimate the quantity of discretionary spending for the upcoming year. This spending will typically represent elements of product- and customer-sustaining expenses, plus spending at higher hierarchical levels (brand and product line; channel and region). The analysis of discretionary spending will complement the activity-based budgeting process for the resources required to perform the more repetitive and predictable activities.

Once the activity-based budget has been determined, managers will authorize the supply of resources to meet the demand for the next year. At that point, users can run their ABC model in the traditional direction, north to south, to calculate activity cost driver rates for the coming period. These prospective driver rates can be used in the several ways identified in the ABM chapters, such as motivating continuous improvement and learning programs; making product- and customer-based decisions on pricing, order size, and order acceptance; and helping product engineers design new products.

In practice, of course, ABB is not a simple exercise. The organization will have to specify far more details about how production and sales demands will be met, about the underlying efficiency of all organizational activities, and about the spending and supply pattern of individual resources. When ABB is performed successfully, however, managers will have greater control over their cost structure, in particular more control over their so-called fixed costs.

How Activity-Based Management and Budgeting Lead to Variable Costs

Early advocates described activity-based costing as supplying information about *long-term variable costs*. In retrospect, this term, although rooted in economics and accounting literature, was vague. Activity-based budgeting makes the somewhat fuzzy notion of long-term variable cost much more precise and operational. As discussed earlier, costs become variable via a two-step procedure. First, demands for resources change. The demand for resources performing unit-level activities increases because of growth, leading to increased volume of activity. Demands for resources performing batch-, product-, and customer-sustaining activities increase because of increases in the variety and the complexity of products and customers. The direction of causality runs in the opposite direction as well. Demands for resources decrease as operational ABM improves the efficiency of activities and strategic ABM reduces the demand for activities.

Activity-based budgeting is the necessary second step to make costs become long-term variable. When demands for organizational resources exceed the available supply, additional spending must occur to provide the required additional capacity. Otherwise, at current levels of efficiency and capacity, the existing resources will be incapable of sustaining the higher and more complex level of activity demands without extensive delays, poor quality, or overuse of equipment and personnel. Conversely, should demands for organizational resources be less than the projected supply, the budgeting process can force the redeployment or reduction in the resources no longer expected to be needed. Contrary to conventional thinking, so-called fixed costs can indeed be made variable in the downward direction as demands lessen for the activities performed by organizational resources. Activity-based budgeting systems calculate the reduced demands for organizational resources by incorporating forecasts of changes both in volume, variety, and complexity as well as improvements in activity efficiency and associated increases in resource capacity. But the costs of resources supplied will decrease only if organizations, through their budgeting and management processes, eliminate excess capacity.

Activity-based budgeting gives managers the information to make almost all organizational costs variable, either up or down. To reemphasize this point, what makes a resource cost variable in a downward direction is not inherent in the nature of the resource; it is a function of management decisions—first, to reduce the demands for the resource, and, second, to lower the spending on the resource. Activity-based budgeting must be part of any Stage IV system so that resource supply can be matched well with future resource demands.

What-If Analysis

Managers use activity-based budgeting to predict resource supply and spending levels for upcoming periods, and to calculate the expected future costs of products, services, and customers. An important feature to couple with activity-based budgeting is what-if analysis, which helps managers predict the consequences of their decisions about individual products, customers, and suppliers. Such decisions, taken in the current period, have important implications for changes in activity levels in the future.

At a simple level, consider the introduction of a new product or customer. As long as the change in activity volumes caused by the new product or customer can be handled with available capacity, the existing activity cost driver rates can be used to report the cost of the product. This analysis assumes that flexible resources, such as material and machine power, will vary, but that the supply of committed resources will not change. The

ABC model reports the cost of all the resources used for the new product or customer. This is especially useful if the product or customer is expected to be sustained for at least several periods; it is not a one-time incremental order. But a manager wishing to price an order for a new product or customer below full cost can strip away the cost of resources that are not expected to be utilized by other products and will not be eliminated in the near future.

Such product and customer cost estimations are especially important for firms that, in any given period, produce only a small percentage of their available products (or serve only a small percentage of their potential customers). They cannot predict which products will be produced or which customers served. For example, one manufacturer typically produces only about 50% of its possible products in a given year. This company's managers cannot predict the product mix and volumes for about 60% of their products. The what-if analysis enabled the managers to identify the resource costs of any new order and gave them confidence in negotiating price and delivery terms. Prior to the development of such what-if capability, they could not predict the cost of orders with any confidence. In retrospect, they learned that many of the orders they had accepted turned out to be unprofitable.

If the anticipated changes in activity volumes for new products or customers require additional capacity, a mini activity-based budgeting exercise should be undertaken. This exercise incorporates the additional cost of supplying new resources, the incremental costs (e.g., materials and energy), and the normal cost of using already supplied resources. Understanding both the total cost and the incremental costs—of materials, energy, plus newly supplied resources—helps managers make better decisions on order acceptance and price and delivery terms. Associating increments of resource supply with particular products or customers also produces a more effective resource acquisition process.

What-if analysis also helps in decisions about the use of common components. Consider a proposal to increase the use of common components and decrease the use of unique components. A what-if analysis permits managers to assess the change in resource requirements from increasing the production volumes of the common components and reducing or eliminating the use of the unique components. Without the activity hierarchy in an ABC model, the benefits from the reduced levels of batch and product-sustaining activities (common components produced in larger batches, fewer small batches of unique components, and fewer number of components in the system) cannot be assessed. Further, the what-if analysis shows managers, as they substitute common components for unique ones, which resources are now in excess supply. These surpluses become the targets for actual, realized cost savings.

Similarly, if engineers are contemplating changing the design of a common component, the ABC-based what-if model identifies every product that uses the common component, the total volume of that component, and the quantities of activities and resources currently required for its production. The model can simulate a resource profile for the redesigned common component and calculate the revised resource cost. If the redesign is accomplished, the revised cost can easily be embedded into the reported cost of all products that use the redesigned component.

Another class of decisions relates to changes in operating processes. For example, the introduction of a new production machine will change the demand for activities and resources. Process improvements in any primary or secondary activity will reduce the demands for resources required to perform the activity. A what-if analysis allows managers to model the impact of the operating change and assess the benefits on product and customer costs. The what-if analysis starts with estimates of the volume of products or customers that are affected by the new or improved operating process. Then it calculates the new activity cost driver quantities, the associated changes in the demand for resources, and the resources that will have to be supplied in the future. After completing this south (products and customers)-to-north (resources) analysis, the model can be rerun in the north-to-south direction to obtain revised product and customer costs of the new production process.

Such what-if analyses are important extensions of the ABC methodology. They enable managers to explore the resource supply implications of decisions made about products, customers, and operating processes. The existing ABC model, either retrospective or prospective, provides the starting point. The subsequent what-if analysis enables managers to perform, easily and inexpensively, the special studies to translate an ABC resource usage model into a scenario containing the proposed changes in resource supply and spending. The result is a fact-based benefits case for the proposed changes in products, customers, and processes.

The what-if analysis helps managers to anticipate future resource demands from decisions made in the current period. We close the book by illustrating how managers with real-time access to an ABC model of resource demand and resource supply now have a mechanism that allows continual communication of economic information between their dispersed and organizationally separate units. This facilitates better decision making on the allocation and management of existing capacity resources to meet the demands from dispersed marketing and sales units.

Transfer Pricing

Transfer pricing issues arise when two organizational units interact by having one unit acquire the output from the other unit. If senior management had all the information possessed by the managers in the decentralized units, it could dictate how much output should be transferred from supplying to acquiring unit. It could also make the profit-maximizing decisions about how much of the transferred output should be sold to external customers, and at what price, by the acquiring unit. In general, however, the acquiring unit has a great deal of information about local customers, competitors, and market conditions that it cannot communicate efficiently or credibly to senior managers at company headquarters. Similarly, the supplying unit has a great deal of information about the efficiency and capacity of its production processes, as well as the alternative uses for production resources, that it cannot communicate to senior management. Consequently, senior management wants to allow the managers of the decentralized units to use their superior information to make local decisions on processes, pricing, and output. The transfer price of goods supplied from one unit to the other ideally provides information about the opportunity cost of the transfer between the two divisions.

Historically, however, transfer pricing has been one of the most difficult and controversial problems for senior managers to resolve. Economics and accounting scholars have demonstrated, using simple deterministic examples, that in perfectly competitive markets, the optimal transfer price should be the market price. In this situation, costs play no role other than to allow each division to calculate its own profitability from producing or acquiring the transferred product. When the transferred product cannot be acquired in perfectly competitive markets, scholars recommend using the long-run marginal cost of supplying the transferred good.[7] This cost reflects the opportunity cost to the selling division of supplying an additional unit of the transferred product. In practice, however, there is considerable controversy about how to calculate long-run marginal cost.

Companies use several cost-based methods for transfer pricing. At one extreme, some allow the selling division to calculate a fully absorbed product cost (using the usual arbitrary overhead allocation scheme from a Stage I or Stage II cost system), and add a profit margin so that the division could appear to be a profit center. At the other extreme, managers interpreted the marginal cost rule to include only the short-term variable costs associated with producing an extra unit of the product.

As an example of this application, for many years a pharmaceutical firm transferred products from its manufacturing plants to its geographically dispersed selling units at short-term variable costs, principally materials expenses (ingredients and packaging).[8] All other manufacturing costs were considered fixed. The existing transfer price system, based on such short-run variable costs, had several problems. First, the marketing divisions reported extremely high profits since they were being charged only for the materials costs. The short-run contribution margin approach led to excessive proliferation of the product line, acceptance of many low-volume orders, and the associated large consumption of production capacity for change-overs. In effect, marketing and sales decisions were being made without regard to their impact on production capacity and long-run costs. Another concern was that the operations division was getting credit only for the expenses of purchased materials. There was little pressure and motivation to control the so-called fixed expenses and to improve operational efficiency. Even if the company's manufacturing plants were less efficient than alternative producers of the pharmaceutical products, the variable cost transfer price provided no incentive for the marketing divisions to shift their source of supply.

The company managers considered but rejected several traditional methods for establishing a new transfer price system: market price, full cost, variable cost, and negotiated price. Market price for the transferred product was not feasible because no market existed for the unique pharmaceuticals, especially an intermediate product that had not yet been marketed or distributed to customers. A full-cost calculation, including materials, labor, and manufacturing overhead was rejected since the traditional methods for allocating overhead (using labor or machine hours) did not capture the actual cost structure in the company's plants. Also, the accumulation of all factory costs into average overhead rates might encourage local optimization by each division that would lower the overall profit of the company. For example, manufacturing plants might be motivated to overproduce in order to absorb more factory overhead into inventory, while marketing divisions might be discouraged from bidding aggressively for high-volume orders and encouraged to accept more low-volume custom orders. Also, this system would not reveal the incremental costs associated with short-run decisions, nor the relative use of capacity by different products and different order sizes. The existing system, using short-run variable cost covering only ingredients and packaging materials, was already known to be inadequate for the managers' purposes.

And finally, senior executives strongly believed that negotiated transfer prices would lead to endless arguments between managers in the different divisions, and consume excessive time on nonproductive discussions. They decided to use a recently developed ABC system for calculating transfer prices between plants and the marketing divisions. The system used next year's forecasted costs, based on budgeted expense data, forecasted volume and mix of sales, and projected process utilization and efficiencies, to calculate transfer prices. The company calculated standard activity cost driver rates for each activity. These costs were charged to products based on actual demands for activities during the year. This approach enabled product costs to be calculated in a predictable manner throughout the year. It eliminated monthly or quarterly fluctuations in product costs caused by variations in spending or resource usage.

The structure of the model explicitly recognized the ABC hierarchy of unit, batch, product-sustaining, and facility-sustaining costs. Unit-level costs represented all the direct expenses associated with producing individual product units, such as tablets, capsules, and ampoules. These expenses principally included the cost of raw materials, packaging materials, and direct wages paid to production workers.

Batch-level costs included the expenses of resources used for each production batch. These expenses were mainly the costs of preparation, setup, cleaning, quality control, laboratory testing, and computer and production management. The costs of a production batch could vary among different products and, of course, among different plants.

Product-sustaining costs included the expenses incurred in registering the products,[9] making changes to a product's production processes, and package design. And facility-sustaining costs represented the cost of maintaining the capacity of production lines, including depreciation, cost of safety inspections, and insurance, as well as the general expenses of the plant such as security and landscaping.[10]

Transfer prices were calculated in two different procedures: one to assign unit- and batch-level costs, the second to assign product- and facility-sustaining costs. In the first procedure, the marketing divisions were charged for unit-level costs (principally materials and labor) based on the actual quantities of each individual product they ordered. In addition, they were charged batch-level costs based on the actual number of batches required for each product they acquired. This procedure gave the manager of a marketing division the flexibility to decide, for example, whether to accept a small order from a customer, or how much of a discount he or she was willing to grant for large orders.

In the second calculation, the product- and facility-sustaining expenses were charged to marketing divisions on an annual basis based on budgeted information. The product-sustaining costs were easy to assign since each marketing division had specific and unique products for its own markets. No individual product was sold to more than one marketing division. The facility-sustaining expenses were charged to each marketing division based on its budgeted use of the capacity of the four manufacturing facilities.

The assignment of the facility-sustaining, plant-level costs received much attention, particularly from the managers of the marketing divisions. They wanted to verify that these costs did indeed stay fixed and did not creep upward each period. By separating the unit- and batch-level costs from the product- and facility-sustaining costs, marketing managers could monitor closely the costs incurred in the manufacturing plants. In particular, they ensured that increases in plant-level costs would occur only when one or more of them requested a change in production capacity. Then the responsibility for the fixed cost increment became clearly traceable.

With the integrated budgeting and transfer pricing process, marketing managers planned their product mix with full knowledge of the cost impact of their decisions. When they proposed increases in variety and complexity, they knew the added costs that they would be charged for because of the increased demands on manufacturing facilities. Active discussions occurred between marketing and manufacturing people about the impact of product mix and batch sizes.

Marketing managers could also now distinguish between products that covered all costs of manufacturing versus those that covered only the unit- and batch-level expenses, so that the contribution above these expenses was less their annual product-sustaining and plant-level expenses. Because of the assignment of unused capacity expenses to the responsible marketing division, marketing managers made decisions about pricing, product mix, and product introduction in light of available capacity. The transfer pricing system also motivated cost reduction and production efficiencies in the manufacturing plants.

Both marketing and manufacturing managers in the different divisions agreed with the reasonableness of the calculated transfer prices. Instead of having arguments about cost measurement and assignment, the managers now worked together to identify ways to reduce unit- and batch-level expenses. Manufacturing, purchasing, and marketing people conducted common searches for lower-cost, more reliable, and high-quality suppliers to reduce variable materials costs. Marketing managers compared plant production costs with those of alternative suppliers around the world. This information was shared with manufacturing managers who learned about where process improvements were required, but who could agree to outsource products when the external suppliers' costs were lower than those they could achieve in the foreseeable future. All these actions contributed to increasing the long-term profitability of the company.

To summarize and generalize, activity-based cost systems seem to provide a missing link in transfer-pricing policy. When market prices are unavailable or inappropriate to use as transfer prices, many firms try to simulate market prices either through negotiated prices or through prices calculated as markups over full costs. Neither approach reflects the opportunity cost for either the selling division to supply the product or for the buying division to acquire it. And worse, markups over full cost usually incorporate arbitrary profit margins and arbitrary assignment of overhead costs to individual products.

At the other extreme, the pharmaceutical company's old system could include only short-term, out-of-pocket costs—primarily direct materials expense. This method led to the problems described above: overproliferation of products, small order quantities, little attention paid to plant and conversion costs, and heavy discounting by marketing and sales divisions since these divisions see abnormally high profits measured by selling prices less materials costs.

Activity-based transfer prices enable marketing and selling divisions to see the long-run marginal costs—at the unit, batch, product-sustaining, and facility-sustaining levels—of their decisions on product volume, order size, and mix (i.e., strategic ABM). Manufacturing divisions get signals about cost behavior reflecting the volume, variety, and complexity of the tasks they have been assigned, and can try to lower the costs incorporated in the transfer prices by improving efficiencies at the unit, batch, and product-sustaining levels (i.e., operational ABM). Producing and marketing/selling divisions now share a common (and valid) language about cost behavior, and their efforts and decisions become synchronized to enhance overall organizational profitability.

Conclusions

We started our journey many chapters ago by identifying the serious limitations of using traditional, standard cost systems for managerial purposes. These existing systems focus on materials, direct labor, and overhead costs, with overhead applied to products and customers using only a few possible allocation bases—direct labor, materials, machine hours, units produced, sales dollars. Since all of these allocation bases are proportional to the unit volumes of production and sales, managers and engineers cannot understand the high costs associated with variety and complexity. Also, the operational feedback—monthly variances from standards—from these traditional financial systems do not support continuous improvement activities to enhance productivity and efficiency, raise quality, and shorten customer response times. We described these cost systems as Stage II, adequate for financial reporting but completely inadequate for managerial decision making and process improvement.

We continued our journey by describing the characteristics of new Stage III cost systems, whose financial reporting functionality is the same as Stage II's. Companies retain their existing cost systems to prepare statements for shareholders, creditors, regulators, and tax authorities. But they introduce new systems: one set of systems to promote operational learning and improvement, and a second set (ABC) for measuring the cost and profitability of their activities, processes, products, and customers. Much of the book provided examples of how companies have obtained benefits from Stage III systems. We showed how innovating companies are using rapid feedback, extensive systems of nonfinancial measurement, kaizen costing, and pseudo-profit centers to drive employee learning and improvement activities. We provided extensive coverage of the many aspects of activity-based management in which managers use ABC information for:

- Highlighting opportunities, setting priorities, and providing financial justification for process improvement activities;
- Making improved decisions on product pricing, substitution, and mix;
- Managing customer relationships, including fact-based decisions on pricing and discounting, functionality, order size, delivery arrangements, and supply chain efficiencies;
- Managing supplier relationships to obtain the lowest cost, not the lowest-priced suppliers; and
- Informing the decisions of product designers and engineers at a time when they have maximum leverage to affect cost and functionality.

We concluded our journey with a vision for the future, a vision that we believe is within the grasp of many companies. First, ABC systems can be upgraded to incorporate additional features not presently available in existing Stage III systems. These features include: explicit measurement of resource and activity capacity, accurate assignment of all business- and corporate-level expenses through the use of secondary and primary activities, incorporation of the cost of capital, and comprehensive measurements of life-cycle costs and profitability.

When companies have achieved their desired functionality in Stage III systems, they can migrate to an integrated set of financial, cost, and performance measurement systems that build upon the low-cost availability of information from enterprise-wide systems. In Stage IV, the operational improvement system continually monitors the organization's resource spending as well as the efficiency, quality, and responsiveness of departments and processes. The ABC system reports periodically the cost of activities and processes and the cost and profitability of products, services, and customers.

The systems are integrated in that both the operational improvement and the ABC system provide the information for the periodic financial reports to external constituencies. Further, the operational improvement system updates the ABC system's cost driver rates based on sustainable changes in activity efficiency and capacity. In turn, as we have shown in this chapter, the ABC system is used for activity-based budgeting, where the resources to be supplied to all organizational departments and business processes are determined by the forecasted demands for these resources by products, services, and customers. Using what-if capabilities in their ABC system, managers can consider the resource implications of major changes in product design, product mix, and relationships with suppliers and customers. And the ABC information can be used for transfer pricing, to inform operations departments and marketing and sales units about the economics of product sourcing and customer sales decisions.

Integrated State IV cost and performance measurement systems will provide the timely, valid information organizations need to survive and prosper in today's environment, an environment characterized by global markets and competitors, rapid technological advances, customer focus, and knowledge-based competition. Attempting to navigate through such complex, turbulent competitive environments with cost systems designed for the industrial age—local markets, stable products and customers, and standard, mass production technologies—will surely lead to disappointment and failure. Managers can now see how to deploy cost and performance measurement systems that will provide them with the information they need to meet the challenges of today's information-age competition.

Notes

Chapter 1

1. R. S. Kaplan, "One Cost System Isn't Enough," *Harvard Business Review* (January–February 1988), 61–66.
2. The failings and obsolescence of existing cost and performance measurement systems in the new competitive environment were documented in several articles and books that appeared in the early to mid-1980s. Although these publications amply described the limitations of existing cost and performance measurement systems, they were less clear about what new approaches were available to overcome these limitations.
3. R. Cooper and R. S. Kaplan, "Measure Costs Right: Make the Right Decisions," *Harvard Business Review* (September–October 1988), 96–103.
4. Strictly speaking, some of the operational ABM applications, such as reducing setup times and eliminating completely non-value-adding activities, have strategic implications. Conversely, strategic ABM, such as working from the bill of activities for products and customers, contains useful insights for operational improvements (such as reducing the costs of processing orders, or handling changeovers). Lacking a vocabulary for distinguishing between the two types of complementary management actions, we admittedly oversimplify by referring to operational ABM as improving the efficiency of performing activities, and strategic ABM as taking actions at the product, service, or customer level to modify the demands for activities.
5. This widely quoted estimate appears in B. S. Blanchard, *Design and Manage to Life-Cycle Cost* (Portland, Ore.: M/A Press, 1978), and J. E. Michaels and W. P. Wood, *Design to Cost* (New York: John Wiley & Sons, 1989).

Chapter 2

1. R. S. Kaplan, "The Four-Stage Model of Cost System Design," *Management Accounting* (February 1990), 22–26. Not all companies start in Stage I. Many

organizations can start with a decent system for external reporting (Stage II), but then use this system for decades.

2. See R. S. Kaplan, "Yesterday's Accounting Undermines Production," *Harvard Business Review* (July–August 1984) 95–101; and R. S. Kaplan and H. T. Johnson, *Relevance Lost: The Rise and Fall of Management Accounting* (Boston: Harvard Business School Press, 1987) for examples of this critique.

3. L. F. Jones, "Product Costing at Caterpillar," *Management Accounting* (February 1991), 34–42; R. Cooper and K. H. Wruck, "Siemens: Electric Motor Works (A)," Harvard Business School Case #9-191-006; R. S. Kaplan, "MetaboGmbH & Co. KG," Harvard Business School Case #9-189-146; and B. Gaiser, "German Cost Management Systems Related to Products and Customer Needs," *Journal of Cost Management* (forthcoming).

4. We will discuss this example in more detail in Chapter 8.

5. R. S. Kaplan, "Texas Eastman Company," Harvard Business School Case #9-130-039, 6–7.

6. Many accountants like to report all results using six significant digits since that makes them feel very accurate. In truth, they are merely being precise and usually quite inaccurate (the first digit may be wrong). In management accounting, we prefer to be vaguely accurate (get the first digit correct) rather than precisely wrong.

7. See R. Cooper, "Hewlett-Packard: Queensferry Telecommunications Division," Harvard Business School Case #9-191-067; and R. S. Kaplan, "AT&T Paradyne," Harvard Business School Case #9-195-165.

Chapter 3

1. See Chapters 2 and 3 of H. Thomas Johnson and Robert S. Kaplan, *Relevance Lost: The Rise and Fall of Management Accounting* (Boston: Harvard Business School Press, 1987).

2. In the United States, the standard costing, flexible budgeting approach was embedded in all cost accounting textbooks, and reached its highest expression in the triannual editions of Charles Horngren's cost accounting book, a textbook initially launched from lecture notes prepared at the University of Chicago in the late 1940s by William Vatter. The current edition of Horngren's classic is C. Horngren, G. Foster, and S. Datar, *Cost Accounting: A Managerial Emphasis,* 9/e (Englewood Cliffs, N.J.: Prentice-Hall, 1997).

3. References on German cost accounting theory and practice include P. Riebel, "Core Features of the 'Einzelkosten-und Deckungsbeitragsrechnung,' " *The European Accounting Review* 3, no. 3 (1994), 515–543; and W. Kilger, *Flexible Plankostenrechnung und Deckungsbeitragsrechnung* (Wiesbaden: Auflage, 1988). Material on German cost systems has benefited from discussions with Professor Péter Horváth of the University of Stuttgart

and an article by his colleague, B. Gaiser, "German Cost Management Systems Related to Products and Customer Needs," *Journal of Cost Management* (forthcoming).

4. Although we illustrate the standard costing, flexible budgeting approach with the GPK system, its basic elements would be very familiar to students trained in standard costs and flexible budgeting in North America, the United Kingdom, and virtually all English-speaking countries. We emphasize the German origins primarily because the practice of standard costing, flexible budgeting became more widely applied (versus widely studied in universities) in German companies than elsewhere.

5. The origins of these highly sophisticated German systems can be traced to the period between the two world wars when the German economy became centralized. The performance of each machine class was sent to government officials in Berlin who determined the output from each factory.

6. L. F. Jones, "Product Costing at Caterpillar," *Management Accounting* (February 1991), 34–42.

7. Conversely, when demand is higher than expected, the burden rate decreases.

8. We will develop this point in considerable detail when we introduce activity-based cost systems in Chapter 6.

9. R. Kanigel, *The One Best Way: Frederick Winslow Taylor and the Enigma of Efficiency* (New York: Viking, 1997).

10. R. S. Kaplan and A. P. Sweeney, "Romeo Engine Plant," Harvard Business School Case #9-194-032, 5, 6.

11. See, for example, D. A. Garvin, *Managing Quality* (New York: Free Press, 1988), J. M. Juran, *Quality Control Handbook*, 3d ed. (New York: McGraw-Hill, 1974); P. B. Crosby, *Quality Is Free* (New York: New American Library, 1979); A. V. Feigenbaum, *Total Quality Control,* 3d ed. (New York: McGraw-Hill, 1991); W. E. Deming, *Quality, Productivity, and Competitive Position* (Cambridge, Mass.: MIT Center of Advanced Engineering Study, 1982); K. Ishikawa, *What Is Total Quality Control? The Japanese Way* (Englewood Cliffs, N.J.: Prentice-Hall, 1985); and J. Main, *Quality Wars: The Triumphs and Defeats of American Business* (New York: Free Press, 1994).

12. See J. Champy and M. Hammer, *Reengineering the Corporation: A Manifesto for Business Revolution* (New York: HarperBusiness, 1993).

13. See documentation of the role for financial control systems in nineteenth and early twentieth century companies in Alfred D. Chandler, Jr., *The Visible Hand: The Managerial Revolution in American Business* (Cambridge, Mass.: Belknap Press, 1977), and Johnson and Kaplan, *Relevance Lost*, Chapters 1–6.

14. See J. Womack, D. Jones, and D. Roos, *The Machine That Changed the World: The Story of Lean Production* (New York: Macmillan, 1990).

15. M. Hammer, "Reengineering Work: Don't Automate, Obliterate," *Harvard Business Review* (July–August 1990), 104–112; J. Champy and M. Hammer,

Reengineering the Corporation: A Manifesto for Business Revolution (New York: HarperBusiness, 1993).

16. Jon R. Katzenbach and Douglas K. Smith, *The Wisdom of Teams: Creating the High-Performance Organization* (Boston: Harvard Business School Press, 1992); also, Michael Hammer, *Beyond Reengineering: How the Process-Centered Organization Is Changing Our Work and Our Lives* (New York: HarperBusiness, 1996).

17. For specific examples of step-down and reciprocal methods, see Chapter 13, "Cost Allocation: I," 471–494, in C. Horngren, G. Foster and S. Datar, *Cost Accounting: A Managerial Emphasis,* 9/e (Englewood Cliffs, N.J.: Prentice-Hall, 1997).

Chapter 4

1. R. S. Kaplan and A. P. Sweeney, "Peoria Engine Plant (A)" (disguised name, but one of the U.S. Big 3 company plants), Harvard Business School Case #9-193-082, 3.

2. A more comprehensive treatment of nonfinancial measures, particularly those derived from strategic not just operational improvement considerations, can be found in R. S. Kaplan and D. P. Norton, *The Balanced Scorecard: Translating Strategy into Action* (Boston: Harvard Business School Press, 1996), especially Chapters 4–6.

3. The best yield measure is *first-pass yields*, the percentage of items completed that make it all the way through production, without any rework. Some companies measure total yield (good items produced divided by items started into production) but count items that have been reworked into acceptable finished goods in the numerator of the yield ratio. This measurement indicates that customers may no longer be getting defective items, but does little to signal improvements in the underlying production process.

4. R. S. Kaplan and C. Ittner, "Texas Instruments: Cost of Quality (A)," Harvard Business School Case #9-189-029, 3.

5. See J. Abbeglen and G. Stalk, Jr., *Kaisha: The Japanese Corporation* (New York: Basic Books, 1985); J. Bower and T. Hout, "Fast-Cycle Capability for Competitive Power," *Harvard Business Review* (November–December 1988), 110–118; and G. Stalk, Jr., and T. M. Hout, *Competing Against Time* (New York: Free Press, 1990).

6. A. J. Nanni, J. R. Dixon, and T. E. Vollman, "Strategic Control and Performance Measurement," *Journal of Cost Management* (Summer 1990), 34, 35.

7. Ibid., 38.

8. Ibid., 41.

9. H. T. Johnson, "Managing Costs: An Outmoded Philosophy," *Manufacturing Engineering* (May 1980), 44 and 45.

10. H. T. Johnson, "Beyond Product Costing: A Challenge to Cost Management's Conventional Wisdom," *Journal of Cost Management* (Fall 1990), 15–21.

11. Ibid., 20.
12. H. T. Johnson, "Management Accounting in the 21ˢᵗ Century," *Journal of Cost Management* (Fall 1995), 19.
13. Robin Cooper, *When Lean Enterprises Collide: Competing through Confrontation* (Boston: Harvard Business School Press, 1995).

Chapter 5

1. M. Imai, *Kaizen: The Key to Japan's Competitive Success* (New York: McGraw-Hill, 1986).
2. For a detailed description of kaizen costing, see R. Cooper and R. Slagmulder, *Confrontational Cost Management, Vol. 3; Kaizen Costing and Value Engineering* (Portland, Ore.: Productivity Press, 1997).
3. Robin Cooper, Chapter 11, "Kaizen Costing," 239–254, in *When Lean Enterprises Collide: Competing Through Confrontation* (Boston: Harvard Business School Press, 1995).
4. In practice, there are two types of kaizen costing. The first focuses on reducing the cost of specific products. It is used when a product enters production above its target cost or when long-lived products become or are at risk of becoming unprofitable. The second, general kaizen costing, focuses on production processes and sets out to find ways to reduce their costs and thus the cost of the products that require those processes. In this book, we describe only general kaizen costing.
5. See R. Cooper, "Citizen Watch Company, Ltd.: Cost Reduction for Mature Products," Harvard Business School Case #9-194-033.
6. R. Cooper, "Sumitomo Electric Industries, Ltd.: The Kaizen Program," Harvard Business School Case #9-195-078.
7. R. S. Kaplan and A. P. Sweeney, "Romeo Engine Plant," Harvard Business School Case #9-194-032, 1.
8. Ibid., 9.
9. Ibid., 12.
10. Ibid.
11. Ibid., 13.
12. R. S. Kaplan, "Euclid Engineering," Harvard Business School Case #9-193-031.
13. We put "profit index" in quotes since all the components in the index were cost items. The index contained no revenue items.
14. R. S. Kaplan, "Texas Eastman Company," Harvard Business School Case #9-190-039.
15. Strictly speaking, the Theory of Constraints subtracts material costs from the revenues produced to measure throughput; see E. Goldratt and J. Cox, *The Goal: A Process of Ongoing Improvement*, rev. ed. (Croton-on-Hudson, N.Y.: North River Press, 1986).

16. This section draws heavily from Cooper, "Pseudomicroprofit Centers," Chapter 13, 283–301, in *When Lean Enterprises Collide.*
17. R. Cooper, "Higashimaru Shoyu Company, Ltd. (A): Price Control System," Harvard Business School Case #9-195-050, 8.
18. R. Cooper, "Kirin Brewery Company, Ltd.," Harvard Business School Case #9-195-058.
19. R. Cooper, "Olympus Optical Company, Ltd. (B): Functional Group Management," Harvard Business School Case #9-195-073.
20. Of course, if managers wanted employees to make input substitutions or modify product mix based on short-term changes in input or output factor prices, they would supply actual, current prices to the employee teams. They would then evaluate the performance of the departments and teams using actual, not standard, prices of inputs and outputs. In this case, the departments would become true, not pseudo-, profit centers.

Chapter 6

1. Example taken from R. Cooper and R. S. Kaplan, "Measure Costs Right: Make the Right Decisions," *Harvard Business Review* (September–October 1988), 97–98.
2. Later in the chapter, we extend the ABC analysis outside of the factory to include selling, distribution, marketing, and general expenses.
3. We are describing the development of an organization's initial (Stage III) ABC system, in which expense information is historical, based on actual operating results in the most recent period. When companies move from Stage III to Stage IV, they will use activity-based systems with budgeted and forecasted information. We will discuss this extension in Chapter 14.
4. Excerpt from the "Roche Vitamins ABM Manual."
5. See, for example, J. A. Brimson, *Activity Accounting* (New York: John Wiley & Sons, 1991); G. Cokins, A. Stratton, and J. Helbing, *An ABC Manager's Primer* (Chicago: Irwin Professional Publishing, 1993); T. Pryor and J. Sahm, *Using Activity-Based Management for Continuous Improvement* (Arlington, Tex.: ICMS, Inc., 1995); D. T. Hicks, *Activity-Based Costing for Small and Mid-Sized Businesses: An Implementation Guide* (New York: John Wiley & Sons, 1992); and G. Cokins *Activity-Based Cost Management Making It Work: A Manager's Guide to Implementing and Sustaining an Effective ABC System* (Chicago: Irwin Professional Publishing, 1996).
6. R. Cooper, "Cost Classifications in Unit-Based and Activity-Based Manufacturing Cost Systems," *Journal of Cost Management* (Fall 1990), 4–14.
7. Cost variability actually occurs at the resource, not the activity, level. However, for ease of analysis, the coding of activities as being predominantly fixed or variable is useful because it allows the user to predict cost behavior

from the activity-based costing model. In Chapter 14 we discuss the development of activity-based models for analyzing cost behavior at the resource level. These models generate more accurate predictions of cost behavior and can be used for budgeting and what-if analyses.

8. A transaction driver can be more accurate than a duration driver when the work involved is unrelated to the duration of the activity cost driver. For example, many of the activities associated with a setup or production run—such as scheduling, preparing the tooling, releasing the materials from the stockroom, and inspecting the first few items produced after the setup—are performed for each setup, independent of how long the setup actually takes. Therefore, the costs of these activities are more accurately assigned to the setup via a transaction driver (number of setups or number of production runs) rather than a duration driver (length [hours] of setup).

9. For product- and customer-costing purposes, this assumption is correct since any two activities that share a common cost driver (such as number of setups on a particular machine, or number of customer requests) can be combined into a single activity without any loss of accuracy. For understanding activity and process costs, however, ABC designers may keep the activities separate, even when they share a common cost driver, to highlight all the individual activities triggered by an incidence of an activity cost driver (a setup or a customer request).

10. One of the main attractions of integrated, enterprise-wide systems is that many more potential activity cost drivers become automatically available for ABC systems.

11. The term "activity-based costing" was first used in a John Deere pilot study of a new costing approach (see R. S. Kaplan and A. March, "John Deere Component Works (A)," Harvard Business School Case #9-187-107). The term first appeared in R. Cooper, "Cost Management Concepts and Principles: The Rise of Activity-Based Costing—Part One: What Is an Activity-Based Cost System?" *Journal of Cost Management* (Summer 1988), 45–54; and Cooper and Kaplan, "Measure Costs Right: Make the Right Decisions."

12. Willie Sutton was a successful U.S. bank robber during the 1950s; see W. Sutton, *Where the Money Was: The Memoirs of a Bank Robber* (New York: Viking Press, 1976). Willie, who was eventually captured at his home not far from a local police station, was asked during his initial interrogation, "Why do you rob banks?" Willie replied, with the wisdom that had made him successful for many years, "That's where the money is!" When developing ABC systems, we should follow Willie's sage advice (but not his particular application of the insight) to focus on high-cost areas where improvements in visibility and action could produce major benefits to the organization. Applying an ABC analysis to resource expenses that are below 1% of total spending will not lead to high payoffs for the organization.

13. After giving a talk on ABC to a group of controllers and financial managers at Texas Instruments in 1987, one of us was given a factory tour. The hosts pointed with some pride to their "blue pen" factory; a facility that, at the time, did nothing but fabricate 256K DRAMS (memory chips). Thus product costing, even in highly complex production environments like a semiconductor fabrication facility, can still be simple if the product line is narrow.

14. R. Cooper and K. H. Wruck, "Siemens Electric Motor Works (A)," Harvard Business School Case #9-191-006.

15. R. Cooper, "The Rise of Activity-Based Costing—Part Three: How Many Cost Drivers Do You Need and How Do You Select Them?" *Journal of Cost Management* (Winter 1989), 34–46.

Chapter 7

1. Some companies might use the ex post "actual" cost driver rate of $72 per order ($273,600/3,800) for costing out individual orders during the period. This would reverse the whole approach of using a standard rate for costing out current and prospective orders, and would take us back to using ABC only as an ex post costing system rather than as a system to provide data to make better current and future decisions.

2. An even more powerful benefit from using forecasted information can be realized when the ABC model itself is used for budgeting future expenses. We defer discussion of ABC for budgeting purposes until Chapter 15.

3. It is not important that such a practical capacity be estimated exactly. Whether the capacity is actually 4,800 or 5,200 is less important than choosing a particular number to approximate the practical capacity, and to continue to use this number each time the cost driver rate is calculated, until the organization has adequate evidence to obtain a better estimate. Distinguishing between practical capacity and normal volume only becomes an issue when normal volume is substantially below practical capacity. As in many cost measurement issues, it is more important to be approximately correct rather than precisely wrong.

4. A further refinement would distinguish, for equipment resources, how much the practical capacity could be increased through improvements in maintenance and repair activities. For example, the rates could be calculated assuming minimal downtime. Then the cost of capacity that could not be accessed, because of unscheduled stops, downtime, and extensive maintenance and repair activities, would be charged to operations but not to products or customers. Such an assignment would provide incentives for manufacturing operations to adopt effective total preventive maintenance (TPM) programs. For an extensive discussion of capacity measurement, see T. Klammer (ed.), *Capacity Measurement & Improvement: A Manager's Guide to Evaluating*

and Optimizing Capacity Productivity (Chicago: Irwin Professional Publishing, 1996); C. J. McNair and R. Vangermeersch, *Measuring the Cost of Capacity*, Management Accounting Guideline # 42 (Hamilton, Ontario: Society of Management Accountants of Canada, 1996).

5. The distinction between the costs of supplying resources and the cost of using resources appeared in R. Cooper and R. S. Kaplan, "Profit Priorities from Activity-Based Costing," *Harvard Business Review* (May–June 1991), 130–135; and R. Cooper and R. S. Kaplan, "Activity-Based Systems: Measuring the Costs of Resource Usage," *Accounting Horizons* (September 1992), 1–13.

6. See, for example, such confusion in W. Ferrara, "The 21st Century Paradigm," *Management Accounting* (December 1995), 32, "The implications of new categories of variable costs initially suggests a decreased number of fixed costs, but further consideration of ABC leads me to suspect that the supposed additional variable costs are really fixed costs."

7. E. Goldratt and J. Cox, *The Goal: A Process of Ongoing Improvement*, rev. ed. (Croton-on-Hudson, N.Y.: North River Press, 1986).

8. We encountered an exception in R. S. Kaplan and A. P. Sweeney, "Peoria Engine Plant" (Harvard Business School Case #9-193-082), discussed in Chapter 4, where employees were treated as "variable costs" and were sent home without pay when there was no work for them to perform.

9. The discussion in this section appeared initially in Cooper and Kaplan, "Activity-Based Systems," 4–6.

10. Economists attribute the existence of these fixed costs as arising from economies of scale in contracting for the resources. Some service units, like machine capacity, come in lumpy amounts and it is cheaper to acquire them in the quantities that the suppliers prefer to offer than to get the exact quantity the company thinks it will actually use. Managers also find it less expensive and more reliable to acquire many resources (such as engineers and managers) on a long-term commitment basis rather than to contract continually in spot markets to acquire resource capacity as needed.

11. Managers do not seem to have any problem recognizing how costs are variable in an upward direction. Examination of past history will usually reveal how organizational spending has increased to cope with increased variety and complexity of operations. It's the mechanism for costs to head in the downward direction that seems to have eluded most managers and academics.

12. Many organizational resources are fungible; they can perform multiple activities, not the single activity assumed in this simple numerical example. We will deal with fungible resources in Chapter 14.

13. Material in this section has drawn heavily from "Assigning the Expenses of Capacity Resources," Chapter 3, 168–170, in R. Cooper and R. S. Kaplan, *Design of Cost Management Systems: Text, Cases, and Readings* (Englewood Cliffs, N.J.: Prentice-Hall, 1991).

14. Klammer, *Capacity Measurement & Improvement;* and McNair and Vanger-meersch, *Measuring the Cost of Capacity.*
15. This observation was made initially in R. Cooper and R. S. Kaplan, "Measure Costs Right: Make the Right Decisions," *Harvard Business Review* (September–October 1996), 101–102.
16. ABC recognizes capacity in all resources supplied. In principle, TOC could also consider processes constrained by human resources but, in practice, the TOC illustrations, examples, and company stories relate to constraints created by equipment capacity.
17. Goldratt advocates subtracting only materials costs from selling prices to calculate throughput. We believe that a better measure would subtract other directly traceable short-term variable expenses such as the expenses of energy required to operate machines that convert materials into salable goods.
18. E. Goldratt, "Cost Accounting: The Number One Enemy of Productivity," *1983 Conference Proceedings,* American Productivity & Inventory Control Society, 433–435; also extensive ridicule and derisive comments in E. Goldratt and J. Cox, *The Goal: A Process of Ongoing Improvement,* rev. ed. (Croton-on-Hudson, N.Y.: North River Press, 1986).
19. Short-term variable costs can be extracted from an ABC system by appropriate coding of a fixed/variable attribute field, as described in Chapter 6.
20. J. S. Holman, "ABC vs. TOC: It's a Matter of Time," *Management Accounting* (January 1995), 37–40.

Chapter 8

1. Many companies, of course, operate in competitive, not monopolistic, environments. When making pricing, and output quantity and mix decisions, they must anticipate and analyze competitors' reactions as well. These competitive situations are discussed in many books on strategy, such as M. E. Porter, *Competitive Strategy: Techniques for Analyzing Industries and Competitors* (New York: Free Press, 1980), and *Competitive Advantage: Creating and Sustaining Superior Performance* (New York: Free Press, 1985).
2. The Balanced Scorecard provides a framework to enable managers to specify their organization's demand curve. The Balanced Scorecard identifies and links, in cause-and-effect relationships, the drivers of current and future revenues; see R. S. Kaplan and D. P. Norton, *The Balanced Scorecard: Translating Strategy into Action* (Boston: Harvard Business School Press, 1996), and "Linking the Balanced Scorecard to Strategy," *California Management Review* (Fall 1996), 53–79.
3. David Garvin, *Managing Quality* (New York: Free Press, 1988); and Jeremy Main, *Quality Wars: The Triumphs and Defeats of American Business* (New York: Free Press, 1994).

4. J. L. Bower and T. M. Hout, "Fast-Cycle Capability for Competitive Power," *Harvard Business Review* (November–December 1988), 110–118; and G. Stalk and T. M. Hout, *Competing Against Time* (New York: Free Press, 1990).

5. M. Hammer, "Reengineering: Don't Automate, Obliterate," *Harvard Business Review* (July–August 1990), 104–112; J. Champy and M. Hammer, *Reengineering the Corporation: A Manifesto for Business Revolution* (New York: HarperBusiness, 1993); also, F. J. Gouillart and J. N. Kelly, *Transforming the Organization* (New York: McGraw-Hill, 1995).

6. As mentioned in Chapter 3, the Japanese have been practicing much of what we now call "reengineering" under their lean enterprise initiatives. The Japanese refer to their discontinuous improvement activities as "kaiken." Recall, from Chapter 5, that their continuous improvement activities are "kaizen."

7. J. B. Simpson and D. L. Muthler, "Quality Costs: Facilitating the Quality Initiative," *Journal of Cost Management* (Spring 1987), 25–34; M. R. Ostrenga, "Return on Investment Through the Cost of Quality," *Journal of Cost Management* (Summer 1991), 37–44; and W. Morse, H. Roth, and K. Poston, *Measuring, Planning, and Controlling Quality Costs* (Montvale, N.J.: National Association of Accountants, 1987).

8. Initially, the cost-of-quality literature urged managers to spend *more* on prevention and appraisal activities so that they could reduce spending on internal and external failure activities. Empirical research, however, indicated that consistent, diligent application of total quality management principles does not require increased spending on prevention and appraisal in order to reduce internal and external failure expenses; see C. Ittner, "Exploratory Evidence on the Behavior of Quality Costs," *Operations Research* (January–February 1996), 114–130.

9. There are some limitations to benchmarking. Even minor differences in the definition of activities and outputs lead to misleading comparisons. For example, at one site, allocated corporate expenses were included in the cost of inserting components while at another they were not. The result was to make one site look inefficient compared to the other. In addition, being the most efficient department does not guarantee being fully competitive.

10. P. B. Crosby, *Quality Is Free* (New York: McGraw-Hill, 1979).

11. Example drawn from R. S. Kaplan and N. Klein, "Activity-Based Management at Stream International," Harvard Business School Case #9-196-134.

12. Ibid., 3.

13. See, "The CAM-I ABC Basic Model," Appendix B (17–19) in M. Raffish and P. B. B. Turney (eds.), *The CAM-I Glossary of Activity-Based Management* (Arlington, Tex.: CAM-I, 1991).

14. R. S. Kaplan, "Maxwell Appliance Controls," Harvard Business School Case #9-192-058.

15. Ibid., 8.
16. The storyboarding process is described in more detail in P. Turney, "Beyond TQM with Workforce Activity-Based Management," *Management Accounting* (September 1993), 28–31; and T. Pryor and J. Sahm, *Using Activity Based Management for Continuous Improvement* (Arlington, Tex.: ICMS, 1995). See also T. G. Greenwood and J. M. Reeve, "Activity-Based Cost Management for Continuous Improvement: A Process Design Framework," *Journal of Cost Management* (Winter 1992), 22–40, for an excellent description of an approach that supports front-line employees' process cost reduction activities by decomposing complex processes into information about process drivers and spending patterns.
17. R. S. Kaplan and D. P. Norton, *The Balanced Scorecard: Translating Strategy into Action* (Boston: Harvard Business School Press, 1996).

Chapter 9

1. R. Cooper and R. S. Kaplan, "How Cost Accounting Systematically Distorts Product Costs," Chapter 8, 204–228, in W. Bruns and R. S. Kaplan, *Accounting & Management: Field Study Perspectives* (Boston: Harvard Business School Press, 1987); reprinted in *Management Accounting* (April 1988), 20–27.
2. A direct costing- or marginal-costing approach, of course, would show much higher margins for these low-volume products since no fixed overhead would be assigned to them.
3. *Exhibit 9–2* also incorporates a crude ABC analysis that traced marketing, selling, and administrative costs to products so that more than factory overhead costs have been assigned to the individual products.
4. "A Lower Gear for Japanese Auto Makers," *New York Times* (August 30, 1992), Section 3, p. 1.
5. G. Stalk and A. Webber, "Japan's Dark Side of Time," *Harvard Business Review* (July–August 1993), 93–102.
6. Of course, as we discussed in Chapter 7, such a death spiral should not occur in a properly designed ABC system. Activity cost driver rates should be set based on practical capacity of resources supplied so unused capacity costs will not be driven to existing products.
7. R. S. Kaplan and A. March, "John Deere Component Works (B)," Harvard Business School Case #9-187-108.
8. M. Porter, *Competitive Advantage: Creating and Sustaining Superior Performance* (New York: Free Press, 1985).
9. For example, M. Treacey and F. Wiersema, *The Discipline of Market Leaders* (Reading, Mass.: Addison-Wesley, 1995). An alternative view has been articulated by Robin Cooper who describes Japanese companies following confron-

tation strategies that attempt to deploy both low price and high functionality; see Robin Cooper, *When Lean Enterprises Collide: Competing through Confrontation* (Boston: Harvard Business School Press, 1995).

10. Porter, *Competitive Advantage*, 120, 14.

11. Obviously, pricing is more complex than just attempting to recover costs. Even if companies can differentiate products and services at low incremental costs, they can certainly attempt to earn high premiums over cost for their unique functionality and service. Product and service cost information provide a reference point, not a floor or a ceiling, for the pricing decision.

12. R. S. Kaplan, "Maxwell Appliance Controls," Harvard Business School Case #9-192-058.

13. This discussion has focused only on the cost reduction and cost avoidance aspects of JIT and other continuous improvement activities. In addition, the benefit case can be bolstered by the higher customer responsiveness of the improved processes. The benefits from the revenue side, however, while potentially quite important, are often more difficult to quantify than the cost savings revealed from the ABC analysis.

14. One company that finally discovered the high costs associated with its much more frequent runs of small batches decided to check with its customers on whether they would be willing to accept larger, less frequent deliveries. The customers were greatly relieved to have been asked and told the company that their own production process only made sense for large batches. Consequently, the frequent small deliveries raised their costs by requiring more receipts and processing of incoming materials, as well as storage fees until they were ready to convert the incoming materials.

15. W. Skinner, "The Focused Factory," *Harvard Business Review* (May–June 1974), 113–121; R. H. Hayes and S. C. Wheelwright, "Link Manufacturing Process and Product Life Cycles," *Harvard Business Review* (January–February 1979), 133–140.

16. R. Jaikumar, "Postindustrial Manufacturing," *Harvard Business Review* (November–December 1986), 69–76.

17. R. S. Kaplan, "Must CIM Be Justified by Faith Alone?" *Harvard Business Review* (March–April 1986), 87–95; and "Management Accounting for Advanced Technological Environments," *Science* 245 (August 15, 1989), 823.

Chapter 10

1. Strictly speaking, if the compensation of the CEO is a function of sales volume (a part of many compensation schemes), one could argue that although the quantity of the resource (one CEO) is fixed, independent of sales volume, the price of this resource is affected by sales volume. Such a relationship

could be used to assign the variable portion of the CEO's compensation to production or sales volume.

2. Actually, to the extent that a resource is fungible across multiple activities, even the cost of a single unit of a resource could be assigned to its multiple uses. For example, even with only a single accounting clerk, if the person handles accounts receivable, accounts payable, and payroll, the cost of that person could be distributed across these multiple activities in an objective and meaningful way.

3. R. S. Kaplan, "Kanthal (A)," Harvard Business School Case #9-190-002.

4. Ibid., 4.

5. The importance of customer loyalty and customer relationships are the center-piece of research on the service management profit chain. See J. Heskett, W. E. Sasser, and L. A. Schlesinger, *The Service Profit Chain* (New York: Free Press, 1997); and Frederick F. Reichheld, *The Loyalty Effect: The Hidden Force Behind Growth, Profits, and Lasting Value* (Boston: Harvard Business School Press, 1996).

6. R. S. Kaplan, "Kanthal (B)," Harvard Business School Case #9-190-002.

7. Experience recounted by Roger Clark in *Measuring Corporate Performance: Activity-Based Management I* (Boston: Harvard Business School Management Productions, 1994).

8. See B. P. Shapiro, V. K. Rangan, R. T. Moriarty, and E. B. Ross, "Manage Customers for Profits (Not Just for Sales)," *Harvard Business Review* (September–October 1987), 101–108.

9. See, for example, the new price incentives established by Procter & Gamble in order to influence the retail and wholesale trade to adopt more efficient practices in logistics and promotions: *Supermarket News* (September 4, 1995), 1; and *U.S. Distribution Journal* (October 15, 1995), 10.

10. Cited in M. V. Marn and R. L. Rosiello, "Managing Price, Gaining Profit," *Harvard Business Review* (September–October 1992), 84–94.

11. An alternative and more generous explanation is that companies may be exploiting the knowledge of the demand elasticities of different customers. That is, they are granting concessions to high price-sensitive customers and no discounts to low price-sensitive customers. Such price discrimination, based on demand rather than cost characteristics, can be profitable if legal, and if the company can prevent customers receiving high discounts from communicating price information or transferring goods or services to the customers paying list price.

12. This evidence is consistent with companies not managing their pricing water-fall well; see Marn and Rosiello, "Managing Price, Gaining Profit."

13. *Supermarket News,* 1; *U.S. Distribution Journal,* 10.

14. "Enhancing Consumer Value in the Grocery Industry," Kurt Salmon Associates (January 1993).

15. R. S. Kaplan, "Pillsbury: Customer Driven Reengineering," Harvard Business School Case #9-195-144, 8–9.

16. "Peanut-butter" used as a verb refers to the arbitrary spreading of costs uniformly across customers, suppliers, and products rather than doing the more accurate, targeted, ABC approach of cost assignment.

17. See "The Right Measures," Chapter 8, pp. 217–253, in Frederick F. Reichheld, *The Loyalty Effect: The Hidden Force Behind Growth, Profits, and Lasting Value* (Boston: Harvard Business School Press, 1996).

Chapter 11

1. See B. S. Blanchard, *Design and Manage to Life-Cycle Cost* (Portland, Ore: M/A Press, 1978); and J. E. Michaels and W. P. Wood, *Design to Cost* (New York: John Wiley & Sons, 1989).

2. Robin Cooper, *When Lean Enterprises Collide: Competing through Confrontation* (Boston: Harvard Business School Press, 1995).

3. See P. Bennett, "ABM and the Procurement Cost Model," *Management Accounting* (March 1996), 28–32, and L. M. Ellram, "Activity-Based Costing and Total Cost of Ownership: A Critical Linkage," *Journal of Cost Management* (Winter 1995), 22–30, for discussions of ABC related to managing supplier relationships.

4. "Activity-Based Management II," video in *Measuring Corporate Performance* (Boston: Harvard Business School Management Productions, 1994).

5. C. D. Ittner and L. P. Carr, "Measuring the Cost of Ownership," *Journal of Cost Management* (Fall 1992), 42–51.

6. Strictly speaking, such costs should be called component-level costs since they relate to components, not end products. For simplicity, we refer to them as product-level costs.

7. R. S. Kaplan, "Pillsbury: Customer Driven Reengineering," Harvard Business School Case #9-195-144, 7.

8. R. Cooper and P. B. B. Turney, "Tektronix: Portable Instruments Division (A) and (B)," Harvard Business School Cases #9-188-142 and -143; Cooper and Turney, "Hewlett-Packard: Roseville Networks Division," Harvard Business School Case #9-189-117; P. Turney and B. Anderson, "Accounting for Continuous Improvement," *Sloan Management Review* (Winter 1989), 37–47; and D. Berlant, R. Browning, and G. Foster, "How Hewlett-Packard Gets Numbers It Can Trust," *Harvard Business Review* (January–February 1990), 178–183.

9. Experience reported in R. Banker, S. Datar, S. Kekre, and T. Mukhopadhyay, "Costs of Product and Process Complexity," Chapter 9, pp. 269–290, in R. S. Kaplan (ed.), *Measures for Manufacturing Excellence* (Boston: Harvard Business School Press, 1989); and S. Datar, S. Kekre, K. Srinivasan, and

T. Mukhopadhyay, "Simultaneous Estimation of Cost Drivers," *The Accounting Review* (July 1993), 602–614.

10. Cooper and Turney, "Tektronix: Portable Instruments Division (A)."

11. For examples of this process in action, see Cooper and Turney, "Hewlett-Packard: Roseville Networks Division"; G. Foster and M. Gupta, "Activity Accounting: An Electronics Industry Implementation," Chapter 8, pp. 225–268, in Kaplan (ed.) *Measures for Manufacturing Excellence*; and D. Berlant, R. Browning, and G. Foster, "How Hewlett-Packard Gets Numbers It Can Trust."

12. M. Sakurai, "Target Costing and How to Use It," *Journal of Cost Management* (Summer 1989), 39–50; T. Hiromoto, "Another Hidden Edge—Japanese Management Accounting," *Harvard Business Review* (July–August 1988), 22–26; Y. Monden and K. Hamada, "Target Costing and Kaizen Costing," *Journal of Management Accounting Research* (Fall 1991), 16–34; Robin Cooper, *When Lean Enterprises Collide: Competing through Confrontation* (Boston: Harvard Business School Press, 1995).

13. R. S. Kaplan, "AT&T Paradyne," Harvard Business School Case #9-195-165.

14. R. S. Kaplan, "Euclid Engineering," Harvard Business School Case #9-193-031, 8.

Appendix

1. For a more detailed description of target costing, see R. Cooper and R. Slagmulder, *Confrontational Cost Management, Vol. 1; Target Costing and Value Engineering* (Portland, Ore.: Productivity Press, 1997).

Chapter 12

1. Occasionally, when we started to build ABC systems, we found defects in the direct labor and direct materials cost-accounting elements in traditional cost systems. For example, direct labor standards were based on estimates made when the product was released into manufacturing from the product development organization, but which had never been verified or updated to reflect actual manufacturing experience. On materials, many organizations used average scrap rates, across a product line or even for the entire factory, rather than product-specific scrap rates. More subtly, the example provided in Chapter 7 on acquiring the high-grade crude oil materials for a refinery required by a unique final product shows that analysts should think about causal relationships and attribution even when assigning the cost of materials.

2. Some industries, such as transportation and telecommunications, whose prices were heavily regulated, did have to conform to statutory reporting

developed by their regulatory agencies. For example, the Interstate Commerce Commission in the United States required all railroads to report their operations using Rail Form A. The procedures governing the production of information for this form required railroads to estimate the costs of operating different types of service.

3. Or the direct contact that a service employee had with a customer was so brief that detailed measurement of the time elapsed was not considered to be cost-effective.

4. This is an overly broad indictment. Many individual service companies, like United Parcel Service, McDonald's, AT&T, and large retail banks did use industrial engineers extensively to study and monitor labor times and efficiencies for their repetitive work processes.

5. R. S. Kaplan, "Manufacturers Hanover Corporation: Customer Profitability Report," Harvard Business School Case #9-191-068.

6. In Chapter 13, we will argue that these initial expenses to acquire customers should be considered the investments in a total life-cycle perspective of customer profitability.

7. The interplay among customer acquisition, retention, and lifetime profitability is at the heart of the comprehensive measurement system proposed in "The Right Measures," Chapter 8, pp. 217–253, in Frederick F. Reichheld, *The Loyalty Effect: The Hidden Force Behind Growth, Profits, and Lasting Value* (Boston: Harvard Business School Press, 1996).

8. R. S. Kaplan "The Co-operative Bank," Harvard Business School Case #9-195-196.

9. T. D. West and D. A. West, "Applying ABC to Healthcare," *Management Accounting* (February 1997), 22–33.

10. P. Sopariwala, "How Much Does Excess Inpatient Capacity Really Cost?" *Healthcare Financial Management* (April 1997), 54–60.

11. Kaplan, "The Co-operative Bank."

12. We are not completely comfortable with the high costs that the Co-op Bank project team assigned to the business-sustaining category. Many of the resources in this category violate the Rule of One we established in Chapter 10 for identifying a sustaining-level expense. We prefer to treat most of those expenses as providing secondary or support activities to primary activities and will discuss this extension in Chapter 13.

13. See "Managerial Cost Accounting Concepts and Standards for the Federal Government," Federal Accounting Standards Advisory Board Statement of Recommended Accounting Standards No. 4 (June 1995); and T. G. Amos, C. A. Paolillo, and D. A. Joseph, "Enhancing CFO Act, GMRA & GPRA Implementation with Activity-Based Management," *The Government Accountants Journal* (Spring 1997), 26–34.

14. J. Walters, "Count Your Costs," *Government Executive* (May 1997), 17, 24–27.

15. Experiences reported in Dale Geiger, "Federal Management Accounting: Determinants, Motivating Contingencies, and Decision-Making Relevance" (Ph.D. dissertation, Harvard Business School, 1993).
16. R. S. Kaplan, "Indianapolis: Activity-Based Costing of City Services (A)," Harvard Business School Case #9-196-115, 1.
17. Ibid., 4.
18. Ibid., 8.
19. R. S. Kaplan, "Indianapolis: Activity-Based Costing of City Services (B)," Harvard Business School Case #9-196-117, 4–5.

Chapter 13

1. H. T. Johnson and D. A. Loewe, "How Weyerhaeuser Manages Corporate Overhead Cost," *Management Accounting* (August 1987), 20–26. The general context for the Weyerhaeuser experiment with a charge-out system for corporate resources is described in H. T. Johnson, "Organizational Design versus Strategic Information Procedures for Managing Corporate Overhead Cost: Weyerhaeuser Company, 1972–1986," Chapter 2, 49–72, in W. J. Bruns, Jr., and R. S. Kaplan, *Accounting & Management: Field Study Perspectives* (Boston: Harvard Business School Press, 1987).
2. The first layer of complexity is mapping between decisions taken to change resource usage (based on the ABC model) and the subsequent impact on spending (or resource supply); see discussion in Chapter 7.
3. In many factories, not all space is equally costly to supply. For example, in semiconductor-wafer fabrication facilities the expense to provide clean room space is much higher than the expense to provide normal space. In such cases, the analyst should have at least two activities: *provide normal space* and *provide clean room space*. The latter activity would attract much higher utility expenses because of the need to recirculate and filter air continuously. Similarly, space provided for warehousing raw materials and finished goods may be less expensive to supply and support than the temperature- and humidity-controlled space required for sophisticated electronic-controlled equipment.
4. Again, this treatment assumes that all employees demand the same time and other resources from the HR department. It would be straightforward, but more complicated, to allow for the HR activities to be more focused on some employees than on others. One could either construct a weighted HR service index to represent the complexity of demands by different individuals, or one could split what is now a homogeneous activity, *support employees*, into two or more separate categories, *provide complex support*, *provide average support*, and *provide basic support*, with employees associated with one of these three mutually exclusive activities.

5. In general, such a sequential assignment procedure may not be possible if there are reciprocal interactions between service departments. For example, the information systems department could provide services to the human resources department and to the factory maintenance department. These interactions can be easily handled through a system of simultaneous equations. See Chapter 3 of R. S. Kaplan and A. A. Atkinson, *Advanced Management Accounting*, 3d ed. (Englewood Cliffs, N. J.: Prentice-Hall, 1998).

6. A. Rappaport, *Creating Shareholder Value: The New Standard for Business Performance* (New York: Free Press, 1986); and "Selecting Strategies That Create Shareholder Value," *Harvard Business Review* (May–June 1981), 139–149.

7. Cash flow return on investment, and its relation to other financial metrics, is described in B. Birchard, "Mastering the New Metrics," *CFO* (October 1994), 30–38; and R. Myers, "Metric Wars," *CFO* (October 1996), 41–50.

8. G. B. Stewart III, *The Quest for Value: The EVA® Management Guide* (New York: HarperBusiness, 1991); J. M. Stern, G. B. Stewart III, and D. H. Chew, Jr., "The EVA®: Financial Management System," *Journal of Applied Corporate Finance* (Summer 1995), 32–46; and G. B. Stewart III, "EVA®: Fact and Fantasy," *Journal of Applied Corporate Finance* (Summer 1994), 71–84. EVA is a registered trademark of Stern, Stewart and Co.

9. G. B. Stewart, "EVA: Fact and Fantasy," 77.

10. Unpublished consulting report.

11. A "facility" is the term used by bankers to describe an agreement or commitment to lend money when a company needs it. Examples include a line of credit, revolving credit, term loan, and banker's acceptance note. A "loan" refers to the amount actually borrowed by a company under the facility arrangement.

12. See R. S. Kaplan, "Manufacturers Hanover Corporation: Customer Profitability Report," Harvard Business School Case #9-191-068.

13. S. Wheelwright and K. Clark, *Revolutionizing Product Development* (New York: Free Press, 1992).

14. Charles H. House and Raymond L. Price, "The Return Map: Tracking Product Teams," *Harvard Business Review* (January–February 1991), 92–100; also Marvin L. Patterson, "Designing Metrics," Chapter 3, 27–52, in *Accelerating Innovation: Improving the Process of Product Development* (New York: Van Nostrand Reinhold, 1993).

15. Measuring lifetime profitability of customers is a major subject of its own, but a detailed discussion of how to perform this calculation is beyond the scope of this book. For more discussion, see "The Economics of Customer Loyalty," Chapter 2 in Frederick F. Reichheld, *The Loyalty Effect: The Hidden Force Behind Growth, Profits, and Lasting Value* (Boston: Harvard Business School Press, 1996); and "Rethinking Marketing: Building Customer Loyalty," Chapter 4, in James L. Heskett, W. Earl Sasser, Jr., and Leonard A.

Schlesinger, *The Service Profit Chain: How Leading Companies Link Profit and Growth to Loyalty, Satisfaction, and Value* (New York: Free Press, 1997).

16. Marc J. Epstein, "Accounting for Product Take-Back," *Management Accounting* (August 1996), 29–33; also, M. J. Epstein, *Measuring Corporate Environmental Performance: Best Practices for Costing and Managing an Effective Environmental Strategy* (Montvale, N.J.: Institute of Management Accountants, 1996).

17. Epstein, "Accounting for Product Take-Back," 32.

18. J. G. Kreuze and G. E. Newell, "ABC and Life-Cycle Costing for Environmental Expenditures," *Management Accounting* (February 1994), 38–42; see also B. Hamner and C. H. Stinson, "Managerial Accounting and Environmental Compliance Costs," *Journal of Cost Management* (Summer 1995), 410.

19. Examples provided in S. B. Hughes and D. M. Willis, "How Quality Control Concepts Can Reduce Environmental Expenditures," *Journal of Cost Management* (Summer 1995), 15–19.

Chapter 14

1. We have indicated, however, in Chapter 7 how even Stage III (nonintegrated) ABC systems can operate with budgeted rather than historical data.

2. In the early days, these exchanges were usually accomplished by writing special software routines that collected the data and information required and then downloaded it to the PC on which the ABC systems resided. Later, local area networks and more advanced data exchange technologies such as OBDC were used.

3. The elimination of the previous costing system entirely is most prevalent in companies whose main manufacturing process is assembly of electronic components. In these companies, the direct labor costing system was hopelessly obsolete and had to be scrapped anyway. Also, this industry had product costs that were flat to decreasing over time and typically used FIFO accounting for its inventory. Complications from putting LIFO layers at risk for tax purposes did not arise.

4. R. S. Kaplan, "AT&T Paradyne," Harvard Business School Case #9-195-165, 7.

5. In addition, the failure of the system to incorporate batch and product-sustaining activities caused the product-costing features of this system (a Stage III application) to be not nearly as good as could have been accomplished had the system just focused on this application alone. Instead, it attempted to be the single system to serve all organizational costing needs.

6. Whether the expenses hit when supplies are received or when the invoice is paid will vary depending on the company's financial accounting convention for recognition of such an expense. And such variation, because of a financial

accounting judgment, just reinforces our point about not wanting such fluctuations to impact the measurement of activity cost driver rates.

7. For example, railroad companies can estimate reliably when track must be replaced and its roadbed repaired based on the gross ton miles and speed of loads carried over the track. Airline companies must perform scheduled maintenance on engines after a specified number of miles have been flown.

8. Astute readers will already have anticipated another distortion. If the higher expenses incurred during the month of maintenance are divided by the much fewer hours worked during that month (because of the downtime caused by the maintenance), the activity cost driver rate for that month escalates even higher.

9. Returning to the example in Chapter 7, the company budgeted $280,000 of resources to perform an activity, *handle customer order*. The underlying efficiency of this activity is measured by how many customer orders *can* be handled, not the number of orders expected to be handled, or that were actually handled ex post. If the number of orders that can be handled (the practical capacity) from the $280,000 supply of resources is 5,000, the underlying efficiency is $56 of resources per order handled. If only 4,000 orders were received in the period, the people and other resources don't suddenly get less efficient, requiring $70 of resources per order. Unless we have specific information to the contrary (more on this later in the chapter), we should estimate and maintain the activity cost driver rate based on the efficiency ($56 per order) when the resources are fully used. Any operating expenses unassigned by such a procedure will be classified as costs of unused capacity, in effect the costs of products not made and customers not served.

10. Note that the $60 rate is what we would obtain in a single calculation were the expected activity level to be at practical capacity. In this case, the total budgeted costs would be $300,000 (from the $200,000 committed costs and the $100,000 flexible costs [$20 per order × 5,000 orders]) and at the practical capacity of 5,000 orders, the cost driver rate calculates as $300,000/5,000 = $60 per order.

11. See Y. T. Mak and M. L. Roush, "Flexible Budgeting and Variance Analysis in an Activity-based Costing Environment," *Accounting Horizons* (June 1994), 104–109; and "Managing Activity Costs with Flexible Budgeting and Variance Analysis," *Accounting Horizons* (September 1996), 141–146.

12. For example, suppose we had 20 front-line people who are paid for 500 hours of work each quarter. About 20% of this time is used up in breaks, training, and various administrative activities, leaving a practical capacity of 400 hours per person.

13. This rate includes, of course, not only the salary and fringe benefits of the front-line employees but also all the costs of supervisory resources, computing and telecommunications resources, and space and office equipment resources

used by these employees as well as the cost of all secondary activities performed for this department and its employees.

14. If the first-stage resource driver is itself duration based, the Stage III system will automatically adjust for the different activity loads each year. The issue being discussed here arises only when a work-load percentage based upon interview data is used. However, a duration-based first-stage resource driver will not adjust automatically for practical capacity.

15. The other condition is that the cost of performing the activity is relatively small so that more detailed measurements, via duration drivers or direct charging, are not warranted.

16. Lacking such an advance in artificial intelligence and expert systems, perhaps companies can follow Shionogi Pharmaceuticals' practice of assigning highly knowledgeable, skilled, and reliable workers to review operating results and make judgments about when a permanent change has occurred in the efficiency or the cost of performing activities.

17. See Robin Cooper, *When Lean Enterprises Collide: Competing through Confrontation* (Boston: Harvard Business School Press, 1995), 268.

Chapter 15

1. This section has benefited greatly from the ideas and exhibits provided by Ralph Canter of KPMG Peat Marwick.

2. Companies with a complex product mix that changes from year to year may find it impossible to predict future product mixes. Even so, they should be able to predict the mix at the product-type level (e.g., standard versus custom, Product Line A versus B) and use this prediction to estimate activity cost driver quantities. For budgeting purposes, we need estimates of the demanded quantities of the activity cost drivers.

3. Any demand that exceeds the practical capacity of the committed fixed resources cannot be satisfied. Managers must adjust the forecasted product/ customer mix until the demand can be met with the existing supply, or they must authorize a capital expenditure to increase the supply of the constraining resource.

4. These three profiles capture much of the observed variation in resource supply behavior, but by no means all. For example, resource supply often displays different profiles when demand is increasing than when it is decreasing. This occurs because managers may be less willing to release highly skilled individuals when demand decreases than they are to hire new ones when demand increases. In addition, some resources may initially be committed but become flexible above a certain level. For example, floor space is limited to existing buildings until all space is occupied. Then demands for additional space can be used to adapt to almost any demand level. There are a myriad of different resource-supply behavior profiles.

5. Theoretically, if the interviewed individuals identified the unused capacity at the resource level (e.g., I only work 80% of the time), then a retrospective ABC could identify capacity at both the activity and the resource levels. We rarely encounter such responses.

6. A relatively straightforward extension to this procedure is required to model the interaction among primary activities, the secondary activities that support the primary activities, and the resources that are required to perform the secondary activities.

7. J. Hirschleifer, "On the Economics of Transfer Pricing," *Journal of Business* (July 1956), 172–184, and "Economics of the Divisionalized Firm," *Journal of Business* (April 1957), 96–108; D. Solomons, *Divisional Performance: Measurement and Control* (Homewood, Ill.: Irwin and Financial Executives Research Foundation, 1965), 160–228.

8. This example is drawn from R. S. Kaplan, D. Weiss, and E. Deshch, "Transfer Pricing with ABC," *Management Accounting* (May 1997), 20–28.

9. Registration costs include the costs of gaining and maintaining approval from governmental agencies for the right to manufacture individual products.

10. Theoretically, the expenses of machines should have been assigned as a unit-level expense using a machine-hours cost driver. The company, however, wanted to treat machine capacity as a fixed expense and felt that including it as a unit-level expense would create confusion among many people who viewed unit-level expenses as almost synonymous with variable costs. The tradition of this company to treat materials costs as the only variable organizational cost undoubtedly contributed to the approach it adopted.

Index

Abbeglen, J., 236n5
accounting costs, 6, 181, 324n2, 338n1
activity/activities
  attributes, 93–94
  batch-level, 90–91, 93, 98, 103–104, 121,
    161, 168, 176, 178–179, 223,
    261–262, 278, 312
  coding schemes for, 93–94, 156, 159
  cost assignment, 94
  costing, 15–17
  customer-sustaining, 90–91, 312
  dictionary, 85–88, 92–93, 105, 108–110,
    143, 151
  efficiency of, 141–143, 152, 282–283
  fixed vs. variable, 114, 328n7
  forecasting, 116, 123
  hierarchy of, in ABC system, 89–91, 314
  mix, 6
  non-value-adding, 157–159
  order-related, 91
  primary, 263–264, 278, 345n6
  product-sustaining, 90–91, 93, 98,
    103–104, 121, 161, 168, 178–179,
    223, 262, 278, 312, 314
  secondary, 263–264, 278, 345n6
  supplier-related, 207
  time required for, 294–297
  unit-level, 90–91, 93, 98, 104, 106, 178,
    261–262
  unprofitable, 5
  value-adding, 156, 157–159
activity-based budgeting (ABB), 301,
    320–322
  impact of, 301–303

  process, 303–311
  use of, 311–312
  variable costs and, 312–313
  what-if-analysis for, 313–316
activity-based cost (ABC) models, 79, 94,
    105, 223
  activity cost drivers in, 150
  activity hierarchy in, 89–91, 314
  analysis, 315
  for budgeted expenses, 113–116, 240
  case studies, 240–250
  efficiency factor, 286
  fundamental equation in, 117–119
  future-oriented data in, 113–116
  historical data in, 21, 111–113, 252
  ownership of, 85
  resource supply decisions, 125–126
  for service industries, 228–230,
    240–250
  as target-costing mechanism, 115
  theory of constraints and, 132–135
  use of estimates, 100
activity-based cost (ABC) systems, 3–6,
    19–20, 26, 79–81, 106–107, 135,
    145–146, 329n11
  activity and process dictionary, 108–110
  analysis, 92, 107, 113, 165, 166, 169,
    176, 179, 192, 233–234, 236–237,
    239, 252–253, 266, 273–274, 276
  application of, 100–102
  assignment of assets, 265–270
  assignment of corporate- and division-
    level resources, 253–263
  attributes of activities, 92–94

About the Authors

Robert S. Kaplan is the Marvin Bower Professor of Leadership Development at the Harvard Business School. Formerly he was on the faculty of the Graduate School of Industrial Administration at Carnegie-Mellon University and served as dean of that school from 1977 to 1983. He consults on the design of performance and cost management systems with many leading companies in North America and Europe, and he regularly offers seminars in North America, South America, Europe, Asia, and Israel. Currently he serves on the Board of Directors of the J. I. Kislak Organization (in Miami) and on the Academic Committee of the Board of Trustees of the Technion (Israel Institute of Technology). His research focuses on new cost and performance measurement systems, primarily activity-based costing and the Balanced Scorecard. The author or co-author of nine books and more than 100 articles, Kaplan is the recipient of numerous awards for both his teaching and his publications.

    Robin Cooper is a professor of management at the Peter F. Drucker Graduate Management Center at Claremont Graduate School, director of the Institute for the Study of U.S.-Japan Relations in the World Economy, and a visiting professor at the Manchester Business School. He consults with companies throughout the world. A leading architect of activity-based cost systems, Cooper is the author or co-author of five books and a frequent contributor to professional journals, including *Accountancy, Accounting, Accounting Horizons, Advances in Management Accounting, Harvard Business Review, International Journal of Production Economics, Journal of Cost Management, Management Accounting, Management Accounting Research,* and *Sloan Management Review.* He is the recipient of the first Innovations in Accounting Education Award and of the Notable Contributions to Management Accounting Literature Award.